Workers Against Work

Workers Against Work

Labor in Paris and Barcelona During the Popular Fronts

MICHAEL SEIDMAN

UNIVERSITY OF CALIFORNIA PRESS
Berkeley Los Angeles Oxford

University of California Press
Berkeley and Los Angeles, California

University of California Press, Ltd.
Oxford, England

Library of Congress Cataloging-in-Publication Data

Seidman, Michael (Michael M.)
Workers against work : labor in Paris and Barcelona during the popular fronts / Michael Seidman.
p. cm.
Includes bibliographical references.
ISBN 0-520-06915-3 (alk. paper)
1. Working class—Spain—Barcelona—History—20th century. 2. Labor movement—Spain—Barcelona—History—20th century. 3. Middle classes—Spain—Barcelona—Political activity—History—20th century. 4. Popular fronts—Spain—Barcelona—History—20th century. 5. Working class—France—Paris—History—20th century. 6. Labor movement—France—Paris—History—20th century. 7. Middle classes—France—Paris—Political activity—History—20th century. 8. Popular fronts—France—Paris—History—20th century. 9. Front populaire—History.
I. Title. HD8590.S342S45 1991
322′.2′094436—dc20 90–33716
CIP

Printed in the United States of America
1 2 3 4 5 6 7 8 9

The paper used in this publication meets the minimum requirements of American National Standard for Information Sciences—Permanence of Paper for Printed Library Materials, ANSI Z39.48-1984. ♾™

To my parents

Nous voulons voir la fin du sinistre loisir parce qu'il suppose le travail—et que le travail n'est qu'un bon prétexte pour ne rien faire.

La Polycritique, 1968

Contents

Preface

This comparative social and political history of the Spanish Revolution in Barcelona and the Popular Front in Paris attempts to show the potency of revolutionary ideologies in Spain, a country with a weak bourgeoisie, and their decline in France, a nation in which capitalists developed modern industries. It investigates how workers in Paris and Barcelona labored during the Popular Fronts, when organizations that claimed to represent the working class held varying degrees of power. The patterns of working-class actions (and inaction) lead this study to question the dominant paradigms of Anglo-American labor historiography.

The book began as a doctoral dissertation supervised by Professor Arthur Mitzman of the University of Amsterdam; it benefited from extensive research in Paris, Barcelona, and Salamanca in the early 1980s. In Paris, I was assisted by both friends and scholars. I owe much to Sylviane Lavergne, Véronique and Jean-Pierre Bachimont, Arthur Marchadier, Louis Chevalier, and Michelle Perrot. In Barcelona, Joaquín Sirera and Horacio Capel provided knowledge and comfort. Stanley Payne directed me to the incredibly rich but disorganized civil war archives at Salamanca, and Raymond Carr provided needed encouragement.

The manuscript has also benefited from the criticisms and suggestions of Traian Stoianovich, John Gillis, Victoria de Grazia, Allen Howard, and Mark Wasserman. The comments of Robert Seidman have anglicized occasionally hispanic and gallic idioms.

Abbreviations

SPAIN

CEDA	Confederación española de derechas autónomas
CENU	Consejo de la escuela nueva unificada
CNT	Confederación nacional de trabajo
FAI	Federación anarquista ibérica
JSU	Juventudes socialistas unificadas
MZA	Madrid–Zaragoza–Alicante
POUM	Partido obrero de unificación marxista
PSUC	Partit socialista unificat de Catalunya
SEUC	Serveis elèctrics unificats de Catalunya
UGT	Unión general de trabajadores

FRANCE

CFTC	Confédération générale des travailleurs chrétiens
CGPF	Confédération générale de la production française
CGT	Confédération générale du travail
CGTSR	Confédération générale du travail syndicaliste révolutionnaire
CGTU	Confédération générale du travail unitaire
GIM	Groupement des industries métallurgiques
GR	Gauche révolutionnaire
HBM	Habitations à bon marché
PCF	Parti communiste français
PPF	Parti populaire français

PSF	Parti social français
PSOP	Parti socialiste ouvrier et paysan
SACIAT	Syndicat et amicale des chefs de service, ingénieurs, agents de maîtrise et techniciens des industries métallurgiques, mécaniques et connexes
SFIO	Section française de l'Internationale ouvrière
SIMCA	Société industrielle de mécanique et de carrosserie automobile
SNCAN	Société nationale de constructions aéronautiques du nord
SNCASE	Société nationale de constructions aéronautiques du sud-est
SNCASO	Société nationale de constructions aéronautiques du sud-ouest
SNCF	Société nationale des chemins de fer français
SNCM	Société nationale de constructions de moteurs

Introduction

At the outbreak of the Spanish Revolution in Barcelona in 1936, anarchosyndicalist militants and other revolutionaries quickly expropriated the cars and trucks in the city, painted the initials of their organizations on them, and drove around Barcelona at dangerously high speeds. Inexperienced drivers who disregarded traffic laws, these militants caused numerous accidents; their daily newspaper, *Solidaridad Obrera*, called them to order and asked them to drive safely and return the vehicles to the proper authorities. Their actions foreshadowed the era of the automobile in Spain.

During the Popular Front in France at almost the same time, on the occasion of their first annual paid vacations, masses of workers abandoned Paris for the overcrowded Riviera and other specialized areas for leisure. The compulsive exit of summer vacationers in 1936 inaugurated the era of mass tourism and the weekend in France.

At first glance, it may seem odd to treat disparate events from such different countries within a single work. After all, one does not have to agree with Napoleon ("Africa starts beyond the Pyrenees") to appreciate the vast differences between France and Spain. Even during the ancien régime, political, economic, religious, and social developments separated those north of the Pyrenees from the peoples of the Iberian Peninsula. The great movements of early modern European history—the Reformation and absolutism—had a much greater impact in France than in its Iberian neighbor. For centuries before the Revolution, France possessed relatively dynamic urban and rural sectors and a modernizing state, while Spain lagged economically, politically, and culturally. In the eighteenth century, French *philosophes* authored an original and powerful critique of the Church, nobility, and traditional economy. In Spain, the Enlightenment was derivative and less potent.

The advent and effects of the French Revolution further accentuated the differences between the two nations. Proclaiming a program for the future, the new nation opened its ranks to the talented, including Protestants and Jews, and subordinated the clergy to the state. In the Enlightenment tradition the Revolution valued the producer more than the "parasitic" noble or priest. Having developed a much healthier agrarian economy than Spain, France in the twentieth century, unlike its neighbor, possessed no great mass of peasants thirsting for land or jobs. Growing French industry was able to employ not only French laborers from the countryside but also foreigners, including thousands of Spaniards. At the beginning of this century, France separated Church from state and subordinated military to civilian government. Furthermore, the relatively stable Third Republic (1870–1940) forged a new national unity that gradually weakened regionalist and centrifugal forces and largely disarmed violent revolutionary and counterrevolutionary movements.

Spain never experienced a comparable bourgeois revolution. Indeed, in the Napoleonic period large numbers of Spaniards fought a bloody *guerrilla* against the French invaders and their revolutionary principles. This reaction to French rule in 1808 has been seen as the starting point for modern Spanish history just as the Revolution of 1789 has been viewed as the beginning of modern France. Even after the revolutionary era, traditionalist Spanish landowners, backed by the clergy, maintained their economic and social dominance in large regions of the peninsula well into the twentieth century. Unlike France, the Spanish nation never integrated Protestants and Jews, and large numbers of Spain's most dynamic people emigrated. Except perhaps in the Basque country and Catalonia, no class of energetic industrialists ever emerged. Yet even in the latter region, as shall be seen, entrepreneurial dynamism was ephemeral. National unity was never fully consolidated, and regionalist movements grew during the Restoration monarchy (1874–1931) in the wealthiest areas of the peninsula. In the nineteenth and early twentieth centuries, armed confrontation between revolutionary and counterrevolutionary forces encouraged the *pronunciamiento*—direct military intervention in politics. The Second Republic (1931–1939) proved unable to secure the separation of military from civilian government and Church from state.

Precisely because of these dissimilar developments, a comparative approach can aid our understanding of the history of both nations and deepen our comprehension of two concurrent events in twentieth-century European history: the Spanish Revolution and the French Popular Front. The historiography of both events has been dominated by a political or diplomatic perspective within each country's national history. Historians have not yet attempted a socially oriented comparative approach but have for the most part concentrated on party platforms, conflicting ideologies, governmental changes, and—in the case of the Spanish Revolution—military battles. Yet a comparative social history of the developments leading up to the Spanish Revolution and the French Popular Front and a social history of the events themselves can profoundly enhance our comprehension of the political, diplomatic, and even military histories of both phenomena. The comparative social approach has its limits and cannot entirely resolve the problems of causality. One cannot prove that a Spanish "working-class" revolution was inevitable since Spain did not follow the French model. Nonetheless, a review of some of the major social, economic, and political differences between the two nations can illuminate why revolutionaries were more influential south of the Pyrenees.

My comparative approach examines the relation between industrial capitalist bourgeoisies (the owners of the means of production) and working classes in Paris and Barcelona. One class treated separately or in isolation from the other reveals only a fragmented understanding of the dynamic between the two classes and of the society concerned. Again, it is their relation and their interaction that permit a more profound comprehension of *histoire événementielle*. The diverse strengths of the French and Spanish bourgeoisies greatly affected the character of their respective working-class organizations. Facing a more dynamic capitalist elite, the French working-class movement developed differently from its Spanish counterpart. These differences, which must be understood in order to evaluate the Spanish Revolution and the French Popular Front, have been masked by the largely political perspective of many historians and by the similarity of political labels in both countries: Communist, Socialist, anarchosyndicalist, fascist, and so forth. Yet the same political parties or currents had to confront different Spanish and French social realities and therefore acquired divergent roles and meanings.

This study attempts to go beyond the similarity of political names and catchwords to illuminate several issues. First, it investigates two different capitalist elites and industrial structures. Second, it suggests that the differences between these elites and their industries created distinct social and political environments for French and Spanish labor movements, encouraging reformism in Paris and promoting revolution in Barcelona. Finally, it demonstrates how workers, mainly blue- but also white-collar, responded to the revolutionary situation in Barcelona and the Popular Front government in France. I have concentrated on developments in Paris and Barcelona because Paris and its suburbs undoubtedly constituted the most important urban center in France in the 1930s, and Barcelona was the center of the Spanish Revolution and the capital of Catalonia, Spain's most economically advanced region. Each city was the capital of its nation's industrial working-class movement.

The first half of the book highlights the political, religious, and economic attitudes and actions that may have encouraged the growth and persistence of revolutionary movements in Spain in general and Barcelona in particular. Barcelona was one of the most vital cities in the Iberian Peninsula. Under adverse conditions of a poor domestic market and few natural resources, its bourgeoisie had managed to build the largest industrial concentration in the nation. Yet the achievement had definite limits. In the second half of the nineteenth and the early twentieth centuries, foreigners—not Catalans—were responsible for creating many of the most modern industries. Health and living standards were often well below Western European norms. As in other regions of Spain, Barcelona's upper classes remained attached to the traditional faith of Roman Catholicism. In a social climate characterized by terrorism, counterterrorism, and sabotage, many owners were tempted to rely on military force to maintain order.

Leading militants of the Barcelonan working class reacted to the climate of repression, lack of advanced native industries, and to what they considered their low standard of living by adhering to revolutionary and largely anarchosyndicalist organizations. Anarchists and anarchosyndicalists were hardly millenarian or primitive, as some historians have claimed; they remained influential precisely because they offered—in ways similar to revolutionary Marxists—a critique of what they believed to be a parasitic and relatively unproductive bourgeoisie. Anarchosyndicalism was an ideology of work and economic development well suited to an economically impoverished society that had accepted neither the Reformation nor the Western revolutions of the eighteenth century.

When revolution erupted in Barcelona in 1936, union militants of the anarchosyndicalist CNT (Confederación nacional de trabajo) and the Marxist UGT (Unión general de trabajadores) inherited a backward industrial structure that they were compelled to modernize under difficult conditions of civil war in Spain. These militants—whether anarchosyndicalist, Communist, or Socialist—copied elements from the Western and Soviet models of economic development and accumulation. While attempting to build the productive forces, they quickly encountered what I shall call workers' resistance to work. The anarchosyndicalists of the CNT, the most important working-class organization in Barcelona, were forced to jettison their theories of workers' democracy and participation to make the rank and file work harder and produce more. The anarchosyndicalists and Communists in the newly collectivized firms reestablished piecework, initiated severe controls on the shop floor, and embarked on an intensive campaign that included both odes to Stakhanovism and socialist realist art.

The second half of the book suggests why France and specifically Paris, in contrast to Barcelona, offered fewer opportunities for revolutionary workers' control. Placed at the center of a much richer national market, the Parisian capitalist elite had created competitive industries in automobiles, aviation, and other modern sectors. After the Dreyfus affair, anticlericalism and antimilitarism were no longer the burning issues that they remained south of the Pyrenees. Hatred of the Church and the army, which motivated many Spanish revolutionaries, no longer provided a platform for an important revolutionary movement in France. The Parisian factory owners themselves may have been less tied to a traditional faith. At any rate, the Jews and Protestants among them were instrumental in developing some of the most advanced industrial sectors. Regional economic disequilibriums, unlike those in Spain, produced no separatist movements perceived as threats to the unity of the nation. In France, relative détente between Church and state, the resolution of the military-civilian conflict, and gradual but steady economic growth induced a decline of revolutionary movements and ideologies, such as anarchosyndicalism, which had lost considerable influence by the 1930s. Instead of producing revolution and civil war, the victory of the French Popular Front culminated in the Third Republic's most significant social legislation, including the forty-hour week and paid vacations. Despite these gains in rationalized and modernized industries (automobiles and aviation) and in more traditional sectors (construction) of the Paris region, blue-collar workers carried on a kind of guerrilla against work. In contrast to Barcelona, where union militants took over factories literally abandoned by a weak and frightened bourgeoisie, in Paris union militants often acquiesced in or even supported the absenteeism, lateness, sabotage, and indiscipline of the rank and file. The Popular Front brought forth the weekend, and Communists and Socialists acted as agents of tourism, not of revolution. Other wants and new needs superseded the desire for revolution among working-class organizations (or, more precisely, those claiming to represent the working class).

This study examines the *lived* experience of workers in both Paris and Barcelona. Its goals are to investigate wage earners' acceptance of and resistance to work. Acceptance of labor meant a demand for job security and overtime, high productivity, and moonlighting. In both cities, some labored hard to satisfy consumerist, familial, and gender-based desires; all required income to meet their needs. Neither basic nor eternal, these needs were socially determined in ways that remain for historians and social scientists to explore. Workers went into the factories not only because they had to eat and survive but also, to an unknown extent, because they chose to work. If the workplaces of the 1930s were often areas of constraint, they cannot be entirely identified with prisons. The seductive forces that induced workers to labor were varied and changing, but they all encouraged workers to collaborate in the process of production, to bend to workspace and worktime. They included the inculcation of values of consuming, of being a reliable breadwinner, of believing in the revolutionary or reformist project of parties and unions, and of manifesting patriotic conviction.

Desires to consume were more developed in France than in Spain, corresponding to the greater power of both the productive and the seductive forces. In Paris, advertising propagated the virtues of consumption and, prefiguring consumers in postwar Europe, Parisian workers labored for a wide array of new goods and services. An expanding range of leisure possibilities induced some to work hard for future vacations. In Barcelona, where war conditions further reduced the meager purchasing possibilities, socialist realism—that is, the glorification of production and the producer—directly substituted for advertising's odes to consumption. The difficulties of survival in a period of civil war and scarcity forced Barcelonans to struggle literally for their daily bread. They demanded higher wages in a context much more economically harsh and inflationary than in Paris. Yet even in the wartime city, many laborers consumed more than the caloric minimum. Workers continued to drink, smoke, and look for amusement. These urges may have bolstered workers' output in certain instances. After all, except for theft, only hard work provided money to engage in diverse pleasures.

The familial position of workers also seems to have influenced their acceptance or rejection of labor. Couples with many children were compelled to labor more than single men or women. Undoubtedly numerous exceptions existed, especially in France in the 1930s when the system of welfare benefits rewarded large families and sometimes discouraged potential breadwinners from taking a salaried position. Men's and women's responsibilities as breadwinners—both primary and secondary—led them to work to support their families. During the Popular Fronts, family heads sacrificed and labored so that their children could avoid the kind of work that they themselves had to perform.

Commitment to the revolutionary and reformist visions of the parties and unions motivated their activists. Those who wanted to build a prosperous and more dynamic Spain attempted to convince their colleagues through persuasion and propaganda to labor for a greater nation. In France, working-class patriots who feared for their country in a period of increasing international tensions and German rearmament were willing to extend working hours and increase productivity.

During the Popular Fronts these seductive forces—whether patriotic, revolutionary, familial, or consumerist—were not powerful enough to overcome workers' resistance to work, a major focus of this book. By resistance to work I mean both individual and collective actions that enabled workers to avoid wage labor in factories. Absenteeism, fake illnesses, lateness, and strikes constituted direct resistance, which meant an immediate escape from the workplace, and thus a reduction in worktime. Indirect resistance consisted of theft, sabotage, slowdowns, indiscipline, and indifference, activities and attitudes that generally harmed output and decreased productivity. Stealing, for example, might eliminate tools and machinery needed for production and increase the costs of controlling the work force. Slowdowns—workers' control of workspeed—limited output. Indiscipline that challenged industrial hierarchy was hardly compatible with efficiency.

Resistance to work in the twentieth century has been largely ignored or underestimated by many Marxist labor historians and modernization theorists—two important, if not dominant, schools of labor historiography.[1] Although at odds on many issues, both groups have not adopted a sufficiently critical attitude toward work. They view labor primarily as creation, not coercion, and regard the worker as producer, not as resister. Modernization theorists postulate workers as adapting to the pace, structure, and demands of work and the workplace. Marxists, anarchists, and anarchosyndicalists view the working class as eventually desiring to expropriate the means of production. The main currents of Marxism and anarchism take the acceptance of labor to an extreme, if logical, conclusion and propose the construction of a utopia in the workplace. Despite their differences, modernization theory and Marxism (including its anarchist variants) have a similar vision of the workers' acceptance of work. Indeed, it can be argued that modernization theory has merely continued the largely uncritical consensus on labor that Marxists and anarchists articulated in the nineteenth century.

Both theories also postulate a progressive view of history. Modernization theorists see workers' gradual adaptation to an advanced division of labor as inevitable, if not desirable. Marxists view the working class as acquiring class consciousness and moving from *an sich* to *für sich* or, in English terms, "making itself." Despite a Blanquist or a putschist current that also existed in Marxism, anarchists and anarchosyndicalists agreed with their rivals that "the Revolution must be the work of the workers themselves." The ideologies of the Left affirmed that one day in the future the working class would acquire sufficient knowledge or consciousness to make a successful revolution.

The progressive view of history and the acceptance, if not glorification, of work have encouraged the study of certain aspects of working-class existence and discouraged an exploration of others. Until recently, interest in ideologies and in the development of working-class organizations took priority over studies of everyday life of workers. Intellectual and political histories of parties, unions, and their militants dominated labor historiography. Examinations of ideologies, whether variants of Marxism or anarchism, permitted the productivist vision of the class to remain unquestioned. Studies of the growing organizations—which, like the ideologies, claimed to represent the class—strengthened the progressivist current. Consciousness, or at least membership in parties and unions, seemed to expand throughout the nineteenth and twentieth centuries. Legal history also created the impression that the workers' movement was progressing, as organizational elites gained recognition or even integration into the state apparatus. Certain studies disclosed however that working-class organizations such as the PCF (Parti communiste français) were *partis passoires* or sieves;[2] through them workers and others passed with little active involvement, as they did in major political parties and unions during the Popular Fronts. Historians began to question the closeness of the relation between workers and their organizations or between workers and their ideologies even if they did so within the framework of modernization theory, which was equally progressivist and productivist.[3]

Labor historians have continued to dissolve the identification between the class and its institutions and organizations.[4] Popular and, more specifically, working-class *culture* have become objects of research.[5] This approach also began with an examination of ideologies, organizations, and militants but expanded to include large areas of unexplored terrain, including what I call the seductive forces. The cultural approach has made genuine contributions to labor historiography, and this book is indebted to the questions and problems it has raised. Yet the cultural approach has been insufficiently critical and has too often sought meanings in work. Like the Marxists and modernization theorists, it has viewed labor as literally meaningful. The workers described in the following pages often regarded their work as meaningless or, less radically, earned wages to support their families and buy consumer goods. The meanings of their work, if articulated, were frequently instrumental or external to it. Wage earners maintained this attitude despite intense propaganda in both cities to convince them that their work was meaningful for the revolution, the nation, and the Popular Fronts. The culturalists' unrelenting search for meaning and their conception of work has led them—like the Marxists and modernization theorists—to neglect resistance and the consequent coercion needed to overcome it.

A history of resistance to work can contribute to a new vision of the working class. The everyday struggles of workers against labor show that the productivist, progressivist, and culturalist vision cannot adequately encompass essential aspects of working-class behavior. An examination of workers' actions in Barcelona and Paris from 1936 to 1938 in both revolutionary and reformist situations will reveal a persistence of direct and indirect refusals to labor. Wage earners in both cities tried to escape from workspace and worktime by taking unauthorized holidays, arriving late, and leaving early. Another form of direct resistance, strikes, was more common in Paris for several reasons. Walkouts usually needed some form of collective organization, and in Barcelona the ranks of labor militants were depleted because many were managing factories or fighting at the front. Of course, the unions themselves, both CNT and UGT, were largely integrated into the state and committed to the development of the productive forces. Perhaps the very real threat of jail or a stay in a labor camp was effective in convincing the rank and file to avoid strikes. Barcelonan workers may have felt that it was less risky to use other strategies of resistance, particularly faking illness, to escape the workplace. Their refusals took more individual than collective forms.

In contrast to these direct strategies, slowdowns and other varieties of indirect resistance occurred while workers were present in the factory and on the shop floor. Slowdowns did not permit workers to escape from workspace but rather were a means to exert control over worktime. Thus they were manifestations of the familiar struggles between workers and their managers—whether capitalist, anarchist, or Communist—over a "just" or "fair" pace of work. As will be seen, those responsible for the collectives in Barcelona and for the nationalized and private firms of Paris complained often of lethargic output and low productivity. In both cities managers wanted to increase productivity by tying pay to individual output.

Other forms of indirect resistance, such as indiscipline and disobedience, challenged the industrial chain of command that was and remains indispensable for economic efficiency in situations where workers have not completely internalized the work ethic. Even though disobedience indicated the individual worker's hostility to a superior, indiscipline usually had the larger effect of hindering the collective productive process. In Barcelona, persistent disobedience entailed an implicit disavowal of the economic leadership of the unions; in Paris, workers disobeyed both capitalist managers and union militants but were more likely to support the latter than the former. Stealing, another variety of indirect resistance, was a special form of disobedience. Theft and pilfering revealed hostility or indifference to the goals of the Popular Fronts, which needed honest, if not committed, workers in order to prosper.

Spanish working-class militants equated theft with sabotage, another strategy of indirect resistance. Barcelonan revolutionaries defined sabotage broadly to include both intentional and unintentional acts that hurt production, an understandable definition during their struggle. Saboteurs became identified with the "lazy" who became, in turn, "fascist." Militants politicized idleness, which existed in working-class culture long before fascism was born. In Paris sabotage was not as politically charged, but it increased dramatically during major strikes.

Reluctance to labor anteceded the victory of the Popular Front in France and the outbreak of war and revolution in Spain but has particular significance in that it persisted in Paris and Barcelona even after the parties and unions claiming to represent the working class took political and varying degrees of economic power. These continuities of working-class culture pose questions concerning the relations between workers and "their" organizations. Workers, it will be argued, were often more interested in pleasure than in labor. Devotion to pleasure meant that workers' desires sometimes conflicted with those of the organizations that claimed to represent them. The Catalan anarchosyndicalist union and Communist party found truly committed followers among only a distinct minority of the Barcelonan working class; the majority of blue-collar workers maintained a certain distance from the revolutionary unions and political parties. Likewise in Paris, even though workers flocked into the union, they sometimes refused to obey high-ranking union, Socialist, or Communist leaders when urged to work harder. During the Popular Front, blue-collar wage earners continued and in some cases increased their refusals to work. Their actions and inaction undercut the claims of unions and political parties to represent the working class.

The perseverance of workers' resistance created tensions between members of the working class and their organized representatives. In both revolutionary and reformist situations, persuasion and propaganda that aimed to convince the workers to labor harder were inadequate and had to be supplemented by force. In revolutionary Barcelona, piecework was reinstituted and strict rules imposed in order to increase productivity. In reformist Paris, only after 30 November 1938, when massive intervention by the police and the army broke the general strike designed to save the forty-hour week, was discipline restored and productivity raised in many enterprises. In both cities coercion supplemented persuasion to make the workers work.

In both Paris and Barcelona the state played a major coercive role. Pro-anarchist historians have argued that increasing state power was responsible for the demoralization of the workers in the Barcelonan collectives. According to these historians, in the early period of the revolution, when workers were able to control their workplaces, they labored with enthusiasm. Following May 1937, the state increased its intervention, and workers lost control in many enterprises. As a result, wage earners' desires to sacrifice diminished and their enthusiasm declined. This pro-anarchist analysis actually inverts the process. The state—and coercive measures in general—grew in response to workers' resistance to work. Governments in both Barcelona and Paris intervened with repressive measures to counteract varieties of direct and indirect resistance to labor.

It was thus the actions or indifference of the workers themselves that contributed to the bureaucratization and centralization of the anarchosyndicalist CNT, as well as the pressures of the war. One can speculate that if the workers had sacrificed wholeheartedly and enthusiastically, the unions, political parties, and the state would not have become as oligarchic and undemocratic as they did. Within the CNT, those advocating democratic workers' control and decentralization might have gained influence; outside it, proponents of a centralized war economy would have had a reduced audience. State power and bureaucracies proved essential in regulating labor. It was over the role of the state—not the nature of labor or the character of the working class—that anarchist and Marxist analyses began to differ significantly. More clearly than their anarchist rivals, Marxists saw the need for a state that could make wage earners work.

An investigation of workers' resistance to work not only contributes to a theory of the state in modern industrial society but may also link histories of women, unemployed workers, and immigrants. The study of resistance to labor will further integrate women into labor history. Instead of viewing female workers as less militant because they were relatively uninterested in joining parties and unions, an investigation of their struggles over maternity leave, absenteeism, illnesses, and gossip demonstrates that women also participated in the class struggle. Some of their methods, such as absenteeism and low productivity, were similar to those of their male colleagues. Others, such as gossip and biologically based demands for leave, constituted their own particular forms of struggle. Women identified less with the workplace because of the temporary and unskilled character of their jobs, lower salaries, and familial responsibilities. Their relative rejection of organizational or ideological involvement—traditional yardsticks of militancy—did not mean that they were any less conscious than males. If avoidance of the workplace rather than party or union membership is taken as a measure of class consciousness, then many women's minimal identification with their role as producer might lead to the conclusion that females were among the true vanguard or consciousness of the working class.

The same argument may apply to the unemployed. Like women, the jobless cannot be dismissed as marginal. Given the importance of refusals to labor—including theft and pilfering—among some employed members of the class, the deceptions and welfare cheating of a minority of the unemployed are not totally alien to working-class culture. Their indiscipline, indifference, and high rate of turnover may be extreme manifestations of tendencies found among employed wage earners. During the 1930s, the unemployed were not merely victims but actors possessing degrees of choice. Simplistic discourses of both the Left and Right that reduce them to either potentially perfect producers or lazy irresponsibles must be avoided.

Less information exists concerning immigrants' acceptance or refusal of work. Contrary to the implications of modernization theory, certain immigrants and peasants dispensed with a period of adaptation to industrial society. Immediately on their arrival in Barcelona, they became strikebreakers. Provincial construction workers in Paris similarly ignored union control of the World's Fair of 1937 and seemed to have labored more diligently than unionized Parisian workers. Veteran industrial workers, such as skilled aircraft workers in Paris, used their strong bargaining position during the Popular Front to reduce their hours of labor by both legal and illegal means. In Barcelona, refusals were quite widespread in the construction industry, which contained a high percentage of trained personnel. The Sorelian "joy in work" cannot adequately explain the actions of these qualified wage earners.

As in the specific cases of female, unemployed, immigrant, and skilled workers, a broad investigation of refusals to labor questions generalizations concerning unions. Labeling unions an integral part of capitalist society cannot fully explain their actions during the Popular Fronts. Depending on the situation, unions attempted to make workers work or assisted their struggles against constraints of workspace and worktime. In Paris, the unions usually aided the workers in their refusals and therefore created problems for French industrialists and the state. It was in noncapitalist or rather collectivized Barcelona that the unions had some success in motivating workers' labor.

A variety of sources inform us of the existence of workers' resistance to work in Barcelona. The minutes from meetings of the collectives and the factory councils provide the largest depository of information. In these meetings, those responsible for the functioning of the enterprises discussed how to combat direct and indirect resistance. Local union officials composed confidential letters that suggested ways to reduce refusals and punish offenders. More publicly, CNT and UGT newspapers and journals complained about "abuses" and produced plentiful propaganda designed to encourage enthusiastic acceptance of labor. Propaganda proved insufficient and was supplemented by strict rules and regulations to discipline wage earners in the workplace. Unfortunately, the wartime situation with its disruptions of markets, supplies, and labor lessens the value of statistical comparisons of productivity before and during the Revolution. We do, however, have the words of disappointed militants who complained that the rank and file continued to resist work in the same ways as previously or even exerted themselves less than before the Revolution.

Many of the sources on Parisian resistance are from managements that accused workers of working poorly. Some of management's charges seem to have been based on private, relatively unmediated daily reports filed by shop-floor foremen. Third parties, such as the police and insurance companies, confirmed other accusations. Occasionally, but rarely, union militants themselves either complained about the rank and file's rejection of work or celebrated it. A number of investigative reports from government officials and decisions by arbitrators appointed by the Popular Front government confirmed management's suspicions of slowdowns and indiscipline. In the construction industry, much evidence for refusal to work comes from court cases that attempted to assign responsibility for cost overruns. Both sides presented their arguments in cases that sometimes were not settled until the 1950s. Available statistics on productivity indicate declines in Parisian automobiles, aviation, and construction. Yet in France as in Spain, rapid changes in industrial organization and retooling lessen the value of figures and make any numerical comparisons between the Popular Front and preceding periods tentative at best.

Ultimately the problem of how workers labored cannot be entirely resolved empirically. No one can approach such a controversial area in working-class history without some bias. Barring the unsatisfactory option of radical skepticism (which obviously cannot answer the question), perhaps the best I can do is make my perspectives clear and be conscious of how I determine them. The historian's conceptions of work and the workplace will greatly influence his vision of the working class. Those analysts who stress the workers' identification with their vocation or who view the workplace as a potential arena for emancipation will tend to emphasize the disciplined and productivist aspects of the class. They follow the tradition of the Western utopians (Marxists and anarchists included) who have often regarded the workplace as a possible locus of liberation. Thus, those who adhere to the productivist utopian tradition have often deemphasized resistances. This lack of public articulation does not lessen the significance of refusals. Perhaps the reluctance to acknowledge resistance shows how deeply those who claim to represent the working class are immersed in the productivist tradition. Their silences are easy to understand, since in societies devoted to the development of the productive forces, refusal of work approaches the criminal and possesses a subversive side that invites repression.

There is another tradition, which includes this book. It questions the productivist interpretation and regards the factory and construction labor of the 1930s as *trabajo* and *travail* (from the Latin *tripalium*, or "instrument of torture"), not as an arena of potential liberation. This critical analysis of work affects the historian's conception of the working class. It views workers not as potentially perfect producers but as resisters who must be constantly disciplined or seduced to accept work. It promotes investigations of both acceptances and resistances. Given these conceptions of work and the worker, management's accusations—particularly when confirmed by the state and other sources—deserve a hearing. My goal is not to impose some sort of bourgeois morality on a class that suffers but rather to illuminate the reasons behind the gap between workers and working-class ideologies, the character of authority in the workplace, and the repressive role of the state in modern industrial societies.

Furthermore, I wish to bring out the utopian dimension of resistance, a word which I have chosen because of its positive connotations. The importance of resistance in two major European cities in the fourth decade of the twentieth century indicates that refusals of work should not be dismissed as the behavior of "backward" or "primitive" working classes. Certainly, resisters did not articulate any clear future vision of the workplace or of society. Unlike the Marxists, they did not fight to take state power or, in contrast to the anarchosyndicalists, abolish or minimize the role of the state. I do not wish to ignore the fact that workers' refusals to work harmed the fight against Franco and weakened French defenses in a period of Nazi rearmament. Yet one might interpret resistance itself as suggesting a working-class utopia in which wage labor would be reduced to a minimum. Resistance was also a conjunctural and cyclical phenomenon, but refusals remained an intrinsic part of working-class culture and manifested themselves in different periods with various divisions of labor. During the Popular Fronts, workers revolted against a variety of disciplines, including that imposed by working-class organizations. Wage earners certainly wished to control their workplaces but generally in order to work less. One may speculate that the way to eliminate resistance is not by workers' control of the means of production but rather by the abolition of wage labor itself.

The history presented in the following pages is cognizant of its partial character and does not claim to be *histoire totale*, which may at best be a useful illusion. I make no pretense of dealing with the Spanish Revolution outside Barcelona or with French working-class movements in the provinces despite their significance; other omissions are equally regrettable. I have tried to obtain a basic parallelism between the French and Spanish sections but, depending on the sources and the importance of the topic, treat certain issues more in depth in one part than in the other. Leisure and unemployment receive greater coverage in the Paris section; art, propaganda, and punishment figure more extensively in Barcelona. What in 1936 the French called the Ministry of Leisure had no Spanish equivalent, whereas wartime conditions in Spain led to the immediate creation of a Ministry of Propaganda.

I must also warn those readers who are interested exclusively in political, diplomatic, and military events that they must turn to the many other works on the Spanish Revolution and the French Popular Front where such information is more than abundant. Many issues that have concerned historians of Spain—anarchist participation in the government, Communist influence in the Second Republic, the role of foreign powers—will not be directly treated here. The French part of this book largely ignores the history of the Popular Front before its electoral victories in the spring of 1936, the subsequent ministerial changes, and the exclusively political opposition of the Right. Political events are by no means entirely forgotten in the French section. Indeed, my periodization of the French events corresponds to the political victories of the Popular Front in the spring of 1936 and its division and defeat at the end of November 1938. When the social and the political are entwined, as they were during the Popular Fronts, the social historian who ignores the political does so at the expense of social history itself.

1
THE WEAKNESS OF THE BARCELONAN BOURGEOISIE

An examination of the different paths of France and Spain illuminates the origins of the Spanish civil war and Revolution and the tenacity of revolutionary ideologies in the latter country. Politically, the Spanish, unlike the French, never forced a lasting separation of the Church from the state and the military from the civilian government; economically, Spanish industrial and agrarian elites created less wealth than their French counterparts. A comparison of the Spanish and French economies helps place in perspective the separate historiographical debates on supposed Catalan dynamism and alleged French backwardness.

In agriculture, even given France's greater natural resources and fertile soil, the differences were significant. In 1935 French wheat yields were almost double the Spanish, and French vineyards yielded 49.13 hectolitres per hectare compared to Spain's 11.63.[1] In industry, the French made 17 times as much pig iron and 10.5 times as much crude steel as the Spanish. In 1935 France consumed 2.2 times the amount of raw cotton and had 5 times as many cotton spindles. The French industrial infrastructure and service sector were also considerably stronger. In 1930 France possessed 2.5 times as much railway line, carried 4.6 times as much freight, and 6.7 times as many passengers. Spain had 304,000 radios, France 2,626,000. In 1935 France produced 5 times more electrical energy than Spain. Even in tourism the French were in the lead, with foreign tourists spending over 9 times more than in Spain.[2] The two countries developed the nearly classic trading relation of an industrial to an agrarian nation: the French exported manufactured goods, and the Spanish shipped agricultural products. In 1934 the largest French exports to Spain were, in order of importance, automobiles and parts, other motor vehicles, silk, iron and steel, and chemical products. Spain sent to France fruits, sulphur, wine, lead, and fresh vegetables.

Although Catalonia was more dynamic than other Spanish regions, it did not or could not escape the weaknesses that characterized industry in other areas of the peninsula. The Catalan bourgeoisie had industrialized to some extent and had produced a respectable textile industry in the nineteenth century, but by the opening of the twentieth century this industry was in decline, and the Catalans had difficulty forging others to take its place. An exploration of the state of Catalan and particularly Barcelonan industry is essential to any critical understanding of what the unions and their militants desired and accomplished when they seized control of Barcelona's factories and shops.

To comprehend Barcelona's industry and industrialists, we must examine certain aspects of its economic, political, and cultural history in the first third of the twentieth century. First is the feebleness of its economy, compared to France and especially to Paris, where the bourgeoisie built modern and basically national industries in automobiles, aviation, and other sectors. Barcelonan industry remained rooted in the nineteenth century and dominated by branches, such as textiles, that were identified with the first industrial revolution. More advanced sectors, if they existed, were largely controlled and propelled by foreign capital; native industries depended for protection on enormous tariffs granted by Madrid. Second is the backwardness of Barcelona's industrial economy, which paralleled the fragility of the agriculture of most regions of Spain. Industrial backwardness resulted in a low standard of living for workers that promoted a climate of violent social unrest. Barcelonan owners reacted to revolutionary and counterrevolutionary terrorism by supporting militaristic and repressive policies to maintain order; the principle of separation of military from civilian government was as foreign to them as it was to many other Spanish elites. Like many upper-class Andalusians and Castilians, the Catalans supported the pronunciamientos of Primo de Rivera and Franco. Third, from the available evidence, the industrialists shared the religious faith of their Iberian counterparts; some relied on a rigid Catholicism to uphold spiritual order just as others depended on the repressive power of the military to maintain public order. Neither Catalan nor other Spanish owners enthusiastically supported the separation between Church and state.

The lack of industry and the weakness of the urban bourgeoisie in Castile, the center of Spain, is well known, and the Catalan success in fostering a bourgeois culture with its values of work, thrift, and industry is often contrasted with the lack of Castilian development. Yet even at its summit in the middle of the nineteenth century, the Catalan cotton industry, the base of Catalan industrialization, was weak in comparison with its foreign competitors. For example, in the Catalan cotton industry each worker transformed 66 kilograms of cotton per year in contrast to the United States' industry, where each worker transformed 1,500 kilograms of cotton per year. At the end of the nineteenth century this industry's growth rate dropped from 5.5 percent to 2.3 percent per year between 1880 and 1913.[3] This decline would have been even greater if Spain had not retained its protected colonial market in Cuba and Puerto Rico until 1898, the year of the Spanish defeat by the United States. After 1898 exports to the former colonies declined drastically. At the beginning of the twentieth century, the largest spinning mill in Catalonia had twenty-five thousand spindles in contrast to the fifty thousand of the average British or French spinning establishment.[4]

The weakness of their textile industry brought a constant demand from Catalan industrialists (and, notably, some working-class organizations) for tariff protection by Madrid. By the end of the nineteenth century the Catalans' demand for protection had resulted in a pact with conservative and traditionalist Castilian and Andalusian landlords who also desired protection for their unproductive and backward agriculture.[5] Thus, the Catalan industrialists sold their high-priced textiles to a poor but protected market in which the level of consumption was very low.

Although the cotton and textile industries were certainly the most important of the Catalan enterprises, the regional economic growth in the nineteenth century was not limited to textiles. Railroads were constructed, but these were dominated by foreign, mainly French, capital and technology.[6] Mines began to be exploited, but again the exploiters were often foreigners, not Catalan or even Spanish. It is estimated that 50 percent of Spanish mines belonged to foreigners who were responsible for much of the concentration and modernization of Spanish industry. Orders for agricultural, textile, and transportation machinery went mostly to outsiders since the Catalans had failed to build a potent metallurgical or machine-tool industry. At the turn of the century, Catalonia did not even have a blast furnace.[7]

Vicens Vives, the influential Catalan historian, has attributed the responsibility for Catalonia's failure to develop heavy industry to "the absence of large seams of iron and soft coal."[8] The lack of mineral resources, however, only partially explains the weakness of heavy industry in Catalonia in the nineteenth century. The geographical and geological factors may be important, but the Catalan bourgeoisie often neglected to invest in modernization of the productive forces. Catalans preferred other forms of investment, such as secure foreign bonds or real estate. Vicens Vives himself noted that in 1865, when phylloxera destroyed French vines and Catalan wine prices soared, some growers "quickly parted with their accumulated wealth in a life of lavish expenditure and pleasure in Barcelona."[9]

By the end of the century the Catalan bourgeoisie was losing what little industrial dynamism it had possessed. It had built a textile industry that, while respectable, nonetheless suffered from low productivity and undermechanization. Being incapable of exporting in great quantities, it depended on an impoverished home market. Other established industrial sectors, such as shipbuilding, shipping, and Barcelona's port activity, were also declining.[10] From 1870 to 1910, the Spanish gross national product fell rapidly relative to the rest of Western Europe.[11] On the eve of World War I, Spain was dependent on foreign nations for many raw materials, finished products, and even foodstuffs. The limited growth of metallurgy, chemicals, electricity, and urban transportation (tramways), like the railroads of an earlier period, was propelled by foreign capital and technology, but these imports compensated only partially for the reluctance of Spaniards to invest in national industries.[12] Spanish and Catalan industries were unable to fulfill the demand for machinery, steel, iron, ships, coal, and coke. In 1914 the cotton industry, largely located in Catalonia, imported 98 percent of its spindles from Britain.[13] Even leading Catalan businessmen such as Guillermo Graell, the head of the Catalan employers' association (Fomento de trabajo nacional), lamented the foreign control of Spanish industry.[14]

Many Catalan employers missed a great opportunity to modernize and develop their businesses during World War I. Neutral Spain was able to sell to all the warring nations and to the markets that the combatants had previously controlled. Since its imports of capital goods and advanced machinery from the belligerents decreased substantially, Spain created new firms that relied on the use of inexpensive labor.[15] Spanish exports quickly expanded; the country unexpectedly had a favorable balance of trade for the first time in many years. The Catalan and Barcelonan entrepreneurs profited greatly by supplying European and Latin American countries that could not purchase English goods.

Despite the windfall profits, the major defects of Barcelona's industry—small size, atomization, technical backwardness, and lack of organization—persisted.[16] Industrialists electrified and mechanized certain textile firms, but much of the profits that they could have used to modernize antiquated machinery, concentrate atomized firms, develop new industries, and free the region from foreign economic domination went elsewhere.[17] The Barcelonan bourgeoisie preferred to buy new foreign cars, speculate in German marks or Berlin real estate, or build luxurious houses. The enormous opportunity of the First World War was dissipated and a predictable postwar crisis hit Catalan industry.[18] Many small chemical and drug firms initiated to provide substitutes for German exports were quickly eliminated when normal commerce resumed. The great industrial powers rapidly recovered the markets they had ceded to Spain.

In Spain in general and Barcelona in particular, entrepreneurs often relied on outright repression to control or subdue a combative working class, which had been adversely affected by the inflation that the war provoked. Repeated acts of sabotage, terrorism, and assassination occurred; they were much rarer phenomena in Paris after World War I. Perhaps above all, Barcelonan employers feared state weakness or impotence. In 1919–1920 the industrialists claimed that ineffective local and national governments had permitted the shortening of the working day to eight hours, allowing "intolerable" indiscipline inside the factories where management's authority was ignored and workers became the real bosses.[19] The Fomento believed that only strong measures by the state could restore normality. The climate of strikes and assassinations, in which "two hundred fifty martyrs of the employers' cause" lost their lives, led to "no other solution, as bad as it seems, than the lock-out." The first duty of the state was to uphold the law in the face of a syndicalism that exploited "bourgeois cowardice."

Barcelonan employers' organizations had a long history of directly subsidizing the *Guardia civil* and other policing agencies.[20] Apparently through funds to a number of governmental agencies, the employers claimed to have boosted the morale of the forces of public order. The Fomento praised the "wonderful performance" of Generals Martínez Anido and Arleguí, who by "attacking the union . . . and its leaders . . . diminished terrorism."[21] These officers had instituted repressive policies, and union officials had accused them of supporting employers' hitmen (*pistoleros*) against those of the CNT. Barcelonan industrialists were disturbed when the generals were transferred in 1922. Large numbers of the Catalan upper class (the list of organizations and personalities was almost endless) regretted the removal of the fearsome pair. In a farewell ceremony for General Arleguí, the president of the Fomento praised the general for "imposing special methods of public order and social hygiene," which halted "anarchy" and restored "authority."[22] After the dismissal of both generals and the legalization of the CNT, employers asserted that terrorism became even more violent than previously. They demanded that the government destroy the union by whatever means available, if necessary by declaring a state of siege and suspending individual liberties.[23]

In this tense atmosphere, influential Catalan employers clung to the Church. Many believed that the moment was not ripe for the separation either of Church from state or of military from civilian government. Guillermo Graell was perhaps the most striking example of an important Catalan businessman whose clericalism was unshakable. He was a militant Catholic, and his writings, *The Religious Question* and *Essay on the Necessity to Return to Religion* (1921), demonstrated the close spiritual ties between the Catholic church and an important part of the Catalan bourgeoisie. Graell's writings won the full endorsement of his colleagues at the Fomento, who called them "brilliant"; in 1934 a monument was erected to honor the "lamented master."[24]

Graell's essays were revealing. He scorned almost every non-Catholic conviction. He attacked "excessive Greek anthropomorphism," along with Descartes, Bacon, Hobbes, Kant, Leibniz, Hegel, and (needless to say) Marx. Adam Smith he criticized for assailing both the Roman Catholic and Anglican churches. In general, the secretary general of the Fomento sustained the "failure of reason against faith":[25] "More science" only created "more grief." Graell's opinions were supported thirteen years later by Victor González, whose *Catechism* "for all social classes" assailed the Reformation, Enlightenment, French Revolution, Rousseau, and all those—such as the anarchists—who believed that man was good.[26] Only belief in God could restrain men and secure the social order.

Graell attacked Protestantism because its variety of sects produced "anarchy." Protestantism was the result of the instinctual refusal of the "Anglo-Saxon race, especially the German" to submit to the great capital of the Latin race, Rome. Protestant individualism was undesirable, as were Lutheranism and even Jansenism.[27] The reformed religion disturbed the conscience: "The result was . . . [that] every Protestant was a pope, a Bible in his hand. This is anarchy."

The head of the major Catalan employers' association despised materialism and believed that Jesus offered more to impoverished workers than pagan utility did. According to Graell, resignation and suffering led to God's love. Indeed, paradise on earth consisted of knowing the art of suffering. Graell advised a friend who complained of his poverty, "Contrary to popular opinion, you will be happier in your poverty than the rich man who has become wealthy through questionable means." "The wealthy" were "an insignificant minority, and they lived less joyfully than the poor. Idleness created boredom, which was the scourge of the upper classes." Graell affirmed that the poor who hated poverty were "uncontrollable" and lamented that the impoverished had lost their patience and resignation, "which were the sunshine and charm of their life."

From his position in the Catalan employers' association Graell did not propagate the Spanish equivalent of Samuel Smiles's thoughts on self-help, the American Horatio Alger stories, or the French *carrière ouverte aux talents*. Instead he preached resignation and submission. The present "colossal social war" was the result of the loss of "the belief in anything beyond worldly existence." Contemporary workers were filled with hatred and blasphemy, in sharp contrast to their peaceful and joyful ancestors who belonged to guilds, attended religious processions, and were generally devout. It is significant that Graell declared that the new leaders of the proletariat were "almost all climbers (*arrivistas*)." The term *arrivista* (from the French) revealed Graell's dislike and condemnation of the social climber, who was often the object of at least ambivalent praise in more dynamic societies.

The Catalan employers' desires for religious order and their fears of revolution led many to search for a power that could restore what they considered stability. In 1923 they supported the pronunciamiento of General Miguel Primo de Rivera, who promised them religion, regional autonomy, high tariffs, and, above all, "social peace." Following in the footsteps of Martínez Anido and Arleguí, Primo—who had been the Captain-General of Barcelona in 1922–1923—won the support of Catalan employers through his repressive policies against anarchosyndicalists. In fact, Catalan employers proved willing to subordinate their demands for regional autonomy to their need for social stability. The Catalan bourgeoisie appreciated the sharp drop in "social crimes" under the general's dictatorship.[28] According to the businessmen, only when the authorities took a firm stand could strikes be quickly terminated. This reliance, if not dependence, on the police power of the state was a constant in the 1920s and 1930s. Prominent Catalan businessmen such as Guillermo Graell had hoped that Roman Catholicism could furnish an ideology to aid in maintaining order, but their colleagues in the Fomento felt more secure with the police and army behind them. It should be noted that the forces of order were Spanish, not Catalan.

The Spanish state protected not only the persons of the industrialists but also their businesses. The government under the dictatorship of Primo de Rivera provided the region's industrialists with one of the highest tariffs in Europe to save industries unable to export sufficiently and still dependent on a miserable domestic market. Catalan industrialists were delighted with the protectionist zeal of Primo's rule, which had eliminated the threat of the previous constitutional government to reduce tariffs.[29] Laws of 1926 and 1927 led to the charge by the League of Nations that Spain was the most protectionist country in the world.[30] If its goal was to provide the time necessary for Spanish, particularly Catalan, industry to expand to compete with more advanced nations, protectionism failed. Indeed, even for the Catalan entrepreneurs it was a two-edged sword that could obstruct Catalonia's development. It was a policy that Barcelonan employers' organizations generally defended; for example, the Fomento blamed the failure to establish an automotive industry in Catalonia on the lack of tariffs.[31]

Considering the state of their industries, Catalan businessmen were understandably not in the forefront of scientific organization of work. Taylor's *Dirección de los talleres: Estudio sobre la organización del trabajo*, was published in Barcelona in 1914, but his *Principles of Scientific Management* was not translated until 1970. A knowledgeable analyst of Taylor's system argued that it could not be applied in Spain.[32] The "primitive level" of organization in Spanish workshops rendered workers apathetic and totally unfit for the new system; except for "small groups" in Catalonia and other "advanced" regions, the undisciplined workers would reject new methods of organizing work and remain impervious to incentives of pay. Although an international meeting on scientific organization of work was held in Barcelona in 1921, the following year one author noted "the nearly complete lack of literature concerning the subject."[33] Although one major concern—the Maquinista, which made locomotives—introduced certain Tayloristic techniques in 1924, its engineer asserted that Spain lacked qualified personnel and needed to train workers in time-measurement techniques.[34]

In 1925 Spain significantly increased its participation in the International Congress on Scientific Organization of Work and sent one of the largest delegations to the convention at Rome. Yet according to industrialists, the conventioneers "gave the impression that they were sight-seeing tourists who had come to admire the beauty of Rome rather than scholars who were seeking information on one of the most interesting problems of production in our times."[35] Taylorism had been applied only "in fragments" in Spain, and the Spanish did not comprehend the "essence" of the system. The employers' journal, *Exito*, revealed considerable ignorance about Taylorism. It claimed that "all those who work in scientifically organized factories eventually regard their bosses as their best friends, instead of enemies."[36] Taylor's method had doubled production in a "great number of American factories" and had completely eliminated strikes. Employers who adopted scientific organization of work did not fire workers but taught them the best way to perform their tasks.[37] Gual Villabí, the head of the Fomento in 1929, confirmed that Spain was considerably behind England, France, Germany, and even the Soviet Union in Taylorization.[38] Although Spain did participate in the congress at Amsterdam in 1932, only a small number of industries found limited applications for new methods of organizing work, which explains in part the persistently low industrial productivity during the growth decade of the 1920s.

The Second Republic (1931–1939) had little choice but to increase the protective barriers that Primo de Rivera had maintained. For example, Hispano-Suiza, which employed fifteen hundred workers, threatened to shut down in part because of the "recent decision by the Ministry of Economy" to liberalize automobile trade.[39] Its workers asserted that "national factories" could not compete with foreigners.[40] Spanish exports dropped from 10.3 percent of national income in 1930 to 4 percent in 1935.[41] The increased trade barriers had paradoxical consequences. While they isolated Spain from the worst effects of the Great Depression, they forced Catalan and Barcelonan industry to continue to rely on the markets of the peninsula; despite some growth in the first third of the twentieth century, these domestic markets were too poor to stimulate industry.

Even though the Second Republic attempted to respond to industrialists' complaints by raising tariffs, Barcelona's employers distrusted it. They saw a direct correspondence between political instability and strikes, and from 1930 to 1936 they complained that the lack of an energetic government resulted in disturbances inside the factory and on the streets: "It is the state which has the unavoidable obligation to control social peace and the calm development of labor."[42] With the advent of the republic, moderate Catalan republicans who wanted to imitate the French model—which, as shall be seen, was able to integrate prominent revolutionary syndicalists to the state apparatus—were frustrated by their capitalist elite's stubborn adherence to a repressive and militaristic concept of authority.[43]

In 1931 businessmen felt that the government would not defend them and that the unions had again grown too powerful. The *sindicatos*, they claimed, were controlling hiring and firing, raising salaries, diminishing working hours, and abolishing piecework. Two hundred employers' organizations protested the "anarchy" of the opening months of the republic.[44] "No civilized country," they asserted, would tolerate the atmosphere of "violence" and "lawlessness" that would eventually lead to "catastrophe." In addition, "intense political activity" had aggravated "social problems."[45] Increased social tensions brought a mass of worried new members to the Fomento. For these recent adherents, the Second Republic meant only disorder and laxity; the entrepreneurs were dismayed by the passivity of the authorities in the face of the "absurd burning of convents," which had taken place outside Catalonia. Simultaneous but seemingly uncoordinated protest movements in the countryside and in the city outraged property owners. In the summer of 1931 CNT unions campaigned for a 40-percent reduction in urban rents, and in the fall sharecroppers and smaller tenants (*rabassaires*) appropriated the owners' share of the harvest.[46] According to the owners, sabotage and assassination attempts were again on the rise. The Catalan upper class, represented by twenty-six associations, protested against a gun-control law that many thought would disarm them in the midst of multiplying robberies and assaults.[47] In the summer of 1932 rural proprietors feared that peasants who kept the owners' part of the harvest might come under CNT influence.

Given the explosive political and social situation, Catalans' increased reluctance to invest in the region's industries is not surprising. In 1931 the Fomento de trabajo nacional censured "many" Catalans who had exported their capital.[48] Those who had lost money because of the catastrophic situation of the German economy were told not to complain. "The antipatriotic attitude of the timid" had caused great damage to the Spanish economy, which, the Fomento claimed, was basically in good condition despite political problems. The Fomento wondered "how many Spaniards will suffer serious losses because they foolishly believe that it is safer abroad than in their own country." Private investment did fall considerably between 1931 and 1933.[49] The Spanish propensity for depositing money in savings banks was generally much less pronounced than the French. In the early 1930s one savings account existed for every 6.6 Spaniards, compared to one for every 2.1 Frenchmen.[50] Furthermore, important Spanish savings institutions were reluctant to invest in industry during the Primo dictatorship and the Second Republic. Many savers preferred what they considered the safest forms of investment—real estate and government bonds.

The Fomento, however, could on occasion find kind words for the Republican government when it crushed the "revolutionary strikes" of January 1932 in Alto Llobregat and other Catalan towns. According to the employers, the authorities had reacted with energy, and the republican prime minister, Manuel Azaña, had spoken to the *Cortes* (legislature) with "fortitude and sincerity." The Fomento demanded harsh punishment for those responsible for the revolutionary strikes but in August 1932 pleaded for leniency for the organizers of General Sanjuro's failed pronunciamiento of that year.[51] Again in 1934, the Fomento wanted to impose severe punishment on revolutionary offenders and implied that in towns where the Guardia civil was few in number rebellions were more likely to occur. Because the Catalan employers needed the Spanish state to defend their enterprises, they rejoiced at the lack of support given to the Catalan nationalist uprising of 6 October 1934. The Fomento cited with approval an editorial in the *Diario de Madrid* that lauded the great number of "good Spaniards" in Catalonia who were completely unresponsive to "separatist craziness."[52] Even during the so-called *bienio negro*, the period of right-wing rule in 1934 and 1935, the Fomento criticized the ineffectiveness of the government to stop attacks against people and property and called for even more repression. Considerable unrest persisted in the streets and in the factories, where workers often showed only "a minimal desire to work." In addition, many Catalan industrialists disliked what they considered the frequent capitulations of the regional government of Catalonia, the Generalitat, to working-class demands.

During the Second Republic, the Barcelonan capitalists continued to subsidize the police directly. On 21 September 1931 the Fomento reported that it had collected money for the families of the guardias injured or killed in the general strike.[53] It praised the heroism and discipline of the guard and other policemen whose presence, it believed, guaranteed that normal life could continue. In October the Fomento, the Cámara oficial de comercio y navegación, the Cámara oficial de propiedad urbana, the Sociedad económica barcelonés de amigos del país, and other organizations of the economic elite amassed 111,117 pesetas for the Guardia civil and security forces. Publicly, the Fomento announced that new barracks for the increased number of guardias were necessary because the population of the city had grown, but privately the Fomento was franker and expressed its doubts concerning the wisdom of locating these barracks in working-class neighborhoods where they might be attacked during periods of "revolutionary unrest."[54] This barracks' construction project had originated during the era of General Martínez Anido, when Catalan organizations promised to buy the necessary land on which the state would erect the buildings. With this agreement in mind, the Cámara de comercio and the Asociación de banqueros had already donated 50,000 pesetas each by the spring of 1932. During the Second Republic contributions to aid strikebreaking soldiers and guardias amounted to hundreds of thousands of pesetas. These direct subsidies to the police and military demonstrated the strong links between employers and the repressive forces of the state. Under these circumstances, the Catalan owners were hardly enthusiastic about the separation of the military from the civilian government.

Likewise, the most prominent Catalan industrialists did not advocate separation between the Church and the state and believed that military power assured public order as the Church guaranteed spiritual order. Upper-class educational opportunities were largely parochial; although some of the Catalan elite may have been Voltairean about religion—believing it to be necessary for the people and not for themselves—their representatives were often publicly devout and their businesses frequently ostensibly pious.[55] Catholic religiosity remained an essential component of the social system of many Catalan industrial communities.[56] The representatives of the Lliga regionalista or Lliga catalana, which was the party of many property owners, identified Spanish culture with Catholicism.[57] The Lliga accused the entire Catalan left of desiring to dechristianize the region and its schools, as had occurred in the Soviet Union and Mexico. During the election campaign of 1936 the Lliga appealed to the conservatism and piety of women, who had been granted the vote during the Second Republic.[58]

During the Second Republic, many Barcelonan enterprises deteriorated. With perhaps over fifty thousand workers in textiles, the city of Barcelona was the most important textile center in Spain.[59] On the eve of the Revolution, the firms that working-class organizations would control remained largely artisanal.[60] Although the textile industry included several large factories with modern equipment, it was generally dispersed into "industrial crumbs," small family firms lacking modern machinery and organization; their primitive equipment and ignorance of methods of rationalization prevented cost-cutting measures.[61] Often when these small and uneconomical units closed down, another industrialist would buy their old machinery at bargain prices to employ it again. Production was rarely standardized or specialized, and a seemingly infinite number of producers manufactured a wide variety of products. Many textile firms could perform only one process, for instance weaving; they were forced to give their fabric to other, equally small, firms for staining or dyeing. This entailed expensive and slow production. Fierce competition among large numbers of firms kept profits and wages low and also hindered modernization and rationalization of the industry. When the post-1932 economic crisis decreased consumption and increased unemployment, the Generalitat took steps in 1936 to prevent overproduction by limiting factory expansion and growth.[62] The Generalitat's solution obviously did not provide a long-term answer to the problems of an industry characterized by underconcentration and undercapitalization.

Metallurgy was plagued by similar problems. In the mid-1930s most of the Barcelonan metallurgical industries' thirty-five thousand workers were dispersed into tiny companies and workshops that averaged fewer than fifty workers per firm and often depended on foreign technicians and technology. As in the rest of Spain, metalworking did not propel the region toward self-sustained industrial growth. Even exceptionally large enterprises in this sector were industrially backward. The pride of Barcelona's mechanical construction, the Maquinista Terrestre y Marítima, with over one thousand workers, made locomotives and railroad cars. Thus well into the twentieth century its production centered on the railroad, originally a nineteenth-century industry. The Maquinista did not export significantly; its main customer was the Spanish government, from which it constantly demanded protective tariffs against foreign competition.[63]

It is important to note that by 1936 Spain had not developed a substantial motor-vehicle industry. Many Spanish automakers, discouraged by the poor market of the peninsula, had left Spain for the more favorable commercial climate of France. For example, Hispano-Suiza, founded in Barcelona with Spanish capital and workers, moved the majority of its operations from its native city to the larger Paris market before the First World War.[64] Most automotive factories in Spain failed in the 1920s, and in the 1930s only a handful continued to produce vehicles.[65] In 1935 Spain imported over 95 percent of its automobiles.[66] In contrast to France and even to Italy, a country which also had a limited national market, neither Spain nor Catalonia succeeded in establishing a powerful automotive industry.

The aviation industry was as weak as the automotive. Some small planes were built in Barcelona in the 1930s, but the industry was far from complete or independent. Here also the market was dominated by foreigners, as a consequence of Spanish industrial backwardness.[67] Prior to the civil war, with the exception of motors, Spain made only obsolete aviation components with foreign patents and licenses. Both observers and combatants often remarked on the domination of foreign equipment in aviation and weaponry during the civil war.

In this bleak portrait of Catalan and Barcelonan industrial development, the electrical industry with twelve thousand workers in Catalonia seems at first glance exceptional. The growth of this industry had been rapid after World War I; in the 1930s Catalonia reported that its level of electrical consumption per inhabitant was comparable to that in England and France. Despite this claim, the Catalan electrical industry lagged considerably behind the French. With 612 different enterprises in Catalonia and Barcelona, the electrical industry lacked the concentration that characterized its French counterpart; competition between these "industrial crumbs" produced uneconomical and unnecessary duplication. The Catalan industry lacked standardization, and firms often had substations for electrical transformation and distribution that produced energy with diverse characteristics.[68] In contrast to the Parisian electrical industry, which had standardized and unified diverse companies around the beginning of World War I, the electrical industry in Barcelona remained a hodgepodge of small, often obsolete, power plants and distribution centers.

As in other modern sectors, the largest electrical companies were ruled by foreign capital and technology.[69] A certain Pearson, an American, had promoted hydroelectric development in Catalonia; Belgian and English capital were also involved in this branch. Spain was not economically healthy enough to wrest control from the foreigners. The manufacture of electrical equipment was particularly retrograde, and the most important manufacturers were also foreign. Once more, the smallness of the Catalan firms producing electrical equipment kept their prices high and placed them in an uncompetitive position. Most of the companies made domestic, not industrial, products such as radios, lamps, and small appliances.[70]

Like the electrical, aviation, and automotive industries, the chemical industry depended on foreigners, and Catalan firms were relatively backward. The statistics available on sixty-nine chemical firms in Barcelona indicate that nineteen firms had between one and ten workers; thirty-five firms had from eleven to fifty workers; eight had between fifty and one hundred workers; and only six employed between one hundred and five hundred workers.[71] The most important exception, the Cros Company with about two thousand workers in branches in many Spanish cities, was linked to English capital; it monopolized Spanish fertilizer production before the Revolution. Although the output of fertilizers grew significantly in the first third of the twentieth century, Spanish production was insufficient to supply the country's needs.[72] Spain imported well over one hundred thousand tons of fertilizers per year from France, Italy, and Germany.

In urban transportation, Barcelona's metro was "the product of private initiative of little ambition" compared to the one in Paris, where "the metropolitan network had been a great and democratic municipal project."[73] Port facilities stagnated during the 1930s, and in 1934 the number of tons handled by the port of Barcelona was only slightly higher than in 1913. In 1932 Barcelona, the greatest port in Spain, handled less tonnage than Cherbourg, the third largest port in France.[74] The port was in the hands of those who displayed "a suicidal indifference"; its high costs discouraged ships from docking there.[75] The Catalan presence on the seas had disappeared, and one expert recommended establishing a new shipping and passenger line with aid from the state, which would prohibit the purchase of vessels two years or older (since Spanish and Catalan companies had the habit of acquiring leftover ships from ports in northern and central Europe). In Spain itself, no ships were suitable for the new line, and the Catalan shipbuilding industry was termed completely decadent and abandoned. Political influence in Madrid, not efficiency or sound shipping practice, was necessary to obtain governmental contracts, and the directors of railroad and maritime companies that received state subsidies were often political appointees who had little concern for competent management.[76]

In contrast to France and, as will be seen, particularly the Parisian region, Barcelona did not develop major industries, such as motor vehicles and aviation, which were connected with the second industrial revolution. In religion, the city's capitalist elite generally supported the Church, and in politics, the military. How the situation in Barcelona affected the everyday life of Catalan workers and the ideology of the organizations that claimed to represent the working class is the subject of the next chapter.

2
ANARCHOSYNDICALIST IDEOLOGY

The weakness of the Catalan bourgeoisie and the consequent economic and social situation in Barcelona favored the growth and tenacity of anarchosyndicalism. Analyses of this ideology—which I broadly define as including those anarchists who believed that the union would be the basis of the future society, those anarchists who merely accepted the *sindicato* as one organization among several that would participate in the revolution, and also revolutionary syndicalists, most of whom were influenced by anarchist theoreticians—have often been clouded by misunderstandings and polemics.[1] Some historians have concentrated on its antistatism and have thereby overemphasized its utopianism or millenarianism.[2] One has underlined anarchosyndicalism's intense "hostility to industrial life," its hatred of the "constraints of organization," and its "hatred for the present": "Syndicalism could be a roaring success where, as in Catalonia, ex-peasants, already aggrieved by rural hardship and injustice, were newly exposed to industry and looked to an idealized past."[3] Not only academics but also revolutionary Marxists have used this sociological explanation to characterize anarchosyndicalism in Catalonia:

> The Andalusian peasant has given our anarchist movement its spiritual constitution. The simplicity of the village vision has dominated it totally. For our anarchists, the only problem to resolve is that of the prison and the Guardia civil.
>
> This is the essential. The rest remains in a nebulous and incoherent state. . . . The Catalan proletariat, to whom history has given the critical responsibility of being the most important agent of the social transformation of Spain, has not been able to form its prole-

tarian consciousness because of the constant peasant emigration from Spain to Catalonia.[4]

The sociological explanation, however, with its characterization of anarchosyndicalism as anti-industrial and backward-looking, deforms the nature of this ideology and misrepresents the actions of the Catalan workers. While some laborers from Andalusia were involved in violent incidents against the Guardia civil and foremen, others accepted work at wages below the union scale and acted as strikebreakers. In Barcelona during the 1930s, only approximately one-third of the workers were non-Catalans. Not all of these non-Catalans were peasants from Andalusia or elsewhere;[5] many were experienced industrial workers from other urban areas of Spain. Other working classes—the French or the German, for example—were partially composed of former peasants, but their sociological composition cannot explain French anarchosyndicalism or, for that matter, the lack of anarchosyndicalism in Germany. Anarchosyndicalism had firm roots in Barcelona, not because of the supposed non-Catalan origins of Barcelonan workers nor because of its alleged anti-industrialism, but because it articulated the desires of an important minority of discontented workers who were frustrated by social, economic, and political conditions in their country and city. Thus it was not millenarianism that underlay anarchosyndicalism but, on the contrary, a rational reaction to the relative poverty and misery of Spanish workers. This rational response constituted both the strength and, as we shall see, the weakness of anarchosyndicalism.

In Spain in general and Barcelona in particular, salaries, health, and education were often below Western European norms. Just before World War I, Spain had the lowest salaries in Western Europe (Portugal excepted).[6] A French consular observer noted that abnormally low salaries and tariff protection were the reasons for the survival of Catalan industry. Even though 65 percent of its budget was spent on food, a Barcelonan working-class family in the 1930s ate little meat or butter.[7] Only marginal progress had been made since 1914. By comparison, in 1936 the family of an employed working-class Parisian spent 55 percent of its income on food (and that of an unemployed worker spent 64 pecent of its budget on food).

Sanitary conditions still left much to be desired, even though Spanish public health improved considerably during the first third of the century.[8] Available, if incomplete, statistics show persistent differences between Spanish and French public health. In 1936, 109 per 1,000 Spanish children, compared to 72 per 1,000 in France, died before they reached their first birthday.[9] In proportion to population, during the early 1930s Spain had twice as many deaths from bronchitis and pneumonia. In 1935 the mortality rate in Paris for these diseases was .89 per 1,000 compared to 2.58 per 1,000 in Barcelona. Deaths from scarlet fever and measles were proportionally almost four times higher in Spain. Again, in proportion to population, Barcelona reported twice as many deaths from measles as Paris. Much higher mortality caused by measles is characteristic, even today, of underdeveloped nations. In the early 1930s typhoid fever, which was linked to a contaminated water supply and poor hygiene, was almost four times more lethal in Spain than in France. In 1935 Barcelona declared 17 typhoid deaths per 100,000 inhabitants compared to 2 per 100,000 in Paris. Only cancer and tuberculosis were consistently more prevalent in France and in Paris. In 1930 a French woman could expect to live 59 years and a French man 55.9, but a Spanish woman only 53.8 years and a Spanish male 51. Spaniards had one of the lowest life expectancies in either Eastern or Western Europe.[10]

Accident and unemployment insurance were less available in Barcelona than in Paris during the 1930s. Jobless Spanish wage earners "were completely abandoned to their fate," particularly in light of the shortage of hospitals and lack of health insurance.[11] In 1932 only 25,261 received unemployment benefits from the Caja nacional contra el paro forzoso. In France, with an active population approximately 2.6 times larger, 312,894 unemployed workers received some sort of state assistance in December 1933.[12] With a national population not quite twice as large as the Spanish, French hospitals and hospices accommodated more than four times the number of patients.[13] In 1933 Parisian hospitals and hospices admitted ten times more patients in a population three times larger than Barcelona's.

In December 1933 both the partial and complete unemployment in Spain totaled 618,947. Spanish joblessness during the

Second Republic usually reflected structural, not momentary, economic difficulties, and many of the jobless were farm or construction workers. Unemployment increased throughout the 1930s in Spain in part because the possibilities of emigration, a safety valve for the poor of certain regions, were reduced. The more advanced nations, such as France, which were adversely affected by the depression, discouraged new immigration and encouraged foreigners to return home. The Spanish and Catalan economy had difficulty providing jobs for returning nationals.

With numerically unimportant exceptions, education for workers was either lacking or controlled by the Catholic church until the advent of the Second Republic.[14] The level of illiteracy in Spain and the number of priests per capita were among the highest in Western Europe, matched only by Portugal, the Balkan countries, and Latin America.[15] Although the percentage of illiterates certainly declined in the first third of the twentieth century, absolute numbers of illiterates remained stable.[16] A recent study has noted that in 1930 33 percent of the Spanish population was illiterate; another has stated 40 percent, and an older source estimates 45.46 percent.[17] In 1930, 60 percent of Spanish children did not attend school.[18] Even in 1934 the number of children of school age who were literate was hardly greater than the number who were not.

Guillermo Graell, the head of the Fomento, wrote in 1917 that 60 percent of the Spanish population could not read or write, although in Barcelona the percentage was 41 percent.[19] In November 1922 the Fomento noted that "perhaps the majority" of workers was illiterate and therefore uninterested in printed documents.[20] Estimates vary, but in the 1930s Barcelona had an illiteracy rate of at least 22.3 percent.[21] In 1936 the percentage of children in Catalonia who did not attend school rose to 36 percent.[22] A Catalan glassworker, Juan Peiró, who was to become the CNT Minister of Industry in the government of Largo Caballero, learned how to read and write in a Barcelonan prison at age twenty-two.[23] Prison seems to have been the university of many other anarchosyndicalist militants. Many working-class children were unable to attend classes because they had to work at an early age; others were discouraged by prohibitive costs, because the state gave little support to education. Spain spent 1.5 pesetas per year per inhabitant on education, whereas France spent what amounted to 5.6 pesetas, or almost four times as much.[24] Spanish technical education was insufficient, with only 1,527 students in both state and Catholic technical schools in 1935. In contrast, France was training 40,000 technical students in 1940.

The higher illiteracy, lower health standards, and weak economy must be taken into account in any evaluation of revolutionary ideologies in Catalonia. In Barcelona, revolutionary ideology took the form of anarchosyndicalism and not of Marxism, which workers identified with "reformism," that is, participation in parliament and collaboration with the hated bourgeoisie. Before World War I a French observer noted the "moderation and restraint" of Spanish Socialists, who were Marxists, and remarked that their "leaders became collaborators in the work of practical reforms realized by the state."[25] After the First World War, the Socialists and their union, UGT (Unión general de trabajadores), continued to cooperate with the government; the dictator, Primo de Rivera, even appointed Largo Caballero, the head of the UGT, as state counselor. Largo Caballero used his position to strengthen the UGT while the CNT (Confederación nacional de trabajadores) was outlawed by the government. Within the Second Republic, Socialists occupied important ministries during the first *bienio* (1931–1933) and after the victory of the Popular Front.

The anarchosyndicalists' rejection, in principle if not always in practice, of collaboration with state and bourgeoisie as well as their criticism of Socialist reformism should not be dismissed too quickly as irrational or illogical. As we have seen, the bourgeoisie in Spain and Barcelona was less frequently the progressive elite that it was in France. Cooperation with the Spanish state, which often responded with repression to social problems and workers' agitation, was clearly unpopular among militant sections of the proletariat.[26] The neutrality of the state was, to say the least, questionable when, as has been shown, industrialists directly subsidized the low-paid Guardia civil. Therefore, anarchist and anarchosyndicalist strength among groups of Spanish and Barcelonan workers should not be seen as a result of the immaturity of workers or their nostalgia for a rural utopia but as a revolutionary response to a society where repression and direct recourse to military rule were frequent.

Until recently, historians have stressed the antistatist character and the political thought of anarchosyndicalism and have therefore ignored its economic doctrines. Although many anarchosyndicalists wished to abolish the state or radically reduce its functions, they were not opposed to economic organization and coordination. In fact, they favored a strong union as the basis of both the revolution and the future society. If anarchosyndicalists desired democratic control of the factories by the workers themselves, they by no means opposed industry, science, or progress in general. Indeed, few were more fervent believers in progress and production than Spanish anarchosyndicalists; they criticized their bourgeoisie because of its inability to develop the productive forces.[27]

By glorifying labor as emancipatory, the dominant forms of anarchism and, later, anarchosyndicalism led not only to the acceptance of industrialization but also to its active promotion. In 1872 the regional conference of the First International in Zaragoza asked, "How can women be free?" and responded to its own question, "through nothing but work."[28] In 1910 the founding congress of the anarchosyndicalist CNT again espoused the idea, which became common among many sectors of the Left, that women were to be liberated by labor. In the textile industry, where women often received half the wages of men, the Barcelonan union advocated equal pay for equal work and elimination of the double exploitation of women at home and at the workplace. The union, whose leadership was exclusively male in a branch where women composed the majority, believed that the "liberation (*redención moral*) of women, who are today subordinated to their husbands, must be brought about by work, which will make them equal to men."[29]

Anarchosyndicalism called on workers in their unions to take over the means of production and, just as important, to develop them. The French thinker Georges Sorel articulated certain ideas common to European and Spanish anarchosyndicalism. Although Sorelism in France was limited to small groups of intellectuals, it nevertheless expressed "certain tendencies of revolutionary syndicalism."[30] Probably referring to CNT militants, a prominent Catalan industrialist asserted that "our workers are more likely to accept the ideas of revolutionary syndicalism of Sorel and Labriola." Sorel, who rejected what he considered the bourgeois notion of progress, nevertheless believed that true progress existed in the workshop and in production:

> Revolutionary syndicalism is the greatest educational force that contemporary society has in order to prepare the work of the future. The free producer in a progressive workshop must never evaluate his own efforts by any external standard; he ought to consider the models given him as inferior and strive to surpass everything that has been done before. Thus, the constant improvement of the quantity and quality of production will always be assured; the idea of continual progress will be realized in a workshop of this kind.[31]

Sorel also criticized the French bourgeoisie for what he considered its failure to develop the productive forces, and he faithfully expressed the productivism that was common to both anarchosyndicalist intellectuals and militants. In 1906 in a speech before one hundred striking comrades, an anarchosyndicalist carpenter, Léon Jamin of the French federation, CGT (or Confédération générale du travail), attacked the "parasitism" of the bourgeoisie and defended modern methods of production:

> I am a fervent supporter of machinery everywhere it can be used. . . . To install machines everywhere will make the final work of the social revolution easier. The only practical way to dispense with the middlemen, the employers, who are between the producers and consumers, is first to participate in your union in order to be able, later, without striking a blow, to take over the means of modern production.[32]

The CGT carpenter concluded that exploitation would not cease until the union realized "scientific organization at work."

Jamin was not the only French anarchosyndicalist to endorse scientific organization at work. Even such a harsh critic of Taylorism as Emile Pouget, a CGT leader, approved the principle of scientific organization of the factory. What Pouget objected to in his pamphlet, *L' organisation du surmenage: Le système Taylor,* was Taylor's pseudoscientific method, which exhausted workers both physically and mentally. According to the CGT leader, in Taylor's system "at all times the scientific point of view, the rational organization of work becomes . . . secondary, and the primary objective is . . . to force workers to overwork."[33] Pouget uncritically approved the system of two American pioneers of scientific organization of work, Frank and Lillian Gilbreth, who, according to the French anarchosyndicalist, wanted only to make work easier and more efficient through the elimination of "useless" movements and the "simplification" of the work process.[34] According to one historian of work organization, the Gilbreths had studied the causes of workers' motivation and sought ways to reduce workers' fatigue.[35] They were in the avant-garde of the movement to wed industrial psychology to scientific management and to secure the "consent" and "contentment" of workers. In addition, the Gilbreths, unlike Taylor, accepted labor unions. Pouget was able to admire the Gilbreths' work since he shared with them a faith in the ability of the scientific organization of labor to bring about, under the proper circumstances, progress in production and the reconciliation of workers to their jobs.

Whereas in France anarchosyndicalism gradually faded in the first two decades of the twentieth century, in Spain anarchosyndicalism grew even after World War I. During the war the Catalan bourgeoisie refused to break its alliance with conservative and traditionalist politicians, and the attempt to make a democratic revolution and establish a republic in 1917 failed miserably. In addition, wartime inflation and the immediate postwar economic crisis fueled working-class discontent throughout Spain, particularly in Barcelona, where violent strikes brought brutal state repression. An atmosphere of class hatred reigned in the Catalan capital, and syndicalist terrorism battled counterterrorism by the state and employers, resulting in 809 major felonies (*delitos sociales*) between 1917 and 1922.[36] Revolving around the CNT, the anarchosyndicalist movement grew in response to the climate of violence and economic crisis, and of disappointment after the failed revolution of 1917.

Within the working-class movement, those anarchists who believed that the union would be the basis of the future society of libertarian communism gained ground over other anarchists who held a more individualist position or who considered that the building blocks of the new society would be the municipalities or the communes of the countryside.[37] The anarchosyndicalists regarded the union—which, of course, totally depended on the existence of the workplace and wage labor itself—as the organizational foundation of libertarian communism. Their attitude reflected the growing acceptance of industrialization among libertarian militants, although, it should be noted, historians have often exaggerated the anarchists' hostility to the machine age.

Diego Abad de Santillán, a leader and theoretician who later represented the CNT in the Generalitat during the Revolution, exemplified the shifts in Spanish anarchosyndicalist ideology. Santillán had favored the rural municipality and opposed the domination of the *sindicato* (union) in the anarchist movement but became one of the most ardent defenders of the *sindicato* as the basis for the revolution. He also shifted from being a zealous critic of capitalist technology and organization of work to being their enthusiastic supporter. In 1931 he could write, "Modern industrialism, in the manner of Ford, is pure fascism, legitimate despotism. In the great rationalized factories the individual is nothing, the machine is everything. Those of us who love freedom are not only enemies of statist fascism but also of economic fascism."[38] Yet two years later, in 1933, Santillán described modern industry as a source of pride for the human race since it had led to the domination of nature. He noted approvingly that Taylorization had eliminated the "unproductive movements of the individual" and had increased "his productivity":

> It is not necessary to destroy the present technical organization of capitalist society, but we must make use of it.
>
> The Revolution will end private ownership of the factory, but if the factory must exist and, in our opinion, improve, it is necessary to know how it operates. The fact that it becomes social property does not change the essence of production or the method of production. The distribution of production will change and become more equitable.

Santillán's abrupt shift was perhaps induced by the Depression, which led many militants, including some who were more anarchist than syndicalist, to conclude that the fall of capitalism was inevitable and that they must be able to manage the economic transition to libertarian communism.[39]

Like many other libertarian militants, the CNT leader underlined the necessity of eliminating "parasitism" and of providing work for all. Work would be both a right and a duty in revolutionary society, and he approved the old saying, Those who do not work, do not eat:

> In the factory we are not seeking friendship. . . . In the factory what interests us above all is that our fellow worker knows his job and does it without complications because of his inexperience or ignorance of the functioning of the whole.
>
> Salvation is in work, and the day will come when workers want it [salvation]. The anarchists, the only tendency which does not seek to live at the expense of others, fight for that day.

He made it clear that in libertarian communism the producer would replace the citizen.

Santillán, a member of the radical Federación anarquista ibérica (FAI), which often controlled key positions within the CNT, was not alone in his support of work, modern technology, and the union as the seeds of the new society. More moderate and more reformist members of the CNT also advocated most of the *faísta*'s goals. Angel Pestaña, a leader of the *trentistas* (the anti-*faísta* moderates of the CNT), called for a reorganization by the union to improve both production and consumption.[40] Marín Civera, who attempted to synthesize Marxism and anarchosyndicalism in his review, *Orto,* confirmed that *sindicalismo* "revered technology, welcomed it with jubilation and cherished it as the greatest part of its dream."[41] Civera, whose journal published contributions from many prominent CNT leaders, favored big unions to compete with capitalist trusts. For Juan López, another CNT moderate, the union should take control of production from the employers and impose "order and moral discipline" on the shop floor.[42] According to López, the unions would intensify production and surpass the technical level of capitalism. Technical commissions would run each industry, in accordance with the popular will.

Even venerable CNT members like Issac Puente, who downgraded the importance of the union in favor of the municipality or the commune, nevertheless stressed their faith in technological progress and production. For these rural-oriented anarchists, everyone had the obligation to produce: "All citizens will become equal in the single category of producers."[43] Another militant who was close to Puente asserted that "life would be so beautiful if everyone worked" so that eventually the "producers" could labor less.[44] Like the anarchosyndicalists, these anarchists asserted that in the revolution the "identity card of the producer," issued by the union, would be necessary to obtain any rights at all. Their goal was to eliminate "parasites," "idlers," and "good-for-nothings." In May 1936, several months before the outbreak of war and revolution, the CNT celebrated its congress at Zaragoza where it recognized the "producer" as the basic unit of libertarian communism.[45]

Foreign anarchosyndicalists, who were influential within the CNT, also emphasized the virtues of work, technology, and industrial democracy. Christian Cornelissen, the Dutch anarchosyndicalist whose *Libertarian Communism and the Transitional Regime* was translated into Spanish in 1936, pleaded for a libertarian communism that would be "modern" and represent "technical progress."[46] He feared that if anarchosyndicalists were not "progressive" and did not ally with technicians and scientists, they would fail as others had in the Russian Revolution and the Italian factory occupations. Unlike many anarchosyndicalists who believed that the state would be replaced by the union and economic coordinating councils, Cornelissen admitted that the state would not completely disappear in the future society but would be organized democratically, "from the bottom up." Although Cornelissen accepted the domination of smaller enterprises in certain sectors, he also attacked numerous comrades who criticized big industry. He favored the extension of the Spanish road network and the use of automobiles to integrate more fully the regions of the peninsula.[47]

The works of Pierre Besnard, secretary of the Anarchist International and head of the French anarchosyndicalist union in the 1930s, exerted a "great influence" over the CNT leadership.[48] Besnard argued that "the period of revolutionary romanticism was over" and that a "constructive plan" of revolution must be elaborated.[49] He termed "labor, technology, and science" the "constructive forces of the revolution"; the future society, from which the state and "all authority" would be completely eliminated, would be based on *"the producer or worker"* (italics in original). "The union," whose "character was biological," constituted the "natural grouping of producers and workers." "Technical sections" under union control would study the best ways to increase workers' output while diminishing their workweek and fatigue. A "work card" containing the number of hours they worked would permit their consumption of goods, which the commune would largely organize. Consumption, which Besnard claimed was not as "creative" as production, would also be rationalized; for example, bakeries that used the "most modern techniques" would produce "on a great scale" to avoid long queues that wasted a "great deal of worktime." In other services, the revolution would turn "ill-tempered and peevish" employees into "lively and conscientious" workers.

According to Besnard, the commune would also take charge of education, to follow the plan sketched in 1876 by the anarchist, James Guillaume. A follower of Bakunin, Guillaume envisaged a perpetual work study program that would begin in childhood and continue through adulthood:

> At the same time that the child develops his body and acquires knowledge, he will learn how to be a producer. . . . As a young man of sixteen or seventeen . . . he will have learned a skill and therefore will join the ranks of useful producers so that he can work to pay back society for having educated him.[50]

Foreshadowing the Maoist period in China, professors would double "as producers who perform manual labor." Although Besnard envisaged the long-term possibility of liberating producers from the "servitude of work," the immediate goal of his social revolution was "to organize production" to allow all "to live and work freely."

Gaston Leval, another French anarchosyndicalist who was influential in both the CNT and the FAI, wanted the economy of the future society to be organized with the consent of the masses but believed that technicians should have important "regulating functions":[51] "Anarchism has always envisaged the functional organization of economic activities. . . . Industry must be directed, administered, and guided by industrial workers and their technicians."[52] For Leval, the fundamental link among human beings was work.[53] He wanted to promote total interdependence and economic unity among regions and criticized "the absurdity of regional patriotism."[54] It is interesting to note that Leval, Besnard, and Cornelissen were much more influential in the Spanish working-class movement than in their native countries, where anarchosyndicalism continued to die slowly.

The revolutionary productivism of Spanish anarchosyndicalists was probably reinforced by the relatively backward state of Spanish industry and agriculture. Their fervent anticlericalism may likewise have become more deeply rooted in reaction to the upper classes' strong links to the Church. For many workers, only a revolution could eliminate the "parasitic" Church, whose priests were exempted from military service and, they claimed, from productive labor. Anarchosyndicalists linked the Church to an economy controlled by "*rentiers,* hoarders, speculators, and dealers," an economy that favored mediocrity and persecuted intelligence.[55] According to one CNT leader, "the lack of culture and the destitution of the Iberian people" were "rooted in the Church."[56] The CNT even blamed the "meanness" (*mezquinidad*) of its class enemy on the Church's influence. A libertarian historian of Portuguese origins viewed the Inquisition as the "defeat of the worker by the warrior, the builder by the destroyer." Many rank-and-file workers shared the anarchosyndicalist militants' intense dislike of the Church; one right-wing Frenchman observed a marked anticlericalism and dechristianization among workers in Barcelona when he visited that city before World War I.[57]

To break Catholic control of education and to end illiteracy, anarchists and anarchosyndicalists demanded that *escuelas racionalistas* be initiated by unions and workers' organizations. Spanish anarchosyndicalists picked up the banner of science and progress, which, they thought, most of their bourgeoisie had dropped. Anselmo Lorenzo, a prominent anarchist militant, denounced the bourgeoisie for turning its back on progress and praised the rationalist "Modern School" for teaching the laws of evolution and for freeing education from "mysticism, metaphysics, and legend."[58] Libertarians attempted to provide a secular, positivist education for the illiterate urban masses.[59]

Diego Abad de Santillán's *Economic Organism of the Revolution* provided one of the most influential outlines of anarchosyndicalist plans for modernization. The book, which first appeared in March 1936, a few months before the outbreak of the civil war, was republished twice during the conflict and prefigured many of the industrial programs of the CNT during the Revolution. Santillán began his essay with a critique of capitalism, which he believed had failed to dominate nature effectively: "Capitalism does not even exploit [natural] resources. Everywhere we observe uncultivated land, unutilized waterfalls, and natural resources that are uselessly lost."[60] In addition, capitalism was unable to extract the highest output (*rendimiento*) from its workers. Because Spanish capitalists had not exploited the natural resources of the country, foreign businessmen had colonized the nation. Without demanding appropriate concessions, the government had permitted the foreigners to become the "absolute masters" of the peninsula. The CNT leader lamented that the tendency to live without work had been present throughout Spanish history, and he argued that the number of Spanish workers—three to four million—should be doubled. Leisure, laziness, and parasitism were degrading and must be eliminated. Other libertarian militants attacked the Spanish state precisely because, in their view, it encouraged this parasitism.

According to Santillán, Spain had to accomplish in several years what capitalism had not achieved in decades; the anarchosyndicalist militant called for national self-sufficiency in oil, cotton, and other raw materials. Agriculture should become specialized and modernized as in England, Holland, and France. Santillán wanted an ambitious program of industrialization. Railroads, highways, and dams were to be built, and Spain needed a potent automobile industry (perhaps on the American model):

> Not so many years ago the automobile was a rarity. . . . Today it is almost a proletarian vehicle, common in our culture, and it must be within the reach of all, absolutely all, the inhabitants of a country. . . . We prefer the Ford factory in which speculation is ended, the health of the personnel is maintained, and salaries are increased. The result is better than a minuscule firm in Barcelona.

Not only anarchosyndicalist leaders and theorists, such as Santillán, Leval, Cornelissen, and Pestaña, recognized Spanish industrial backwardness, but local CNT militants lamented the failures of the Barcelonan bourgeoisie and wanted to take steps to rationalize and modernize their industries. The Barcelonan Metallurgical Union accused the bourgeoisie of maintaining "a series of useless and superfluous industries."[61] In the inaugural issues of the monthly journal of the Catalan Federation of Metallurgy, CNT militants deplored the lack of "progress" in the factory and underlined "the misery, the lack of light, of hygiene, the same outdated tools, poor organization and imperfection of work because of the ineptness and poverty of the Spanish metallurgical bourgeoisie, which was always lagging behind the bourgeoisie of other nations."[62] In particular, the Barcelonan militants criticized the inability of the Spanish industrial elite to mass-produce cars, and they dreamed of the "hot" Spanish car of the revolutionary future: "The cute little car (*cochecito*) will be constructed . . . to shelter two lovebirds. Its construction will take into account the most modern advances, . . . lightning rods, aviation equipment, swimming equipment, radio, fire alarms and extinguishers."

The sailors of the CNT rebelled against the decadence of the Spanish merchant marine. According to the militants, Spain had never acquired a modern fleet because of greedy politicians, corrupt bureaucrats, and visionless shipowners who purchased "old 'junks' from the flea markets of foreign countries . . . receiving big allowances from the state for services totally foreign to any national interest."[63] Similarly, shipbuilders had never really been interested in producing but in living off governmental subsidies and political influence. Thus the Spanish merchant marine was filled with vessels that other nations had discarded after World War I. In sum, "our fleet means economic ruin for the state, a moral and material torture for the workers, and a shame for the Spanish people, while the shipowning vultures get rich on governmental subsidies for navigation, construction, and reparation."[64] According to the militants, Spanish shipping was therefore subjected to "humiliating control" by foreigners who managed two-thirds to three-quarters of commercial traffic from 1900 to 1936.

CNT construction workers also criticized the bourgeoisie for lacking initiative, and they charged that its incessant speculation and its failure to construct new housing had boosted rents for many Barcelonan workers with scant resources.[65] To remedy the "old Spanish vice of laziness," the construction militants proposed the building of new lodgings that would provide fresh air, light, and space for many who were trapped in unhealthy, dark, smelly, and overly dense apartments in the middle of the city. CNT militants were highly influenced by the urbanism of Le Corbusier, the Swiss architect whose ideas for a city of large apartment houses and for improved automobile circulation were quite popular in the anarchosyndicalist union. Thus, the CNT desired to build a modern and "progressive" city, one they asserted the Barcelonan bourgeoisie had never been willing or able to construct.[66]

Like their colleagues in construction and metallurgy, the militants of other major industries—textiles, chemicals, and electricity—decried the backwardness of Barcelonan industries and called for concentration of small workshops and factories, modernization of old plants and equipment, standardization of parts and products, and rationalization to reduce labor costs and increase production. In the textile industry, CNT militants wanted to concentrate small firms and standardize production in order to reduce the number of articles manufactured.[67] Collectivization, that is, workers' control, would decrease needless competition, improve quality, and augment needed exports. It should be noted that the CNT was not alone in its desire to rationalize industries in textiles and other sectors. The POUM (Partido obrero de unificación marxista), a revolutionary Marxist party, also demanded "concentration," "modernization," and "rationalization," and it criticized the Catalan bourgeoisie for wasting the windfall profits of World War I. The workers must do what the bourgeoisie had failed to accomplish, said the *poumistas*, who asserted that "the unions and the factory are the best schools in theoretical and practical education of the working class for the realization of socialism."[68] The UGT, a minority union in Catalonia that was close to the Catalan Communist party (PSUC, or Partit socialista unificat de Catalunya), called too for the rationalization and standardizaation of industry. Communists criticized the dominance of "foreign capital" in the "most important and thriving sectors" and wanted to construct an "independent" and "national" economy.[69]

Activists of working-class organizations demanded the establishment of technical schools. CNT and UGT militants desired the creation of educational institutions to produce technicians for a large public-works program. Militant sailors attacked the lack of educational opportunities in Spain and declared that the schools established by employers were insufficient and obsolete. The majority of sailors remained illiterate, and activists complained that, unlike English seamen, Spaniards were not able to receive training in order to advance through the ranks and that only officers' sons could become officers.[70] Thus, in addition to the accusations that the Barcelonan bourgeoisie had not developed the means of production, anarchosyndicalist militants charged that it had proved incapable of opening careers to talent and ability.

Furthermore, bourgeois weakness permitted foreign domination of large sectors of Catalan industry. Like their leaders, rank-and-file activists of both the CNT and UGT resented and resisted foreign control of their industries. Militants in metallurgy criticized the Spanish bourgeoisie for its subordination to English, American, and German automakers.[71] Fully aware of the poverty of the national aviation industry, the CNT Metallurgical Union wanted to "create a powerful air force, capable of assuring national independence at all times."[72] The Confederación deplored the minimal development of the chemical industry; the UGT Catalan Chemical Union complained that the bourgeoisie had left this sector in an "embryonic state."[73] Both the CNT and UGT noted the advanced state of foreign chemical firms and stressed the need for economic liberation of domestic industry from the foreigner.[74] During the early years of the Second Republic, the Sindicato nacional de teléfonos charged that the government favored "American interests instead of those of our nation."[75] CNT telephone workers protested the government's jailing of "honorable comrades" by "gunmen in the pay of Wall Street." CNT sailors declared plaintively that even the maps of the Spanish coast were English, although the activists concluded that English maps were not necessarily a handicap since if navigators used Spanish maps, "the ships would end up on the rocks."[76]

The militants of the electricity and gas industries were particularly sensitive to foreign control, which, as we have seen, prevailed in this branch of the Catalan economy. The CNT Federation of Water, Gas, and Electrical Workers lamented the "bleeding" (*sangría*) of the economy caused by the imports of electrical equipment and called for an effort to manufacture the material in Catalonia.[77] An account of one of the most important strikes in Spanish history, mounted in 1919 against the Barcelonan power company significantly labeled "La Canadiense," showed how CNT militants fought foreign control of electricity. The article appeared in a CNT publication in 1937.[78] It remarked that foreigners had developed Spain because the indigenous bourgeoisie was too lazy and aristocratic; the English who managed the company were arrogant and treated the Spanish as inferior. In 1919 when the power company dismissed seven workers, blue-collar workers joined white-collar workers in a strike. Instead of meeting the demands of the workers, the government and the Barcelonan bourgeoisie responded with repression; the strikers replied by sabotaging power lines and transformers.[79] A general strike ensued, and it again met repression by government and employers. The official response to this strike contributed to the climate of terrorism and counterterrorism that reigned in Barcelona until the pronunciamiento of Primo de Rivera in 1923.

Confronting what they considered to be a shortsighted and visionless class of employers, Spanish anarchosyndicalists adopted many of the goals that the bourgeoisie in more advanced countries such as France had already accomplished. Thus, anarchosyndicalists desired to develop Spain's productive forces to create national self-sufficiency and a more prosperous national market. This economic nationalism of Spanish anarchosyndicalism has been obscured by the nationalist ideology of the Spanish Right and by its own ideology of "proletarian internationalism." Yet, as we have seen, both anarchosyndicalist leaders and militants demanded the end of foreign industrial domination and the strengthening of Spanish, not international or regional, control of the means of production.

The anarchosyndicalist ideology of economic development included a democratic political philosophy extended to the workplace. The means of production were to be developed with the consent—and control—of the workers themselves. This extension of democracy to production and faith in the union as the agent of revolution distinguished anarchosyndicalist ideology from some forms of Marxism, particularly bolshevism, which stressed the priority of the party. Anarchosyndicalists wanted what is now known as *autogestion,* or workers' control in the factory. The great majority of anarchosyndicalist theorists posited worker-elected democratic councils, to be coordinated by the unions, as the decision-making bodies of the revolution. According to Santillán, power would be exercised by the workers themselves, who could revoke the council at all times. Local and regional councils would be coordinated by the Federal Council of the Economy; it would plan and direct industry and agriculture in accordance with instructions from below.[80] Issac Puente proclaimed, "Technicians and workers united in assemblies will decide the internal regime of a factory, and the federation of unions will have control of production."[81]

Anarchosyndicalist theorists never explored in depth a potential conflict between the democratic form of the councils and the content of the program for economic rationalization and industrialization. Faced with a choice between workers' participation in production and efficiency in production, some libertarians did hint at their response: "Libertarian socialism has never refused the right to resist those who can harm collective life."[82] Anarchosyndicalists would be justified in punishing an individual "who, because of ill will or another motive, would not want to yield to the previously agreed-upon discipline."

According to the French anarchosyndicalist Pierre Besnard, special clinics and schools would care for morally and physically "abnormal" individuals and reeducate them to participate in everyday life.[83] Santillán noted that "in a regime of organized work it is very difficult to live outside of production"; Leval warned that a "parasite" could obtain "nothing" during the

Revolution.[84] Even though Pestaña advocated industrial decentralization, he too wanted "work identity cards" to control slackers. Juan Peiró—who, with Pestaña, was a leader of the *trentistas*—complained that Spain was a "semicolonial country" whose people might need a good dose of repression to make the revolution succeed.[85] Another militant asserted that a libertarian communist society would not use force on those who did not wish to labor but would instead treat them as mentally unbalanced and allow them to wander about as long as they did not disturb social peace. One visionary advocated, when money was abolished, that "vagrants" be required to have their identity cards stamped by a union official to ensure that they could not avoid work. The 1936 CNT Congress of Zaragoza, which reunited moderate *trentistas* and more extremist *faístas,* proposed popular assemblies to discipline those who "do not fulfill their duties either in the moral order or in their functions as *producers.*"[86] The libertarian communist revolution had an obligation:

> [to] seek from every human being his maximum contribution in accordance with the necessities of society. . . . All useful men will be ready to fulfill their duty—which will be transformed into a true right when man works freely—by collaborating in the collective.[87]

The prewar CNT congress demanded not merely sacrifices but also "willing cooperation in the social reconstructive work that everyone will carry out unanimously."

The question of what would happen, however, if the workers themselves resisted the anarchosyndicalist desire for modernization remained unanswered. Would leaders and militants opt for democracy or production? Before we can understand how they handled this problem, we need to examine the relation between the CNT and Barcelonan workers.

3
THE CNT IN BARCELONA

The CNT possessed a dual role in Barcelona. First, in the context of economic backwardness and political repression, it was a revolutionary organization at its inception and—unlike the French CGT—remained revolutionary during the 1930s. Second, the CNT was a union that, like others, defended the everyday demands of its members. An examination of the two roles is indispensable for understanding the political and social situation that eventually led to revolution in 1936.

The Confederación nacional de trabajo was born in Barcelona in 1910, its birth an indication that many anarchists who continued to reject political parties had temporarily put aside terrorist tactics to accept the union as the basis for the libertarian revolution. At its origin and throughout most of its history, the CNT had a very loose and antibureaucratic structure.[1] It first built the organization around the Catalan regional Confederación and later included other regional confederations, coordinated by a national committee. The individual unions kept a great deal of autonomy, since the anarchosyndicalist CNT had a horror of overcentralization and consciously tried to avoid bureaucracy. The union had very few paid officials and minimal strike funds.

The main weapon of the CNT was to be the insurrectional general strike, the day when workers would put down their tools and take control of the means of production from a government and bourgeoisie in disarray. It supplemented this goal with other forms of anarchosyndicalist direct action—sabotage, boycotts, a virulent antiparliamentarism, and antipolitical propaganda.[2] From its birth the Confederación was frequently declared illegal as the government reacted to strikes, acts of terrorism, or other forms of direct action.

After the First World War, persecution of the revolutionary CNT often contrasted with official tolerance of the reformist UGT. The Spanish government and, to a lesser extent, capitalist elites were willing to accept and sometimes even encourage the existence of this union, which was linked to the Socialist party and which generally advocated parliamentarism and cooperation with the state and political parties. Even the CNT was, at moments, willing to ally with its less revolutionary rival. In August 1917 the CNT supported a strike initiated by Socialists and the UGT to bring about a republic. Pro-anarchist historians have characterized its demands:

> The strike proved to be entirely political, its demands influenced not by Anarchist ideas but by those of the Socialists. The CNT program in Barcelona . . . went no further politically than a demand for a republic, a militia to replace the professional army, the right of labor unions to veto (not enact) laws, divorce legislation, the separation of church and state.[3]

Certain of these demands went well beyond the standard Republican platform and frightened reformist elites. The Spanish state and the Catalan bourgeoisie were unable to enact even the moderate parts of the CNT program and thereby helped to push a large part of the organized working-class movement into a more revolutionary and antipolitical direction.[4]

Such inaction and timidity of the state and Spanish elites obstructed reformism in Barcelona and revealed "the weakness of the bourgeoisie as a revolutionary force."[5] Historians have viewed the failed revolution of 1917 as another example of the collapse of the "bourgeois-liberal revolution" in Spain. The Catalan bourgeoisie, they have argued, wanted a democratic revolution that would de-Africanize Spain and render it European. The Socialists and, significantly, moderate sectors of the CNT wanted to assist the liberal bourgeois revolution; however, when working-class organizations called a general strike to usher in a republic, the Catalan elite became frightened and consequently abandoned the fight to democratize Spain. In 1936, only when the CNT and other working-class organizations took nearly total power—political, economic, military, and police—did they secure a republic and the separation of Church from state and military from civilian government, basic features of what was known in the rest of Western Europe as the bourgeois revolution.

According to anarchist historians, the Confederación suffered brutal repression following the First World War and the failed revolution.[6] From 1919 to 1923, anarchosyndicalist militants were tortured, assassinated, and imprisoned. Police falsely charged that "hundreds" of activists had died "attempting to escape." The *cenetistas* retaliated by assassinating "intransigent bosses, policemen . . . the president of the government . . . the archbishop." According to employers, in Barcelona from approximately 1911 to 1921, there were 848 victims of class violence, of whom 230 died and 618 were injured; another 400 were assaulted.[7] Most of the victims were workers. In 1919–1920 the social climate deteriorated further because of a shortage of raw materials and food. In an inflationary economic climate, workers began demanding a guaranteed minimum salary and striking more frequently. According to industrialists, the CNT gained support through boycotts and threats to force workers to join the union and through payments extorted from businessmen. By the end of March 1919, a general strike had shut down Barcelona, and a new state of war had been declared. As we have seen, the employers demanded from the authorities an energetic campaign to eliminate the CNT and initiated a lockout. In addition, the Fomento recommended that Catalan employers adopt a variety of repressive techniques—blacklists, strikebreakers, armed guards, and mutual aid against boycotts.

Syndicalist moderates in the CNT, such as Salvador Seguí and Angel Pestaña, who were willing to compromise with the state and the UGT and who relegated the realization of libertarian communism to a relatively distant future, could not bring moderation to prevail in an atmosphere of terrorism, repression, and economic stagnation. Although the moderates remained a minority in the 1920s, they did not disappear; in response to them in 1927 the Federación anarquista ibérica was formed to ensure that the revolutionary virtues of the CNT were not diluted by syndicalists and reformists. The FAI's membership included the most famous anarchist activists and theorists: Diego Abad de Santillán, Juan García Oliver, the Ascaso brothers, and the legendary Buenaventura Durruti. In its quest for revolutionary purity the FAI exhibited a tendency toward centralism. Thus, the Federación resembled Lenin's Bolshevik party in very significant ways. Like the Bolsheviks, the FAI fought against "trade-union consciousness" among the working class and sought to keep revolutionary ideals alive. In fact, a historian has labeled one current within the FAI "anarchobolshevik." Juan García Oliver, one of the most important anarchobolsheviks, argued for the "conquest of power," a kind of anarchist dictatorship.[8] Like many Leninists, the FAI considered itself the "elite," the "vanguard," or the "consciousness" of the CNT and the working class. If in the end the *faístas* were successful in keeping a significant part of the organized working class on a revolutionary path, they were aided immeasurably by a state and a bourgeoisie that assassinated or jailed moderates in the CNT.

Like the CNT, the FAI did not always maintain its revolutionary purity and sometimes negotiated with political parties in violation of its own principles. These deals and negotiations were important because they prefigured the participation by both CNT and FAI in the Republican government during the Revolution. They also revealed that anarchist and anarchosyndicalist antiparliamentarism and antistatism were often abstractions. During the dictatorship of Primo de Rivera, anarchists who were exiled in France agreed to cooperate with antimonarchist political parties.[9] Unofficially, radical and moderate sectors of the CNT collaborated with Catalan nationalists even though the organization condemned Catalan separatism.[10] The FAI even played a role in the creation of the Second Republic:

> The FAI did not always behave as a pure flame of Anarchist consistency; on the contrary, it was ready to bend its antiparliamentary principles almost to the breaking point when crucial situations arose. Thus, in the municipal elections of 1931, *faísta* delegates joined their moderate opponents in supporting a Republican-Socialist coalition.[11]

The electoral victory of the Left in the large towns convinced King Alfonso XIII to abdicate.

One historian has attributed these contradictions between anarchist ideology and practice to the personality of the *faístas* and has argued that in 1930 their impulsiveness led them to abandon doctrinal purity to collaborate with politicians.[12] Paradoxically, in 1931 the same impulsiveness induced them to invoke doctrinal purity to avoid reformism. However, such an important separation of theory from practice cannot be attributed merely to the "always impulsive" character of the *faísta*. On the contrary, these contradictions revealed the bankruptcy of anarchosyndicalist apoliticism.

The revolts of 1932 and 1933 demonstrated this contradiction. In January 1932 the FAI, which largely controlled the CNT at this time, attempted to incite a social revolution and proclaimed libertarian communism in the Catalan mining districts of the Alto Llobregat and Cardoner. In a number of towns, the rebels confiscated the weapons of the Somaten, Catalan police auxiliaries.[13] In Sallent, syndicalists seized the powder kegs and dynamite of the potash factory and raised the red flag on the town hall. The revolutionaries took control of the telephones and the roads. After guardias had been fired on and injured, the governor sent the military "to intimidate the disobedient villages."

In February other Catalan towns were affected by the movement:

> In all the localities where libertarians dominated the situation temporarily and tried to make the social revolution, they found themselves forced to constitute executive committees charged with maintaining order and guarding the disgruntled and opponents. Even if they wished to abolish laws, install a society without authority or compulsion, and permit freedom for the creative spontaneity of the masses, they imposed their domination by force through decrees they modestly called proclamations. Far from realizing "anarchy," the revolutionary leaders, armed and possessing dynamite, established what could be called the "dictatorship of the proletariat" without taking into account the opinion of the peasants and the petty bourgeoisie.[14]

A left-wing communist has noted that the insurrectionaries of January "did not behave apolitically but politically."[15] The first act of the victorious revolutionaries was to take political power and rule through an executive committee.

The failed revolts also revealed the tendency of the libertarian militants to plan in secret rather than democratically consult with the rank and file. Both the CNT and the FAI alternated between a kind of Blanquist belief in the conspiracy of the few to bring about the revolution and a counterfaith in the revolutionary spontaneity of the masses. The revolt of January 1933 demonstrated the failure of both the conspiratorial and spontaneous ideologies: a strike of CNT railwaymen had been planned for the beginning of January 1933, despite the fact that the UGT largely controlled this sector and that many CNT railway workers were reluctant to strike.[16] Elements of the FAI, led by García Oliver and other anarchists, nonetheless disregarded the lukewarm revolutionary sentiment among the workers and prepared to launch an insurrection. On 8 January 1933, CNT bands in Barcelona attacked military barracks; in several villages and towns throughout Catalonia libertarian communism was proclaimed. Money, private property, and exploitation were abolished—until government troops arrived to suppress the revolt. The lesson of the January revolt was not that the FAI lacked realism, since the social situation during the Second Republic was such that even a small group of conspirators could frequently spark revolts in Catalonia and throughout Spain. What was at issue here was the contradiction between democratic theory and conspiratorial practice, a contradiction that reemerged during the Revolution.

Responding to the government's repression of anarchists, peasants, and workers after the failed revolts of 1932 and 1933 and acknowledging the government's inability to realize reform, the CNT enthusiastically propagated its antipolitical ideology and advocated abstention from the elections of November 1933. Durruti told seventy-five thousand workers in the Barcelona bullring, "Workers, you who voted yesterday [i.e., in previous elections] without considering the consequences: if they told you that the Republic was going to jail nine thousand laborers, would you have voted?"[17] It is hard to determine how widely workers followed the CNT's call not to vote, but in the province of Barcelona abstentions reached almost 40 percent, compared to 30 percent in the rest of the country.[18] Perhaps popular apathy was responsible, or commitment to anarchosyndicalist positions may have explained the high percentage of abstentions in the Catalan capital.

After the electoral victory of the Right, the CNT attempted yet another revolutionary takeover in December 1933.

> To the people: The CNT and the FAI summon you to armed insurrection. . . . We are going to achieve libertarian communism. . . . The women in their homes. The worker at his job. . . .
>
> Private property is abolished and all wealth is at the disposition of the collective. The factories, shops, and the entire means of production will be taken over by organized proletarians and put under the control and administration of the factory committee, which will try to maintain the current dimensions and characteristics of production. . . . The CNT and the FAI will be represented by red and black colors. . . . Any other flag must be considered counterrevolutionary. . . . You must be ready to give your lives in defense of the revolution that offers all of you the two most stable means of life: economic independence and liberty.[19]

Although this revolt, limited to Aragon, failed as disastrously as its predecessors, the point here is not so much to criticize the CNT's and FAI's tactics (although they were certainly ill-conceived) but to show the nature of the Confederación's revolutionary practice. First, the proclamation announced the advent of libertarian communism and liberty in general, but this new social organization demanded absolute obedience to the CNT and the FAI ("any other flag will be considered counterrevolutionary"). Second, the decree ordered the revolutionary worker to stay on the job and his wife to stay at home. As anarchosyndicalist theorists had noted, in libertarian communism the factory committee would not change the nature of production or, in this case, the sexual division of labor. In fact, the FAI and the CNT declared that the size and dimensions of production would be preserved, at least momentarily. Prefiguring the post-July 1936 period, only the *control* of the productive forces, not production itself, would change. In the social revolution the worker would labor for the factory council.

With the Right bolstered by its electoral victory and the subsequent failure of the CNT insurrection at the end of 1933, Socialists feared that fascism could soon take power in Spain as it had recently done in Germany and Austria. The Socialist cry became Better Vienna than Berlin; the armed resistance of the Viennese workers was preferable to the passive submission of the German working class. The Socialists began to seek partners for an antifascist alliance. In addition, sections of the Socialist rank and file, particularly rural workers, were becoming increasingly radicalized because of ineffective governmental land reform projects and difficult conditions in the countryside. Disappointed with the results of his collaboration during the first two years of the Second Republic, Largo Caballero adopted a more radical position and proposed a "revolutionary" alliance with the CNT; but many CNT militants remained understandably skeptical. After all, the Confederación had sometimes obtained less than expected from its compromises with the Socialists and the UGT. As has been seen, in 1917 the coalition had even failed to bring about a republic, and anarchosyndicalist militants remembered how Largo Caballero had profited from his position as Primo's state counselor to win adherents to the legal UGT and undermine the banned CNT.

In the 1930s the rivalry continued. In 1930–1931 the libertarians' contacts with other left-wing parties and unions had aided the formation of the Second Republic, and workers flocked into the Confederación's unions. In Barcelona and other regions neither the repression of the dictatorship nor its incomplete modernization had eradicated the social base of the CNT.[20] The anarchosyndicalists' militancy and successful struggle to reestablish their organizations provoked countermeasures by the Socialist-backed government, which again attempted to suppress the CNT and jailed many of its activists. The UGT used its influence in Madrid to attack the CNT's power base in the port of Barcelona.

Despite the coolness of most of the Confederación to an alliance with the Socialists and the UGT, certain anarchosyndicalists were ready for a revolutionary coalition. In February 1934 a widely distributed essay by Valeriano Orobón Fernández was published, urging a revolutionary alliance between the CNT, Socialists, and the tiny Communist party:

> In order to defeat an enemy who is gaining ground on the proletariat, a granite-like block of working-class forces is indispensable. . . .

> The alliance is going to occur on the revolutionary terrain that the CNT has always occupied, terrain which the Socialists now approach after the resounding failure of their experiences with bourgeois democracy.
>
> Platform of the alliance: . . . Revolutionary working-class democracy is direct social action by the proletariat. . . .
>
> The present theoretical position of the Socialist and Communist parties bestows excessive importance on the role of the political instrument in the revolutionary process. This attitude is odd in the official parties of historical materialism, which ought to see in the influence of the economy the touchstone of all real social transformation. We [anarchosyndicalists], despite the label of utopians which we are given, believe that the security of the revolution depends above all on the *rapid and rational articulation* of the economy. And so the mere slogan of political order is insufficient to embrace the fundamental problems of a revolution. What . . . is essential is the socialization of the means of production and extensive labor coordination and organization, which the construction of a new economy entails. And this cannot be the work of a central political power but of unions and communes which, as immediate and direct representatives of the *producers*, are in their respective areas the natural pillars of the new order.[21]

Orobón's article prefigured, however imperfectly, the CNT's alliance with other working-class organizations, particularly the increasingly radicalized UGT, during the civil war. He also stressed the economic basis of the workers' alliance. The anarchosyndicalist militant realized that the common ground between the CNT and Marxist revolutionaries was their vision of the economic future. Both tendencies agreed on the need to socialize production, to "reintegrate the unemployed into the productive process, to orient the economy toward an intensification of output and to raise the standard of living. . . . Work is, henceforth, an activity open to all and from it emanate all rights."[22]

Orobón's appeal for a revolutionary alliance with Socialists and Communists had only a limited influence within the CNT because the Catalan section, by far the most important branch, rejected such a coalition. The relative influence of Catalan anarchosyndicalism had increased at the expense of the rural sections of Andalusia, after the First World War.[23] Furthermore, the Catalans did not have to contend with a strong Socialist or Communist party in their region. In the eyes of CNT militants, Catalan Socialists had discredited themselves by allying with the Catalan nationalists of the Esquerra.

Many CNT militants came to regard the nationalists as enemies of the Confederación and considered them petty bourgeois. The atmosphere of collaboration that had existed between some sectors of the libertarian movement and Catalan nationalists quickly disappeared during the opening months of the Second Republic when the Esquerra joined with the forces of order to "save" the Catalan economy from strikes and agitation promoted by "irresponsible" elements in the CNT.[24] In return, the Confederación accused the nationalists of profiting from CNT votes and then betraying the libertarian movement.[25] As its name indicated, the CNT made its main priority to create a *national* workers' organization, not to strengthen Catalan nationalism. Catalan nationalists, particularly the right-wing Estat català, persecuted and outlawed the CNT even as the Confederación was being legalized in other regions of Spain.[26] The CNT would ally with the Socialists and the UGT only if they would clearly break with the Catalan nationalists and firmly declare their revolutionary intentions.

Although the Catalan CNT was resistant to Orobón's proposal, the Asturian section of the Confederación was more receptive to a working-class alliance. In contrast to its organization in Catalonia, the CNT was a minority union in Asturias; its local leadership understood that it could participate in the revolution only by cooperating with its rivals.[27] The coalition prepared the way for the Asturias revolt, which was to be ignited by the political events of 1934. In October of that year, the CEDA (Confederación española de derechas autónomas) entered the government. The CEDA was a right-wing Catholic party that many on the Left feared would acquiesce in a "fascist" coup d'état in Spain. Even the moderate—and Catholic—president of the republic, Niceto Alcalá Zamora, doubted that the leader of the CEDA, Gil Robles, would be loyal to the republic and was reluctant to call him to form a government. Nevertheless, on 4 October Alcalá Zamora permitted the formation of a government that included three ministers from the CEDA. The following day in Asturias the coal miners, who had been increasingly politicized by what they viewed as the failure of the republic and radicalized by deteriorating working conditions, began the famous Asturias insurrection, the prelude to the civil war that was to erupt two years later. It is not necessary for our purposes to describe in detail the bloody repression of the revolt by the elite Foreign Legion and the Moorish troops of General Franco. It is important to note, however, that local committees composed usually of Socialists, Communists, and—depending on the town—anarchosyndicalists, attempted to put their plans for social revolution into practice; in various towns and villages of the region, the means of production and distribution were collectivized.

In Catalonia, at the time of the Asturias revolt, the "Catalan state within the Federal Spanish Republic" was declared by Lluis Companys, the leader of the Catalan nationalists grouped in the Esquerra. This attempt at Catalan independence failed miserably. It clearly demonstrated the limits of Catalan nationalism, whose social base was too weak and narrow to form an independent nation. As we have seen, the Catalan bourgeoisie had long made its peace with Madrid and the traditionalist elements of central and southern Spain; it lacked the strength to overcome their influence and the dynamism to dominate the entire nation economically and politically. Thus, radical Catalan nationalism could not count on the support of a large part of the upper bourgeoisie that depended for protection and favors on Madrid. Lacking the support of the upper class and the CNT, radical Catalan nationalism in the 1930s was the province of what for lack of a better name we call the petty bourgeoisie—technicians, shopkeepers, *funcionarios*, clerks, artisans, and sharecroppers. Their nationalism was not only political but cultural and involved as well a renaissance of Catalan as a spoken and written language. The economic possibilities of a nationalism that called for a separate Catalan state were severely restricted, because the feeble Catalan industries depended both on protection granted by Madrid and on the impoverished markets in the rest of the peninsula. Catalan nationalism might mean a desirable political and cultural independence from a bureaucratic and centralized Spanish state, but many Catalans of varying social origins realized that, given the condition of regional industries, a separate nation might well lead to their economic destruction.

The failed insurrections in Catalonia and Asturias generated rather severe repression of the Left by the right-wing government. Various estimates placed the number of political prisoners in Spanish jails between twenty thousand and thirty thousand individuals. In Catalonia the number of prisoners has been estimated at four thousand, most of whom were Catalan nationalist, not working-class, militants.[28] Throughout 1935 the Left feared a continued crackdown and repression by the Right. On 14 April 1935, the fourth anniversary of the Second Republic's founding, the military officers who defeated the October revolution in Catalonia and Asturias received medals in a public ceremony in the center of Madrid.[29] The government desired to create—perhaps as the French had done after the Paris Commune of 1871—a republic of order that could protect private property and the Church. The effort was, of course, unsuccessful. Republican stability proved difficult to achieve in a country whose rural population was thirsting for land and whose working-class militants were often enrolled in revolutionary organizations.

The Left drew together to end the Right's repression. In January 1936 the Socialists, republicans, POUM, UGT, Catalan nationalists, dissident syndicalists (Partido sindicalista), and the Communists signed the program of the Popular Front. It was basically an electoral coalition designed to preserve republican institutions and offered only vague solutions to socioeconomic problems. In fact, the French Popular Front, which was hardly a revolutionary alliance, was much bolder than its Spanish counterpart when it demanded nationalization of defense industries. In Spain, paradoxically, where many fundamental social and economic problems were yet unsolved and where land reform and economic modernization were needed to develop agriculture and industry, the unity of the Popular Front remained almost exclusively electoral. The representatives of the moderate republican parties who signed the program made it clear that they rejected the three major proposals of the Socialists—nationalization of land and its distribution to the peasantry, nationalization of banks, and "workers' control."[30] Although some rightists were favorably impressed by the moderation of the program of the Popular Front, the failure of the Left to agree on some of the most important social and economic issues anticipated the tensions and ruptures that would recur during the Revolution.

The Catalan Left also forged its own Popular Front—or more precisely, Front d'Esquerres—which included Communists, Socialists, *poumistas, rabassaires* (smaller Catalan tenants), and a variety of Catalan nationalists who supported the Second Republic. Its program demanded the restoration of regional self-government guaranteed by Catalan statute, which the right-wing government had suspended after the failed revolution of October 1934. In addition, the Catalan leftist coalition called for preservation of the "social advances of the Republic" and for application of the repressive Law on Vagabonds of August 1933 against "those who are really vagabonds," not against unemployed workers. Although the entire Left, including anarchosyndicalists, agreed on the need to eliminate "parasites," the CNT and some rank-and-file *poumistas* considered the content of the program of the Catalan and Spanish Popular Fronts insufficiently radical.

The CNT had reasons of its own to fear continuation of the *bienio negro,* or the government of the Right, since many of its militants had been jailed, and some were facing the death penalty, which had been restored in 1934. During April 1934 in Zaragoza the Confederación had embarked on a two-month general strike, of which one goal was the liberation of jailed militants. The Popular Front did offer amnesty for the prisoners; in return, the CNT toned down its campaign for abstention. Although some unions and leaders reiterated the official position against political participation, others—such as the influential Construction Union—deviated from the classic anarchist position.[31] This policy, of "the negation of the negation," gave the green light to the rank and file to vote for the Popular Front.[32] Even the famous *faísta* Durruti openly advocated that CNT members go to the polls.[33]

As might be expected, the electoral campaign aroused passions all over the country and especially in Barcelona, where the electorate became increasingly polarized. The Right was divided, and its more moderate elements isolated. The abstentionism urged by the Unió democràtica de Catalunya, which represented Catalan Christian democrats, was condemned by more extremist Catholics as a "desertion and betrayal of the homeland and a flagrant disobedience of the principles that the Holy See and the Spanish episcopate have recently affirmed."[34] In February 1936 the Popular Front won an important victory. Nationwide, it captured from 47 to 51.9 percent of the votes, compared to the 43 to 45.6 percent for the Right. In Catalonia, 59 percent voted for the Left, 41 percent for the Right.[35] To an unknown extent, the CNT contributed to the victory by covertly recommending against abstention ("we must free twenty thousand workers still jailed and obtain amnesty").[36] In Barcelona and Zaragoza, where anarchism was influential, the number of abstentions fell to 27 percent and 31 percent respectively, as opposed to 40 percent and 38 percent in 1933. Even allowing for the CNT's exaggeration of its own importance, the increase in the number of voters was indisputable; according to another estimate, abstentions fell in the city of Barcelona from 38 percent in 1933 to 31 percent in 1936.[37] Even in 1936, however, popular apathy continued to cause many abstentions.

The victory of the Left heightened the fears of the Right that the Popular Front would violently secure the separation of Church from state, reduce the power of the military, encourage regional nationalisms, and perhaps put land reform into practice. In addition, the failed revolts of 1932, 1933, and 1934 raised the specter that it would not be the moderate republicans such as Manuel Azaña or Martínez Barrio who would secure certain features of the unfinished bourgeois-liberal revolution but rather, as in Russia in 1917, working-class revolutionaries who had no respect for private property. CNT militants, leftists in the Socialist party and the UGT, *poumistas,* and Communists might not only institute lay and civilian rule; they might also nationalize or collectivize the means of production.

Throughout the Second Republic military officers dealt with threats to the traditional order and "separatisms" of the periphery by plotting against the republic, but those in uniform were not solely responsible for the lack of social peace. Workers continually pressed their demands through strikes, many of which the CNT led. The CNT's ideology and political activity have already been examined, but its day-to-day functions as a *union,* representing its membership and strengthening its organization, have not. An investigation of the CNT's role as a union that demanded less work, job security, better benefits, and higher pay for its male and female membership is necessary in order to understand the character of the CNT from 1931 to 1936 and the demands of the Barcelonan working class. When the Revolution erupted in July 1936, the CNT would find itself having to combat desires it had encouraged during the Second Republic.

With the advent of the republic, many CNT unions experienced a massive influx of new members, estimated at over 100,000 in Catalonia.[38] In 1931, CNT members were 58 percent of the working class from the city of Barcelona and 30 to 35 percent from the province.[39] Barcelona's workers followed their previously established pattern of disregarding ideology and switching to the union that they thought would best protect them. As in 1922, after the repressive Generals Martínez Anido and Arleguí had been transferred, workers abandoned the right-wing Sindicato libre and joined the reopened anarchosyndicalist unions.[40] In 1931 the Metallurgical Union of Barcelona reported that its membership had jumped in several months from 18,500 to 29,000 and that it had exhausted its supply of union cards.[41] The Construction Union issued 42,000 cards in a brief period. Workers joined the Confederación in large numbers but, complained CNT officials in Barcelona, did not pay their dues or attend meetings. "Many adherents are not up to date with their dues. All membership cards must be checked, and we must make everyone who is behind realize the necessity of being up to date. In case someone refuses, he must not be permitted to work."[42]

If reluctant to pay dues, workers were not hesitant to strike. In 1931 the Chamber of Commerce of Barcelona described the situation immediately after the establishment of the republic:

> The petitions for new working conditions, and the strikes that the workers launch when the employers refuse to accept these [condi-

> tions] coincide with violent demonstrations by groups of the unemployed. The tactic that is followed is to present new demands only to a small number of firms and then to call on other firms if these demands are accepted or, if not, to call a partial strike.[43]

A Catalan republican criticized the workers for wanting to satisfy all their desires immediately after the proclamation of the Second Republic.[44] At the end of May and the beginning of June 1931, agitation continued unabated. The CNT admitted that it could not control the strikes that erupted in the summer of 1931. The government felt forced to take measures to guarantee the right to work. In July the governor, Carlos Esplá, and military authorities led by General López Ochoa threatened to replace striking electricians and other workers with military personnel.

A wide variety of issues provoked strikes; prominent among them were disputes over piecework. A number of unions demanded the "total elimination of piecework and incentives."[45] This demand had been voiced as early as the founding congress of the CNT in 1910 in Barcelona and would continue to be popular among the city's workers even during the civil war and Revolution. Other persistent desires were a slower pace of work and a reduction of the workweek. In 1912 a right-wing French observer remarked that Spanish workers were not fond of laboring quickly and often engaged in slowdowns.[46] During World War I Gaston Leval, the anarchosyndicalist militant who worked at various jobs in both France and Spain, was pleasantly surprised at the much slower rhythms of production, more frequent breaks, and the relative absence of overtime and piecework in Barcelona compared to Paris.[47] In the 1920s an engineer of the Maquinista, who introduced pay incentives based on a system of "scientific" organization of work, feared workers' "laziness" and "tricks . . . to deceive" the time-measurement monitors.[48]

Historians have correctly asserted that the numerous strikes and demands for a shorter workweek were responses to the increasing number of unemployed in Barcelona in the 1930s. As has been seen, unemployment insurance was practically nonexistent in Barcelona, which made workers' solidarity with the jobless critical. Various CNT unions proposed schedules to share the limited amount of work equitably among all workers. In addition to solidarity with the jobless, Barcelona workers wanted to diminish the workweek simply to work less. As will be seen, a reduced work schedule was only one method—and not necessarily the most efficient—of decreasing the number of jobless. When the forty-eight hour workweek was reimposed in November 1934 during the *bienio negro,* strikes erupted, and workers refused to labor more than forty-four hours.[49]

This *bienio negro* (1934–1935) was a period in which the labor movement found it difficult to protect its gains. In 1934 workers went on strike less frequently than previously and lost labor conflicts more often than in 1933.[50] Following the victory of the Popular Front in 1936, the forty-four-hour week was reestablished, and both CNT and UGT metallurgists demanded reimbursement for the extra four hours' work per week that had been required during 1935. The Generalitat mediated this dispute and resolved it by a wage increase. Many metallurgists remained dissatisfied with the settlement, however, and embarked on work slow-downs, which cut production in half. In various political and social climates throughout the Second Republic, Barcelona's workers fought hard over bread-and-butter issues. From 1931 to 1936, although the unions' attempts to win a six-hour day were unsuccessful and the goal of a thirty-six-hour week went unfulfilled, a forty-two-hour week was established in several important sectors of Catalan industry.

In order to avoid work, workers in the CNT and other unions even injured themselves. The Maquinista reported that during a bridge construction project in Seville, workers provoked minor infections by cutting themselves to take advantage of sick pay. As a result, the Maquinista was dropped by its insurance company.[51] Employers feared that if they had to shoulder the entire burden of accident insurance and indemnities, counterproductive consequences could be expected:

> Protection for the worker could encourage desires to obtain a permanent disability. . . . This is a fact verified by the broad experience of insurance companies and mutual associations. To receive indemnities for a longer period of time, treatment for many accidents has been prolonged beyond any real need through the use of caustic and corrosive agents (*cáusticos y corrosivos*), even at the risk to one's health.[52]

The struggle for a shortened workweek assumed another dimension: though highly dechristianized and often anticlerical, Catalan workers nevertheless defended the traditional fiestas with vigor. In 1912 a French Catholic described such an occasion:

> the strength of popular feeling, the need for rest and amusement . . . were so urgent that, in spite of their abolition, the Spanish people spontaneously celebrated the customary work stoppages of Saint John on Monday and Saint Paul the following Saturday. Disregarding the employers, they deserted all the workshops. Republican anticlericals gave into the [popular] pressure by organizing balls and operettas.[53]

The CNT Textile Union protested against the suppression of twenty-three paid, interweekly holidays.[54] Barcelonan workers were ready to invoke "tradition" in order to struggle against working time. In 1927 the Fomento noted that the employers who attempted to make their workers make up or recover feast days that were not Sundays could expect trouble.[55] Indeed, strikes lasting a considerable number of days to protest the schedule did occur in the spring and summer of 1927, in 1929, and in 1931.[56] In addition, workers would sometimes skip the day before or after a holiday, traditional or not; legislation was formulated to restrict this custom.

Working women, who composed 57.3 percent of the work force in the Barcelonan textile industry, seem to have been particularly combative about the work schedule and other issues that directly concerned them, such as maternity insurance.[57] Women wanted the prohibition on night work to apply to the hours of 11 P.M. to 5 A.M. instead of 10 P.M. to 4 A.M., since they did not wish to rise one hour earlier. When a law prohibiting night work for women was altered, the change of schedule "was not welcomed by the workers," who then went on strike.[58] Women laboring at a textile factory in Badalona refused management's proposal for a split workweek, half the women to work three days and the other half to labor the three remaining days; the women favored a workweek of the same three days for everyone.[59] The CNT Textile Union demanded that pregnant women receive four months of maternity leave.[60]

Judgments concerning women's militancy must be mixed. Many Spanish women were less likely than men to join and lead unions because they considered their employment to be temporary. In 1930, the 1,109,800 working women constituted 12.6 percent of the total work force and 9.16 percent of the female population.[61] Only 43,000 to 45,000 joined unions; of these, 34,880 to 36,380 belonged to the Catholic trade-union movement. Some began to labor at age twelve or fourteen and quit immediately after they were married, usually between the ages of twenty-five and thirty. If widowed, some returned to the labor market. In 1922, Barcelonan industrialists asserted that most women workers left their jobs to get married and that very few labored until retirement age.[62] In 1930, 65.6 percent of working women were single, 19.29 were married, and 14.26 were widowed.[63] In Barcelona, 65 percent of the active female population worked in industry.

In many families that sought to acquire a small business or a piece of land, women controlled the family budget and may have hesitated at the loss if they or their husbands were to join walkouts. Some female workers, who labored for a wage that complemented the earnings of other family members, were also reluctant regarding strike action. Women from the impoverished middle classes, who worked to keep up appearances, may have resisted participation in militant movements. In July 1931, 560 employees—mainly office personnel and repair workers—struck against the telephone company.[64] Young women seem to have been among the first to return to work. During the conflict three male strikers, who were probably members of a CNT affiliate that claimed to represent 8,500 workers in this branch, were stopped by police for trailing three non-striking young women. The strike ended in failure, perhaps because it generally lacked the support of working women, who were much less likely to strike than their male fellow-workers but who often received half the mens' wages.[65] Militancy, though, should not be exclusively identified with strikes or union membership, and as has been seen, women were capable of defending what they considered to be their own interests against those of entrepreneurs.

Conflicts arose not only between employers and workers—male or female—but also, significantly, between employers and their foremen, who also refused to work during fiestas.[66] On 8 and 24 September 1932, foremen skipped work, and their employers denied them their wages. The industrialists claimed that if foremen were absent, even though workers were present, the day would be totally wasted. The employers asked for the state's help in persuading the supervisory personnel to fulfill their duties. The government mediated the dispute, and it established that the foremen's union, El Radium, had petitioned the employers' federation several times for retirement and health insurance without receiving a response. In October 1932 the authorities concluded that foremen must come to work during interweekly holidays but that insurance for sickness must also be established. The civil governor insisted that foremen abide by the recognized work schedule.

These tensions between the foremen and their employers showed that the industrialists had stubborn adversaries even among the supervisory personnel of their own factories. In fact, class conflict between foremen and employers was frequently as intense as were struggles between workers and bosses. In contrast, during the same period in France foremen were the sergeants of industry, generally committed to the success of their enterprise and to industrial discipline. Indeed, supervisory personnel often exceeded their employers in concern for the smooth functioning of the firms. Yet in Catalonia the foremen seriously contested the authority of their bosses and occasionally even held them hostage during strikes. At times, the supervisors detonated explosives and destroyed property.[67] The 1934 foremen's strike took on "a violent character with bombs, acts of sabotage, and the entire repertory of extremism," which the entrepreneurs thought was "inappropriate" for this category of personnel: "Although it might seem strange, the foremen, who should be models of equanimity, serenity, and reflection during social troubles, forgot their role and adopted a rebellious attitude that matched the most extreme working-class organizations."[68] Even non-CNT foremen of certain textile factories committed acts of violence. These members of the so-called workers' aristocracy were involved in assassination attempts against "scabs" and sometimes planted bombs in factories that continued to operate during the strike. Their acts demonstrated the incapacity of the entrepreneurs to impose or implant what might be called capitalist hegemony upon a group whose allegiance was absolutely necessary to industry's effective functioning.

Throughout the 1930s, workers staged violent strikes to protest layoffs and firings. In September 1930, firings provoked a widespread strike in construction.[69] In the same year, another strike in metallurgy demonstrated how workers' power obstructed dismissals. On 2 October, 760 workers walked out of a foreign-owned metalworking factory that employed 1,100 workers in Badalona.[70] Two days later, police arrested and jailed two workers for violation of the right to work. The authorities then detained four women, whose militancy and solidarity with strikers had provoked their brutal treatment from the Guardia civil. Metallurgical workers protested the arrests and charged that police, who were engaging in loading and unloading goods for the factory, were acting as strikebreakers. On 24 October, the Unión patronal de Badalona agreed to reinstate the dismissed workers but affirmed the employers' right to discharge personnel for "justified motives." Furthermore, the bosses prohibited union delegates from acting inside the factory but pledged not to dismiss workers who had a year of seniority. Workers were to return to work the following Monday. Without notifying the authorities, they continued their illegal strike.

Tensions increased on 29 October, when strikers disobeyed a summons to disperse given by mounted police armed with sabres. The guardia arrested five men and four women who were carrying stones. The next day, 250 "scabs," in the governor's words, entered the factory. When a truck accompanied by policemen left the firm, strikers, "presumably from the Sindicato único (CNT)," attacked the vehicle with small arms. Those in the truck, perhaps guardias themselves, fired back and killed two strikers. The day after, the governor responded to the workers' deaths by jailing the presidents of the transportation and construction unions of Badalona. During the funeral of the strikers, the Guardia civil "was forced to charge" the crowd of three to four thousand persons. Little wonder that both workers and bosses who wanted to encourage a moderate and nonrevolutionary trade unionism of the northern European variety were unsuccessful in Barcelona. Such close collaboration between private industry and the state, which seems to have acted not only to ensure the right to work but as an armed strikebreaker, also reinforced anarchosyndicalist ideology in Barcelona.

Strikes over firings continued during the Second Republic. Catalan workers had long memories, and workers and civil servants who had been "unfairly" dismissed during the general strike of 1917 demanded compensation.[71] Large metalworking factories, such as the Casa Girona, also found it difficult to discharge workers without suffering a strike.[72] Until the *bienio negro* Catalan employers found it very hard to lay off personnel; even during 1934–1935, dismissals led to strikes. From April 1935 to January 1936 out of thirteen strikes only four or five were caused by salary demands. The majority were provoked by the discharge of a comrade or the desire to share more equally the limited number of jobs.[73] With the victory of the Popular Front, employers were pressured to rehire and indemnify workers who had been dismissed for subversive activities. Wage earners and foremen in transportation, textiles, and dyeing and finishing—workers who had been associated with acts of sabotage—returned to their posts. Those who had been discharged for nonpolitical reasons were also able to return to the payroll. In June 1936, rural proprietors joined urban industrialists who voiced fears that they would no longer be able to fire workers.

The violent atmosphere in Barcelona sprang not only from conflict between classes but also from rivalry between unions. During the 1930s the struggles of the CNT and the UGT produced bloodshed, particularly in the port of Barcelona where the CNT dominated. The UGT posed a threat to anarchosyndicalist control there since, in addition to a reformist ideology that attracted some workers during Primo's dictatorship and the early years of the Second Republic, the Socialist union was able to use its influence in the government to win benefits for its members. In 1930 the government backed the UGT and the Sindicato libre against the "communist and anarchosyndicalist" Sindicato único.[74] In November and December of that year, the CNT seemed to have successfully resisted the drive of its rivals, who had acquired the reputation of strikebreakers, to control hiring on the docks. One can only speculate whether the CNT remained a potent force in Barcelona despite or perhaps because of its largely illegal status until the opening years of the Second Republic. What is certain is that Primo's repression and modernization did not eliminate the Confederación. When the UGT leader, Largo Caballero, became Minister of Labor in 1931, violent conflicts continued in the port. In this dangerous atmosphere, workers had to be cautious and shrewd enough to choose the "correct" union, that is, the one that could protect their persons and their employment.

In 1933 the conflict resumed.[75] In April the CNT called a strike, and several workers who continued to labor were killed. According to the employers, the struggle between the two organizations prolonged the strike in March 1934 by gas and electrical workers. When one union achieved its demands, the other would attempt to outbid it and initiate a new walkout. In October 1934, the UGT-influenced Alianza obrera attempted to show—with some success, according to one observer—that it could initiate a general strike without CNT approval.[76] The rivalry between the unions was further aggravated by the desire of each to place its members in the limited number of available jobs. After a strike, workers would flock into the victorious union—whether CNT or UGT.[77]

There was however another, less dramatic, side to the relation between the two unions. The CNT and the UGT also collaborated during the Second Republic, and their oscillation between conflict and cooperation would continue throughout the Revolution. The united front of the unions in 1936 again stimulated the long memory of Barcelonan wage earners. After the victory of the Popular Front, metallurgical workers demanded and received compensation for working a forty-eight-hour week during 1935 and the first few months of 1936.[78] Both unions supported wage earners' demands for back pay for those workers who had struck in October 1934. In March the CNT and the UGT demanded the rehiring and indemnification of telephone workers fired during the strike of 1931.[79] In May the number of strikes, particularly those protesting dismissals of employees, increased rapidly.[80] Even the Generalitat's Minister of Labor, who was sympathetic to the labor movement, began to complain of "endemic" walkouts that threatened to destroy the Catalan economy. Unity of action between the two major Barcelonan working-class organizations produced a wave of work stoppages that, if less violent than those in 1931 and 1934, was more powerful. As could be expected, the capitalist elite repeated its hoary warning that "the reigning anarchy" might destroy its firms. The power of unions—especially of the CNT—increased on the shop floor as rank-and-file workers sought admission to the Confederación.[81]

During the Second Republic, the Barcelonan working class managed to maintain its standard of living. More than 35 percent of the workers obtained the forty-four-hour week, that is, a 9 percent reduction of the working day. Approximately 55 percent won wage increases of various kinds. About 33 percent achieved both wage increases and reduction of the working day. These gains were considerable since the price index was stable in Barcelona from 1931 to 1936. It might be added that the forty-four-hour week in metalworking was attained over the strident protests of the major Barcelonan manufacturers, who declared that no other region had reduced the workweek.[82] Thus, in a period of political instability, worldwide economic depression, and high unemployment, Barcelona's working class demonstrated a remarkable ability to win somewhat higher wages, a shorter working week, and, occasionally, an end to piecework. The CNT and, to a lesser degree, the UGT were instrumental in many of the workers' victories. Yet there were two sides to the prewar CNT, which was not only a union fighting for the immediate gains of its constituency but also a revolutionary organization struggling for control of the means of production. During the Revolution these two functions of the Confederación would come into conflict because the Barcelonan working class would continue to fight, under even more unfavorable circumstances, for less work and more pay.

4
AN OVERVIEW OF THE REVOLUTION IN BARCELONA

Given the background of conflict between workers and bourgeois, the outbreak of revolution in Barcelona should come as no surprise. Weaker than its French counterpart, the Catalan bourgeoisie had developed only primitive productive forces, and workers' living standards remained relatively low. Into the 1930s, working-class militants of major organizations such as the CNT continued to adhere to revolutionary ideologies. During the Revolution these militants would take control of the means of production and attempt to put their ideologies into practice. Like other twentieth-century revolutionaries, the Barcelonan activists were forced to confront not only their declared enemies but also the indifference of those they claimed to represent. They reacted with both coercion and persuasion: terrorist tactics and labor camps supplemented patriotic propaganda and socialist realism. Before these topics can be explored, however, the eruption of the Spanish Revolution in Barcelona must be examined.

It was, ironically enough, the failure of the revolt against the republic by a large part of the military that detonated in Barcelona the revolution that those in uniform had dreaded. In the first half of 1936 mounting social and political violence throughout Spain and fears that the traditionalist order would soon be dismantled provoked the pronunciamiento of the Spanish generals, eventually headed by *Generalísimo* Francisco Franco. In Barcelona the military revolt of 19 July was defeated because of the combined actions of republicans, Socialists, Communists, Guardia civil who remained loyal to the republic, and, most important, CNT militants. The CNT and the FAI became the strongest forces in Barcelona and dominated public power in the city after the failure of the revolt. Despite their supremacy, these libertarians decided to form a Central Committee of Antifascist Militias with the other left-leaning parties and unions of Catalonia.The committee was a government in everything but name; with CNT and FAI backing, the new regime created the "necessary patrols" and "disciplinary measures" to maintain order.[1] Most observers have noted that the "anarchobolshevik" Juan García Oliver was the central figure of the committee. Once again, as in the unsuccessful revolts of 1932 and 1933, the antipolitical, antistatist ideology of anarchosyndicalism turned out to be an abstraction.

With power in the hands of the libertarians, popular anticlericalism manifested itself spectacularly in the first weeks of the Revolution. The "masses" violently reinforced the separation of Church and state that had been achieved only tentatively with the advent of the Second Republic. The Church was often hated by the popular classes because of its identification with the traditionalist order and its unproductive and "parasitic" nature.[2] The efforts of a small group of sincere Christian democrats were not able to alter working-class militants' perception of the Church as reactionary. During the 1930s in Spain many concluded that the Church was, in effect, allied with "fascism." Anarchosyndicalist and other forces wanted to make certain that it would no longer act as a brake on the productive forces through its control of education or its influence on mores. Like many republicans, anarchists believed that "to secularize is to modernize."[3] *Solidaridad Obrera* proclaimed, Down with the Church, and the CNT daily reported attacks on churches in working-class neighborhoods.[4] Nearly every church in Barcelona was set afire; in the so-called red terror almost half the victims were ecclesiastics. According to clerical sources, 277 priests and 425 monks were assassinated.[5]

The attacks, the deaths, and the defeat of the army revolt in Catalonia prompted the flight of the great majority of the bourgeoisie from Barcelona. One anarchosyndicalist source has estimated that 50 percent of the bourgeoisie fled, 40 percent were "eliminated from the social sphere," and only 10 percent remained to continue work: "Bosses, managers, engineers, foremen, and so forth," feeling endangered, left the city.[6] Thus many factory owners literally abandoned their firms, which, as working-class militants claimed, they had often neglected and underdeveloped. This surrender, with scarcely a struggle, had little precedent in Western Europe and revealed that the Barcelonan bourgeoisie had failed to build a broad social base of support and ultimately depended on police power for its control of the productive forces.

Unsure of future developments, some employers delayed their departure for several weeks or months after the pronunciamiento. An unknown number stayed in the city and worked in various capacities, presenting the unions with the problem of whether to admit them and their sons as members and how much to pay them.[7] Some militants favored their admission and integration into the revolutionary economy, whereas others viewed the former bosses as potential saboteurs and feared their ability to manipulate revolutionary legislation to their advantage. In fact, to avoid workers' control, employers did form cooperatives; one year after the Revolution began, cooperatives had increased fivefold.[8]

As in many other social revolutions, the flight of the monied classes deprived many workers of their sources of income. Large numbers of domestics lost their jobs. With the approval of the Generalitat, bank accounts that had been either frozen or abandoned by employers were used to pay former servants (who sometimes inflated the amount of their back wages).[9] As other employers departed, were arrested, or became destitute in 1937, the numbers of unemployed servants grew. Joblessness affected other areas of the economy: for example, two hundred construction workers were obliged to seek other employment when their project, which had been funded with utility bonds, was forced to close.[10] Another firm, employing forty workers to make dresses for "high society," lost the majority of its clients.[11] When firms were unable to pay workers, the latter—sometimes successfully—appealed to the Generalitat to put them on its payroll.

The flight of capital began well before the pronunciamiento, but was aggravated by the outbreak of the Revolution. In these first months, the Generalitat attempted to combat the problem by issuing decrees that prohibited hoarding of currencies and precious metals. Even small savers were tempted to hide their nest eggs or transfer them abroad. Throughout the war police charged hundreds with the offense of "evasion of capital." Even though it declined during the course of the war as local and national governments reasserted their authority, tax evasion by both individuals and collectives remained significant. Funds that could have been used to develop the productive forces or modernize equipment were often smuggled out of Catalonia or hidden to be divided among a firm's personnel.

Militants of the CNT, often in collaboration with members of the UGT, whose leaders followed the line of the PSUC (Communist), took charge of many abandoned factories. Some of these new managers had been shop stewards before the Revolution. Their dynamism contrasted sharply with the attitude of most of their colleagues, who preferred to stay at home in July 1936. They immediately reorganized many firms, especially those with over one hundred workers, into collectives; in each collective workers elected a factory council from both CNT and UGT militants to run the factory. Other workshops and firms, especially those that had fewer than fifty workers and whose owners had remained in Barcelona to work during the Revolution, were jointly managed by the owner and a control committee of CNT and UGT militants.

In the weeks that followed the defeat of the pronunciamiento in Barcelona, unions and political parties of the Catalan Left recognized the need to legalize and coordinate the various forms of workers' control that had emerged after 19 July. On 14 August 1936 the Economic Council of Catalonia was created, and its members included Diego Abad de Santillán of the FAI, Juan P. Fábregas of the CNT, Estanislao Ruiz Ponseti of the PSUC, Andrés Nin of the POUM, and others from the UGT and the Esquerra. The CNT, FAI, and the dissident Communists of the POUM pushed for as much collectivization as possible and for severe limits on private property. On the other side, the Esquerra, UGT, and PSUC, which combined Catalan nationalism with allegiance to the Third International, wanted less collectivization and more protection for the small industrialists and shopkeepers who were numerous in Catalonia. Paradoxically, a large number of these petty bourgeois joined the UGT and the PSUC because they considered that the two Marxist organizations constituted a needed counterweight to the revolutionary and collectivist tendencies of the CNT and because the Esquerra, the most likely political party of Catalan nationalists and petty bourgeois, was considered too weak to defend their interests.

The Decree on Collectivization of 24 October 1936 was a compromise of the various unions and political parties that composed the Catalan Left, but the decree clearly revealed the dominance of the CNT:

> After the nineteenth of July the fascist bourgeoisie deserted its posts. . . . The abandoned enterprises could not remain without direction, and the workers decided to intervene and to create Control Committees. The council of the Generalitat had to authorize and orient what the workers accomplished spontaneously. . . .
>
> For the collectivization of the firms to be successful, their development and growth must be aided. To this end, the Economic Council . . . will financially aid the collectives and will group our industry in large concentrations that will assure maximum output. . . .
>
> Former owners and managers who have technical and managerial capabilities . . . will serve the needs of the firm.
>
> A factory council, named by workers in a general assembly, will be responsible for the management of the collectives.[12]

First, this decree implied that workers' control was a *necessity* because a large part of the bourgeoisie had fled. Second, although it paid homage to the "spontaneity" of collectivization by the workers, the edict asserted that the collectives had to be channeled toward "maximum output," "large concentrations," "growth," and "development." Third, the decree urged cooperation with technicians and former employers and therefore encouraged a continuation of the organization of work and the division of labor that existed before the Revolution. Finally, the revolutionary content of the edict was its legalization of workers' control. The workers themselves and their representatives would be responsible for managing the collectives.

If the decree was the outcome of a compromise among the various forces of the Catalan Left, its conception of collectivization and workers' control largely reflected the preponderance of the libertarian movement that still held political, police, and, of course, economic powers in October 1936. Juan Fábregas, a CNT member who became president of the (Generalitat's) Economic Council, was instrumental in attaining this "greatest legal achievement of the libertarian movement."[13] Fábregas's quick ascent to power revealed a great deal concerning the economic thought of the CNT. He had joined the Confederación immediately after the attempted coup of the generals. Before the Revolution, he had been linked to the Esquerra and had been the director of the Institute of Economic Sciences of Barcelona; nonetheless, he loyally served the CNT in the Economic Council and thus earned the enmity of the Communists and some Catalan nationalists. In December 1936 he was replaced on the council by another anarchosyndicalist whose thought we have examined, Diego Abad de Santillán. Fábregas's similar economic vision disclosed key aspects of the Spanish Revolution. The economist called for the rational reconstruction of the Spanish economy under the supervision of the technocrats whose cooperation was "necessary to acquire, at whatever cost."[14] Like Santillán, Fábregas advocated the formation of a network of councils that would orient production "under technical and scientific principles."

Fábregas wanted easy credit to stimulate industry and to create what the Spanish economist called "national labor" (*trabajo nacional*), which would solve the problem of unemployment. The CNT economic advisor called for a "vast plan of public works," including roads, canals, dams, and artificial lakes: "We must declare loudly . . . that work is not a punishment but a pleasure. . . . It is the glorious time of the exaltation of work. We will transform work into the maximum exponent of true wealth, into the unique sign of social prestige, making it the greatest source of pride for emancipated workers."[15] During the Spanish Revolution, anarchosyndicalism was an ideology of labor; this tenet helps to explain why a former bourgeois economist such as Fábregas came to represent the CNT in positions of the greatest importance.

The CNT abandoned its antipolitical ideology not only to join the Generalitat but also to participate in the central government of the republic. In November 1936 four CNT leaders were named ministers in the government of Largo Caballero: Juan García Oliver, Minister of Justice; Juan Peiró, Industry; Federica Montseny, Health and Public Assistance; Juan López, Commerce. Libertarian participation in both the Generalitat and the central government ended shortly after the famous May Days of 1937 when CNT and FAI militants fought Communists and Republicans in the streets of Barcelona and other towns throughout Catalonia. This is not the place to describe in detail the political struggles and violent skirmishes between the libertarians and the Communists; they have been amply reported elsewhere. What is important for our purposes is the periodization, or the beginning and end, of workers' control in Barcelona. As we have seen, immediately after the failure of the military uprising in Barcelona, the Confederación occupied the most important political, economic, and police posts in the city. While other forces—Communist and Catalan nationalist—reorganized and gained strength, the CNT, although retaining its arms, began gradually to lose its political and police powers in Barcelona. Many, if not most, historians have focused on the decline of the CNT's political power and its withdrawal from both the Generalitat and the central government after May 1937; they have wedded the CNT's loss of political power to a collapse of its economic power in the factories that its militants had collectivized or controlled. In other words, consonant with the *political* perspective of most historians—whether Communist or anti-Communist, pro-CNT or anti-CNT, Stalinist or Trotskyist—the periodization of the collectives has been subordinated to the CNT's participation or nonparticipation in government.[16] The end of the CNT's membership in both the central and Catalan governments, after the street fighting of May 1937, has therefore been identified with the successful counterrevolution against the Confederación's economic power in the factories that it controlled.

The identification of political and economic periodizations has some, but only limited, value. When forces opposed to the CNT—whether Communist or Republican—controlled the government, they probably withheld the foreign currencies and financial assistance that CNT factories needed to procure raw materials and machinery. After the CNT withdrew from politics in May 1937, Communist strength increased and large attacks took place on collectives in certain regions, notably Aragon. Nevertheless, in Barcelona, which was the CNT's strongest bastion as the CNT was undoubtedly its most important union, the Confederación's economic control of industry did not collapse when its enemies gained political power. Even with Republican and Soviet aid, the Catalan Communists would have had difficulty in eliminating the Catalan CNT, which may have had as many as 1,000,000 members in April 1937. In contrast, the Catalan UGT reported 475,000 members in January 1937.[17]

After the initial defeat of the pronunciamiento, the Confederación never regained the offensive but, often with the participation of the UGT, retained control of many of the largest industries in Barcelona until just before the end of the war. The Generalitat did gain preponderance in several industries, but its legislation was ignored in many others. Numerous articles in the libertarian press attested to the CNT's command of most collectives in Barcelona after May 1937. In November 1937 a CNT publication for the exclusive use of member unions stated that those who had attempted to destroy the Confederación had failed and that the CNT was successfully managing a great number of cooperatives and collectives and even cooperating with official economic organizations, including the Executive Commission of Agricultural Credit, Committee against Unemployment, Postal Savings Bank, and the Fuel Regulation Commission.[18] The anarchosyndicalists also continued to occupy seats on the Generalitat's Economic Council, where they effectively opposed many Communist-inspired proposals. The CNT was able to remain influential in the key sector of the defense industries despite the Generalitat's increasing financial and legal intervention during the first year of the Revolution. Until the end of 1937 the Confederación actively resisted the attempt by the central government, backed by the Communists, to take more than nominal control of the Catalan war industries, where—according to the CNT's own estimates—the union controlled 80 percent of the work force.[19]

During 1938, after the national government's Subsecretaria de armamento assumed control of the defense sector, the CNT was still able to place its members in the factories. The Communist technician M. Schwartzmann has confirmed the Confederación's tenacious hold on Barcelona industry after May 1937; in branches such as transportation and woodworking, CNT control was so monopolistic that in May 1938 the UGT complained of the persecution of its militants in these sectors.[20] In April 1938 militants advised the dissolution of the Commission on Behalf of Prisoners and a reduction of the number of the Confederación's lawyers because the "CNT prisoners are few and soon all will leave jail."[21] On 10 May 1938 the German anarchosyndicalist A. Souchy wrote in *Solidaridad Obrera:* "The base of economic life rests, in spite of everything and everybody, in the hands of workers' organizations."[22] As late as October 1938 Juan Comorera, a PSUC leader, admitted the existence of two economies in Spain, one largely private and the other dominated by the CNT.[23] A CNT militant insisted that despite the campaign against the collectives "the system of collectivization was deeply rooted in Catalan economic life . . . becoming the most solid base of our resistance in the domain of production."[24] An anarchosyndicalist historian has called the preservation of CNT economic power a "miracle" produced by union "toughness," which "stopped the government in its tracks."[25]

Legislation often existed only on paper. In October 1937 Juan Fronjosá, a Communist and the secretary general of the UGT, declared that "three great sectors"—republicans, Marxists, and anarchosyndicalists—were leading the struggle against "fascism."[26] The UGT leader went on to complain that although the Decree on Collectivization required that the Generalitat's Economic Council name controllers, the collectives themselves were choosing them "in the great majority of cases." He protested that the Economic Council intervened only to endorse the workers' nominations. According to the union leader, this procedure resulted in an "intolerable farce" in which the controller was usually "only the plaything" of the collective and even acquiesced in its "illegal activities." Fronjosá's complaints cannot be dismissed as mere Communist propaganda since in the chemical industry, for example, the Generalitat's controllers either refused or were unable to fulfill their duties during much of the Revolution.[27] As late as October 1937, the Generalitat's plan for a bank devoted to industrial development, although authorized by the Decree on Collectivizations, had not been enacted.

The Confederación could retain control in many collectivized and controlled firms because it possessed a variety of sources of income and influence in the revolutionary economy. At least in the first months of the Revolution and probably considerably afterwards, unions were more likely to receive urban rents (if paid) than were either landlords or governmental organizations.[28] In addition, unions held a near monopoly on the labor market and collected dues from both the old and the many new members. Certain collectives also contributed to the unions' treasury, which retained considerable revenues even though local and national governments gradually consolidated their powers of taxation as the war continued.

Some historians have tied the decline of the supposed revolutionary fervor among its members to the CNT's loss of political and economic power and to the anarchosyndicalist leadership's decision to collaborate with other parties and unions in the government: they consider that the CNT constituency became increasingly estranged from its leaders because of the leaders' political cooperation with former adversaries.[29] In their view, the rank and file were especially concerned to put the Confederación's Zaragoza program into practice. From July to October 1936, the "libertarian and collectivist economy" was able to "develop *autogestion* without obstacles."[30] Thereafter, the historians argue, a "spontaneous" and "militant" base of members, devoted to democracy and workers' control in the factory, was prevented from realizing its goals by an increasingly bureaucratic leadership. The proletariat's willingness to sacrifice receded as military objectives took priority over the social revolution.[31]

Yet even in the first days of the Revolution, and despite a general 15 percent pay raise, workers may not have pursued *au-*

togestion with such eagerness and enthusiasm. Indeed, after 19 July, anarchosyndicalist newspapers and radio broadcasts continually called for workers both to return confiscated cars and return to work:

> It is urgent that all [bus] workers belonging to the section justify their absence from work.
>
> [We] notify those [Hispano-Olivetti workers] who are illegitimately absent that sanctions will be applied to whomever deserves them.[32]

In one large metallurgical factory, the return of blue-collar workers was "gradual" during the two weeks that followed 19 July.[33] On 15 August the Control Committee of public transportation demanded that all workers justify their absences with a medical certificate.[34] Five days later a committee member and a physician were assigned to inspect the ill in their homes. The worker-managed power company dispatched a physician to a worker's house for the same purpose.[35] In transportation, dismissals for absences without permission were "common" in the first weeks of the conflict.[36] A POUM printer reported that his workmates had to "hunt down" their absent colleagues and convince them to continue to labor.[37]

According to one witness, the Generalitat's decision to pay wages for days lost because of the Revolution "corrupted" the workers. This measure, which was supposed to last only several weeks, became permanent, and a number of factory councils continued to receive money even though their firms produced nothing. The author claimed that laziness and idleness were encouraged and that "some sectors of the working class" became complacent.[38] The Confederación considered the Generalitat's decree establishing a forty-hour week "ruinous, suicidal, and counterrevolutionary"; the reduction of work hours and increase of wages amounted to a "serious mistake."[39] One Catalan power station celebrated the arrival of the Revolution with extended feasting; during one month the workers in Camarasa "consumed 270 bottles of 'Castell del Remei' wine, 40 chickens, 20 geese, and other items."[40]

Yet some did sacrifice to serve the cause. In the Casa Singer, which had a long tradition of CNT militancy, fifty of one hundred workers volunteered for fortification work with "great enthusiasm and revolutionary spirit." An undetermined number of workers in the power industry asked to labor overtime for the war effort. *Solidaridad Obrera* reported "Sunday work volunteers."[41] Revolutionary and patriotic beliefs motivated an unknown number to accept work.

Many others, though, displayed only a superficial commitment to the cause. In December 1936, eight hundred construction workers at Flix offered to dig trenches at the front. When their site was bombarded several months later, the workers deserted or fled.[42] The unions often had to threaten the conscripted to ensure that they would obey mobilization orders. In February 1937, UGT phone workers were certain that a number of comrades would not report for military training. Several months earlier fortification work had become "obligatory" for telephone workers.[43] The CNT-UGT managers of the power industry agreed to pay a month's salary for each of their workers age eighteen to twenty who were in military training. They nevertheless stipulated that once the training was completed, the recruits must go to the front "without any excuse."[44] Even Prime Minister Azaña noted that "to stimulate recruitment, each soldier received ten pesetas per day, which was five times more than the usual wages of Spanish troops."[45]

When the Republican army had almost one million men, soldiers' pay became an "exorbitant charge" for the governmental treasury. In November 1936 in a large Barcelona collective, not even one of the mostly UGT-affiliated workers was listed in the military; in July 1937, 16 of 280 were in the armed forces; in January 1938, the total was 45 of 318.[46] By 1938 many recruits from Barcelona were discouraged, as one of their officers, a libertarian commissar, reported:

> In this training camp there are 470 recruits; 85 percent belong to the CNT. Seventy percent are manual workers, 15 percent peasants, and 15 percent shop assistants . . . from the Barcelona region. . . . They come demoralized and without enthusiasm, constantly worried about their families whom they have left without means during this economic crisis. . . . Many are without shoes and complain about it. . . . They are aware of the economic favoritism

> shown to bureaucrats and police forces. . . . They always say, "If there have to be sacrifices, they should be equal for everyone."
>
> They object to insignificant things, for example, a late distribution of tobacco, a meal without wine, or hard bread. . . . They are really bothered by having to join the army to fight.[47]

Many workers tried to avoid military duty, and in 1938 it also became difficult to recruit officers from libertarian ranks.[48]

The declining military fortunes of the Second Republic certainly reinforced this lack of commitment, but it appeared almost immediately after the conflict began. At that time most Barcelonan workers belonged to no union; in July 1936 they flocked into the CNT and, to a lesser extent, the UGT. The social base of these two unions differed somewhat: the Confederación had more blue-collar members than the UGT, which tended to attract white-collar workers, technicians, and small businessmen. Although some manual laborers and blue-collar workers did enter the UGT, this minority union was generally more popular among workers who were literate and those who had technical training. It should be underlined that many workers joined the unions not for ideological reasons but because life in revolutionary Barcelona was quite difficult without a union card. To eat a meal in a collective kitchen, to acquire welfare aid, to find or keep a job, to attend a technical training center, to obtain housing, to be admitted to a clinic or hospital, to travel outside of Barcelona, and so forth, a union card was often desirable, if not necessary. Union membership and connections were ironically the only way opportunists could avoid military service, by being declared "indispensable" in the workplace.[49]

According to the CNT's figures, it represented only 30 percent of the Catalan industrial workers in May 1936, down from 60 percent in 1931.[50] "Tens of thousands" of workers with little "class consciousness" joined the two unions in search of social protection and stable employment.[51] On 4 August 1936, for example, several weeks after the outbreak of revolution, a majority of members of the union of workers at dog races held a general assembly. One member reported that many of the affiliated believed they needed to join either the CNT or the UGT "in order to defend our interests."[52] Another argued that the CNT offered "more guarantees for the workers since it controlled the majority of entertainment workers." A certain Cuadrado insisted that the CNT had always defended the workers, but another objected that the Confederación might suspend the dog races. A participant addressed this fear by asserting that there was also an equal danger that the UGT would cancel the races. At the end of the discussion the assembly voted "unanimously" to join the CNT. "After discussions with managers of both unions," workers who specialized in insulating and waterproofing materials also decided to join the CNT because the Confederación's construction affiliate was more experienced in the workers' speciality.[53] Other unions voted to adhere to the UGT for similar reasons. The president of a union representing market laborers suggested that "it was advantageous and useful" to join a national organization, and the majority agreed to enter the UGT.[54]

A CNT manager of the power company thought that "one of the principal errors of the unions was to force the workers to join one of them. We are not really sure about many of the huge number of new members, although it's not worthwhile to discuss this outside of the union."[55] In June 1937 H. Rüdiger, a representative in Barcelona of the revived First International, wrote that before the Revolution the CNT had only 150,000 to 175,000 members in Catalonia.[56] In the months following the outbreak of the war, Catalan CNT membership jumped to nearly 1,000,000, of which "four-fifths are, thus, new people. We cannot consider a large part of these people revolutionaries. You could take any union as an example of this. Many of these new members could be in the UGT." Rüdiger concluded that the CNT could not be an "organic democracy." In the rival union, the situation was little different: one UGT official asserted that the Catalan federation of the UGT had 30,000 members before 19 July and 350,000 to 400,000 afterwards; he recommended a new organization of the union since many affiliates lacked energy and experience.[57] A number of CNT unions discouraged the election of new members to posts of responsibility in the organization or in collectives unless they received unanimous approval. Therefore, this large influx of adherents to Catalan unions and political parties was not simply an indication of ideological conversion to anarchosyndicalism, socialism, or communism but an attempt by rank-and-file workers to survive as best they could in a revolutionary situation.

During the Revolution, many workers were reluctant to attend union meetings or, of course, to pay union dues.[58] One collective, Construcciones mecánicas, changed its plans to hold assemblies on Sundays since "no one would attend" and instead chose Thursdays.[59] In fact, activists often claimed that the only way to get workers to appear at assemblies was to hold them during working hours and therefore at the expense of production. Twenty-nine of seventy-four workers in a UGT-dominated clothing firm attended an assembly in October 1937.[60] In one large metallurgical concern, only 25 percent of the personnel participated actively in assemblies.[61] The most active workers were over thirty and had technical ability and at least five years' seniority. Frequently, assemblies merely ratified decisions taken by smaller groups of militants or technicians. Some workers felt coerced and were reluctant to speak, let alone protest, during meetings. Even when the rank and file attended, they often arrived late and left early. In construction, the UGT Building Union warned that if delegates did not attend meetings and if members did not fulfill their duties, their union cards would be withdrawn. He meant, in effect, that they would be fired, a serious threat in an industry characterized by high unemployment, especially when joblessness in Barcelona was aggravated still further by an influx of refugees from other parts of Spain.

Even supposedly committed militants often missed meetings. Members holding positions of responsibility were warned.

> The comrades of the Control Committees must consider themselves workers no different from others and are thus obligated to work. They are able to meet as much as they wish but always after working hours. . . . When a comrade—whoever he is and whatever position he holds—sabotages our labor, he will be immediately expelled from the workplace.[62]

UGT telephone personnel criticized working women, the majority of whom had joined the union after 19 July, as never having attended even one assembly. Female workers remained even more apolitical than their male colleagues, perhaps because of lesser interest in social promotion and little representation in the unions. Working women were burdened with both wage labor and domestic chores, such as Saturday shopping. Some activists unsuccessfully proposed fines for members of either sex who did not appear at meetings. Other militants threatened sanctions.[63]

Apathy and indifference contributed to the disintegration of workers' democracy and the reappearance of a managerial elite during the Spanish Revolution. The new elite of union militants employed both old and new techniques of coercion to make workers labor harder and produce more. As will be seen, statist, medical, and unionist bureaucracies expanded in response to workers' resistance. For example, early in the Revolution employees and security guards of the Barcelonan newspaper *La Vanguardia* met at a tavern to drink and gamble during working hours. To end such "irregularities," local union officials—like the national authorities—proposed issuing "identity cards" and imposing rules against leaving the workplace. In another case, the UGT headquarters needed to send out inspectors to affiliated unions to collect dues because an average of only one-third of UGT members in Barcelona met their obligations.[64]

The managing class of union militants, who must be distinguished from mere union members, was largely responsible for the collectivization of the Barcelonan factories. Assisted by skilled workers and technicians, they controlled the daily functioning of the industries. The militants of both the CNT and the UGT were, of course, influenced by the economic thought of their respective organizations. The CNT demanded workers' control, which the factory councils and the unions were to coordinate, whereas the UGT desired nationalization and governmental control. Nevertheless, despite these differences over the *forms* of decision making that the new order would adopt, that is, the choice between state or union control of production, the organizations were in basic agreement concerning industrial goals. Both advocated concentration of the many small factories and workshops that dotted the Barcelonan industrial landscape, standardization of the variety of industrial products and equipment, modernization of tools and capital goods, and establishment of an independent Spanish economy, free from foreign control. In brief, the unions wanted to rationalize the means of production in a Spanish national framework.

The tasks the unions wanted to perform were often ones the bourgeoisies of more advanced nations had completed. As we have seen, the Spanish and Catalan bourgeoisies had been unwilling or unable to rationalize, modernize, standardize, and free the economy from foreign control. The Spanish Revolution in Barcelona meant an attempt by working-class organizations to accomplish these goals. Collective control was instituted to develop industries that had stagnated under the regime of private property. In this respect, the Spanish Revolution resembled the Russian, where organizations claiming to represent the working class took over the privately owned productive forces from a bourgeoisie that had not developed a strong industrial economy. In Spain, as in the Soviet Union, the effort to rationalize the productive forces was accompanied by technocratic thought and methods propagated by Fábregas, Santillán, and other CNT and anarchosyndicalist thinkers. Like Soviet planners, the Spanish revolutionaries desired, at least in theory, to build enterprises on a large scale. They often employed the same methods, such as Taylorism, highly preferential treatment for managers and technicians, and strict control of rank-and-file workers. Certain CNT unions even copied the Stakhanovism of the Bolsheviks in order to promote production.

In another fundamental aspect, internationalism, the Spanish and Russian Revolutions exhibited important similarities. Although Marxist and anarchosyndicalist ideologies shared the cosmopolitanism of the First International and called for a worldwide revolution and solidarity with the proletariat of all nations, this theoretical internationalism conflicted with nationalist practice. Both revolutions attempted to free their industries from foreign capital and control and to develop the productive forces within the national framework. Despite its federalism, the ideology of the CNT called for a strong and economically independent Spain. *Solidaridad Obrera* declared in May 1937, Spain for the Spanish and Our Revolution must be Spanish. Its Madrid paper affirmed that libertarians were the true patriots since they defended the Spanish Revolution, which would "unleash our capacity for work and free Spain from its colony status."[65] In May 1937 Juan López, the CNT Minister of Commerce in the Republican government, declared that he had "aspired to attain the economic unity of Spain."[66] López attacked the "foreign invasion of Spain" and demanded "national independence." According to the CNT daily, the Spanish Revolution would produce "an ethnic and psychological transformation that has been, for many years, in the heart and soul of the race (*raza*)." A CNT journalist proposed a plan of "national reconstruction": "What is produced in Asturias does not belong to Asturias. What is made in a certain municipality does not belong to that municipality. . . . We must guarantee the consumption of everyone, the equal right of all to consume."[67]

Juan Peiró, a Catalan himself, was hostile to Catalanist demands for regional economic control and instead desired a unified national economy. He sharply criticized the Generalitat and the Basque government for hindering and even sabotaging the national economy. In 1939 Peiró demanded a "national xenophobia," which would inspire all classes to rebuild the Spanish economy.[68] After the war, the anarchosyndicalist leader asserted, Spain would pursue the "ideal" of economic self-sufficiency. Another CNT minister from Catalonia, Federica Montseny, who was the first woman ever to hold a ministerial post in Spain, believed that "we are the true nationalists. We are a people . . . who lead all nations." A. Schapiro, a prominent official of the First International, sharply condemned the "panegyric of revolutionary nationalism" and warned his comrades against "chauvinism."[69] During the Revolution other foreign anarchosyndicalists criticized the CNT's nationalism and "chauvinism."[70] Helmut Rüdiger, a German anarchosyndicalist, judged that the nationalism of the Confederación had greatly harmed the Spanish libertarian movement.[71] It should be noted that this nationalism was further exacerbated (but certainly not created) by the failure of Western democracies to aid the Spanish Republic and by anti-Stalinists' fears that the one great power that did help—the Soviet Union—was interfering in Spain's internal affairs.

The Spanish Revolution, like the Russian, also had its labor camps (*campos de trabajo*), initiated at the end of 1936 by Juan García Oliver, the CNT Minister of Justice in the central government of Largo Caballero. As we have noted, García Oliver was a very influential *faísta* and the most important figure in the Central Committee of Antifascist Militias, the de facto government of Catalonia in the first months of the Revolution. In no way could this promoter of Spanish labor camps be considered marginal to the Spanish Left in general and to Spanish anarchosyndicalism in particular. According to his supporters, García Oliver had established the principle of equal justice under law that the Spanish bourgeoisie had previously ignored. The work camps were considered an integral part of the "constructive work of the Spanish Revolution," and many anarchosyndicalists took pride in the "progressive" character of the reforms by the CNT Minister of Justice. The CNT recruited guards for the "concentration camps," as they were also called, from within its own ranks. Certain militants feared that the CNT's resignation from the government after May 1937 might delay this "very important project" of labor camps.[72]

García Oliver's reforming zeal extended to the penal code and the prison system. Torture was forbidden and replaced by work:

> normal labor with weekly monetary bonuses and a day off per week when the prisoner's conduct merits it. If this is not enough to motivate him, his good conduct will be measured by vouchers. Fifty-two of these vouchers will mean a year of good conduct and thus a year of liberty. These years can be added up . . . and thus a sentence of thirty years can be reduced to eight, nine, or ten years.[73]

The abolition of torture has usually accompanied the modernization of a prison system. Modern justice has been ashamed to use corporal punishment, and the modern prison has acted principally on the spirit of a prisoner, not the body. Anarchosyndicalists like García Oliver believed that a prisoner's soul and values must be changed in ways that would benefit the productivist society of the future.

To a great degree, the labor camps were an extreme, but logical, expression of Spanish anarchosyndicalism. It was in the labor camps that the CNT's "society of the producers" encountered Fábregas's "exaltation of work." Understandable resentment against a bourgeoisie, a clergy, and a military whom workers considered unproductive and parasitic crystallized into a demand to reform these groups through productive labor. Anarchosyndicalists endowed work with great moral value; the bourgeoisie, the military, and the clergy were immoral precisely because they did not produce. Thus penal reform meant forcing these classes to labor, to rid them of their sins through work. The Spanish Revolution was, in part, a crusade to convert, by force if necessary, both enemies and friends to the values of work and development.

The ministry of the *faísta* was proud of its "advanced" ideas and considered its camps more progressive than those in the Soviet Union.[74] García Oliver promised humanized detention, and CNT representatives investigated complaints of gross negligence, in the Lérida prison, for example.[75] Sometimes, however, the tone of the reformers shifted:

> The weeds must be torn out by their roots. There cannot be and must not be pity for the enemies of the people, but . . . their rehabilitation through work and that is precisely what the new ministerial order creating "work camps" seeks. In Spain great irrigation canals, roads, and public works must be built immediately. The trains must be electrified, and all these things should be accomplished by those who conceive of work as a derisive activity or a crime, by those who have never worked. . . . The prisons and penitentiaries will be replaced by beehives of labor, and offenders against the people will have the chance to dignify themselves with tools in hand, and they will see that a pick and a shovel will be much more valuable in the future society than the placid, parasitic life of idleness that had no other aim than to perpetuate the irritating inequality of classes.[76]

According to a CNT historian, "delinquents, reactionaries, subversives, and suspects were judged by popular tribunals composed of CNT militants and, if found guilty, jailed or condemned to forced labor. Fascists, soldiers who looted, drunkards, criminals, and even syndicalists who abused their power were put behind bars or in work camps where they were forced to build roads."[77] Inmates of the work camps reported that they also dug trenches and built railroads. One avid *franquista* lamented that "duchesses, marchionesses, countesses, wives and daughters of military officers" were forced to harvest grain.[78]

Most who were sent to prisons and work camps were convicted on political charges—which included violating public order, possessing arms, and engaging in fascist activities.[79] A much smaller number received sentences for robbery, murder, hoarding, and black marketeering. This last category increased markedly in 1938 when, for example, revenue guards arrested a mason with 2,200 pesetas or another individual carrying 179 eggs.[80] The number of prisoners in Catalonia multiplied fivefold during the war. In November 1936, 535 were in Catalan jails; in November 1938 the figure was 2,601. The greatest increase was of women inmates, whose numbers jumped from 18 in November 1936 to 535 two years later. Deserters from the Republican army (more numerous than those from the Nationalist army) filled their own camps, and their numbers increased dramatically in Catalonia during 1938.[81]

The art of the Revolution reflected its problems and expressed its values and morality. The clearest expression of this art were the posters of the Spanish Left—Communist, Socialist, and anarchosyndicalist. The major organizations gave considerable time and money to produce this propaganda even after paper and other resources became scarce and expensive. Many of the poster artists had been active in advertising before the war, and they worked not for one organization but for many. For example, an official of the Professional Designers' Union made placards for the CNT, UGT, PSUC, and the Generalitat. His union even produced posters for the POUM, the dissident Communist organization. An ecumenical style emerged that, despite slight thematic differences, portrayed both the workers and the productive forces in nearly identical images. Even as anarchosyndicalists and Communists killed each other on the streets of Barcelona in May 1937, the aesthetic unity of the Popular Front persisted. Ideological disputes and power struggles did not prevent competing organizations from accepting similar representations of their supposed constituencies.

In these posters, which greatly resemble the style of Soviet socialist realism, workers were either working, fighting, or dying for the cause. These men and, just as important, women—for in the Spanish Revolution women and men were theoretically equal in war and work—always struggled heroically and untiringly for the victory of the Revolution or the Second Republic in farms, factories, and on battlefields. In fact, the sex of the subjects in many posters was nearly indeterminate, and what was important was neither the qualities nor the character of the individual portrayed but his or her function as soldier or worker. Spanish socialist realism expressed the progressive "masculinization of the iconography of the workers' movement."[82] One CNT sign, made to combat pessimism and defeatism, pictured two figures, a man and a woman, who looked alike. Both possessed huge forearms and biceps, broad shoulders, and very small heads, suggesting that it was physical, not mental, effort that was required of them. The figures were almost identical except that one had longer hair and inconspicuous breasts, the only hints of femininity in the image. One detail distinguished the other figure: rolled-up sleeves, an easily recognizable symbol of manual labor.

This art was solely concerned with the constructive or destructive capacity of its subjects who were simultaneously its objects. The artists deemphasized differences between soldier and producer, defense and civilian industries as much as between woman and man. One PSUC poster identified industries of war and peacetime. In the picture the long chimneys of the latter repeated the shape of the large cannons of the former. A famous CNT-FAI poster conveyed the same message. In the foreground a soldier firing his rifle complemented a worker in the background harvesting wheat with a sickle, itself a symbol of labor in socialist-realist iconography. The figures would have been indistinguishable except by their implements and positions. Vivid reds and blacks, the colors of the anarchist movement, strengthened the forms of the powerful workers. The caption read, Comrade, work and fight for the revolution. Artists never depicted the workers and soldiers of the posters as tired, hungry, or ill. The means of production—the factories, farms, and workshops—no matter how ugly, were idealized equally with the brave, strong, and virile men and women who lived and died for the cause. This portrait of the productive forces reflected the Left's productivism and its desires for modernization. Both machines and humankind were heroic and larger than life.

Given the Marxist and anarchosyndicalist conception of the worker, it is hardly surprising that revolutionary art would stress her or his productive capacities. These ideologies, which glorified labor and the laborer, consequently portrayed the female and male wage earners as muscular and powerful beings capable of creating objects both for consumption and for the struggle. Thus the importance of the arm and particularly the hand, a symbol of *homo faber* and the focus of many compositions. Interpreting the posters helps us both to understand how Marxists and anarchosyndicalists literally imagined the working class and how revolutionaries responded to workers' actual behavior during the civil war and Revolution. Spanish socialist realism attempted to persuade the workers to fight, work, and sacrifice more. It was propaganda that was always humorless and sometimes menacing.

The art of the Frente popular aimed to diminish workers' resistance to work, which was, as we shall see, one of the most pressing problems for the entire Left. Barcelonan workers were known to miss work on holidays, particularly during the Christmas–New Year's season. The PSUC responded to such absenteeism with a poster that pictured a soldier whose bayonet was slicing through Saturday on a calendar. The poster's caption called for the end of fiestas and demanded that a new "war calendar" be imposed. Another picture demanded that May Day become, not a holiday, but a day of "intensification of production."

Spanish militants sometimes equated excessive drinking and laziness with sabotage and even fascism. One CNT poster, which was made in Barcelona for the Departamento de orden público de Aragon, pictured a corpulent man smoking a cigarette and comfortably resting in what appeared to be the countryside. The colors of this piece were unlike those of most other posters; the figure was not red or black but yellow, reflecting the tones of sunny Spain. At the bottom was printed the caption, The lazy man is a fascist. Another CNT poster, made again for comrades in Aragon, displayed a man who was also smoking a cigarette, a symbol, one may speculate, of indifference and insolence since committed workers and soldiers were not shown smoking. This individual was surrounded by tall wine bottles, and the poster contained the caption, A drunk is a parasite. Let's eliminate him. This was particularly tough talk during a period when threats of elimination did not always remain oral, and work camps for enemies and the apathetic were in operation. Both Marxists and anarchosyndicalists were hostile toward non-producers.

A number of posters addressed the problem of workers' indifference. One showed a strong red figure who was digging the earth with a shovel and who asked laborers to join voluntary work brigades (many of which became obligatory during 1937). Another, from Madrid, requested disabled veterans to aid the fight by working in factories and thereby releasing as yet uninjured workers for combat. A third contained a very direct appeal: Worker, Work and We shall win; it showed a bare-chested red figure with a well-defined muscular torso, blacksmith or metalworker, underneath whom a row of soldiers was firing their weapons at the enemy.

The artists of the Revolution also developed a genre of posters for the literacy campaign. This theme reflected the poverty of Spanish education, the high rates of illiteracy among workers, and the Left's need for trained workers and cadres. A modernist poster showed a soldier in red and black with several yellow books and contained the caption, Anarchist books are weapons against fascism. The theme of books as weapons, which blended nicely with the utilitarianism of the Left's literacy campaign, echoed in another poster that showed a blindfolded soldier holding a large book. Underneath the fighter was inscribed, Illiteracy blinds the spirit. Soldier, learn! The relation of education to fighting paralleled that of work to fighting. There was a rapprochement, if not an identification, of the two activities. The literacy campaign posters, like those representing the means of production, were modernist. One striking promotion of the anarchosyndicalist publications *Tierra y Libertad* and *Tiempos nuevos* combined soldiers, rifles, factory chimneys, newspapers, and books in a sophisticated cubist composition.

Spanish socialist realism was not exempt from what Nikita Khrushchev once called "the cult of personality." Massive representations of Marx, Lenin, and Stalin appeared in public places. The libertarians replied with photographs, sketches, and portraits of Durruti, whose image seems to have been as pervasive in the anarchosyndicalist press as that of Stalin was in Communist publications. On the anniversary of the death of the legendary anarchosyndicalist leader, who died on the Madrid front early in the war, CNT and FAI publications were filled with tens of articles and pictures of the fallen hero. *Tierra y Libertad,* the review of the *faístas,* even included a somewhat sentimental essay entitled, "Durruti: A Giant with a Heart of Gold," even though before his death the libertarian martyr had advocated mobilizing the "infinity of loafers and libertines in the rear."[83]

The anarchosyndicalists developed their own form of visual expression that differed little from the Marxist variety. This similarity reflected shared values—a glorification of labor, a respect for the development of the means of production, and the vision of the worker as producer. When workers in the collectives did not conform to this productivist conception, the CNT and the UGT alike responded by creating persuasive and coercive images that were designed to convince them to work harder. This art should be seen as reflecting the views of the militants, not working-class culture in its entirety. Indeed, it aimed to combat a deep current in the everyday life of Barcelonan wage earners—workers' resistance to work and reluctance to fight. To estimate the posters' effects on the behavior of Barcelona's working class is unfortunately difficult, if not impossible: vandals or graffiti artists *avant la lettre* tore down or covered over many posters as soon as they appeared on the walls. As yet little evidence exists that the socialist realism of the Frente popular boosted production or increased combativeness.

The nature of the Spanish Revolution can only be partially discovered in the political categories of most historians. By concentrating on the political struggles among the CNT, PSUC, and other organizations and the consequent counterrevolution of May 1937, historians have distorted the periodization of workers' control in Barcelona and have not fully explored the more fundamental question of the significance of the Revolution itself. Yet the art of the Revolution, its labor camps, and its vision of the future revealed its essence: the development and rationalization of the means of production of the nation. Everything else yielded to this central goal, and in the process workers' democracy disappeared, if it had ever existed. The following chapters will examine how the union militants developed the productive forces in Barcelona and the problems that they encountered among the workers whom they claimed to represent.

5
RATIONALIZATION

Although the war increased the pressures to produce, the urgent effort to rationalize the productive forces should not be attributed solely to the necessities of this conflict. Anarchosyndicalists of various shades of opinion advocated the development of the means of production through rationalization before the civil war and Revolution erupted. Indeed, one cause of the civil war and Revolution was the inability or unwillingness of Spanish capitalists to create and sustain modern industries. It was the resulting low standard of living for many workers that inspired working-class organizations—with varying degrees of success—to concentrate, standardize, and modernize the backward industrial structure.

In textiles, the most important industry in Barcelona, both the CNT and the UGT of Badalona, the city's industrial suburb, agreed on collectivizing and merging the firms into "a single industrial organization."[1] The unions argued that concentration would improve productivity and encourage mass production. It would not only eliminate the many small and inefficient firms but would also end work done at home, *trabajo a domicilio,* which was often considered responsible for low wages. After 19 July 1936 such work was said to have disappeared; some collectives paid a weekly sum to workers who brought their sewing machines into the factory. Concentration would also lay the basis for a thriving national economy, and the CNT planned to reduce imports by planting cotton, pita, hemp, and other plants to free the textile industry from foreign sources of raw materials. The collectives would strive for Spanish economic independence.

The unions had similar plans for the construction industry. As in even advanced capitalist nations, this industry was dispersed into small units and employed approximately thirty-five thousand workers in Barcelona, the great majority of them in the CNT. The unions concentrated and coordinated many small firms and gradually consolidated an amalgamation, which employed approximately eleven thousand workers in workshops of twenty-five to four hundred members.[2] By the beginning of September 1937, the CNT Building Union claimed—perhaps with some exaggeration—that it had eliminated "parasitic" intermediaries and had concentrated three thousand shops into one hundred twenty "great producing centers" that supposedly mass-produced.[3] It retained a number of former employers as technical advisers at the standard wage for workers.

The tanning and leather industry of Barcelona, however, revealed a considerable distance between desires for concentration and the harsh reality of a wartime economy. Both unions noted that despite the profits of World War I, the industry remained backward.[4] According to the CNT, after 19 July the seventy-one tanning factories of Barcelona were collectivized, and their number was quickly reduced to twenty-five, in which, "with the same personnel and the consequent savings of machinery and tools, the same amount of production was realized as in the seventy-one tanneries under bourgeois administration."[5] Distribution was centralized, and an energetic attempt to export was organized "with the goal of independence from the rapacity of the capitalist system."

Yet the concentration of this and other industries was more difficult than the CNT admitted. The subservient status of Catalan industry, which the anarchosyndicalists had so decried, haunted the revolutionaries during the war. The need for foreign materials, markets, and transportation facilities hindered the grouping and integration of companies belonging to foreigners. Since the peseta's value continued to fall and Republican carriers might be sunk by the enemy, British currency and English ships were necessary to transport indispensable chemicals and fuels. The protests of the British consulate delayed plans to concentrate the leather and shoe industry, whose larger firms had attracted British investors.[6] Likewise, the directors of Catalan railroads, telephones, and (as we shall see) utilities were obligated to negotiate with their former owners and managers.

In the chemical industry the process of concentration was slowed by the difficulty of coordinating the needs of individual firms, the unions, and the state. The Generalitat's Chemical Council, composed of four technicians, four UGT representatives, and four CNT delegates, was not empowered to take coercive measures against workers. When UGT workers' "indiscipline" harmed production in a glue factory, the council was forced to call on that union to restore order.[7] In June 1937, the concentration of the soap industry, which employed eleven hundred workers in forty firms in Barcelona, was still being "studied." A month later the council was able to fix soap prices, but concentration of the industry seemed no more definite. The opposition of the Italian firm, Pirelli, which was by far the largest producer of cables and insulating materials, was also a major obstacle.[8] Perhaps in order to maintain their autonomy, collectives were reluctant to provide the Generalitat's Chemical Council with information and statistics. In June 1938 inspectors were ordered to investigate enterprises that had not responded to census questionnaires.[9]

The division of power and the lack of a strong state not only hindered the process of concentration but also blocked the rational distribution of raw materials. Republicans and revolutionaries needed the equivalent of the Raw Materials Section that had functioned in Germany in the early years of World War I. In a situation where supplies were costly or impossible to acquire, some CNT firms and unions would hoard their stock of fuel or other necessities; others might sell them without authorization or at inflated prices.[10] The Barcelona UGT undoubtedly used precious foreign currencies for partisan purposes when it sent militants to Paris to purchase arms.[11] The power industry devoted valuable time and money to electrifying the town of Llivia, a small Spanish enclave inside France, in order to improve the image of Catalonia in the eyes of foreigners. Despite the opposition, which argued that resources should be used to unify the industry and bring electricity to more important Catalan towns, the committee decided "to demonstrate to the foreigner that the workers do things better than . . . the previous economic organization."[12]

Regional divisions complicated the problem; both CNT and UGT leaders complained that the national government at Valencia ignored Catalan needs. The Valencian administration supposedly refused to supply required chemicals to Catalan textile firms that had not paid their taxes.[13] Catalan railroad workers asserted that Valencia had not rationally organized the distribution of wagons, and that outside Catalonia many cars sat vacant and inactive, even though the railroads had been declared a key industry.[14]

In many industries, wartime conditions made concentration and reorganization necessary. Military conscription opened positions and required a redistribution of manpower; in addition, the loss of markets and raw materials made many workers redundant. Bombardments destroyed capital goods and forced a new division of machinery and personnel. For example, despite opposition from those who were transferred, the CNT Automobile Union was determined to move workers where they were needed.[15] Other enterprises made a special effort to ensure that "indispensable" status was granted only to workers who were absolutely necessary for production. Managers gained the authority to transfer personnel specifically for disciplinary purposes.[16]

The best documented example of industrial changes may be in Catalonia's industries of gas and electricity where militants attempted to unify and coordinate the 610 electrical companies. It is interesting to note that the figure of 610 was uncertain; the problematic state of statistics was itself a sign of the industrial backwardness that hindered the unification of the industry. A leading CNT militant of the Water, Gas, and Electricity Union commented in November 1936:

> Unification creates many difficulties. The figures are not exact. We do not know if there are 605 or 615 small ex-firms (*ex-empresas*) that exist in Catalonia, and I have put the average at 610.
>
> Of these 610 ex-firms there are only 203 that are producers of energy. . . . This means that some 407 ex-firms resell electricity. This is intolerable and is the fruit of the situation before 19 July.[17]

Although all militants agreed on the principle of unifying an industry so dispersed and scattered, the actual process of concentration was slow and full of obstacles. The new managers of the CNT and the UGT immediately confronted the problem of how to deal with technicians in restructuring this branch. Not surprisingly, given the conditions of the most advanced industries in Catalonia, the problem of the experts was complicated by the fact that many of them were foreigners. The nationalism of union leaders approached xenophobia; some committee members admitted that they had a "phobia against foreigners."[18] Others asserted, "Everything that is within Spanish territory must be exploited by Spaniards." The Control Committee dismissed some of the most unpopular or incompetent technicians, whether Spanish or not.[19] Yet the managing committee feared difficulties if the foreigners abandoned their former companies en bloc. After many—but not all—did depart, the ruling committee found it hard to find replacements and had to confront the resistance of the local committees, which sometimes refused to accept the technicians recommended by the head office.[20] In addition, the power industry found it difficult to retain its own experts whose skills were also demanded by the military.

Managers not only depended to an extent on foreign technicians but also on foreign capital and, more generally, international goodwill. Because of the cutoff of its usual supply of Asturian coal and the poor quality of Catalan coal, the region needed foreign coal to produce gas. Fearing Nationalist attacks and suffering the blockade of loyal shipping, Catalans had to use foreign ships to transport energy supplies. The latter could be purchased only with gold or foreign currencies. Therefore, some gesture was required to demonstrate to non-Spanish investors that the new managers were not, as the right-wing press charged, "gangsters." Even as the British consulate protested the refusal of the electric companies to pay their foreign "coupon clippers," Spanish authorities rescheduled the debt to Swiss investors.[21] Although in September 1937 the Generalitat declared a moratorium on interest payments, it delayed the formal legalization of the electrical industry in order not to alienate the English. British, Soviet, and, surprisingly enough,

German coal found its way to Barcelona. Evidently, German commercial and mercantile policy conflicted with its diplomatic support of Franco's forces, and deutsche marks seem to have been easier to acquire than other currencies. The difficulties of obtaining foreign coal and other goods stimulated the inventiveness of Catalan scientists and technicians who experimented—often successfully—with new materials and energy sources.[22]

The five major gas and electricity companies disagreed over the extent of the sacrifices and the contributions that each firm would have to make to unify the industry. The prewar financial situation complicated matters since companies with a healthy balance sheet did not wish to pay off the debts of unprofitable enterprises.[23] The numerous smaller enterprises feared that the large firms would take advantage of their comparative weakness and force them to work without proper compensation. Many former executives or foremen with needed technical and administrative skills were frightened that unification would mean a loss of their pay, power, and prestige. Workers feared that concentration by transfer to another branch might destroy their job security. They were reluctant, for example, to be moved to the gas section; not without reason, they considered it a dying enterprise.[24] The Catalan companies had used coal to produce gas, but supplies—and thus gas production—became extremely precarious during the conflict. To encourage wage earners to adjust to a new workplace and to accept new transportation costs, managers proposed to award a bonus to transferred workers. By contrast, the Central Committee of gas and electricity had to discourage other employees who demanded new posts for reasons of personal advantage.[25] In addition, the Decree on Collectivization of October 1936 granted firms with over one hundred workers the right to collectivize as they desired, and some of these firms preferred not to join the concentration in order to retain control of their resources and administration. Control Committee members complained that the decree suited neither the needs of their industry nor the necessities of the war, which required centralized command to shut off power and lights during an aerial attack.[26] In response, the Generalitat attempted to amend legislation to fit the needs of the power industry.

The infinity of committees that sprang up at the beginning of the Revolution blocked centralization of the industry. The Control Committee threatened to replace them if they did not follow its orders.[27] "Only concentrations . . . can permit undertakings of such importance as the electrification of the railroads and electrochemical industries. To break up our industry would shackle progress and would mean the destruction of an extremely important part of the national economy."[28]

Yet resistance to unification remained significant throughout the Revolution. On 11 January 1937 the Cooperativa popular de Villanueva y Geltrú accused the Barcelonan Central Committee of acting more rapaciously than capitalist enterprises. Representatives of the cooperative, backed by local CNT and UGT delegations, asserted that the newly unified power industry, SEUC (Serveis elèctrics unificats de Catalunya), was merely a cover for four earlier enterprises that were trying to absorb the weaker firms. A CNT delegate from Barcelona replied that the SEUC had been created in the interests of the war effort and of the Catalan economy. The representatives of the cooperative and the local CNT protested that the SEUC had divided profits as had the bourgeoisie and, unlike railroads, had acted irresponsibly by granting its employees a year-end bonus. Another local CNT delegate threatened that the 2,300 members of the Villanueva cooperative would not pay their bills unless their rights were recognized. Local residents believed that their interests deserved a consideration equal to that given to foreigners. A member of the town council noted that his citizens were disappointed with the cost and the services of the new concentration. Barcelona's Central Committee members replied that their enterprise was protecting the general interest but agreed to study the proposals of the cooperative.

The local committees ignored recommendations of SEUC's Control Committee concerning promotions and ranking of personnel. They also refused to relay information about their excess personnel, which was vital in a situation of war and revolution.[29] In September 1937 both the Barcelonan committee and the UGT criticized the persistent egoism of individual firms that prevented complete consolidation of the industry.[30] Even in 1938, when the Generalitat controlled the industry, it declared that unification progressed slowly "owing to the reluctance of the former companies to transmit data that have been requested several times."[31] Nor was this problem limited to the power industry. The control committees of other enterprises, such as the MZA (Madrid–Zaragoza–Alicante railroad), found it difficult to centralize command in the face of disobedient subcommittees. As in gas and electricity, workers of some companies resisted concentration because they feared that they might lose pay, benefits, or job security in the new organization.[32]

In the dramatic times of war and Revolution in Barcelona, the metallurgical and metalworking industries were arguably the most essential productive forces. The backwardness of this sector and its lack of competitive automobile and aviation branches has already been described. Of the metallurgical and metalworking factories surveyed, thirty-six employed between one and ten workers, fifty-two had from eleven to fifty workers, and twelve had between fifty-one and one hundred workers. Four factories employed from one hundred to five hundred workers, and only two employed over five hundred workers. Out of one hundred six factories, eighty-six had a CNT majority and twenty had a UGT majority, although the UGT tended to be slightly stronger in larger factories. The physical size of these firms was often minuscule; some measured 150 square meters, some only 50, or even 17 square meters. The scale of these enterprises limited production.[33] For example, when the Fundición Dalia was asked if it could increase the number of its workers in order to augment production, it responded that it had already doubled production for the war effort. With thirty-seven workers, it was working at peak capacity and could not absorb any more personnel. Another firm, Talleres Guerin, whose eighty workers made electrical equipment, reported that its production was limited by its lack of machinery.

In April 1937 the CNT and the UGT agreed "on the need to socialize the metallurgical industry on the basis of industrial concentration."[34] The Confederación's Metallurgical Union in Barcelona declared that, despite the opposition of the petty bourgeoisie, it had unified the industry's small workshops and had thereby increased output. Seven major concentrations were planned, including iron and steel production, aviation, and automobiles. The last amalgamation would integrate all activities of automotive production, from casting and the production of parts to delivery on the market.

The Marathon Collective, formerly the General Motors plant in Barcelona, provides a good example of coordination if not concentration of an industry in mechanical construction. After the fighting of 19 July, part of the management left, and instructions came from the United States to shut down the factory. Instead, militants of the UGT and the CNT (the latter dominated in the collective) took control of the firm; technicians began to coordinate, finance, and advise many of the small metalworking firms that began to manufacture previously imported auto parts. The Marathon Collective embarked on an ambitious program to assemble parts made in Catalonia and to mass-produce a truly national truck. In July 1937 the collective celebrated the first anniversary of the 19 July victory by displaying the first mass-produced truck and motor that had been built in Catalonia.[35] Ninety different factory councils and control committees that had cooperated in the construction of the Spanish truck participated in the festivities. A Marathon director praised the labor of twelve thousand workers in the Catalan automobile industry, and he stated that the production of a mass-produced vehicle was part of "our war of independence." He concluded that the bourgeoisie had neither the knowledge nor the will to mass-produce automobiles.

The CNT was quite proud of its role in the concentration of the auto industry: "The achievement of our Revolution is its power to control all enterprises. . . . Another very important point is . . . to be able to reduce the cost of cars that before 19 July we had to buy from foreign nations."[36] Faced with the interruption of foreign parts and equipment, CNT militants had rationally reorganized production by coordinating and concentrating small workshops. Anarchosyndicalist productivism merged with Spanish economic nationalism to produce the beginnings of an independent automotive industry.

Standardization of parts and equipment often accompanied concentration. CNT metallurgical militants wrote in their review that standardization had three advantages: interchangeable parts, speed of repairs, and economy. They concluded, "The degree of standardization is the gauge that determines industrial progress. Proof of this is that nations which have the best industry are those that have the greatest quantity of standardized parts."[37]

The Industria Metalgráfica, a collective of 220 workers, 91 of whom were men, offered an excellent example of rationalization that was accompanied by standardization in what was, for Barcelona, a relatively large factory.[38] Of the collective's workers, 206 belonged to the CNT and 14 to the UGT. The 8 technicians of the firm were in the CNT, whereas the 14 administrative personnel were in the UGT. With machinery that was over two decades old, it had produced metal boxes, metal cases, and lithographic equipment. After revolution broke out, the factory converted its output to war production. On 5 November 1936 the collective's ruling council acknowledged that it intended "to reduce labor as much as possible" by eliminating certain processes. The council argued that it was "absolutely necessary to revamp the manufacturing process, and we consider that 'standard' manufacturing is the most advisable." Standardization would reduce the time needed for manufacture and open vistas of "almost unlimited" production of items such as beer cans. In September 1938 the UGT Metallurgical Union of Catalonia called for standardization of production and the use of the "most modern practices."[39]

The militants of the construction industry also embraced standardization. CNT activists in its Building Union argued against "archaic norms" and "rudimentary methods" in favor of new techniques such as reinforced concrete, "whose good results are unquestionable."[40] The CNT approved "modern construction" with its solidity, cleanliness, airiness, and roominess. This desire for light, space, and hygiene was quite understandable in Barcelona, where working-class housing often lacked these qualities. The anarchosyndicalist militants admired methods of building in the Soviet Union, "where construction acquires the characteristics of a marvelous beauty."[41] Their urbanism was highly influenced by Le Corbusier's ideas, and CNT journals included pictures of "cities of the future"—large modern metropolises of huge high rises linked by expressways.[42]

The Confederación modernized the machinery in the factories that it controlled. Modernization required a considerable effort during the war and Revolution since much of the needed machinery had to be imported. In addition, the CNT's adversaries in the central government and the Generalitat sometimes controlled the necessary foreign currencies. Many CNT unions nevertheless pursued modernization of equipment. The electrical industry illustrates the obstacles that attempts to modernize equipment sometimes encountered.[43] As in the case of raw materials, Spanish substitutes for foreign products were hard to find. In January 1937 the industry's Central Committee discussed a request to change the billing system for its customers from monthly to bimonthly and to bill gas and electricity charges simultaneously as part of its program for the unification and concentration of its industries. However, the billing machines were in poor condition and continually required replacement parts from Paris; new personnel had to be trained to use the machines properly. Managers concluded, under the circumstances, that billing reforms would have to be delayed.

Wartime conditions obstructed industrial development. A shortage of vulcanized wire limited the use of hydroelectric power. The industry could not quickly repair the damage caused by bombardments of power stations because much of the needed material had to be acquired abroad and purchased with foreign currencies. American-made material became so valuable that it was once proposed as collateral for an Aragon firm's loan.[44] Even when machines could be purchased or were available, a shortage of qualified personnel—perhaps conscripted or departed—may have prevented their operation.[45]

Industries' unwillingness or inability to pay bills on time disturbed plans for their rationalization. Several weeks after the Revolution erupted, the Control Committee of gas and electricity considered employing the Antifascist Militias to collect debts from "elements who are taking advantage of the present circumstances to avoid paying their bills."[46] Two months later, the committee complained to a representative of the CNT

Construction Union that neither ordinary consumers nor a great number of institutions—which included the Generalitat, municipality, prisons, railroads, streetcar companies, journalists' union, police headquarters, and even the barracks of the Antifascist Militias—had met their payments.[47] Furthermore, the departure of the upper and middle classes meant a 37 percent decline in revenue. Many of the remaining consumers were dishonest, "always trying to find a way to swipe free kilowatts. . . . Unfortunately, working-class comrades are among the defaulters (*morosos*). If we catch an upper-class defaulter, we give him what he deserves, but we cannot do anything to the workers since many plead that they don't have a job."

Committee members sharply attacked the railroads not only for their debt to the electric industry but also for their reduction in fares for passengers. Although the reduced price bolstered the railroad's image among the public, electricity managers accused the railroads of charging considerably more for bulk transportation to compensate for the loss of passenger revenue. According to the power company, the transport of coal had become more expensive than its purchase; these added expenses and defaults delayed the industry's plan to construct a modern headquarters in the plaza Cataluña. One member concluded sardonically, "The Revolution means not paying." Another worker (the representative of the Construction Union who had not succeeded in getting funds from the Control Committee for workers about to be laid off) added, "It's true there are many abuses. Many comrades have policing and defense tasks. They get free meals and clothes, bonuses and compensation. Then they go out on a spree, leaving their families to pay the gas and lighting." Militants wondered why, despite the purchase of all available electric stoves, no increase in use of electricity had been recorded, implying that customers were tinkering with their meters. At the end of the year the Control Committee studied a proposal for a special section to fight fraud.[48] Members suggested that gas and electric meters no longer be read separately; joint readings would save labor and would also threaten potential defaulters with the interruption of both sources of power. The committee wanted to take strong measures to force consumers who had moved to pay bills that had accumulated at their former addresses; one militant asked the Housing Commission to refuse to rent to anyone who did not possess a receipt from a recently paid electric bill.[49]

In the spring of 1937, the shortage of coins in Barcelona made it difficult for clients to use pre-pay, coin-operated meters. Consumers were apparently hoarding silver coins. To solve the problem, a member suggested that the industry mint its own company tokens for use in its meters; another participant objected that the tokens would be immediately counterfeited.[50] When the merchants of one town, La Rapita de los Alfaques, petitioned for a lower electricity rate, the committee agreed to study the problem, but one activist was certain that during the investigation "those merchants won't pay."[51] In May the famous collectives of Aragon owed the Catalan electrical industry over 300,000 pesetas.

The Control Committee of the centralized power companies, which criticized other institutions for slow payment, was itself reluctant to pay the Generalitat's newly imposed taxes.[52] Other collectives and controlled enterprises were also disinclined to meet their obligations. The MZA refused to contribute to the Ministry of Public Works since railroad traffic—and thus income—had declined dramatically.[53] The War Industries Commission was a notorious debtor, and its delays caused economic problems for creditors such as the Plastic Industries Company.[54] Movie theaters seemed also to have been in debt.[55] During 1937 many enterprises began demanding payment in cash. For example, the CAMPSA, the state energy company, would not deliver fuel to the railroad unless it received hard currency.[56]

Regardless of problems of cash flow, many committees significantly improved working conditions. CNT factory councils recognized the effects of hygiene on production and wanted to imitate modern American firms that had industrial physicians. The textile factory, España industrial, established a day-care center for working mothers and a new dining room.[57] In Badalona textile firms, CNT activists improved retirement and medical benefits. The UGT established a clinic and expanded health-care and retirement benefits.[58] Breaking with prerevolutionary practices in certain industries of employing children from twelve to fifteen years old, the CNT Graphic Arts Union prohibited the employment of those under fourteen. CNT loaders debated the difficult questions of the physical capacity and output of aged laborers. The power industry dealt with the delicate problem of how to divide fairly the burden of the retirement fund.[59]

Yet in many cases the disruption of the economy and the diminution of resources blocked the improvement of working conditions.[60] For example, managers refused a request from a workshop for new windows. In another case, the high price of paint prevented the repainting of the offices of a train station. When the personnel of the Gerona-Llansa line became demoralized by poor working conditions, they were told to sacrifice for the war. The electrical industry was reluctant to give permanent payroll status to temporary personnel, such as construction workers or miners, even though it demanded "maximum output" from the latter in the admittedly hazardous mines.

Laudatory accounts of the Catalan war industries have ignored the dangerous conditions in the newly built armaments industry.[61] Fumes from dynamite and tolite, used in explosives' production, made the personnel sick. "To avoid possible poisoning" they asked for milk and coffee and suggested that two nurses be employed so that each shift had access to medical care in case of an accident. The personnel also demanded a bomb shelter where they could be safe from enemy bombardments and friendly (but often inaccurate) antiaircraft fire. Their CNT-backed delegate declared that after the national government had taken over the factory, the families of accident victims had not received compensation. He cited four workers who had perished because of an explosion on 4 September 1936, six who had died in another explosion on 22 September 1936, and one in an explosion in March 1938; two others had been seriously injured in accidents in October 1936 and November 1937. Only one of the victims had been insured.

In their efforts to improve working conditions and to develop the productive forces, both the CNT and the UGT built schools and centers to train technicians. These schools survived and even prospered despite political and ideological tensions within and between the unions. In metallurgy, both unions made a special effort to train technicians from their own ranks. The

UGT established schools for "professional preparation," "without which there is no prosperity."[62] The CNT Metallurgical Union established a school called Labor, which was free from the "false education" of the Church. In the Marathon Collective (CNT-UGT), professors taught "love of work" and studied the "magnificent" automobiles of General Motors.[63] The largely CNT-dominated Foundry Collective and the UGT Metallurgical Union of Badalona instituted scholarships for children. Hundreds of children from working-class families received financial aid from the government or the unions for various types of schooling. In construction, the CNT encouraged young workers, who often ignored the promulgated "union values," to study in the libraries which the union had built and to attend the classes which it offered.

Even before the Revolution, the CNT had led efforts to raise the cultural level of the working class. Continuing this tradition, the CNT and, to a somewhat lesser extent, the UGT established libraries in many collectives to encourage reading and educate the many illiterate workers. Illiteracy remained significant among wage earners. The CNT Maritime Union stated that out of twenty sailors, fifteen could not sign their names. Members of the control committees of the remaining privately-owned enterprises were required to be able to read and write.[64] The twenty-thousand-strong women's organization, Mujeres libres, which had close links to the anarchosyndicalist movement, began a large campaign during the Revolution to instruct women, who had higher rates of illiteracy than men.[65] The UGT also wanted to hold classes for illiterates. Even though anarchosyndicalist and Marxist militants were often genuinely committed to improving workers' cultural life, the unions' attitude toward education resembled, in part, the literacy campaigns and educational practices of various Marxist regimes with their utilitarian emphasis on learning in order to increase production.

Historians favorable to anarchosyndicalism have often regarded the CNT's educational efforts as part of its unique global culture, which transcended trade unionism and conventional politics to influence aspects of everyday life.[66] The CNT and the UGT along with Catalan political parties organized the

CENU (Consejo de la escuela nueva unificada), designed to replace parochial schools. The CENU desired both the rationalization of work and the social promotion of workers; its goal was to enable capable workers to attend the university. With other organizations, the CENU undertook the schooling of over 72,000 children who had been without any formal education before the Revolution. In one district, elementary-school enrollment jumped from 950 students to 9,501 during the conflict. In the entire city, 125,000 new students were registered.

The desire to create a rational educational system and to train students and technicians was thus not unique to the CNT and formed an essential part of both unions' revolutionary project of developing the means of production. For the CNT and organizations close to it, the elimination of illiteracy and the development of the productive forces were intimately linked. Well-rounded and educated workers were to be integrated into a society of production and order. One libertarian militant described their goal:

> The producers in a libertarian communist society will not be divided into manual laborers and intellectuals. Access to arts and sciences will be open, because the time devoted to them will belong to the individual and not to the community. The individual will be emancipated from the community, if he desires, when the workday and his mission as producer are finished.[67]

> The more work is esteemed, the more idleness will be repulsive. In other words, the more the child loves good . . . the less evil will affect him.[68]

In fact, the content of the CNT's technical education was hardly different from that of the more advanced capitalist nations or even that of the Soviet Union. An article published during the Revolution claimed that the United States showed the way in vocational education and that the Soviet Union perfected it.[69] The Confederación criticized the Spanish bourgeoisie precisely for its inability to provide the training more accessible to workers in other nations.

The urgent need to train technicians in order to secure the Revolution strengthened the Confederación's technocratic tendencies, which were potent, if not dominant, even before the war. The conflict—with its conscription, disruption of supplies, and creation of defense industries—undoubtedly dramatized the importance of technicians who had to find substitutes for missing materials, build new industries almost from scratch, and replace their colleagues who had fled abroad or had gone into the army. One must keep in mind, though, that the war merely reinforced the technocratic tendencies of anarchosyndicalism: libertarian communists envisaged a postwar society where technicians would continue to direct the development of the means of production. The CNT's glorification of science and technology attracted some technicians and managers to its ranks while the union frightened away others by its leveling tendency, by the dominance of blue-collar workers in its membership, and by its relative indifference to Catalan nationalism. In turn, the Confederación distrusted the experts and kept detailed records of their personal, professional, and political histories.[70] Many technicians, managers, and particularly white-collar workers joined the UGT, closely aligned with the PSUC, which supported many demands of the Catalan nationalists and often accepted large wage differentials without question.

Yet throughout the Revolution the CNT sought, and partially won, the support of the technicians. The journal of the CNT National Federation of Water, Gas, and Electricity, *Luz y fuerza*, believed that it had learned from the past:

> The experience of the Russian Revolution taught us, the Spanish workers, how to treat the technicians because without them a total revolution cannot be made. Once everything rotten and archaic that exists in Spain is destroyed, the efforts of all will be needed for reconstruction. If we did not have this clear vision, we would find . . . at the end of the war that nothing would have been accomplished, and, what is worse, that we would have to submit to foreign technicians.[71]

The CNT Maritime Union asked, "Can an engineer be mistaken for an unskilled worker? The engineer symbolizes creative thought, and the unskilled worker [symbolizes] thought's object. . . . The social revolution . . . has its engineers . . . and its unskilled."[72] The union admitted that "we need technicians." Revolution or not, the captain was still responsible for the organization of work and would remain the "primary and legitimate authority." By January 1938 the CNT approved a proposal to grant technicians "coercive powers."[73] Its militants also criticized police actions that harassed needed technicians whose revolutionary credentials were not impeccable.[74]

Within the amalgamated construction industry and other collectives, the technicians were often in command. In the amalgamation, the CNT and the UGT agreed that "technicians of different sections must fix a scale of minimum output within twenty days and this must be ratified *necessarily* by the assembly of each section, attempting as much as possible to utilize the minimum output established before 19 July 1936."[75] The Chemical Council agreed after long debate that former bosses with indispensable knowledge should be permitted to work as technicians.[76] Experts in the newly developed defense industries were clearly essential because they had to improvise and create products that had never been produced in Catalonia. Presses, lathes, pistols, rifles, machine guns, grenades, and various chemicals for explosives were all manufactured, often for the first time in Spanish factories, under CNT auspices.[77]

The unions, though, could not always convince their members to obey and respect the technicians. Early in the Revolution the CNT-UGT managers of the power industry felt that they had to impose "authority and discipline" on local committees that wanted to dismiss technicians and managers with doubtful revolutionary credentials.[78] In October 1936, a certain Menassanch stated that the central Control Committee had encountered difficulties in some power stations after foreign technicians had departed and three out of four local committees had rejected the central Control Committee's recommendations on replacements for the foreign technicians "in spite of our instructions and warnings":

> We could not convince them. . . . We must not forget that both unions have a certain number of adherents who have recently joined [them]. This growing number weighs in the balance, and it is possible that they are more Catholic than the pope and maybe even more extremist than union veterans. We can easily be dragged down by these new elements. . . . In a word, it is necessary to require that the local committees strictly comply with our agreements with the juntas of the unions.[79]

On 27 November 1936 a large meeting of the central Control Committee, local committees, and both unions reached a compromise in which the central and local committees agreed to share power over the appointment of technicians.

Other sectors also refused to acquiesce in the leadership's technocratic desires. The CNT Maritime Union often demanded that sailors obey their officers and criticized the "crew's hatred of the technicians."[80] The union warned sailors not to disturb ships' officers in the exercise of their technical functions. Salary differences certainly aggravated these tensions, and the rank and file's indiscipline provoked a kind of creeping democratic centralism of the Leninist variety:

> Anarchosyndicalism and organized anarchism are governed by majority rule. . . . Members are required to accept the decisions of the majority even if they oppose them.[81]

> The liaison between the union and the crew should not be understood only from the base to the top but also from the top down.[82]

Since the majority of the sailors "did not have the ability to occupy the positions which the organization [union] can entrust them today," the union needed "organization men" (*hombres de organización*) to accomplish its tasks.[83]

Thus during the Spanish Revolution traditional anarchist and anarchosyndicalist desires for a nonhierarchical leveling of salaries conflicted with the urgent need to develop the means of production with the aid of scientists and technicians. The CNT's plans for modernization and its campaign to win and retain the support of the technicians opposed the leveling tendencies of its largely blue-collar base. In January 1937 in the CNT National Committee of the Textile Industry, a Barcelona delegate attacked the higher salaries that technicians were receiving and claimed that many of them had joined the Confederación only because of opportunism.[84] In a response that certain members of the audience booed, Juan Peiró, the CNT Minister of Industry in the central government, criticized the Barcelona delegate for desiring to level salaries. According to Peiró, this attempt went against the syndicalist and libertarian principle, "to each according to his work": "The technician has many more needs [than the ordinary worker]. It is necessary that he be duly compensated." Peiró's viewpoint dominated the CNT's practice during the Spanish Revolution in Barcelona.

An examination of salary differences in the Barcelona textile industry confirms the preferential treatment that the CNT and, of course, the UGT accorded to the skilled. Available statistics confirm that although there was some leveling of salaries, the militants in charge of the factories retained considerable wage differentials, ranging from 2:1 to 7:1. The Central Committee of the large textile factory, España industrial, was controlled by the CNT. The factory employed 1,800 workers; its skilled workers and technicians received between 92 and 200 pesetas per week in December 1936.[85] With 302 workers, the Industria Olesana reported in December 1936 reductions of 10 percent in the salaries of its directors; 21 other technicians received salary increases.[86] While salaries for directors may have decreased, with or without UGT participation, the Confederación maintained higher wages for technicians and skilled workers in the dyeing and finishing branch of the Barcelonan textile industry. Even in cases of salary leveling, pay differentials increased as workers took on more responsibility or as their technical skill increased. Salary differences in other branches were similar to those found in textiles. Claims that the CNT-inspired contraction of salaries led to a great decrease in production must be qualified.[87]

The Revolution destroyed neither the lower wages of women nor the traditional gendered divisions of labor. When the Federación local of the UGT needed secretaries or cleaners, it invariably searched for women.[88] In the Comedor popular Durruti all the waiters, cooks, and dishwashers were males. Workers in the first two jobs earned 92 pesetas and the third 69, whereas the seven cleaning women earned 57.5.[89] In the large factory of España industrial, where over half the personnel were female, women earned 45 to 55 pesetas per week; men received 52 to 68.[90] In a large metallurgical collective, women in the same professional category as men earned lower pay.[91] For telephone workers the proposed minimum weekly wage for men was 90, for women 70.[92] As lower wage earners, women gained from the general leveling of salaries, but many collectives continued the prerevolutionary practice of paying them less.

When UGT telephone workers assembled to discuss military training, female and male participants agreed that women would receive instruction as nurses, not soldiers.[93] In certain cases women were the first to be fired. When box makers encountered economic problems, CNT militants approved the motion not to pay female workers "who had other means of support."[94] Committees also attempted to prevent pregnant women from using maternity insurance to receive more than their usual salaries.

Yet when compared to prewar employers, revolutionaries reduced wage inequalities and offered more job opportunities. In November 1937, with the assistance of the government, Catalan organizations set up an Instituto para la adaptación profesional de la mujer, in which women trained not only as secretaries and cooks but also as engineers, electricians, and chemists. The CNT-supported Mujeres libres—whose active role in the literacy campaign among women we noted earlier—wanted to create a technical training school for women to enable them to replace mobilized males.[95] Militants of this organization offered to "scour factories and workshops exhorting workers to produce the maximum" and encouraging them to volunteer for the front and for fortification work.

Anarchosyndicalist activists and Mujeres libres members—who admired the supposed Soviet success in eliminating prostitution—argued for the reform of prostitutes, of course through the therapy of work.[96] Federica Montseny, the CNT Minister of Health and Public Assistance, asserted that the Revolution offered prostitutes the chance "to change their lives and become part of the society of workers." This choice was indeed ironic since there is some evidence that before the conflict certain women had opted to become prostitutes precisely to avoid factory jobs and poor working conditions.[97] Although abortion was legalized and birth-control information made available, some militants recommended that workers refrain from sexual relations and childbirth during the Revolution.

The UGT took a special interest in adapting women's roles to meet the demands of the war and wished to cooperate with the CNT in training female apprentices. According to the secretary general of the Barcelona UGT federation, "Catalan women had always demonstrated a love of work and great ability in the workplace."[98] He demanded that certain collectives end their practice of paying women less than men for equal work. He also urged the unions to promote women to leadership in their organizations. In some workshops women began agitating for equal salaries.[99] In others, mothers received a twelve-week paid maternity leave and thirty minutes daily for nursing.[100]

In August 1938 a UGT official (a woman) asked member unions about the possibilities of hiring more women.[101] The responses of union leaders revealed both the state of Catalan industries and male attitudes toward female workers. The secretary general of the Woodworkers' Union replied that the lack of raw materials and electric power prevented the integration of women into his branch. He asserted that women did not possess the skills to substitute for woodworkers in this still unstandardized sector. In addition, the UGT leader believed that "with honorable exceptions" women were qualified only for "simple" tasks, such as varnishing, not for heavy or dangerous work.

In other sectors, the necessities of war introduced changes in the traditional division of labor. In rural post offices, women occupied the places of mobilized or deceased male relatives, and in the cities they began to labor as mail carriers. Despite their memory of female strikebreakers in the early 1930s, UGT Postal Union officials recommended that women also serve in offices. The secretary general of the UGT Paper Union believed that with proper training women would be able to perform most jobs in paper production but not in carton manufacture, which demanded more brute strength. The UGT Health Workers' Union claimed that the CNT job monopoly prevented it from hiring more women, who were "biologically" better suited for health-care positions.

Male and female wage earners learned to labor in new ways. The wartime priority on concentrating and standardizing productive forces reinforced the technocratic tendencies of anarchosyndicalist and Marxist theory and led to the most modern techniques to rationalize the means of production. For the CNT, the development of the factory system was a prerequisite for libertarian communism, and both unions adopted many of the methods that characterized capitalist production. In

October 1938 *Síntesis*, the review of the CNT-UGT Collective Cros, the major Spanish chemical firm, frankly stated that "many of the methods employed by the capitalist system to obtain a greater output cannot yet be replaced and should be used by proletarian society."

Both the CNT and the UGT promoted Taylorism, a system of scientific organization of work proposed by the American engineer, Frederick W. Taylor. Although it may seem odd, Taylorism, which was developed by a Philadelphia engineer of bourgeois origins in the most advanced capitalist nation, shared one basic feature with anarchosyndicalism and communism: the elimination of the class struggle. Taylor did not seek union, communist, or socialist control and development of the means of production; he believed that the bourgeoisie, when scientifically instructed, would be able to terminate the class struggle through prosperity, that is, through unlimited production and its counterpart, unlimited consumption. Taylor viewed workers not only as producers but also as consumers (or savers) and sought to increase their ability to be both. The American engineer therefore advocated the most efficient ways to increase production.

His system involved breaking down a task into its component parts, thus deepening the division of labor and terminating artisan-like production. Standardization was an essential element of "scientific management," and he demanded "the standardization of all tools and implements used in the trades, and also of the acts or movements of workmen for each class of work."[102] Management would accomplish this standardization and direct the rank-and-file workers. The underlying principle of Taylorism was management's appropriation of the direction of the work process itself and the reduction of workers to mere executors of management's wishes. Thus, Taylorism enlarged the division between those who planned or thought and those who executed orders. Taylor himself had a real disdain for workers' intelligence, and he feared their laziness. He felt, not without reason, that workers would resist scientific management through work slowdowns and even sabotage. Therefore, he made certain that scientific organization of work could coerce laborers, if need be.

> Human nature is such, however, that many of the workmen, if left to themselves, would pay but little attention to their written instructions. It is necessary, therefore, to provide teachers (called functional foremen) to see that the workmen both understand and carry out these written instructions.
>
> [In the construction industry he demanded] the careful selection and subsequent training of the bricklayers into first-class men, and the elimination of all men who refuse to or are unable to adopt the best methods.
>
> It is only through *enforced* standardization of methods, *enforced* adoption of the best implements and working conditions, and *enforced* cooperation that this faster work can be assured.

Scientific management shared with anarchosyndicalism an emphasis on efficient production through control of the work process by technicians. Santillán had endorsed Fordism, which other CNT militants also praised as a "model" of "wise lessons."[103] On 19 November 1938 a letter from a CNT technician called Taylor "the greatest organizer known."[104] The technician thanked the workers and the director of the Labora factory for their cooperation. He regretted that he had to leave the arms-producing firm, but he was confident that if Labora continued on its present path, it would become one of the most important metallurgical firms in Spain. Another letter of 23 November 1938 to the administrative *junta* of the CNT Metallurgical Union confirmed that "during my stay at Labora I explained to the management of the factory the road to follow for the best output."[105] An article entitled "Professional Selection" in the CNT metallurgical journal praised the research done at Bethlehem Steel, Taylor's factory, where the optimum-sized shovel for coal stokers was developed and employed;[106] this shovel permitted the most efficient use of the workers' strength. The article also lauded a disciple of the Philadelphia engineer, H. Gantt, who had eliminated workers' unnecessary movements and therefore increased productivity. In addition, it argued for a careful selection of apprentices since the metallurgical industry had some jobs that required only brute strength and others that needed intelligence. The review of the CNT-UGT Collective Marathon also praised Taylorism, and it concluded that the American engineer had achieved "scientific organization of work" that chose the best workers for each job in the factory.[107] In July 1937 the Catalan Institute of Economic Sciences called for "speed bosses" and a system of incentives in collectives.[108]

It is essential to underline that Taylorism and the other techniques employed by the unions were not merely a consequence of a wartime situation that demanded rapid production but were also the unions' response to the prewar social and economic incapacities of the Spanish and Catalan capitalist elites. In this regard, the Left continued to pursue an industrial modernization that the bourgeoisie had barely begun. The union militants envisaged a future of rationalized and developed productive forces within an independent national economy. The base of the anarchosyndicalist project was the rationalized, standardized, and even Taylorized factory, which, in its details, greatly resembled the plants of the advanced industrial nations. The Collective Marathon (formerly General Motors of Barcelona) constructed an automobile factory whose long aisles were suitable for assembly lines and whose space approximated the Renault factories in the industrial suburbs of Paris.

Plans for a functionalist city of the future paralleled the addition of the techniques of advanced capitalism in the workplace. Anarchosyndicalist militants wanted to construct cities of apartment houses and mass automobile circulation. In fact, the Marathon Collective declared that the economic potential of a nation could be measured by the number of motor vehicles per inhabitant, and it hoped that the automobile would soon become an accepted part of everyday life in Spain.[109] Nevertheless, the unions' and parties' visions of a rationalized and modernized future did not end the secular struggle against workspace and worktime, the subject of the next chapter.

6
WORKERS' RESISTANCE

As we have seen, the prerevolutionary Barcelona working class was extremely combative. Before the outbreak of the civil war, the workers frequently went on strike—sometimes with violence, sabotage, and work slowdowns—over demands that included a shorter working day, higher wages, end to piecework, and defense of traditional holidays. Despite an economic crisis, the workers were generally successful in defending their living standards; they demonstrated a remarkable ability to win many of their claims.

When the unions took control of the factories, the traditional working-class demands did not cease, and many wage earners continued to ask for more pay and persisted in their attempts to avoid constraints of factory space and time. The CNT and UGT militants who ran the collectives opposed many of the workers' desires that they had once supported; in the difficult times of war and Revolution, they called for more work and sacrifice. Rank-and-file workers frequently ignored these calls and acted as though the union militants were the new ruling elite. Direct and indirect resistances to work became major points of conflict between the base and the militants, just as they had been when the bourgeoisie controlled the productive forces. In Barcelona and in Paris, industrial managers of various political convictions were compelled to confront this aspect of working-class culture.

The rank and file's continuing exactions and actions revealed the productivist assumptions of anarchosyndicalist and Marxist theories of *autogestion.* Without changing the nature of the factory itself or by merely rationalizing it, anarchosyndicalists and Marxists called on workers to participate and control their workplace. Union activists were asking workers to endorse enthusiastically their role *as workers.* In effect, given the content of the militants' project for the development and rationalization of the means of production, workers were being pressured to participate willingly in their own bondage as wage earners. It is hardly surprising that many of them were reluctant to take part in the developmental democracy of the Spanish Revolution, and it is little wonder that union militants often lamented the unattended factory assemblies and unpaid union dues.

Union activists did attempt to satisfy one persistent rank-and-file desire. At the beginning of the Revolution, the CNT union of the textile and garment industry carried out a demand that it had been making for years: the abolition of production incentives, especially piecework—"the principal cause of the miserable conditions" of the workers, according to the union.[1] The UGT too had condemned piecework and had asked the government to do away with it. Yet the abolition of piecework soon came under attack by the Confederación itself:

> In the industrial branches that were in our [CNT] union and where before 19 July a great amount of piecework prevailed, now that there is a fixed weekly salary, productive output has declined.
>
> With all this, there is nothing to give our economy a firm base, and we hope that all workers . . . will use with the maximum care tools and raw materials, and will give their maximum productive output.[2]

The Casa Girona offered one of the most significant and spectacular examples of the problems of workers' control in the Spanish Revolution. Casa Girona, also known as Material para ferrocarriles, employed eighteen hundred workers and was one of the most important metallurgical factories of Barcelona. It had made railroad equipment before the Revolution, and after July 1936 it produced war materiel.[3] A report by the CNT-controlled factory council of Casa Girona to the CNT Metallurgical Union of Barcelona declared that costs before 19 July 1936 had been 31,500 pesetas and had increased to 105,000 pesetas. Charges for the retired personnel rose from 688 pesetas before 19 July to 7,915; for accidents from 950 pesetas to 5,719; for the sick from 0 to 3,348. Weekly payroll costs jumped from 90,000 to 210,000 pesetas. With all these cost increases a "rather intense production" was expected and needed. However, the factory council stated, production had actually diminished despite greatly improved benefits and an increase in the number of workers from the prerevolutionary total of thirteen hundred to eighteen hundred.

Girona's factory council did not believe that lengthening the working day would solve the problem since it had already added eight hours per week to the schedule; the additional time had not only failed to increase production but had not even succeeded in stopping its decline. Thus, despite a 38 percent increase in personnel, a 233 percent increase in benefits, a 133 percent rise in weekly paychecks, production declined 31 percent. The council suggested certain "practical" measures to correct the situation: "*To establish a war bonus that will be adjusted to completed production* [italics in original]." According to the management of Girona, no other solution was possible, since pay increases and the establishment of minimum production levels had failed. The council asked the Metallurgical Union for authorization to establish the bonus and to initiate "rigorous control" through its production committee and engineers. The council denied that its proposals meant a return to the "old times of exploitation" since "the prices of all work will be agreed upon by those who manage and those who execute." Workers whose work was superior must be rewarded. If not, the council argued, initiative would be discouraged.

A commission that the administrative board of the CNT Metallurgical Union delegated to investigate the "abnormalities" at Casa Girona confirmed the Girona factory council's difficulties. The investigators reported that a worker who received 18 pesetas produced 30 pieces, whereas an apprentice who received only 5 pesetas produced 80 pieces in the same time. According to the commission, the workers themselves had agreed with the factory council to establish a system of piecework. The commission concluded that the new system of production incentives clashed "fundamentally . . . with our most intimate convictions" because the CNT had always fought against piecework. Yet the workers were carried away by their "egoistic instincts" and (the commission claimed) egged on by Communist and UGT agitators. The commission declared despondently that Casa Girona would not be the last case where production necessities would contradict "our ideas of equality and liberty." It attacked the "un[class-]conscious and irresponsible" workers who refused to produce without a monetary incentive and judged that the Girona council was justified in establishing piecework since "[class-]conscious workers" were a minority in the factory.

Although it received scant mention in the press, the case of Casa Girona created a dramatic debate within the CNT. In a meeting of officials of the Metallurgical Union on 27 May 1937, its president, Rubio, declared that in a war and Revolution workers must work until exhaustion.[4] A prominent militant, Gómez, disagreed: he supported the forty-hour week in Casa Girona and rejected additional hours. In another meeting on 1 June, President Rubio stated that producers could not enjoy the Revolution during the Revolution; he attacked advocates of the forty-hour week in Girona and argued in favor of a longer workday in the war industry. According to Rubio, supporters of the forty-hour week in Girona "have been scabs and think only of their stomachs and nothing more." Gómez, champion of the forty-hour week, resigned in protest. He declared that he had seen the discontent among Girona workers, and that they could not produce because of apathy and physical and moral fatigue. Yet the workers were still sacrificing, according to Gómez. He protested that certain privileged persons were receiving several thousand pesetas per month. The bars of Barcelona were still full, the Ramblas (a main thoroughfare) was crowded, and "millions of slackers and idlers" were loitering in the city. He demanded CNT action to stop such abuses. If the CNT put the malingerers to work and granted the forty-hour week in Girona, these admittedly "un[class-]conscious" workers would zealously defend the Revolution to preserve their gains. The debate between Gómez and the union's president ended in a compromise that both criticized the attitude of workers in Casa Girona and condemned the alleged conspiracy of political parties against the CNT's revolution. It asked Gómez to change his attitude and rejoin the union and requested Rubio to continue as president. The resolution concluded that "socialization," that is, control by a CNT union of concentrated firms and collectives, would be the "salvation of our social and economic achievement."

Similar problems in other industries—whether controlled by CNT or UGT—nonetheless showed that neither Communist nor UGT agitators were primarily responsible for low output and productivity. One CNT militant in the Loaders' Section lamented that "production was 50 percent of what it should be" and complained that the section did not possess sufficient coercive powers to improve output.[5] For several months the slow workpace continued to cause damage to perishable fruits, and militants criticized the rank and file for lacking "union and revolutionary spirit." At a private meeting of UGT railroad officials, one militant insisted that a forty-eight-hour week with Saturdays off was in effect at the branch in San Andrés, a Barcelonan suburb, but "the number of machines repaired is smaller than before the Revolution."[6] An office workers' petition, eventually withdrawn, to restore the six-hour day that existed before the Revolution, demoralized Communists.[7] Thus, the declaration of the CNT Metallurgical Union at Casa Girona, which blamed Communists for its production problems, reduced complex industrial and social difficulties to a rather simplistic political level. Except for changes in the industrial decision-making process that the theory of *autogestion* introduced, neither the CNT nor the UGT provided an alternative model to develop the productive forces. When the unions were faced with industrial problems such as poor productivity and workers' indifference, they were forced to tie pay to output, just as the capitalists had done.

Problems over piecework persisted throughout the Revolution. The tailoring collective F. Vehils Vidal, with over four hundred fifty workers who made and sold shirts and knitwear, imposed, as early as February 1937, an elaborate system of incentives to stimulate its personnel.[8] In October 1937 the Casa Alemany, which received heavy orders for pants and other articles, subcontracted at piecework rates.[9] In May 1938 Barcelona railroad workers were notified of the nearly total reestablishment of piecework:

> The orders of the managers must be obeyed.
>
> The workers will receive a reasonable rate per piece. They must not forget the *basic rule* of collaboration and must not try to deceive the management.

> A list of work accomplished . . . must be presented monthly, and it must be accompanied by a report that compares the results obtained with those of previous months and justifies work outputs and variations.[10]

In the construction industry, the technical-administrative council of the CNT Building Union proposed in August 1937 a revision of anarchosyndicalist salary leveling.[11] The council posed the following dilemma: either we restore work discipline and abolish the unified salary or we encounter disaster. The council recognized bourgeois influences among the workers and called for the reestablishment of incentives for technicians and professionals. In addition, it recommended that only "profitable (*rentable*) works" be undertaken: "The masses must be reeducated morally" and their work remunerated according to effort and quality. In July 1937 a joint declaration by the CNT-UGT Construction Amalgamation of Barcelona agreed that pay should be tied to production: "In case of the nonfulfillment of the minimum [output] by a comrade, he will be penalized and then expelled if he repeats his error."[12] The CNT-UGT report recommended the posting of graphs on output as well as propaganda to raise morale and increase productivity. It determined that low output often resulted from construction workers' fears of layoffs after the termination of a project.

Both publicly and privately the UGT advocated that salaries be linked to output and that sanctions be imposed on offenders. The UGT Masons' Union reported on 20 November 1937 that a pay dispute in the Construction Amalgamation had led to a work stoppage and even sabotage. It also noted that other workers did not want to work because they were not receiving 100 pesetas per week. The Masons' Union called the attitude of these workers "disastrous and out of place in these moments."[13] On 15 December it stated that lower-paid workers wanted to equalize their salaries and that it was discussing with the CNT how to establish minimum outputs. On 1 February 1938 the UGT told its members not to make demands in wartime and urged workers to work more.[14]

The conflicts in the construction industry revealed that the rank and file continued to press wage demands as they had done before the Revolution. Wartime inflation certainly aggravated workers' wage demands, as wholesale prices increased more than two and one-half times during the war.[15] Certain collectives and industries did benefit from the inflationary economy. Brick, cement, and transportation firms were overbilling, complained the Construction Amalgamation, and it demanded guarantees that all work proceed normally and that prices correspond to normal outputs.[16] Most workers, though, were penalized by the price hikes. At the end of 1936 and at the beginning of 1937, women demonstrated against the shortage of bread. Other demonstrators continued the Barcelonan tradition of popular seizure of food supplies. On 6 May 1937, "a large group of women descended on the port of Barcelona where they looted a number of vans filled with oranges."[17] Furthermore, basic foodstuffs were rationed, and householders were forced to spend time in long lines. By 1938 milk, coffee, sugar, and tobacco were in short supply. No deaths from hunger were reported in 1936 and only 9 in 1937, but in 1938 the figure rose to 286.[18] Enterprises and unions established cooperatives or continued company stores to save workers time and money. Yet an explanation of salary conflicts based solely on physical or economic needs is inadequate; any analysis must include an examination of the problematic social relations between the workers and the directors of the collectivized and controlled firms. These new industrial managers, who were usually technicians or union militants, were continually beseeching the rank and file not to demand wage hikes during the difficult times of war and revolution, but their pleas for more work and sacrifice were frequently ignored in various industrial sectors.

For instance, CNT and UGT members of the Control Committee of gas and electricity encountered a serious problem early in the Revolution, and considerably before the May Days of 1937. On 3 December 1936 rank-and-file workers of this industry began collecting signatures demanding a joint CNT-UGT assembly to solicit the year-end bonus.[19] The reaction of the Control Committee was angry. One member qualified the petition as "counterrevolutionary and fascist" and asked that those who had signed it be locked up. UGT and CNT committee members alike feared that the proposed assembly would not only claim the annual bonus but might raise the potentially embarrassing question of salary differences among workers, technicians, and administrators. One Control Committee member declared that the "unions exist to direct and channel the aspirations of the masses"; others concluded that an assembly must be avoided at all costs. Some feared that in an assembly the three hundred who signed the petition demanding more money could easily be joined by another two thousand or even four thousand workers. A certain García stated, "Either we have no authority over the masses or we impose it on them." The meeting finally agreed to pay the bonus to avoid the assembly. Members were requested not to discuss the meeting with outsiders since the committee wished to learn who had initiated and agitated for the petition in order to take possible punitive measures against them.

An equally dramatic debate occurred in the Cros Collective, whose review, *Síntesis*, frequently told workers to postpone their demands for salary increases and vacations. Not all workers followed *Síntesis*'s advice. On 30 June 1937 the collective and its associated unions—representatives of the collective's offices and factories in Alicante, Lérida, Valencia, and Barcelona as well as delegates of fourteen different UGT and CNT unions—met in Barcelona to discuss a petition from sailors and ships' technicians in the CNT and UGT maritime unions. The workers demanded back pay for overtime and work on Sundays and holidays performed for the Cros Company from November 1935 to 19 July 1936.[20] In other words, the sailors wanted back pay for work done before Cros had been collectivized. Both the CNT and the UGT National Federations of Chemical Industries opposed the sailors' claim, but they hoped for a compromise since many other sailors had received back pay. Other delegates resisted a compromise because of the needs of the war and those of the collective itself.

During the meeting, tension flared when a sailors' representative, frustrated by the long discussion, stated that if the assembly was not in a hurry to achieve a solution, the sailors were: a ship was scheduled to sail shortly. Delegates interpreted the statement as a threat, and the president of the assembly warned that the meeting could not be coerced. Other delegates criticized the sailors for threatening to strike and for their "indiscipline." A representative from Alicante noted that workers in his factory had been hungry but had still sacrificed for the good of the collective. The Badalona delegate protested the sailors' demands and argued that they should not treat the collective like "bourgeois" since all agreements had been adopted by majority vote. He insisted that no accord could be reached until the sailors' representatives ceased threatening to strike. The UGT maritime delegate replied that he was not aware of any strike threat. His CNT counterpart declared that all the sailors wanted for risking their lives at sea was fair and equal treatment. Another participant replied that the collective had always given the highest consideration to its sailors but that on occasion the sailors had refused to sail if their demands were not met and that the factory council had been forced to accede. Finally, the assembly accepted a proposal that delayed a solution to the problem of back pay until economic conditions permitted. In other collectives, workers' long memories posed problems for the new managers who had to decide about the rehiring and back pay for those fired during the *bienio negro* or even as early as 1919.

Another full session of the representatives of unions and factories of the Cros Collective debated the question of a 15 percent salary increase for workers at its Barcelonan factory. The local CNT and UGT chemical unions of Barcelonan had previously supported the wage claims of their workers and had even threatened to shut down the plant if salary hikes were not granted. The director of the Barcelonan factory and officials from other factories and unions urged the Barcelonan unions to oppose the increases that, even if justified, endangered the "new economy." The president of the assembly declared that the Barcelonan workers, like the sailors, were trying to win augmentations with coercive methods. He asserted that it was not the time to make demands; workers should not create new problems for their councils, which they themselves had elected. The president believed that he could permit only transitional cost-of-living increases, but that this concession did not mean the right to make further demands. When the central office of the collective presented a proposal arguing against the augmentations, the Barcelonan factory's delegates then threatened to leave the assembly. The delegation from Madrid responded that it was shameful to lose time in "such materialist" debates when there were great tasks to accomplish. Subsequently, the pay hike for the Barcelonan plant was voted down by all except the factory concerned, and the president reminded Barcelona's delegation of its wartime obligations. The debates over raises for the Barcelonan workers and back pay for the sailors demonstrated that the threat of strikes and actual strikes were present during the Spanish Revolution.

The constant demands of the workers, which began very early in the Revolution, frustrated the union leaders. In November 1936 the work of cleaners employed by the railroad reflected their dissatisfaction with their salaries; according to one member of the UGT council, "the cleaners had always met the wagons and discharged the toilets. Now in many cases they do not."[21] They and other indisciplined workers had accepted tips, a practice that had been banned in this and other enterprises. Some railroad employees, such as cooks, resisted working on hospital trains. Members of the council asserted that most of the personnel lacked "goodwill," which committee members thought they had earlier demonstrated by working in the medical cars. The cleaners continued to complain frequently about their salaries and were eventually rewarded back pay.

Although the CNT-UGT unions of the amalgamated power industry agreed that demands for more pay and fewer hours "should not be discussed now," they had to confront workers from some poorer companies who felt that their salaries and work schedule should equal those of their colleagues from more privileged firms.[22] To protest what they considered an unfair system of salary classification, employees of the power industry seem to have engaged in an organized slowdown strike in which they performed morning work in the afternoon.[23] In a meeting of the CNT Metallurgical Union on 3 July 1937, a militant exhorted "our comrades" to become "idealist" and cease being "materialist." Several months earlier, the Metallurgical Union had concluded that higher living costs necessitated a salary increase, but it had hoped that the raises might end the "malaise" and keep order in the factories.[24]

Workers sometimes demanded pay for volunteer work or refused to sacrifice for the war effort. The UGT Sindicato de vestir had requested four men and women to collect clothes for the troops. The volunteers did not "understand" that they would not be remunerated for their services and demanded their wages.[25] The MZA Central Committee suspended seven volunteers, sent to unload coal at the French border, who abandoned their posts because of an argument over meals.[26] Although some did sacrifice for the front by making clothes for soldiers or by donating money to the injured, others were reluctant to be taxed for the war. The CNT Graphic Arts Union dispatched a functionary to the well-known publishing house of Seix y Barral to ensure that the personnel paid the 5 percent contribution to the militias. The CNT *sindicato* promised to investigate other noncontributors.[27] In January 1937 when workers of a jewelry collective were informed that they were required to give 5 percent of their salary to the militia, they "refused to work overtime."[28] The union responded by rejecting any pay increase.

Wage conflicts were far from the only manifestation of workers' discontent: the unions were also forced to confront major problems of absenteeism and lateness, phenomena that have existed in varying degrees throughout the history of labor. In the nineteenth century, Catalan workers, like their French counterparts, sustained the tradition of "dilluns sant" (Holy Monday), an unofficial and unauthorized holiday that many workers took to prolong their Sunday break. In the twentieth century, the largely dechristianized and anticlerical Catalan working class continued to respect traditional interweekly religious holidays. During the Revolution the anarchosyndicalist and Communist press often criticized the workers' adamant defense of these traditions; *Solidaridad Obrera* and *Síntesis* proclaimed that the traditional religious holidays must not be an excuse to miss work. Some unions prohibited the celebration of interweekly fiestas. An initiative from local committees of the power industry forbade Christmas vacations in 1936 but retained New Year's Day as a fiesta.[29] The observance of religious holidays during the working week (observers never noted Barcelonan workers in significant attendance at Sunday mass) along with absenteeism and lateness indicated workers' continuing dislike of the factory, however rationalized or democratic. These acts of avoiding wage labor perhaps revealed a deeper detachment from the ideals of the Spanish Revolution than did struggles over salary issues.

Long and heated debates occurred concerning how—and if—vacations should be organized and paid.[30] Many wage earners seem to have been determined not to miss summer vacations in 1936 and 1937 regardless of the political and military situation.[31] Several weeks after the pronunciamiento, the Control Committee of gas and electrical industries decreed that 15 August would not be a holiday. In 1937 as the summer approached, some unions prohibited vacations entirely.[32] In many collectives Saturday labor was highly unpopular. In November 1937 the UGT condemned the indiscipline of a number of railroad workers who refused to work Saturday afternoon.[33] A CNT union penalized three loaders who had continually rejected Saturday work with the loss of ten days' pay and, significantly, of fifteen holidays.[34] One militant added that the penalty for pilfering should be working six Saturdays. Women laboring in CNT offices ignored its slogan, During war there are no holidays, and militants felt compelled to take disciplinary action against a female typist who refused to work on Sunday; they feared that if the offender was not disciplined, "many [women] comrades would miss Sunday work."[35] The famous days of May 1937 offered some wage earners an unexpected vacation before the CNT and the UGT campaigned vigorously for an immediate return to work.

Sickness multiplied the number of workdays missed. In construction many comrades were often "ill." The CNT Technical Commission of Masons noted "the irresponsibility of certain workers. We refer to those who fake illnesses and do not work, thus causing heavy economic damages to our collectives."[36] The commission was astonished at the "astuteness and the wickedness of the unscrupulous workers" who invented all kinds of strategies to get sick pay. It singled out one case where a worker certified as an epileptic was surprised by a visit of members of the Technical Commission while he was gardening. This and other types of deceit "seriously threatened" the commission's social policies; it demanded a "crusade" by union delegates "to radically stamp out the abuses." Another technical commission, that of the CNT woodworkers, established a Committee on the Sick that required a worker to visit one of its physicians in order to obtain sick pay. It also alerted "union delegates and workers in general" to watch out for abuses. The CNT mutual did catch one woodworker who, continuing the tradition of self-inflicted wounds, had provoked an infection in his index finger. In November 1937 militants of the UGT Masons' Union claimed that, in addition to the excess of personnel, lack of credits, and transportation difficulties, an important reason for the "failure" of the Construction Amalgamation was the "excessive sum of pesetas paid to the ill."[37] The Executive Committee of the UGT federation in Barcelona confirmed these findings:

> [there were] many abuses regarding sicknesses since factory councils did not institute a severe control. Control is difficult because the presumed sick person often had a close relationship with the members of his committee. However, if the workers were insured by a firm, which would carefully watch the situation, this fraud might be avoided. It was agreed to consult with the comrades of the insurance union about this.[38]

Among loaders and stevedores, abuses by accident victims resulted in a heavier payment to the workers' mutual. One loader, who had been hospitalized for almost a year, was able to save a significant sum from his pension.[39] The assembly urged the Control Committee to take measures to ensure that physically capable workers labored. The committee's effectiveness was doubtful, since several months later a militant denounced workers who had been absent for several days but appeared on Saturday to pick up their paychecks. In December 1936 a prominent militant of the Tinsmiths' Union complained of the "abnormalities committed in almost all workshops with respect to illnesses and [work] schedules." In January 1937 another tinsmith noted "licentiousness" in several workshops: "There are many workers who miss a day or a half-day because it suits them and not because of illness."[40] In February 1937 the CNT Metallurgical Union declared frankly that some workers were taking advantage of work accidents.[41]

In this context the physician, ignored by historians, became a major figure of the Spanish Revolution. In the early months, some committees replaced individual company physicians but by no means eliminated their supervisory role. The revolutionary managers of the electric and gas industries urged that the Physicians' Union immediately remove a doctor whom the personnel distrusted; his replacement would have to "make house calls to verify the illnesses of those treated by other physicians."[42] Many unions and collectives reserved the right to mandate their own medical personnel to examine sick workers. One collective required that victims of work accidents immediately inform the physician of its insurance company.[43] Physicians had the power not only to excuse absenteeism but also to demand less difficult tasks for their patients. Their medical experts served to judge if control committees and other bodies were guilty of favoritism in granting sick leave.

Yet physicians were not all paragons of revolutionary virtue. A number sympathized with the military rebellion, and others took advantage of their position. The UGT clinic reported a series of abuses: the sick were badly treated, nurses were "coerced," milk destined for patients was consumed by others, and the official car was used for personal purposes.[44] Among railroad workers, although the number of injured had declined, their compensation had grown. The union delegate blamed "this irregularity on the lack of a spirit of sacrifice among the personnel, but much more on the indifference of the physicians, who do not do their duty. In many cases, the injured receive the entire weekend off."[45] To end the abuses of some, the militants decided to increase the surveillance of the sick. The Communist cell agreed to warn physicians that unless they became stricter, they would be dismissed. It decided furthermore that only a physician who was unknown to the workers was qualified to judge "the dubiously ill."

Tobacco and alcohol, subjects of reprobation in socialist realist posters, contributed to the loss of worktime. Early in the Revolution, employees and security guards of the Barcelona newspaper *La Vanguardia* would meet to drink and gamble during working hours. A militant from the CNT Metallurgical

Construction Union complained that workers abandoned their jobs to get cigarettes. After many warnings, the Central Committee punished a porter who was often drunk on the job by transferring him to another, perhaps harder, post for two months.[46]

The confused situation of war and revolution could provide a good cover for absenteeism. Control committees became skeptical when workers claimed that the "events" of July 1936 prevented them from returning to their jobs. An executive of *Solidaridad Obrera* warned that without the authorization of the CNT regional committee, those who were absent from work would not be paid. The managing committee of the power industry planned to examine "an infinity of cases of duplicity."[47] Militiamen, who had been employed by the power companies, ignored a notice published in the newspapers asking them to return to their jobs. Furthermore, militants complained that many militiamen remained in the rear. Railroad managers dismissed a number of workers for what the union committee judged unauthorized absences; in turn the workers became distrustful of their committee, which, they suspected, wanted to encourage their enlistment in the armed forces as a way of reducing payroll costs.[48]

In addition to absenteeism, sabotage and theft—implying a great distance from the libertarian or communist principles of cooperation in production—continued during the Spanish Revolution. Sabotage was often defined in the broadest terms:

> Leaving before the finishing time. . . . Complaining violently. . . . Taking holidays without reason. Finishing a job and not asking for more work. Waiting on customers impolitely. Eating during working hours. Talking. Distracting other workers. . . . Telephoning or receiving telephone messages that are not urgent. Workers who commit these infractions will lose one day's pay.[49]

A prominent CNT journalist from Madrid assessed the situation.

> You can find comrades who do not know how to measure the value of things and carelessly permit them to be wasted. . . . Others, who are aware of and able to help the cause of antifascism, criminally tolerate the employers' sabotage for a guaranteed wage. They do

> not care if the machines are working or not as long as they get paid every Saturday. If they can eat, they don't give a damn if others lack the necessities.
>
> Some act equally badly when they take over an industry and live off its capital. Others reduce the workweek so that no comrade remains unemployed. They labor maybe one whole day per week and then raise prices seven- or tenfold to maintain their wages.[50]

Given the shortages of gasoline and auto parts, a Central Committee charged that local committee members who used cars for unneeded trips were guilty of "sabotage" and might be dismissed.[51] The CNT Junta de hierro expelled four workers who had "sabotaged" the rationalized foundry collective.[52] The four, who had acquired "indispensable" status, had slept on the night shift; since he had allowed the skilled workmen to nap on the job, their foreman was also fired for permitting "serious damage to the Economy and the War [effort]." The CNT Metallurgical Union of Badalona—where, as we have seen, militancy was especially intense in the early 1930s—had a particular problem with saboteurs, and it requested its Barcelonan counterpart not to give work to Badalonan metallurgists without its express approval.

On 17 March 1938 the CNT delegate of the Collective M.E.Y.D.O. reported to the machinery section of the CNT Metallurgical Union that sabotage was endangering the life of the collective.[53] Over an extended period a great number of parts and tools, valued at 50,000 to 60,000 pesetas, had disappeared. The collective had attempted to convince its workers that these thefts were equivalent to stealing from themselves. Persuasion failed, since the thefts continued and even increased. As a result, the collective laid off its workers until the stolen equipment reappeared. After two days without work (and apparently without pay), several workers on their own initiative went to the home of a certain Juan Sendera and found much of the stolen equipment. The accused Sendera was dismissed from the collective.

Stealing was reported in other workshops and collectives, although its extent or growth is hard to estimate. Petty larceny was rampant among loaders, who stole eggs and grains.[54] Placing the stolen products in their bags, the laborers would make several trips a day to their homes, having apparently intimidated their colleagues and controllers to the point that the latter would not denounce any pilferer. One militant complained that "during work hours many comrades sit down, smoke, and don't behave as they should. When this is called to their attention, they are insolent with the comrades of the committee." The assembly voted to fine thieves 100 pesetas for the first offense and to expel recidivists. In the first weeks of the Revolution, the union of market laborers tried to reduce simultaneously both pilfering and unemployment by employing its jobless members as guards.[55]

Some union militants and officials of the collectives were even accused of embezzlement and misuse of funds.[56] The lack of qualified cadres and devoted union militants may have led, in certain cases, to the promotion of opportunists. A former member of the conservative Radical party, who had been quickly promoted to important positions within the CNT local of Castellón, fled to Barcelona; the Castellón union accused him not only of running off with funds destined for refugees but also of taking a female comrade with him.[57] A CNT metallurgist was suspected of siphoning off union dues into his own pocket.[58] Anarchosyndicalist sources reported corruption concerning the collection of funds belonging to the Textile Union.[59]

The most spectacular case of theft occurred in the power industry.[60] The gas and electric committee had a secret—and illegal—bank account in Paris that was supposedly destined for the purchase of coal. In 1936 the managing committee, acting perhaps with the complicity or knowledge of the Generalitat, had authorized a delegation to deposit funds in a Parisian bank. In September 1937 the managing committee ordered a new delegation to return to Paris to change the francs into pesetas. Several colleagues accompanied the two members of the original delegation—one in the CNT, the other in the UGT—who had placed the bank account in their own names. When the spouses of the two men joined them in the French capital, suspicions awoke in other members of the delegation. Tempted by such a large sum, over one million francs, the duo had become embezzlers. They disappeared with the women and the money.

The tabloid reader would be stimulated by this evident corruption in high places. For our purposes, though, the story —which so discredits the revolutionaries that one wonders whether it was fabricated by imaginative *franquistas*—demonstrated the lack of qualified and committed CNT and UGT personnel for positions of power and responsibility in certain industries. The scandal provoked the direct intervention of the Generalitat in October 1937 and the subsequent end of the industry's autonomy. Truly dedicated CNT and UGT militants knew that such cases of corruption among their leaders could only demoralize the rank and file and make them even more resistant to any appeal to work hard and fight hard for the cause. Under such circumstances, cynicism was a highly contagious disease. There were, of course, many examples of the other sort: dedicated activists who showed countless times that they were willing to sacrifice at the front and at home. For example, the treasurer of the CNT Woodworkers, assassinated by "vile thieves," was praised for having given his life to defend the collective's interests.[61]

In an odd twist, one agricultural collective in Barcelona felt compelled to defend one of its guards, who had killed a child. The collective explained that well-armed neighborhood gangs of twenty to thirty members employed children—some of whom were refugees—to steal produce that the gangs then sold on the black market; the collective's determination not to permit local "good-for-nothings" to live off its labor had resulted in the unfortunate "accident."[62] The CNT charged that pilfering by "ignorant troublemakers" was the most serious problem of the Barcelonan Agricultural Collective, which possessed 1,000 hectares (for 24,700 acres) throughout the city.[63] Militants often regarded stealing, waste, and other forms of sabotage and disobedience as fascist, again reducing a fundamentally social and industrial problem to a political level where they could more easily solve it through repression.

It was hardly surprising that petty larceny and welfare cheating became major issues in Barcelona, where thousands of unemployed refugees from other parts of Spain congregated. In July 1938 the city held approximately twenty-two thousand refugees.[64] Communist activists complained that some employed refugees deceived welfare personnel and ate in collectives' soup kitchens.[65] The PSUC militants demanded that the authorities purge the cheaters. Toward the end of 1938 tensions between natives and the uprooted grew; incidents—especially stealing from the fields—multiplied as food became scarcer for nearly everyone, and Catalans increasingly resented the presence of the newcomers.[66] Welfare officials tried to be generous, and the refugee population in Catalan industrial cities sometimes received rations more regularly than the natives; however, certain towns siphoned rations designated for the new arrivals to the indigenous population.[67] The uprooted suffered from typhoid epidemics, which in Barcelona resulted in 144 deaths in 1936, 261 in 1937, and 632 in 1938.[68]

In less desperate circumstances than the refugees, wage earners also deceived officials. Historians of the Spanish Revolution have ignored the fact that workers sometimes took advantage of the rivalry between the CNT and the UGT to advance their own interests, searching one union and then the other for support in their demands for less work, higher pay, vacations, and job security. A Communist UGT leader found that the naming of factory councils according to the proportion of workers enrolled in each union produced "confusion" and "instability" because of the workers' switches.[69] In a private meeting of the UGT Railroad Union on 23 January 1937, the CNT was accused of attempting to attract UGT members by reneging on an agreement by both unions to require work on Saturdays.[70] A UGT official asserted that "laziness at this moment is absurd and antirevolutionary," but other UGT activists insisted that unless the CNT consented to work on Saturday, their members would also refuse to labor. UGT militants also charged their rival with "manoeuvring" to attract disgruntled UGT clerks; the CNT supposedly advocated fewer working hours and more vacations for telephone employees.[71]

In the power industry, which was overwhelmingly CNT in the early days of the Revolution, the UGT tried to win adherents by advocating a shorter workweek of thirty-six hours instead of the CNT's proposed forty-four hours.[72] The dispute revived in 1937. In July the UGT proposed either a thirty-six or forty-hour intensive schedule, which meant a minimal lunch break; the CNT wanted the normal workweek of forty-four hours.[73] Given the division, the workers began choosing the workweek that suited their individual preferences. A libertarian militant charged that "if the CNT had proposed the establishment of an intensive working week of thirty-six hours, don't you think that we would have won the majority? The workers, in general, do not think beyond their stomachs." He implied that the UGT was campaigning to attract CNT members on the platform of a thirty-six-hour week and believed that "it was not now possible to manage the industry because of this problem." He feared the demoralization of comrades at the front when they learned about the scheduling conflict: the soldiers "will request that the English return to see if they can straighten out things." Many workers apparently adopted the shorter workweek. CNT activists accused the UGT Gas and Electrical Union of favoring a "do-nothing" working week in order to promote a situation that would force the government to take control of the industry.[74]

On 4 October 1937 a CNT delegate admitted, "We can't make the workers do what they reject," but "if we give them what they want, we are heading for slaughter." A member of the managing committee declared, "This indiscipline of the workers, without a doubt, comrades, stems from the disagreement between the two unions."[75] An adherent of the UGT, upset at the indiscipline, added that the committee's orders were not being followed and recommended the expulsion of disobedient workers. He asked his CNT colleague if the Confederación could enforce the work schedule.

> I'm afraid not. They [the disobedient workers] will maintain the same attitude as always, and they will not want to compromise. . . . It is useless to try anything when they ignore the agreements and instructions that come from the Building Committees, the Section Commissions, and so forth. They do not pay attention to anything, whether the orders originate from one union or the other.[76]

A representative from the Barcelonan UGT also feared the increasing "collective indiscipline." The meeting ended without a solution.

In Casa Girona the UGT workers were "fervent partisans" of the forty-hour week, and, according to CNT sources, they threatened to abandon the UGT if its leaders remained opposed to the shorter working week.[77] One CNT delegate feared that workers in the distribution sector might join the other union if the Confederación did not raise their salaries. The CNT Tinsmiths' Union worried that if it did not pay for vacations, Communists would profit from its consequent unpopularity.[78] An unknown number of workers became members of both unions, a shrewd but risky tactic. When one such laborer was discovered during an identity check by a control patrol, union militants planned to take "energetic action" against him. The CNT Automobile Union tried to expel General Motors workers who held membership in both unions.[79]

The tensions between the two unions persisted throughout the Revolution, despite their daily cooperation and the similarity of the problems they confronted. The historiography has largely stressed the political and ideological differences between the two organizations. Some historians have focused on the program of the UGT and the Catalan Communist party for nationalization or government control of industry, in contrast to the CNT's policy of collectivization or union control. Others have pointed to the ambivalence of the CNT and anarchosyndicalists toward political action and governmental responsibility, as opposed to the willingness of the UGT and the Catalan Communist party to participate in elections and to control the state. However significant these ideological and political tensions were, the day-to-day conflicts over economic and industrial control were at least equally important.

The two unions competed constantly for new members, each adherent yielding new dues and increased power. In addition, competition for available jobs was fierce; only those holding an appropriate union card could get them. In certain branches where the CNT dominated, it could place its members in positions. A UGT building union reported in its meeting of 8 December 1936 that workers were joining the Confederación because it could offer them better chances for jobs.[80] A serious struggle in the collective Fabricación general de colores, which had a slight CNT majority, erupted over which union would be able to place its members in a limited number of new jobs.[81] The UGT members of this chemical firm declared that the

CNT had acted illegally and arbitrarily by monopolizing new employment. In September 1937 UGT delegates and council members even threatened to call a strike if their rights were violated again.

Throughout the Revolution the unions traded charges of unjustified use of force and unfair tactics. The UGT protested that CNT collectives would ask the Generalitat for assistance when in debt but, when profitable, would hoard the surplus.[82] Likewise, the Confederación accused "socialists" of dividing profits among themselves.[83] Both unions asserted that their rival used "indispensable" status to protect favorites, not irreplaceable workers; others said that many workers became "demoralized" because of the large numbers of "dodgers" (*emboscados*) protected by the unions' organizations.[84]

The tensions and struggles between the unions, however important, were overshadowed by the similarity of the problems that they encountered in managing entire industries. Despite their ideological disputes and membership raids, they were responsible for production and therefore for industrial discipline; they cooperated to keep workers compliant. In many industrial branches the CNT and UGT agreed not to rehire workers who had been fired for indiscipline or low productivity.[85] In Barcelona both unions' federations tried to act in unison to eliminate the New Year's bonus and prevent the celebration of Christmas.[86] The *sindicatos* would sometimes combine forces to oppose government initiatives that they perceived to be harmful to the interests of their constituents.[87] In some industries and particularly in textiles, joint CNT-UGT committees overcame their feuding and agreed on hiring practices that divided the number of jobs between the two organizations.[88]

As has been shown, the unions were in basic agreement concerning the issues of industrial reorganization: concentration, standardization, rationalization, and development of the productive forces of the nation. In October 1937, a Communist UGT leader declared that as the struggle continued, the "ideological and tactical differences between the two branches of the militant proletariat" were narrowing.[89] At the UGT congress the following month, some militants demanded "first, unity of action [of the CNT and UGT] to increase and improve production; second, work discipline to eliminate loafing, saboteurs, and the unthinking."[90] UGT leaders desired an alliance with the CNT not only to domesticate the "uncontrollables" but to avoid the formation of a third union, which, UGT militants feared, could easily attract large numbers of wage earners. The secretary general of the UGT federation of Barcelona supported the workers' right to choose—but only between the CNT and the UGT.[91] In March 1938, as the eastern front collapsed, the CNT and the UGT signed a program for unity designed to bolster the defense of the Second Republic, whose armed forces experienced increasing desertions.

> The CNT and the UGT will cooperate in the rapid constitution of a potent war industry. The unions will have to establish, as an urgent and indispensable task, a strict spirit of vigilance against any kind of sabotage and passivity in work and the improvement of the latter in order to increase and ameliorate production.
>
> The CNT and the UGT believe that a salary that is tied to the cost of living and that takes into account professional categories and productivity must be established. In this sense the industries will defend the principle of "the more and better the production, the greater the pay."
>
> The two organizations yearn for the recovery of the national wealth, coordinating the economy and ordering it legally so that the independence of the country is assured to its fullest extent.[92]

The Communists termed the program "a great victory for the Popular Front and for democracy."[93] Many in both unions considered this pact a synthesis of Marxism and anarchosyndicalism, a fraternal embrace of Marx and Bakunin. If so, this joining of hands aimed to make the workers labor harder and to produce more for the unions and the nation.

Faced with sabotage, theft, absenteeism, lateness, false illness, and other forms of working-class resistance to work and workspace, the unions and the collectives cooperated to establish strict rules and regulations that equaled or surpassed the controls imposed by capitalist enterprises. On 18 June 1938 the CNT and UGT representatives of the Collectivá Gonzalo Coprons y Prat, which made military uniforms, reported a serious decline in production that lacked "a satisfactory explanation."[94]

The representatives of the two unions demanded respect for production quotas and the work schedule, strict control of absences, and "the strengthening of the moral authority of the technicians." The tailoring collective F. Vehils Vidal, which had established an elaborate system of incentives for its four hundred fifty workers, approved a rather strict set of rules in a general assembly on 5 March 1938.[95] One individual was appointed to control tardiness, and too many latenesses would result in a worker's expulsion. Comrades who were ill would be visited by a representative of the council of the collective; if they were not at home, they would be fined. As in many collectives, to leave during work hours was forbidden, and all work done in the collective had to be for the collective, meaning that personal projects were banned. Comrades leaving the shops with packages were required to show them to guards who were charged with inspection. If a worker observed incidents of stealing, fraud, or any dishonesty, he had to report them or be held responsible. Technicians were required to issue a weekly report on the failures and accomplishments of their sections. Comrades were not permitted to disturb "order inside or outside the firm," and all workers who did not attend assemblies were fined.

Many other collectives of the clothing industry issued similar sets of rules. In February 1938 the CNT-UGT council of Pantaleoni Germans prohibited unauthorized movements by threatening a suspension of work and salary ranging from three to eight days.[96] The CNT-UGT Control Committee of the Rabat firm (employing mostly women) allowed only conversations concerning work during working hours. Other collectives, such as Artgust, which had unsuccessfully asked workers to increase production, also enforced rules forbidding conversations and even receiving phone calls.[97] In August 1938 in the presence of representatives from the CNT, UGT, and the Generalitat, the workers' assembly of the Casa A. Lanau prohibited lateness, false illness, and singing during work.[98] The CNT and UGT unions of Badalona initiated a supervision of the sick and agreed that all workers must justify their absences, which were, they claimed, "incomprehensible" and "abusive," considering that the working week had been reduced to 24 hours.[99] In several collectives workers received a maximum three-day leave for a death in their immediate family. Enterprises also demanded that their personnel return to the workplace immediately after an air raid or alarm; the CNT Metallurgical Union urged militants to take measures to ensure that production could recommence "without any excuse."[100]

The severity of these rules and regulations would seem to have been a consequence of the decline of production and discipline in many textile and clothing firms. On 15 June 1937 the accountant of the CNT-UGT Casa Mallafré issued a report on its tailoring shops. He concluded that the administration of the collective had been honest and moral; however, production continued to be "the most delicate part of the problem" and "in production lies the secret of industrial and commercial failure or success."[101] If output of the workshops continued at its current extremely low levels, the accountant warned, the firm—whether collectivized, controlled, or socialized—would fail. Current production did not even cover weekly expenses; output must increase if the firm were to survive. Another CNT-UGT garment collective, Artgust, reported in February 1938, "In spite of our constant demands to the factory personnel, we have not yet succeeded in improving output."[102] The small clothes-making firm J. Lanau, with thirty workers, had similar problems. According to its accountant's report of November 1937, the mostly female personnel had been insured for accidents and illness; they had maternity benefits.[103] The workers reportedly had good relations with the owner and a control committee composed of two representatives from the CNT and one from the UGT. Production was off 20 percent, however; to correct the problem the accountant recommended establishing "clear production quotas" in both the workshops and sales. In other enterprises where workers had cordial relations with management, accountants similarly recommended measures for increasing productivity.[104] The director of a clothing firm told the assembled workers, "All this revolution against the economy must stop. You must maintain maximum productivity because the firm . . . is seriously ill and needs intensive care. It will only recover with the required injections of work. If this does not occur, the surgeon will be called to amputate the necessary members."[105] He warned that if some were fired, "it is your fault for producing little and badly." The CNT representative added that those who did not do their job "were rats of the collective"; the assembly approved the dismissal of three workers. In other collectives individual wage earners were fired or suspended for a variety of reasons: malingering, absenteeism, unauthorized holidays, and "immorality."[106] The latter charge was not infrequent during the Spanish Revolution and revealed that union activists considered any inadequacy or failure at work and vagrancy in general as "immoral," if not downright sinful.

In February 1938 the National Council of Railroads established penalties, which included fines and suspensions, for absenteeism, indiscipline, poor productivity, drunkenness, and lateness. The council aimed to eliminate "all types of intensive working days that are shorter than eight hours (the legal working day) and weekly breaks that, without being endorsed by any competent organization, have arisen spontaneously and that cannot and should not continue a day longer."[107] The MZA required that workers who claimed to be injured on the job report immediately to its health service during working hours.[108] Carelessness that caused accidents led to new rules and new techniques of supervision. In March 1937 a collision resulted in serious "moral" and "material damages," the latter estimated at "many thousands of pesetas, which the collective had to pay because of certain comrades' desertion and negligence."[109] The Comité decided to impose sanctions and discussed the eventual "creation of a study concerning a psycho[logical]-technical examination of all railroad workers."

In January 1938 at its economic session, the CNT determined the "duties and rights of the producer." It established the position of a "task distributor" who would "be officially responsible . . . for the quantity, quality, and conduct of the workers." This task distributor could dismiss a worker for "laziness or immorality"; other officials were to check if minor work accidents of "suspicious origin" were legitimate or "make-believe." In addition, "All workers and employees will have a file where the details of their professional and social personalities will be registered."[110]

Even as early as March 1937, when the CNT was participating in the government, all citizens between eighteen and forty-five (only soldiers, functionaries, and invalids were exempted) had to possess a "work certificate."[111] The authorities could ask for this card "at any time" and would assign those who did not carry it to fortification work. If violators were found in "cafés, theaters, and other places of amusement," they could be jailed for thirty days. Right-wingers and others had to employ all kinds of subterfuges to obtain the documentation necessary to avoid fortification work.[112] The Confederación thus realized the old anarchosyndicalist desire for the "identity card of the producer" that would inventory his moral, that is, productive, capacity.

Although most restrictions were designed to make workers work, one rule confirmed the existence of workers who held two jobs or who demanded overtime. These wage earners accepted labor because of individual or family needs, not those of the Revolution or the cause. Continuing the tradition of the prerevolutionary workers' movement, which desired to integrate the unemployed into the work force, collectives often prohibited dual employment and overtime. In certain collectives, workers were not allowed to have two sources of income. Communist militants planned to fire both those who received a double salary and rumormongers who made such false accusations.[113] CNT union officials scheduled an inspection at the home of one "wheeler-dealer" who was thought to have a small business as well as his regular salary from a controlled enterprise. The UGT railroad union forced militiamen to declare in writing their sources of income.[114]

Although some management committees sharply discouraged overtime, they were not inflexible. When one firm claimed that it could not find the necessary qualified personnel during a busy period, it received permission for employees to work extra hours.[115] Given the demand for skilled personnel in both military and civilian sectors, overtime was a prerequisite for victory, and it was authorized for war-related work. Unions sometimes insisted, however, that extra hours be paid at the ordinary rate. In December 1936 a militant in the jewelers' section of the CNT Metallurgical Union demanded the expulsion of a colleague who had refused to work extra hours in a CNT collective because overtime pay was low.[116]

During the Spanish Revolution in Barcelona, workers continued to engage in direct and indirect refusals to work. Their acts conflicted with the militants' urgent need to develop the backward productive forces they had inherited from a weak bourgeoisie. Militants therefore adopted repressive techniques to make workers work and to reduce resistances. They implemented piecework, dismissals, elimination of holidays, medical inspections, and strict rules. Like the capitalists and state managers in Paris, anarchosyndicalists and Marxists in Barcelona struggled against secular resistances. The following chapter will evaluate the activists' achievements and limitations.

7
THE END OF THE SPANISH REVOLUTION IN BARCELONA

Under the extremely difficult circumstances of war and Revolution, union activists fought to create a competitive national market and to modernize and rationalize industry. Despite the shortages in food and raw materials, the effects of the bombardments on factories, and the loss of traditional markets, the militants and technicians bought and manufactured new machinery, created products, improved working conditions in many firms, opened new sources of raw materials, and eliminated some of the most glaring inequalities in the workplace.

Even their adversaries often praised their control of industry. The pro-Franco historian of the large textile firm, España industrial, wrote that the "reds" had permitted technicians to act skillfully and efficiently and "thus they were able to manage the ship in the best way despite the absence of the captain."[1] The conservative historian of the Maquinista Terrestre y Marítima noted that at the end of the war and Revolution, the factories of his company were in much better condition than its directors "had ever hoped."[2] The union militants who controlled the gas and electricity industries of Catalonia maintained their equipment so well that after the war production quickly returned to prewar levels once problems of coal supplies were resolved.[3] French diplomats confirmed the rapid return of industry, and one observer noted that trams and electric railways offered normal service shortly after Franco's occupation of Barcelona.[4] Despite their contribution to the productive forces, many union militants who participated in the management of collectives and controlled enterprises were purged or imprisoned, as their colleagues watched, afraid or indifferent.[5]

It is difficult to present an overall evaluation of the purely economic performance of workers' control in Barcelona for various reasons. First, the interruptions in supplies of food and raw materials lowered production in many collectives and controlled factories. Second, the traditional markets for Catalan industry—Andalusia and other regions—were under *franquista* control, and exchange was often impossible. Third, the difficulty of acquiring foreign currencies and the fall of the peseta hindered purchases of needed foreign-made machinery; domestic enemies of the collectives were often reluctant to provide capital and equipment. Fourth, beginning in the spring of 1937 and continuing much more intensively in the first months of 1938, enemy bombardments reduced industrial output. Fifth, the transformation of many Catalan industries to war-related activities distorted productivity. Therefore, industrial production dropped between 33 and 50 percent during the civil war.[6]

Yet an approach that seeks to judge only the economic performance of workers' control will, like the purely political appraisals of the Spanish Revolution, surely miss the significance of this Revolution, which some have called the most profound of the twentieth century. My concern has been to avoid an exclusively political or economic evaluation and instead to explore the social relations in the collectivized factories and workshops. In this regard, the technicians and union militants who took control of the productive forces confronted the same problems that have affected both the Western bourgeoisies and the Communist parties that have rapidly developed the means of production. The new factory managers often ran into the resistance of the workers themselves, who continued to demand more pay, fake illness, sabotage production, reject the control and discipline of the factory system, and ignore calls to participate in managing the workplace.

In response to workers' resistance, the union militants disregarded their democratic ideology of workers' control and opted for coercive techniques to increase production. Many collectives gave technicians the power to set production levels; piecework reappeared, and incentives tied pay to production. The new managers established strict control of the sick, severe surveillance of the rank and file during worktime, and frequent inspections. Firings and dismissals for poor performance and "immorality," that is, low productivity, occurred. The CNT realized its plan for the "identity card of the producer" that would catalogue workers' behavior. Socialist realist posters glorified the means of production and the workers themselves so they would produce more. Labor camps for "parasitic" enemies and "saboteurs" were founded on the modern principle of reform through work.

The reactions of the leaders of the working-class organizations to the rank and file's actions in the collectives and controlled firms were revealing. Federica Montseny, the CNT Minister of Health and Public Assistance in the republican government, posited a theory of human nature to explain the problems in workers' control. According to this prominent *faísta,* who was the daughter of a well-known anarchist theoretician, human beings "are as they are. They always need an incentive and an interior and exterior stimulus to work and to produce the maximum production in quality and quantity."[7] As for the CNT Metallurgical Union, "the collectives . . . have underlined the bad side of human nature. This has consequently led to a decrease of production when it is most necessary to produce."[8] At the end of 1938, Felipe Alaiz—a *faísta* who was elected editor of *Solidaridad Obrera* in 1931 and was later named director of *Tierra y Libertad*—defined the "essential problem of Spain" as "the problem of not working."[9] "In general," he complained, "there is low productivity, and low productivity means . . . irremediable ruin in the future."

The CNT activist asserted that the "strikes were partially responsible for the decline of the work ethic." Though strikes were necessary on occasions, workers had abused the right to strike. Political, general, sit-down, slowdown, and other kinds of strikes may have been useful in the past, but now they only hurt the new "consumer-producer." Likewise, holidays on Sundays, weekends, May Day, and numerous other public holidays as well as vacations injured the cause. Sick leave, work accidents, featherbedding, and job security hurt the "proletarian economy" and food production: "To be on the payroll for a year really means working a half year. This shortfall has deservedly ruined many firms, but if it continues, it will ruin all the workers." Enlarging the focus, Alaiz reiterated: "If we do not work, we will lose everything, even if we win the war." One of the most important UGT leaders and a prominent Communist agreed that it was the conduct of the workers that most endangered the collectives.[10] In a confidential conversation with CNT members of the Optical Collective Ruiz y Ponseti, this UGT economist said that though few would state so publicly, the workers were merely "masses," whose cooperation was unfortunately necessary for the success of the enterprises.

The union leaders were joined by lower-ranking militants who embarked on extensive propaganda campaigns to convince and compel the rank and file to work harder. *Solidaridad Obrera* claimed that the women who were making uniforms in the new CNT tailoring shops were content; it contrasted the space, lighting, and machinery of the Confederación's workshops with the unhygienic conditions that prevailed before the Revolution.[11] The CNT daily proudly stated, "We are organizing some workshops with the same system as in the United States." Yet in June 1937 the tailoring union's Central Committee criticized the "immense majority" of workers for misunderstanding the Revolution.[12] The rank and file had not yet realized that they must sacrifice and, as a result, the tailoring industry had had to postpone plans for collectivization. Women, who were the majority in the textile industry, received special criticism since they used the factory not merely as a workplace but also as a social space. One CNT militant complained, "It is not rare that many women come to work, gossip too much, and do not produce enough. If the lack of raw materials is added to this, the collapse of production is considerable."[13] *Síntesis,* the magazine of the CNT-UGT Collective Cros, attacked laziness and vice, and it warned workers who considered "work a punishment" that they had better change their attitude quickly. *Petróleo,* the organ of the UGT petroleum militants, criticized workers who, "as in the time of black capitalist domination," wanted to celebrate traditional holidays and to receive pay hikes. "The Revolution," it bluntly stated, "is not a party time (*juerga*)."[14]

Not surprisingly, sailors were singled out as an especially undisciplined group of workers. In March 1937 *CNT Marítima* stated that, with some exceptions, the majority of sailors had not been working energetically. In July 1937 it rebuked them for low productivity, fake illness, and absenteeism. A "lamentable majority" of CNT sailors felt that they had fufilled their union duties when they paid their dues; *CNT Marítima* estimated that only 20 percent were working as hard as they should. A report of July 1938 stated that sailors who had been receiving pay on shore for months had resisted orders to sail.[15] Near the end of the civil war and Revolution, the CNT Maritime Union became extremely blunt: "The majority of workers are an inert mass who, carried by circumstances, came to the unions because life was impossible without a union card. . . . You must guess what the sailors are thinking because they are not able to express themselves in assemblies and meetings."[16]

Under the circumstances, even anarchosyndicalist militants admired the Soviet model, since the Bolsheviks had built new industries and had modernized the old, thereby securing the economic base of the Revolution. According to one *faísta,* the Soviet Union continued to progress despite capitalist attempts to strangle its triumphant revolution.[17] The CNT Building Union esteemed not only Soviet art and architecture but to a certain extent the Soviet economic model as well: "The gigantic thrust of industry and agriculture in Russia derives from the producers and not from the rulers."[18]

This statement revealed the Confederación's belief that workers must construct an economy without coercion from above. However, given the industries that the unions wanted to build and the division of labor that they had decided to impose, coercion proved to be as necessary in Barcelona as it had been in the Soviet Union. Therefore, with UGT cooperation, the CNT came to accept and even to promote Stakhanovism, a Soviet technique for increasing production. In February 1937 the CNT Textile Union of Badalona called on workers to imitate Stakhanovism, which had aroused "keen enthusiasm" among Soviet laborers.[19] The CNT review even published a photograph of the Communist work hero. "Here is an example that the Spanish worker must strive to imitate for the benefit of the industrial economy." The CNT and UGT militants of the Collective Cros lauded Stakhanovism and determined to make work "a sporting game, a noble competition" in which the victor could achieve a great prize: "the title of distinguished worker of production."[20] The collective called the Soviet Union an example of "successes obtained by rationalization and efficient work organization." For the Collective Marathon, formerly the General Motors branch in Barcelona, the Soviet Union was the "guide and example for the world."[21] The UGT Metallurgical Union and other organizations friendly to the Communists supported the Soviets' ideal of work; the CNT Building Union proposed a five-year plan "of technical modernity and stringent morality" that would liberate Catalonia from "international capitalism" and orient the economy in the postwar period.[22]

In a pamphlet, *The Front of Production,* F. Melchor—one of Communist leader Santiago Carrillo's principal lieutenants—cited Stalin's and Molotov's praise of Stakhanovism, which, said Molotov, produced "a happy and cheerful working class" that went to the factory "joyously."[23] Melchor advocated a popular front of production; he praised the example of a shock brigade in a Catalan munitions factory where four comrades—two from the Communist-dominated JSU (Juventudes socialistas unificadas), one from Estat català, and one from the CNT—"encouraged" their comrades to work "intensively." A Barcelona UGT leader claimed that shock workers offered a contagious example of higher output that other workers felt inspired to emulate.[24] He cited the feats of various "production heroes," among them one truck driver who worked overtime to maintain his vehicle in good repair and had driven more than 95,000 kilometers without a breakdown. The UGT activist warned that workers must remain vigilant in the workplace since "saboteurs" and "Trotskyists" were trying to wear down workers' enthusiasm by mouthing slogans such as We should work only if the government feeds us.

In practice, though, the shock brigade seemed to have arisen not from a spontaneous demonstration of enthusiasm but rather as a response from above to workers' indiscipline. In a PSUC cell meeting, militants reported that the head of the Sabadell aviation factories had agreed to establish shock brigades because "even though the majority of the workers belong to the

[Communist] party . . . new members lacked the spirit of sacrifice that, given the present circumstances, they should have."[25] To give the Sabadell workers the proper example, it was "an absolute necessity" to form a brigade with several comrades who were "accustomed to this kind of work." The activists decided to appoint several dismissed UGT subway militants as shock workers in the factory. After meeting with their Sabadell colleagues, the shock workers returned disgusted by the aviation workers' lack of "political and union education and spirit of sacrifice." According to the militants, what really concerned the Sabadell workers was "to hold jobs that would let them avoid work. [They gave] the impression of a fascist, not Communist, cell meeting." On the other hand, CNT militants "provided an example worth imitating." PSUC shock workers recommended a purge of the Sabadell cell.

The unions made it perfectly clear that the workers had to build a new society based on work. The Revolution must create a "new dawn" where "work was essential."[26] Whereas true art and science had been destroyed by capitalism, work was "the only value that remains unblemished."[27] One CNT activist wrote that "work is the source of life"; the Confederación itself praised the "sublime song of work."[28] The anarchosyndicalist militants came to accept uncritically a value that in other European countries had accompanied the rise of the bourgeoisie, and they lauded the union as the basis of the new economy because its productive capacity was supposedly superior to that of private property: "The union is the form par excellence that permits the extraction of the maximum of efficiency and output from its members." The journal of the UGT petroleum workers, *Petróleo,* explained, "We want to make a new society in which work and the worker will be everything."[29] The Confederación fervently desired to "lay the foundations of a society based on love of work"; activists composed poems dedicated to work as "the divine sun" that "gives light to nations."[30] The future society would not revolve around religion, sex, art, or play: the workers would be central, and it was certain that they must labor.

Even though production was the top priority and coercion served to increase output, the unions and the state provided leisure activities to attract the rank and file. Before the Revolution, spectators and participants enjoyed a wide choice of hobbies and sports.[31] Swimming, cycling, tennis, boxing, jai alai, bullfights, wrestling, and soccer had aroused great interest in the early and mid-1930s. The playing of basketball and baseball were signs of incipient Americanization, and nonpolitical clubs promoted hiking and other activities. The Amateur Soccer League coordinated the activities of approximately two hundred clubs.[32] In fact, during the election campaign of 1936 the Left accused the Lliga of distributing, significantly enough, soccer balls and sport shirts to buy votes.[33]

The Revolution continued most prewar leisure activities and politicized Catalan sports. The National Federation of Catalan Students declared that sports offered a way of mobilizing youth to defend Spain. The Amateur Soccer League was proud to be the "sporting organization that has the most militants at the front." The Boxing Section of the CNT asserted that some of its thirty boxing clubs had 80 percent of their members in the military.[34] In addition, the unions held festivals and established rest homes.

Certain groups of CNT militants tried to purify more traditional leisure and sporting activities. In the nineteenth century, anarchists had argued for the elimination of bullfights. During the Revolution, libertarian militants continued to distinguish between educational and noneducational leisure activities but often maintained the latter to avoid an increase of unemployment. Some CNT activists demanded greater taxation on noneducational entertainment—bullfights, *frontones* (pelota courts), dog tracks, boxing, and even soccer.[35] Reduced numbers of dog tracks and *frontones* operated throughout the struggle.

Licentious popular culture was attacked but did not disappear. Anarchosyndicalist and Communist militants criticized the lazy for congregating in bars and cafés.[36] Some CNT activists wanted to end immorality by shutting down such unproductive activities as bars and music or dance halls by 10:00 P.M.; several music-hall managers reduced the number of bars. Authorities executed a number of drug dealers and pimps and supposedly cleaned up "neighborhoods of vice."[37] In general, the Left frowned on pornography. One CNT militant equated pornography with "evil influences that make children turn pale."[38] According to a military publication, pornography produced masturbation that provoked tuberculosis; the militant CNT Graphics Union even destroyed "a pornographic novel."[39]

The campaign against prostitution, with posters and propaganda, did not eliminate the major problem of venereal disease in Barcelona. The sailors' port also attracted many soldiers, who usually had a good deal of disposable income. Indeed, venereal disease was the primary cause for discharging militiamen, who received repeated warnings against the malady.[40] In July 1938 army physicians were ordered to inspect brothels located away from the front lines and to check their men every two weeks. If soldiers became infected more than once, they could be sent to a military prison. Three-time offenders were subject to the accusation of self-inflicted wounding and might receive the death penalty, a certain cure.

Besides traditional streetwalking, new vices prefiguring the consumerist future arose. The use of the automobile was one of the most frequent. Countless members of committees and councils drove vehicles without proper authorization. Even the most dedicated revolutionaries were fascinated by the car. Many collectives took measures to limit the use of automobiles since members were wasting precious gasoline. Militants spent great amounts of time and energy discussing the unauthorized trips, accidents, insurance, repairs, confiscations, and the enormous expenses of what would become the centerpiece of twentieth-century consumption. Anticipating Spaniards of today, the activists pleaded for safe driving and proper care of vehicles. The telephone, not yet banalized and vulgarized, became a symbol of power and authority. Committee members were awarded a phone when elected and forced to relinquish it when their term expired.[41] As with automobiles, abuses developed: many activists demanded phone service on the slightest pretext, and former committee members avoided having their phone disconnected when they left office. The elevator completed the modernist trilogy and became, like the car and the telephone, a necessity for unions and their militants.

Anarchosyndicalists' plans for a rationalized, modern Barcelona within an economically independent nation failed to inspire many of the rank and file to wholehearted sacrifice. In fact, direct and indirect resistances were a negation of the values of the Spanish Revolution, which glorified the development of modern productive forces and production itself. The workers' refusal to participate enthusiastically in workers' control demonstrated that their class consciousness differed from that of their new industrial managers. For the union militants, class consciousness meant active participation in the building of socialism or libertarian communism; many workers expressed their class consciousness by avoiding the space, time, and demands of wage labor.

Despite their proclaimed Marxism, even historians of the extreme Left—Trotskyists, pure anarchists, and *autonomes*—have viewed the conflicts of the Spanish Revolution as essentially political. Some have criticized the CNT leadership for its participation in government, increasing bureaucratization, and compromises with other parties and unions, particularly with the Communists. Extreme leftists have often seen Los amigos de Durruti, a group that was active in the street fighting of May 1937, as offering an alternative to the CNT's compromises and bureaucratization. Los amigos proposed to strengthen the collectives at the expense of the private property still remaining in Catalonia, and it desired to revitalize the CNT so that the Confederación could exercise a revolutionary dictatorship against the Republican and Communist opposition. Nonetheless, it is difficult to believe that even the extremists of Los amigos offered a response to the fundamental problems of the Spanish Revolution. As the CNT and the UGT did, this group called for more work, sacrifices, the end of salary increases, and even "forced labor" (*trabajo obligatorio*).[42] Los amigos de Durruti failed, of course, to take power, but its type of anarchobolshevik program would not have resolved the differences between the militants and the base. Like its opponents, Los amigos offered basically political solutions to problems that had deep social and economic roots.

The rank and file's daily negation of the values of the Spanish Revolution, which were also the values of Communists, anarchosyndicalists, and even many progressive Republicans, did not mean that these workers agreed with the military and clerical Right. The rank and file's resistance to the modernization and rationalization of the productive forces desired by the militants should not be identified with political conservatism or reaction. Their opposition was diffuse, unarticulated, and both individual and collective. They proposed no alternative to party, union, or private control of the means of production; yet their refusal to participate enthusiastically in workers' control must not be dismissed as false consciousness or unconsciousness. Nor should it be attributed to the peasant or preindustrial character of the Barcelonan working class since over two-thirds of the workers were natives of Barcelona or veteran industrial laborers. As shall be seen in Paris, direct and indirect refusals are present in much more advanced industrial societies; these phenomena indicate that resistance to workspace and worktime is not confined to developing countries but occurs through many stages of industrialization.

Historians of the Spanish Revolution have focused on the political and ideological divisions among Communists, Socialists, and anarchosyndicalists and have thereby neglected the central problem of the divorce between militants committed to a certain vision of the future and workers who were reluctant to sacrifice to fulfill this ideal. The militants used coercion to force the workers to work harder both to win the war and to build the new society. The war merely reinforced, but did not create, the need for coercive methods. The war was thus not the cause of the coercion and repression of the rank and file but, like the militants' vision of the future, the result of a long historical process with prewar roots.

Ironically, after the defeat of the Left, Franco's governments adopted many aspects of the militants' vision of the future. After two generations of stagnation, in the late 1950s the means of production began again to be rationalized and modernized. Spain strengthened its agriculture, improved its infrastructure, and developed its industrial base. New needs—such as the automobile and the telephone—were refashioned, and no longer could CNT militants lament that "Spanish backwardness derived, to a great degree, from racial laziness that leaves [the Spaniard] satisfied with a crust of bread."[43] Cars began to be mass-produced, and the anarchosyndicalist project of cities of large apartment complexes and massive automobile circulation was partially realized. Considering the ability of postwar Spain to achieve much of the CNT and UGT militants' dream, it is no wonder that anarchosyndicalist and other large-scale, working-class, revolutionary movements have nearly disappeared in present-day Spain.

The decline of revolutionary movements can be traced to the rapid economic growth from the late 1950s to early 1970s. For our purposes, it is important to note that the spurt to increased prosperity did not result from an industrial revolution undertaken by the Spanish bourgeoisie but rather from Spain's proximity to the expanding labor and capital markets of post-World-War-II Europe. A mass tourist industry grew to accommodate northern Europeans attracted by the sunny beaches and the cheap peseta. Spanish workers traveled in the opposite direction and sent a hefty part of their salaries back to the Iberian Peninsula. The Franco regime kept wages low, limited strikes, and maintained a repressive order, which established a climate favorable to investments by multinational corporations. In addition to the old model of the pronunciamiento, Spain can now offer certain Hispanic and Third World countries a new model of democratic consumer society.

8
THE STRENGTH OF THE PARISIAN BOURGEOISIE

Both Left and Right in France have often described the Popular Front as a *révolution manquée,* a missed opportunity for the working class to take control of the means of production as its Spanish counterpart had done. When French workers occupied factories and staged sit-down strikes during May and June 1936, commentators of various political persuasions believed that the workers were on the road to revolution. Yet despite an unprecedented one million workers occupying factories throughout France, the French capitalist elite, unlike the Spanish, retained its ownership of the means of production. Instead of making revolution during the governments of the Popular Front, the workers demanded—and received—paid vacations and the forty-hour week. In the midst of the greatest economic depression capitalism has never known, France gave birth to the weekend. In the face of high unemployment and the increasing threat of war, French workers fought for their forty-hour week with Saturday and Sunday off. Thus the Popular Front was not only an alliance of unions and leftist political parties to prevent fascism in France, it was also the birthplace of mass tourism and leisure. The demand for a social revolution in which the workers would take over and develop the means of production was superseded by numerous struggles against work. The second part of this book examines the revolts against work in Paris and its suburbs; it details the reactions to workers' aspirations by the Communist and Socialist parties and the massive federation, Confédération générale du travail (CGT), which were, with the Radical party, the main components of the Popular Front.

To recall the different French and Spanish economic, political, and religious evolutions helps us understand the decline of revolution and revolutionary ideologies in France. In contrast to Spain, France had steadily and consistently industrialized from the middle of the nineteenth century and throughout the twentieth; its development of the productive forces had, as in other Western nations, severely restricted the revolutionary possibilities of working-class organizations. The French had created a thriving national market and slowly forged national unity. In the first third of the twentieth century, regionalist movements did not pose a threat to the indivisibility of the nation. Again, in direct contrast to Spain, there were no attempts at a coup d'état in the 1920s, and the conspiracies of the 1930s failed miserably. The French, too, had separated Church from state and the military from the civilian government. After the Dreyfus affair anticlericalism was no longer the burning issue that it continued to be in Spain and seemed after World War I to have become an outdated ideology, its appeal lost. Although anticlericalism did not disappear in the interwar era, it progressively dwindled and declined.[1]

Furthermore, in France and particularly in Paris, careers were open to the talented, regardless of religion. The French bourgeoisie became increasingly decatholicized and widened its ranks to include considerable numbers of Protestants and Jews, some of whom played essential roles in the most modern industries—electricity, automobiles, and aviation—that in Spain were either backward or nonexistent. The assumed aristocratic values of venality, *oisiveté*, and the prestige of titles gradually declined, as that of *réussite* (success) took their place: "The most modern and active part of the bourgeoisie defended the virtues of work and talent."[2] If, in the nineteenth century, *rentiers* were an important minority of the French upper classes, the true idle rich (*véritables oisifs*)—those who never exercised a profession—were much less numerous. As the Socialist leader Jean Jaurès said, "The bourgeoisie is a class that works." Periodic economic crises forced this class to renew itself; in so doing, it enlarged its numbers and broadened its base. The Parisian bourgeoisie was particularly fluid and supported a philosophy of effort and action.[3]

From such diverse national contexts, different paths emerged. In 1936 anarchosyndicalist militants in Barcelona took control of the underdeveloped productive forces that a weak bourgeoisie had abandoned, whereas the militants of the extreme Left in Paris—anarchosyndicalists, Trotskyists, and dissident Communists—who demanded soviets, workers' councils, or some form of workers' control, were largely ignored. They held little interest for the masses of workers and, quite unlike in Barcelona, for militants of the largest working-class organizations—Communist, Socialist, and the overwhelming majority of the CGT. In contrast to the Spanish organizations, by 1936 the largest French unions had relinquished their earlier doctrines of revolutionary workers' control. In Paris the huge majority of workers and even most union militants in the industries under study here did not want to take over and develop the means of production. In fact, many workers often desired to avoid work and had little wish to labor for their employer, state, party, or union. As in Spain, the nature of the productive forces promoted struggles against work. The noise and vast space of the factories, the dirtiness of the workplace, the ugliness of industrial suburbs and anxious boredom of daily commutes, the ever-present danger of accidents, and the meaninglessness of many tasks encouraged workers to flee from the means of production. The spreading rationalization, the increased deskilling of labor, and the consequent necessity of army-like discipline in the factories aggravated resentments that expressed themselves through direct and indirect revolts against work. When closing time arrived in many factories, workers, even if exhausted, rushed madly for the exit. Thus, during the Popular Front in Paris militants and workers waged a daily guerrilla against work and its attendant discipline. This guerrilla became the most important form of class struggle during the Popular Front and damaged the Left's hopes of economic growth through increased production and consumption. The workers' struggles against labor discipline and for the weekend bring into question certain generalizations by historians that French workers had accepted the industrial system and had adapted to the factory.

Paris is the obvious subject for analysis because of its enormous political and economic importance to France, even greater than Barcelona's to Spain. And the choice of the industrial branches is not totally arbitrary. Two of them—automobiles and aviation—formed the advanced sectors that led the working-class movement during the Popular Front; the occupation waves of the spring of 1936 began precisely in these sectors. Because of its more traditional character, the third branch, construction, contrasted sharply with the industrial modernity of the other sectors. The building industry reflected the small-scale, family concerns that, despite the success of the second industrial revolution in France, still dominated in many branches of the economy. In the World's Fair of 1937, it took part in a huge construction project employing tens of thousands of workers that was to be the showcase of the Popular Front. The workers of the industries examined here expressed many of the desires of Parisian wage earners in other sectors (which, when relevant, have also been adduced). To put workers' actions and desires into proper perspective requires a survey of French and particularly Parisian economic and social development.

After World War II, many historians emphasized French industrial backwardness compared to Germany, England, and the United States. More recently the focus of historiography has shifted, and historians have stressed France's development of powerful industries in automobiles, aviation, and chemicals. If the French *patronat* (employers) often remained patriarchical and authoritarian, it was not always Malthusian. The growth of capital equipment in France during the first third of the twentieth century was comparable to that in Germany and the United States and faster than that in Great Britain.[4] Even before World War I, France was "unmistakably a country of advanced industrial capitalism."[5] "In real terms, the French in 1913 enjoyed a standard of living higher than their German neighbors and had made substantial progress with regard to Great Britain." The growth rate per inhabitant in France between 1870 and 1964 increased more rapidly than Great Britain's and only a bit less than Germany's.[6]

The economist Alfred Sauvy, who has emphasized the "Malthusianism" of French employers, has nonetheless declared that between the wars France, "like other industrial nations," imported raw materials and exported manufactured products.[7] From 1911 to 1936 French industry began to dominate a previously agricultural nation, and by 1931 the majority of the population was no longer rural.[8] Although the number of farmers declined by one million from 1911 to 1936, agricultural production increased. Industrial progress surpassed agricultural advances, and from 1898 to 1913 industrial production grew 3.4 percent per year, a very respectable figure.[9] The First World War produced even greater industrial growth, and the industries of the second industrial revolution—automobiles, aviation, and chemicals—expanded rapidly. With the assistance of an activist state, French industry successfully met the test of World War I and then adapted to the loss of the heavy industries of the north and northeast, regions occupied by the Germans. In a remarkably short time, the armaments ministries organized arms and airplane production, and after several years of war, a dynamic Ministry of Commerce regulated trade.[10]

In the 1920s these modern industrial sectors did not suffer a postwar crisis, and the growth rate for French industry was the highest in Europe.[11] Industrial production more than doubled from 1921 to 1929, although population grew only 14 percent in the same period. Thus, industrial expansion occurred in those industries that used machinery extensively and attained levels between 1906 and 1929 that were matched again only in the 1950s and 1960s.[12] In the 1920s Spain too experienced significant industrial growth, but its expansion was based on the employment of large quantities of inexpensive labor, not the introduction of new machinery.[13] Between 1920 and 1930, Spanish industrial productivity increased, at most, by 20 percent, whereas French industrial productivity grew nearly 100 percent. Even during the depression of the 1930s, hourly productivity continued to rise 2.1 percent per year, a rate similar to the gains registered from 1896 to 1929.[14] C. J. Gignoux, the leader of the French manufacturers' association, CGPF (Confédération générale de la production française), during the Popular Front and a supporter of Vichy's Révolution nationale during World War II, nonetheless declared that France had made significant industrial progress from 1919 to 1939.[15] He noted that after World War I the Third Republic had provided the modern infrastructure of the French economy by building roads, airports, power stations, and ports; it constructed or improved schools, hospitals, and telephone and postal communications.

A tendency toward concentration or elimination of small, relatively inefficient firms characterized industrial developments in the first third of the twentieth century.[16] From 1906 to 1931 the number of firms employing from one to five workers decreased approximately 35 percent, whereas the number of establishments with over five hundred workers almost doubled. Even though the majority of French enterprises remained small, the economic significance of very large factories with over one thousand workers increased substantially. The majority of workers labored in firms employing over one hundred workers. Modern metalworking firms began to employ more workers than the older textile industries, which had been the base of the nineteenth-century industrial revolution. In metalworking, those businesses that employed over five hundred workers formed only 1.2 percent of metalworking firms, but these companies employed 37.8 percent of the work force. The technologically most advanced industries—iron, steel, chemicals, and motor vehicles—were the most concentrated. By 1936 French industry had reached a certain balance between large and small firms, a kind of interdependent dual economy in which small and medium-sized businesses coexisted with large enterprises and in which rather backward regions contrasted with the very advanced.

Again, unlike in Spain, the automotive industry played a fundamental role in France in the first half of the twentieth century. The French had been pioneers in automotive construction before the First World War, and they adopted mass-production techniques during the conflict. At the end of the war France remained second only to the United States in production of automobiles.[17] Between 1906 and 1931, the number of workers in the automotive sector grew by a multiple of five. From 1923 to 1938 French motor-vehicle production increased 180 percent, compared to a 20 percent growth in the United States. Throughout the 1920s France remained the largest automaker in Europe, surpassed in exports only by the United States in 1931. Continuing concentration characterized this industry: in 1924 there were 155 firms; in 1932 there were 60, but by 1939 only 31 automakers remained. In 1934 the majority of the eighty-eight thousand workers directly involved in motor-vehicle manufacture labored in firms with over two thousand workers. The three largest companies—Renault, Peugeot, and Citroën—produced 56 percent of the vehicles in 1925 and 70 percent in 1932.

In 1936 the automotive industry, including its spin-off activities such as repairs, sales, and services, was capable of employing up to eight hundred thousand workers, making it perhaps the key sector of the French industrial economy. During the Popular Front, France was second, again, to the United States in the number of vehicles in circulation and in the ratio of automobiles per inhabitant. In 1935 the over two million vehicles traveled on a relatively good road system. By the 1930s the railroads, the transportation achievement of the nineteenth century, were surpassed by automobiles, which had 650,000 kilometers of roads compared to 67,000 kilometers of track and employed directly or indirectly six hundred thousand workers compared to five hundred fifty thousand railway employees.[18]

At its birth the French aviation industry had a symbiotic relation with the automobile industry. Most of the early French aviation pioneers had begun their industrial and technical careers in automobile-related activities; many pilots had been bicycle or race-car drivers.[19] The First World War had considerably promoted investment in this sector, and production jumped from 50 planes per month in 1914 to 629 per month in 1918. Postwar output fell sharply, but the French state, in contrast with the Spanish, actively promoted an independent national aviation industry. The government aided private aviation companies and built the necessary airport facilities.[20] In 1926 France transported 1,067 tons of merchandise by air, compared to 1,050 tons for Germany and 679 tons for England.

The chemical industry closely followed the growth of automobiles and aviation. Rubber and petroleum products were needed to build and fuel the vehicles, in addition to the more traditional uses of chemicals in agriculture and textiles. Prior to World War I the French chemical industry was prosperous but weak in comparison with the German since it did not produce chemicals such as coloring agents, bromine, and chlorine.[21]

During the conflict French industry learned how to replace chemicals that it had previously imported from Germany. After the war the state, with the cooperation of chemical industrialists and sometimes with the participation of labor organizations, created committees—such as the Commission de défense nationale pour les industries chimiques and the Conseil national économique—to assure French self-sufficiency in chemicals and other products. By 1929 the French balance of trade in chemicals was favorable, and in 1932 France had risen to second place in the production of phosphate fertilizers.[22] Although the French chemical industry remained behind its American and German competitors, in the decade that followed the First World War, "France equipped herself with a chemical industry that could stand up to most in Europe."[23]

As in industrial sectors like chemicals, automobiles, and aviation, the French capitalist elite created a powerful electrical industry. On the eve of the First World War the city of Paris had already unified the production and distribution of electricity.[24] In 1907 there were approximately forty plants in the Paris region, but by 1914 their number had been reduced to nineteen. Between 1906 and 1931 the numbers of workers in electrical construction multiplied by 7.5. In the 1920s, "French technology of electrical construction . . . freed itself from foreign techniques."[25] In 1925 the Conseil supérieur de défense nationale concluded that the electrical construction industry was capable of satisfying potential French war needs. In 1930 France produced more electrical power than Japan or England, and in 1933 the nation was reportedly fourth in the world in the generation of electricity.[26] Between the wars, concentration continued. In 1936, 80 percent of the electrical power of the Paris region was generated by six plants, and a significant part of the railroads and the public transportation of the Paris region had been electrified. The French industry contrasted sharply with the backward and scattered character of Barcelonan electrical firms.

The dynamism of French industrialists not only altered the factory and production, but in certain industries it also changed the quality of labor itself. The modern industries of the Paris region, particularly the automotive, were pioneers in the rationalization of work. Unlike in Spain, where union militants were sometimes responsible for the introduction of scientific techniques of rationalization, in France the capitalist elite often proved quite capable of industrial reorganization. It viewed Taylorism and other forms of scientific organization at work as following in the tradition of Saint-Simonian productivism and *étatisme.*[27] French technological and industrial elites often welcomed the latest methods of rationalization and believed that they could bring prosperity and power to the nation. The experts thought that the increasing consumption of goods produced by the new techniques would dampen class conflict and create the material and spiritual climate for class collaboration. As in America, capital and labor would be reconciled on the neutral ground of science and technology. In contrast to the Spanish situation, a collection of Taylor's articles appeared in French in 1907. His famous work, *The Principles of Scientific Management,* was immediately translated and made available to French readers in 1912, less than a year after its American publication. French advocates of scientific management wanted to make the American engineer's writings known to French industrialists to "avoid false interpretations of Taylor."[28] Taylorism was adopted in the French automotive industry before World War I, when its introduction provoked strikes against production speed-ups and the lowering of piecework rates. A minority of workers, mainly skilled personnel, resisted the deskilling of their labor caused by the new methods of organization.

The First World War and its consequent requirements of production accelerated the application of Taylorism and other forms of scientific organization at work. During the conflict, M. Hourst, a Michelin director, defended Taylorism against attacks by arguing that it enabled wage earners to perfect their skills in several days or weeks, as opposed to the years that were previously required.[29] In addition, it allowed unskilled and new workers, including women, to replace qualified personnel. The Michelin executive cited the shorter workweek and the higher wages that would result from the correct application of the procedures of the Philadelphia engineer. To obtain these advantages, the workers must, of course, give up idling (*flânerie*).

The trends toward the deskilling of labor and mass production continued after the war. Several firms that had produced armaments during the conflict reconverted to the mass production of automobiles.[30] During the 1920s assembly lines multiplied throughout the motor-vehicle industry where "the skilled worker with his habits, his own rhythm of work, and his particular consciousness of a job well done" was replaced "by the unskilled laborer, the o.s. (*ouvrier spécialisé*)."[31] At Renault between the wars "intelligence was incorporated into the machine." Workers found themselves before a mechanism that aimed "to replace their own labor; and their initiative was thus more and more limited by the engineer."[32] In 1925 at Renault, approximately 46 percent of the workers were skilled (*ouvriers professionnels*), while 54 percent were relatively unskilled (*manœuvres* and o.s.). By 1939 the percentages were 32 percent skilled and 68 percent relatively unskilled. On the eve of the Second World War in the large automobile factories around Paris, 60 percent of the workers could learn their jobs in three days.[33]

The development of the assembly line gave rise to a new kind of factory space. "Assembly-line work leads to the construction of buildings that have only outside walls. The interior is divided by a very small number of partitions, in contrast to the compartments of the era of specialized and skilled workshops. The new spatial organization permits a large view of the whole production."[34] Presumably, the new space helped managers to oversee and control workers.

In addition to an altered organization of space and labor, a new measure of time was devised in the modern automobile factory. Piecework, or rather production incentives, an intrinsic part of scientific organization at work, became the established form of payment for most autoworkers between the wars. Workers were forced to be conscious of the clock from the time they punched in until the siren ended the working day. Simone Weil, the intellectual who worked in several of the large metalworking concerns around Paris, described factory life in the 1930s:

> Piecework, the purely bureaucratic relation between the various parts of the firm, and the separated production processes are all

> inhuman. Your attention has no worthy goal and is forced to concentrate on a small-minded task, which is always the same with some variations: do fifty pieces in five minutes instead of six, or something similar.
>
> There are two factors in this slavery: speed and orders. To succeed, you must repeat the same movement at a pace that, being quicker than thinking, stops not only reflection but even dreaming. When you are in front of your machine, you must destroy your soul, your thoughts, your feelings, everything.[35]

The unskilled and the semiskilled were subordinated to the operations and the pace of their machines. At best, workers could control their working speed, but certain methods of piecework reduced even this limited degree of autonomy. Working too rapidly might eventually result in a lower rate per piece; a slow pace meant a skimpier paycheck. Important decisions were made by managers and technicians, and hierarchy was an intrinsic part of a metallurgical worker's life. In the huge space of the noisy factory, a stringent discipline was needed to force the semiskilled laborers to perform their repetitive and boring jobs. Foremen and controllers, with virtually absolute authority over their subjects, were hired to ensure that workers produced how and what they were ordered. Sometimes a foreman played the sultan and sexually harassed female subordinates.[36] Every aspect of wage-earning lives was tightly controlled: at Renault the management, not the unions, issued special identity cards to workers.

With other important French firms, Renault participated in the Exhibition on Waste promoted by the Service of Scientific Organization at Work of the Union des industries métallurgiques et minières in November and December 1932.[37] The war against *gaspillage* (waste) was considered by Left and Right alike to be an integral part of scientific management. The goal of the exhibition was to encourage a "spirit of thrift" and economy among French employers and workers in order to reduce waste whenever possible. Renault was determined to "expose the nefarious and sometimes deadly role of waste" through lectures and displays. The exhibition on wasting time displayed a clock that replaced the usual divisions of hours and minutes with calculations that each lost hour cost the factory 175,000 francs. The display on squandering office supplies confirmed that if all the sheets of paper consumed by factories every year were placed end to end, they would reach halfway around the globe. The staples used would have linked Paris to Montargis, some hundred kilometers away. Other stands presented tools and materials broken by carelessness or lack of maintenance and showed parts and materials found in the trash and in the washrooms. The Exhibition on Waste argued that it would be better to "kill squandering" than to rely on protective tariffs to ensure the future of French industry.

Renault's efficiency experts wanted to cut costs by simplifying tasks and eliminating superfluous movements. Renault management understood that its drive to save money needed at least some cooperation from the rank and file:

> A surveillance that is too apparent becomes aggressive and leads to a struggle between the workers and the controllers. Then there is a constant, silent, and underhanded war in which the personnel, more numerous and knowledgeable about the details of the work, always have an advantage. . . . Time used in this warfare is time paid by the employer and lost to production.
>
> [The problem is] how to encourage the personnel to produce more and better without having to watch them constantly.[38]

The company's ideal was to encourage self-control: "The controllers in the workshop ought to be replaced as soon as possible by machines of control and verification, permitting the workers to control themselves."[39]

Yet Renault's efficiency experts were trapped in a logical and practical impasse. For if industrial societies usually exercised surveillance and control of the workers, then they would have no simple task to create conditions under which workers would labor without control and coercion, especially when jobs were becoming increasingly deskilled. Indeed, the demand for the simplification of tasks and for scientific organization of work, including Taylorism itself, arose precisely because workers often resisted work and required the control of supervisors, human or machine. In fact, managements faced the real dilemma of whether to permit the production of inferior and flawed goods or to spend considerable sums to control workers and cut down on defects. Verification of production was costly, and management strove to make certain that the services were as effective as possible. In the early 1930s inspections occurred periodically, but not regularly, to maintain the element of surprise. All controllers were obliged to sign a prepared checklist to verify that they had really inspected what had been assigned. A chief controller spot-checked the inspectors; sanctions were taken when inspectors were negligent.[40] Those who checked payrolls and parts were to receive a certain percentage of the money they saved for the company in order to encourage them to find errors and reduce overall expenses. Inspection was not completely effective, however, and in April 1931 Louis Renault complained that "what kills our country is that nobody wants to be sufficiently disciplined to demand from those who execute that they do what they are told quickly and scrupulously. . . . Those who will not act so that parts without defects are made will first be penalized and then dismissed."[41]

Renault wanted to avoid the predicament of Citroën and certain American companies where the cost of quality control exceeded the damages that an increase in defective parts would have caused if inspections were reduced.[42] It should be remembered that not only the workers but also the controllers themselves had to be monitored. During the Popular Front, the firm tried to reach a proper balance between the number of productive workers and the number of unproductive personnel who watched those who produced. To avoid continuous surveillance, Louis Renault wanted to "make the worker as responsible as possible for his work so that he is interested in it and loves it."[43] As will be seen, this goal was not to be realized.

Management wanted to foster upward mobility. Workers who had demonstrated competence and commitment to the company must be allowed to advance. A Renault executive concluded that "experience has shown that it is indispensable that a good inspector be a good professional who had performed assembly-line jobs before he acquired his position. Besides, this is the method used in American factories."[44] In fact, one major reason that Renault engineers and executives admired American industry was its ability to integrate and promote workers who desired to climb the professional ladder. In 1936 Renault officials who were visiting automotive plants throughout the United States commented on the 4 to 1 salary differential between skilled and unskilled workers: "It is this enormous difference between the salary of the laborer and the salary of the highly skilled worker that allows the quality of the labor force that America possesses. [American] workers make a constant effort to educate themselves in their profession and to advance into a higher class."[45] The Renault engineers lamented that "this mentality is difficult to implant in France." As evidence, they noted that at the Société des aciers fins de l'est (S.A.F.E.), a metallurgical firm controlled by Renault, "we frequently run into difficulties when the laborers protest against the supposedly excessive salaries of an excellent roller (*premier lamineur*) even though the difference between the pay of the rolling-mill hand and an excellent roller is hardly 1 to 2 compared with 1 to 3 or 1 to 4 in America." Management's desire to reward the upwardly mobile was forced to confront the egalitarianism of many French wage earners.

During the Popular Front, management continued to struggle against this egalitarianism and attempted to create its own company culture. One way of assuring that supervisory personnel would be disciplined was to follow their careers from the beginning. Apprentices who might eventually become foremen or superintendents were supposedly subjected to "total training—professional, technical, and moral."[46] Foremen, whose "moral and professional capacities" were absolutely necessary to obtain greater output from workers, must be able "to reach higher ranks through their knowledge, experience and moral values."[47] In other firms, technical knowledge and ability were not the only criteria for selecting supervisory personnel. Michelin, which controlled Citroën after 1935, chose to train not only technicians for its *service des économies* but "above all, former law students." In other words, what was really important was that these efficiency experts be committed to the company values of cutting costs and reducing waste.[48]

The Renault executives admired the Americans not only for their ability to implement policies that promoted social mobility among workers but also for their organizational methods. "Cleanliness," "order," and "discipline" were the terms French visitors frequently employed to describe American factories.[49] At Ford in Detroit, "an extreme discipline governs the entire factory. It is absolutely forbidden to smoke." Although Ford workers were paid hourly and not by piecework, each wore a highly visible number and had to produce a minimum output (recorded by counters on the machines) or be discharged.[50] Walkways raised above the shop floor facilitated surveillance of the rank and file.

Renault officials also praised the organization of the General Motors plant in Antwerp, where the foreman was freed from all tasks other than surveillance of workers. To help the foreman with his job of control, an inspector and his assistants marked each operation on a card that accompanied the automobile on the assembly line. If a customer complained about a defect, the controller could be immediately identified and dismissed.[51] Workers who wore distinctive red and blue hats supplied the assembly lines with tools and parts and "helped the foreman maintain order." By bringing the needed parts and equipment directly to the assembly lines, these specific workers reduced the movements of their colleagues and increased the rhythm and steadiness of production. Renault attempted to copy General Motors and to free its supervisory personnel from tasks other than control; in 1938 new machinery and an innovative system of accounting permitted foremen and superintendents to devote their time to "technical surveillance of production."[52] Thus Renault often succeeded in implementing the latest techniques to reduce the gap in productivity between French automakers and their American competitors.

Not all industries were as rationalized or as concentrated as that of automobiles. Rationalization in the aviation industry was less advanced, and manufacture of airplanes often required a precision and a perfection that was not compulsory in automotive fabrication. Prior to the First World War, to an even greater degree than in auto production, workers in aviation were largely skilled artisans who labored long hours but lived "at the same rhythm as their employer, eating and drinking when he did."[53] The earliest aviation workshops were frequently located near the airfields of the Paris suburbs. When the first large factories were constructed as early as 1911–1912, with management's offices separated from the shop floors, assembly lines were still rare. Between the wars rationalization progressed: in the suburb of Argenteuil, the Lioré et Olivier company replaced its wooden hangars with massive concrete and glass constructions. Visitors to an aviation plant at Mureaux were impressed by the "order and ease of execution that permitted better and quicker production." Despite increasing rationalization in all sectors, workers in aviation remained more skilled than their counterparts in other metalworking industries.

The construction industry was commonly a refuge for workers in various crafts. Compared to the "militarized territory of the factory," the independent employment of plumbers or roofers, for instance, was remarkable.[54] Most construction was decentralized and family-run; whereas in 1931 in metallurgy firms with more than one hundred workers employed 98.3 percent of workers, in construction and public works such firms employed only 23.8 percent of workers. In 1931 construction occupied one million workers, approximately 10 percent of the labor force; about 40 percent of construction workers labored in establishments with fewer than fifty workers.

Yet even within the rather traditional structure of the construction industry, the character of work was changing between the wars. Like aviation, chemicals, and automobiles, construction was among the fastest growing industries in France in the first third of the twentieth century.[55] The use of machinery like bulldozers, cranes, cement mixers, pumps, and jackhammers eliminated considerable amounts of hard physical labor; spray-painting machines and the beginning of mass production in locks and hardware made other old *métiers* obsolete. Large public-works projects in the Paris region, the extension of the subways and the World's Fair of 1937, employed hundreds and even thousands of workers.

The modern industries examined here changed the face of Paris and particularly of its suburbs. The automobile industry started up in the western part of Paris proper, where its wealthy clientele resided.[56] During the war, the industries of automobiles and aviation expanded rapidly and huge factories rose in the *banlieue*. The Renault establishments in Boulogne-Billancourt, employing over thirty thousand workers, were probably the largest in Europe. The Citroën firm was located only a few kilometers from Renault; thus the giants of the French motor-vehicle industry were located inside their largest market. The aviation industry was even more concentrated around Paris than the automotive industry. In 1936, one estimate claimed, 65 percent of the factories manufacturing aircraft bodies and 90 percent of the plants producing airplane engines were in the Paris metropolitan area.[57] Both industries were willing to pay the greater costs and higher salaries that the Paris region entailed in order to be situated in perhaps the largest market on the Continent.

The increasing concentration and intensified division of labor found in the advanced industries of the Paris region were paralleled by a growing specialization of urban space. In eighteenth- and early nineteenth-century Paris, aristocrats, bourgeois, and workers had often lived in the same neighborhood or even in the same building. Many industries were established in the heart of the city, and there was little need to leave one's *quartier* to commute from home to work.[58] During the nineteenth century, neighborhoods began to take on the character of a specific class, and some workers left the center of the city for outlying arrondissements while bourgeois went to the western parts of Paris. The twentieth-century development of the suburbs reinforced the tendency of the working class to move from the urban center to its periphery. The ratio of workers living in Paris to the total Parisian population in 1931 was lower than in 1848.[59]

By 1936 the strength and dynamism of the Parisian bourgeoisie had considerably altered the everyday life of workers in the Paris region. The commute from home to work lengthened as both factories and personnel moved into the suburbs of the city. The graceless nature of the *banlieue* contrasted sharply with the more intimate atmosphere of the traditional working-class *quartiers* of Paris. In some industries, the specialization of urban space was complemented by a further deepening of the division of labor at the workplace, and many workers were reduced to mere executors of orders from superiors. During the Popular Front workers would respond to the changes not by making a revolution but by continuing struggles against work and by fighting for paid vacations and the weekend, which opened the prospect of escape from jobs and residences alike.

9
THE IDEOLOGY OF WORKERS' CONTROL

In direct contrast with its persistence in Spain, the revolutionary anarchosyndicalist program of workers' control and development of the means of production in their unions dwindled in France during the first decades of the twentieth century. Despite a brief flare-up immediately after the war, anarchosyndicalism faded in a country whose advanced industries remained largely in national hands and whose productive powers continued to grow at rates similar to those in the other great nations. The vicious circle of misery, violent revolt, and repression that characterized the social climate in Barcelona found little scope in Paris. The major problem that the French Left confronted was how to adapt a supposedly revolutionary movement to a society where revolution was becoming an increasingly distant possibility.[1] From a political *longue durée,* the Popular Front in France was not merely a short-term alliance of the Left to prevent fascism but also an acknowledgment by Communists, Socialists, and many in the CGT that a Soviet or anarchosyndicalist-style revolution in twentieth-century France was highly unlikely.

The Barcelonan revolutionaries' critique of their own bourgeoisie was more difficult to apply to Parisian capitalist elites. No French counterparts of Diego Abad de Santillán and other CNT militants could lament the lack of a national automotive or aviation industry precisely because French bourgeois were pioneers in both sectors in the early twentieth century. More generally, complaints about the inability of the bourgeoisie to rationalize and modernize, though they surfaced in Paris, did not carry the same weight in a city that was the home of Renault and of exporting aviation firms, and where, as has been seen, industrialists developed electrical industries and others in the interwar period.

Nor by the 1930s could French revolutionaries, unlike the Spanish, assert that the Church possessed excessive power over education and health facilities or that the state had failed to eliminate illiteracy. Paris witnessed none of the spectacular burning of churches, sabotage, and assassinations that occurred in Barcelona and the rest of Spain during the Second Republic and that pushed Spaniards toward the political extremes. French Catholics were not solidly opposed to the Popular Front. Christian democrats, led by Marc Sangnier and his Jeune République, actually supported the "Blum experiment," and certain Catholic intellectuals—such as Emmanuel Mounier and his review, *Esprit*—also endorsed the coalition of the Left.[2] Some Catholics even joined the Ligue des droits de l'homme, a change that demonstrated, according to one observer, that the Church-state struggle had abated. Although most Catholic publications and the hierarchy in general strongly opposed the Left's coalition, some—such as *L'Aube, La Vie catholique,* and *Sept*—adopted more nuanced positions that were seconded by a number of younger priests. In 1936 as political pluralism developed, French Catholics could no longer be classified as solidly right-wing. In contrast to previous elections, the campaign of 1936 relegated the religious question and debates over lay education to secondary importance.[3] Despite right-wing Catholic nightmares and predictions, the violent wave of anticlericalism that had engulfed Spain never materialized in France.

The decline of ideologies of revolutionary workers' control in France was also partially attributable to the role of the state. The French Third Republic had aided large sectors of the working class. It had, for example, established free rationalist education; agitation to establish anarchosyndicalist modern schools was comparatively minor. Unlike in Spain, governments and sectors of the bourgeoisie effectively promoted anticlerical and scientific education. By 1914 almost all French peasants could read and write. The Third Republic's educational efforts no doubt contributed to the industrialization of France, while Restoration Spain's inability to school peasants and workers at least until the 1920s posed an obstacle to economic development.[4] Even from 1930 to 1935, during the era of the great school-building program of the Spanish Second Republic and the multiplication of *escuelas racionalistas,* France had in proportion to its population twice the number of students in secondary institutions.[5] In 1931 the vast majority of illiterates in a number of Parisian factories seem to have been foreign workers, mainly North Africans.[6]

The French state, although it repressed major strikes, also mediated between labor and capital. A socialist, Alexandre Millerand, joined the government in 1899 but without his party's official support. *Millerandisme* was "the first systematic attempt conducted at the highest levels to regularize industrial relations" and to ensure that the Republican state would mediate between the working class and employers.[7] The presence of a minister who was reputed to be a friend of the workers mitigated, at least briefly, antistatist and anarchist attitudes, particularly among post office personnel, miners, railroad workers, and government construction laborers.

The war itself enlarged the powers of the state and contributed to the further integration of Socialists and syndicalists into the nation. Albert Thomas, who became the Minister of Armaments, attempted to increase wages and improve working conditions by cooperating with—and cajoling—employers.[8] Thomas welcomed the interventionist state and believed that planned governmental action, not revolution, could help bring about socialism in France. He was unabashedly productivist and, already during the war, advocated Taylorism. The Socialist minister envisaged a postwar world where the state would both intervene in a rationalized private sector and administer an enlarged public sector. Workers were to be unionized, represented by shop stewards, and employed by large modern industries. Thomas had faith that Socialists would achieve justice through participation in government and collaboration with employers.

Private initiative also led to the improvement of working conditions. In the late 1920s and early 1930s, Renault embarked upon a vigorous campaign to reduce accidents in order to decrease its insurance premiums and improve its labor productivity.[9] The automotive manufacturer created an accident-prevention service to collect statistics on the problem; it determined that new and inexperienced workers were victims in many cases. Sixty-seven percent of the unskilled and 14 percent of the skilled workers who were injured had worked fewer than three months in the factory, and 26 percent of all accidents occurred during their first month of employment. The prevention service established a psycho-physiological examination for the newly employed, evaluating their "hearing, seeing, breathing . . . intelligence, adaptation, dexterity, and reactions." In addition, it set up for potential personnel trial tests that simulated actual working conditions and came from an examination of the aptitudes of the "best workers in each specialty." Thus, from the moment when workers or apprentices applied for a job, they were subjected to physical and psychological analysis by physicians, engineers, and technicians to determine whether their work would be safe and productive.

Renault's campaign against accidents was successful. From 1930 to 1932, the number of workers injured in the first three months of employment decreased 37.8 percent. Accidents during the first days of employment diminished 84 percent. However, these results must be qualified by the economic downturn of the 1930s, which permitted management to select its workers more carefully and retain them for longer than had been possible during the expansion of the 1920s. Renault's experience contrasts sharply with that of the Catalan railroads, for example, where during the Revolution working-class militants introduced scientific techniques to prevent accidents.

A report of the Conseil national économique, composed of representatives of management, major labor unions, and the state, concluded that numerous entrepreneurs wanted to improve safety in factories in order to increase productivity.[10] A physician employed by the CGT, or Confédération générale du travail, announced both a dramatic decline in cases of lead poisoning—from 1,525 in 1928 to 494 in 1936—and decreases in mercury poisoning. The CGT review, *Syndicats,* agreed that social security (*assurances sociales*) had greatly lowered the number of deaths caused by tuberculosis.[11] Nonetheless, it is difficult to generalize about conditions of health and safety in the enterprises of the Paris region. During the factory occupations of

1936, Parisian workers often demanded improvements, and conditions varied greatly from one plant to another.

Perhaps partially in response to private and state intervention that did improve working and living conditions, French *syndicalistes* became more moderate. The career of the CGT's most important leader, Léon Jouhaux, illustrated the decline of an ideology of revolutionary workers' control with the growth of one variety of French reformism. A young revolutionary syndicalist, Jouhaux was elected secretary general of the CGT in 1909 but soon led the organization to a more conciliatory stance toward the state and the Socialist party. Jouhaux was typical of a number of prominent prewar union leaders who gradually abandoned their faith in the revolutionary spontaneity of the French proletariat and came to emphasize bread-and-butter issues.[12] Even before the Great War, support for revolutionary syndicalism was declining among leaders of the French working class.[13] In 1914 Jouhaux congratulated the Socialists on their electoral victory and hoped that their strength in Parliament would lead to new social legislation; influential union militants found it hard to resist "the Socialist seduction."[14] When war broke out, Jouhaux feared that the working class would become isolated from the nation and that royalists and monarchists might destroy the Republic. Like Albert Thomas, he quickly joined the *union sacrée*, the coalition of traditional political adversaries who united to win the war. Increasingly influenced by Thomas, Jouhaux helped to expand the CGT's role in the wartime economy.[15]

In the immediate postwar period, Communists and Bolshevik sympathizers had little more success in realizing their own version of revolution than did other Marxist or syndicalist revolutionaries. Although historians must avoid a crude determinism that excludes a priori other outcomes, I would surmise that revolution was unlikely, even in the postwar unrest, to overthrow a Third Republic bolstered by victory in the Great War. During this period of agitation, radical militants often could not win supporters even in working-class bastions such as Renault.[16] The turbulence that followed 1 May 1919 did not produce the general strike revolutionaries desired. A potential and continually postponed revolutionary movement to defend the Soviet Union demonstrated the difficulty—which would reappear during the Popular Front—of mobilizing French workers over issues of international politics. If in June 1919 some metal workers demanded political power, recognition of the Soviet government, and amnesty for political and military prisoners, many others struck for a workweek of forty-four (instead of forty-eight) hours, pay hikes, and an end to work speed-ups. The strikes remained largely legal and pacific; the French state, assured of the loyalty of its army and police, never lost control of the situation.[17] The Parisian metallurgical strikers were largely isolated from workers in other sectors and in the provinces. Following the defeat of the strike, the rightist bloc national triumphed in elections of November 1919. In May 1920 a general strike, spearheaded by railroad workers, failed because its lack of support from certain sectors of the working class combined with repression by government and employers.

Within the CGT the ideology of revolutionary syndicalism continued to recede. Already at the end of 1918, it had abandoned its radical formula of the "mine for the miners" and called for nationalization.[18] According to the Confédération, producers and consumers from *départements* (state administrative divisions), communes, cooperatives, and other organizations should manage enterprises in collaboration with the state. The CGT leadership—in cooperation with Albert Thomas—sought a new synthesis. In 1919 Thomas introduced legislation that proposed the nationalization of the railroads and autonomy for state-run enterprises. He and Jouhaux advocated a tripartite nationalization managed by representatives of the state, wage earners, and consumers. During the strikes of the spring of 1920, officials of various factions in the CGT also demanded nationalization, not revolutionary workers' control.[19] A number of Socialist activists called for nationalization on "nonradical grounds."[20] Léon Blum introduced in Parliament a CGT-adopted plan for an autonomous public railroad corporation controlled by representatives of workers, management, and consumers. Socialists and the CGT majority proposed a "defensive" nationalization that would restore workers' morale, raise productivity, and rationalize the railroad network. In 1920 the Conseil économique du travail, which was composed mainly of syndicalists and Socialists, defined the term: "An enterprise is nationalized when it is exploited with regard to the needs of the community and has no other goal than to obtain the maximum of utility and economy for consumers."[21] In 1920 the CGT abandoned "the revolutionary nature of the general strike" for more moderate proposals.[22] The reformism of Albert Thomas, questioning revolutionary syndicalism even before World War I, had come to dominate thinking concerning workers' control; from 1919 onwards, nationalization became a permanent CGT demand. At the end of 1920 the powerful Fédération des métaux argued for a nonrevolutionary form of workers' control where committees named by workers would regulate hiring, pay, and discipline.[23]

The CGT's ideological shifts after World War I reflected its participation in the war effort and advances of social legislation, such as the eight-hour law, which passed unanimously in April 1919. It was gradually abandoning its revolutionary syndicalism before the war, but Jouhaux's postwar projects revealed even further distance from earlier syndicalist positions of hostility to class collaboration and advocacy of a general strike. Even though the Confédération retained as its ultimate goal the abolition of wage labor, it embarked on a "policy of presence" in national affairs and systematically tried to penetrate the state apparatus. Its program of 1919 demonstrated that it was playing the democratic game, and it expressed "a genuine kind of socialistic reformism."[24] Jouhaux, having lost faith in the revolutionary potential of the working class, pursued his goal of attaching syndicalism to the nation. The CGT leader defined the revolution as a "long-term evolutionary process which, little by little, penetrates the system."[25] Georges Dumoulin and other prominent CGT leaders followed Jouhaux's path from revolutionary syndicalism to reformism.

In direct contrast to the Spanish CNT, the French Confédération joined *commissions paritaires,* labor-management boards in both the public and private sectors. During the 1920s the CGT leader's opinion on the choice of labor minister was solicited even by rightist governments, and the Confédération collaborated with the Socialist parliamentary group. Despite the opposition of its rival, the Communist-influenced CGTU (Confédération générale du travail unitaire), the CGT began to search systematically for compromises to avoid strikes. In 1925 Jouhaux's immediate postwar suggestion of a National Economic Council of representatives from labor, management, and consumers was adopted by Premier Edouard Herriot, a Radical who accepted unionization of government employees, many of whom joined the CGT.[26] In 1927 the moderate but influential Fédération des fonctionnaires rejoined the Confédération. The passage of housing legislation in 1927 and a social security law in 1928 reinforced the day-to-day reformist policies of the CGT.

Although the CGT's strategy did not lead to a truly mass union movement until 1936, when literally millions of new members joined, its pragmatism proved more popular than the revolutionary sectarianism of the CGTU or the small CGTSR (Confédération générale du travail syndicaliste révolutionnaire), where anarchists and anarchosyndicalists agitated. The CGT's "policy of presence" in the state apparatus "renewed and reinforced its structures, increased the number of its members and its militants, enlarged its audience and perspectives."[27]

In comparison, the strongly Communist CGTU declined continuously after 1926.[28] Although when it began in 1921 it had attracted more members than the CGT, by 1926 the CGTU had 431,240 adherents and the CGT 524,960. By 1934 the CGTU's membership was 264,085 and the CGT's was 490,984; CGTU revolutionary rhetoric, including charges after 1928 that the CGT leaders were "social fascists," was unable to prevent the attrition of its membership. Nor did its opposition in 1928 to social reforms such as social security and workers' retirement funds—which it also termed "fascist"—endear it to the masses. In the 1930s the CGTU, like the PCF (Parti communiste français) to which it was closely linked, emerged from the periphery only when it toned down its revolutionary rhetoric. In 1932 the union began to alter its tactics in the automotive sector. CGTU officials attacked "sectarianism" and "sloganeering," and with renewed vigor supported claims by the smallest groups of workers.[29] In aviation the CGTU's doctrinal refusal to deal directly with the ministries became "outmoded" in the 1930s.[30] During negotiations to merge the two unions in 1934, the CGT held a much stronger bargaining position than its rival. Unification of the two was achieved in March 1936 and contributed to the élan of the Popular Front, reducing even further the tiny membership (between four thousand and twenty thousand) of the anarchosyndicalist CGTSR.[31] Though never entirely disappearing, revolutionary movements such as anarchism and syndicalism were never dominant during the 1930s in Paris or France.

In Spain, significantly, the reverse occurred: the growth of UGT radicalism during the Second Republic, and especially in 1936, mirrored the rise of a revolutionary temper among key sectors of peasants and workers. During the same decade there emerged no French equivalent of Largo Caballero, who led the Spanish Socialists and the UGT in a revolutionary direction after 1933. Spanish historians have debated whether Largo led or merely followed the masses toward the dictatorship of the proletariat. Whatever the verdict on this issue, it was clear that under Largo, Spanish Socialists, unlike the French, were encouraging workers to take over many state functions. Important Spanish Socialists declared that if the Second Republic did not satisfy their demands, they would make revolution.[32] The burning of churches in May 1931, the insurrections of July 1931 in the Seville area, of January 1932 in the Llobregat valley, and of January 1933 in Barcelona demonstrated that Largo had some reason to become "obsessed" that the CNT "might outdistance him on the Left." The harshness of the repression that followed the Socialist-backed Asturias revolt of October 1934 did little to diminish Socialists' revolutionism. After the electoral victory of the Popular Front, Largo continued to call for a proletarian dictatorship and a revolutionary alliance with the CNT. By the summer of 1936, Socialists espousing revolution were dominant in Spain but not in France. Long-term social and economic problems—lack of land reform and slowness of industrialization and modernization—merged with political difficulties—Church-state conflict, paralysis of the administration, and militant regionalisms—to push Spanish Socialists and Spain itself into revolution and civil war.

The French Socialists followed a more moderate path. A distinction between the conquest and the exercise of power, which Léon Blum had elaborated in 1926, continued to be the touchstone of Socialist ideology during the Popular Front. According to Blum, the *conquest* of power could occur when the majority of a population that desired significant change supported the Socialist party (Section française de l'Internationale ouvrière, or SFIO). The Socialists could then take all political power through legal or illegal means to make a social revolution that would alter property relations.[33] By contrast, the *exercise* of power would take place when the SFIO was the dominant party in a leftist majority; a Socialist-dominated administration would govern within the limits of capitalist legality and the rules of parliamentary democracy. During the Popular Front, Socialists exercised power—and relegated revolution further into the future, as did Communists. This rapprochement between Socialists and Communists was indeed ironic, since Blum had elaborated his distinction between the conquest and the exercise of power to criticize the PCF's impetuousness. He had accused French Bolsheviks of blindly imitating their Soviet comrades by attempting to conquer power before the proletariat was ready, and he blamed them for disparaging reforms that would prepare the working class for revolution.[34] On the same grounds, Blum attacked the revolutionary Left within his own party.

The SFIO's leftist wing, which included advocates of revolutionary workers' control, was never to dominate the party; even the commitment to revolution of leftist leaders such as Marcel Pivert has been questioned.[35] On 27 May 1936 in the midst of the wave of sit-downs, Pivert published his famous article, "Everything is possible," in which he implied that the revolutionary moment had arrived. During the first year of the Popular Front government, however, Pivert advocated support for the Blum government, "not . . . revolutionary action outside the legal channels."[36] The leader of the Gauche révolutionnaire (GR), Pivert served in a minor capacity as media consultant in the first Blum administration and hoped to use his position to strengthen his influence within the SFIO. Pivert asserted that it was foolish to condemn a government that permitted "the development of the revolutionary capacity of the masses."[37] Nor did other members of the GR wish to break completely with the government in the fall and winter of 1936.

Yet despite obvious ambiguity, the Pivertists were considered revolutionaries by many supporters and opponents. In early

1937 Pivert resigned from the government, declaring that he would not "capitulate before capitalism and the banks. No! I agree neither to social peace nor to *union sacrée*."[38] During the elections of 1936 in Paris, the Socialists lost ground to the Communists. A police observer attributed the Socialist decline to the departure of the "moderate" neo-Socialists and to the "extremism" of the Fédération de la Seine, where the *pivertistes* and other leftist Socialists were influential; this group "often tried to appear more revolutionary than its Communist neighbors."[39] After the outbreak of the Spanish Civil War, the GR wanted French workers to emulate their Spanish comrades by launching a social revolution and forming a proletarian government similar to that of Barcelona in the summer of 1936. Pivert, though, had to concede that his advice had been ignored by the great majority of the working class: "The gravest obstacles [to the pursuit of revolutionary struggle] seem to come from ourselves as much as from our class enemies. . . . The proletariat lacks an offensive spirit."[40]

In April 1937 the Gauche révolutionnaire won 11.6 percent of the votes in the Socialist party's national council, and in January 1938 it won 18.4 percent.[41] This faction attracted support in regions where Socialist electoral strength was weak and where small groups of radical intellectuals, with little commitment to the parliamentary road to socialism, found *pivertisme* attractive. Even though their strength grew in 1937, the radicals never captured the SFIO, made a revolution, or even acquired a working-class base. In the long run the influence of the GR on the SFIO's workplace cells, the amicales socialistes, was not consequential. During the strikes of the Popular Front, the *pivertistes* were never sufficiently numerous or "well placed to play any decisive role."[42]

The GR's expulsion from the SFIO in June 1938 effectively destroyed it. A number of prominent militants who had been associated with this faction refused to join Pivert's new group, Parti socialiste ouvrier et paysan (PSOP), which rejected "social-democratic reformism," imperialism, and national defense.[43] Cut off from the SFIO, the PSOP—like the Trotskyists—became a sect. Again, the importance of those advocating an immediate revolution was not decisive in the French Socialist movement in the 1930s. The PSOP became neither the revolutionary vanguard of the working class nor the French equivalent of the POUM.[44]

Trotskyists and other leftists have criticized Pivert—as they have attacked Andrés Nin of the POUM—for collaborating with bourgeois governments and for failing to establish a truly revolutionary party at the proper moment. But the question of why the revolutionary groups in France (including Trotsky's own) were not able to acquire solid support in the working class and to make a revolution has been answered only superficially. Leftist critics have offered a basically political explanation for the failure of revolution in France in 1936, and they have emphasized lack of leadership, that is, the absence of a French Lenin. They have also called attention to the counterrevolutionary activity of the Soviet Union, which wanted to bolster the democracies against the growing international threat of fascism. The critiques of the Trotskyists and others have however largely ignored a discussion of social and economic factors that debilitated revolutionary movements—whether Trotskyist, anarchosyndicalist, or Communist—in advanced capitalist countries such as France.

At the end of the First World War, communism replaced anarchosyndicalism as the dominant ideology of revolutionary militants. At its birth in France, communism was, in a sense, another ideology of revolutionary workers' control in the form of soviets, or workers' and soldiers' councils, as opposed to the union. Accordingly, French revolutionaries interpreted bolshevism as an approximate form of syndicalism.[45] Victor Griffuelhes, secretary general of the CGT from 1902 to 1909, declared that both revolutionary syndicalism and the soviets were based on "the producer while neglecting the citizen. What has made and continues to constitute the force of the soviets is the power given to the producers—workers and peasants."[46] Revolutionary syndicalists shared the Communists' disdain for parliamentarism.

Yet communism in France was, in part, an import from another country, the Soviet Union, whose social conditions resembled those of Spain more than of France. Communism, or bolshevism, was unable to maintain its immediate postwar popularity. At the split between Communists and Socialists at the

Congress of Tours in 1920, with 120,000 members the Communists greatly outnumbered the Socialists, with 50,000. Then in the elections of 1924, the PCF won 877,000 votes and the Socialists approximately 1,500,000. In 1933 the membership of the PCF dropped to 28,000, whereas that of the Socialists rose to 130,000.[47]

Before the 1928 elections the French Communist party had adopted a new line of "class against class" that echoed the position of the Communist International. The PCF believed that a new period of capitalist instability had begun and that comrades should take a hard line against the "social imperialists" or "social fascists" of the SFIO. This intransigent tactic was a key factor in the 1928 elections that took place under the reestablished *scrutin d'arrondissement.* According to this system of voting, if no candidate won an absolute majority in the first round, a run-off election was held in which the candidate who obtained the most votes was declared the winner. This system encouraged political alliances in order to win the second ballot, but Communist voters were instructed to disregard "republican discipline" and to vote for no other candidates of the Left in the second round. Although the PCF gained 200,000 votes in the first round or 1,063,000 compared to the Socialist total of 1,700,000, 44 percent of its voters ignored the party's instructions and voted instead for the better-placed Socialist or Radical in the second round.[48] Traditional republican discipline triumphed in the second round, and the PCF lost thirteen of its twenty-seven seats in the Chamber of Deputies. Many Communist leaders—Marcel Cachin, André Marty, and Paul Vaillant-Couturier—were defeated. Maurice Thorez, the future PCF head, was successful only because he was able to attract Socialist votes in the second round.

In 1929 during the wave of repression and arrests of its militants and leaders, the Communist party continued its revolutionary rhetoric. It demanded a revolutionary civil war and accused the Socialists of being "enemies of the proletariat and of the revolution."[49] Yet the attrition of members was not halted, particularly in key industrial regions. From 1924 to 1929, membership declined 45 percent in Paris. The PCF was no more successful on the streets; demonstrations from 1929 to 1933 to defend the Soviet Union against "war-mongering imperialists" and to protest against unemployment failed to attract large numbers.[50] The party continued to lose members and votes at the beginning of the economic depression that, according to its own analysis of capitalism's crisis, should have brought it new popularity. Before the elections of 1932, Maurice Thorez accused his Socialist rivals of being "the principal support of the bourgeois dictatorship. The crisis accelerates the fascistization of the Socialist party and of the CGT [, which are] ever increasingly integrated into the apparatus of the bourgeois state."[51] Regardless of the harsh rhetoric, in 1932 PCF and SFIO votes were 783,000 and 1,964,000 respectively. The Communist percentage of the vote declined from 9.3 percent to 6.8 percent, which was less than in 1924. In the Paris region, it fell from 20.7 percent to 17.4 percent. Only eleven Communist deputies remained in the Chamber.[52]

The Communist party never captured more than 12 percent of the national vote until 1936, when it appeared unabashedly reformist and patriotic. Already in 1934 during the cantonal elections, when the Popular Front was forming, the PCF decided to adhere to republican discipline and support Socialist candidates in the second ballot. The party was moderating its positions to attract the petty bourgeoisie who, it feared, might gravitate toward fascism as it believed the Germans had. At the end of 1934 in discussions concerning a common platform with Socialists, the Communists refused the Socialists' demands for "structural reforms" or nationalizations, fearing major changes that might alienate the middle classes whom the PCF now sought to seduce. Despite difficulties in establishing a common program for the municipal elections of 1935, the agreement to back the best-placed candidate of the Left persisted and resulted in a PCF gain of approximately fifty municipal seats, eight of which were in Paris itself.[53] Significantly, in 1935 the Communists chose Bastille Day, the symbol of modern French nationalism, for a mass rally in support of the Popular Front.

During the elections of 1936 the PCF instructed its militants to avoid any slogan that was revolutionary and to participate in the singing of the Marseillaise.[54] According to Thorez, the "most successful" Communist campaign slogan was For a Free,

Strong, and Happy France. Comrades offered an "outstretched hand" to Catholics. To elect Communist candidates, militants were permitted to deviate from the " 'political line' of communism." The PCF's votes nearly doubled, and it acquired 72 seats in the Chamber, compared to 116 for the Radicals and 182 for the SFIO and similar groups. For the first time the PCF became a major parliamentary force and, until recently, "a source of lasting attraction to the French masses."[55]

In Paris, the Socialists lost ground to the Communists in the 1936 legislative elections, which a police observer attributed to the departure of the "moderate" neo-Socialists and to the "extremism" of the Fédération de la Seine, where left-wingers dominated. Paradoxically, the PCF managed to reassure many moderates of the Left and to calm their fears.[56] The adoption of a "national and democratic" strategy also permitted the PCF to increase its membership significantly: from 42,500 in 1934 and 87,000 in 1935, membership jumped to 235,000 in 1936 and to 302,000 in 1937.[57] During the Popular Front, Communist separation between theory and practice came to resemble that of the SFIO: the parties cooperated to achieve major reforms, postponing both revolution and dictatorship of the proletariat to the distant future.[58] The greatest PCF gains in votes and members took place at a time when it argued against any immediate application of revolutionary workers' control or soviets. It advocated instead "significant improvements" for the workers within the capitalist system. CGTU and Communist support for the reforms of the Popular Front can be seen not only as a tactical maneuver that would bolster Franco-Soviet cooperation against Hitler's Germany but also as belated acknowledgment of the relative success of the CGT's and the Socialists' strategy of compromise and their synthesis of reform and revolution, nationalism and internationalism. The Communist synthesis included active support for the Soviet Union and Republican Spain.

As revolutionary currents weakened, consumerist desires rose. New needs accompanied the acceptance of the most modern techniques of production and consumption. In both 1919 and 1935 the CGT proposed that nationalized enterprises be controlled by delegates; the state would choose one-third of them, and the producers (workers and technicians) would choose another third. The remaining delegates would come from consumers. The Confédération's desire for the participation of consumers revealed that it was moving from a focus on control of production toward an appetite for consumption. Although the CGT continued to advocate the development of the productive forces during the interwar years, it altered its emphasis and began to view the worker not only as producer but, just as important, as consumer.

In return for wider and more equal distribution, French unions were willing to accept both the goods produced by capitalism and the methods used to manufacture them. Even the most revolutionary union, the CGTU—which, in the 1920s, included both revolutionary syndicalists and Communists and which continued to demand workers' control—allowed and even lauded the most modern techniques of rationalization, especially if they were employed in the Soviet Union. In 1927 when a revolutionary syndicalist asked O. Rabaté, a CGTU leader and future architect of the Popular Front, where rationalization did not brutalize workers, Rabaté responded, "In Moscow."[59] According to a 1927 article by Maurice Thorez, workers' rationalization equaled socialism. In the 1930s *Humanité* praised Stakhanovism, which produced "brilliant results." On the occasion of a working visit of French Communist miners to the Soviet pits, they reported, "We have doubled or quadrupled normal production without special effort, *something that is absolutely impossible in the conditions of the capitalist countries.*"[60] In the Soviet Union, "to be a Stakhanovist is a matter of honor for every worker." *Humanité* remarked that visiting French comrades had experienced a happy surprise when they learned that the wages of their Soviet colleagues were nearly ten times higher than French wages: "This is the system of pay in the Soviet Union! Nowhere in the world is there anything similar."[61]

Yet once in the West, French Communists were much more critical of scientific organization of work, even though they accepted it in principle. In 1927 Rabaté censured—in a manner reminiscent of Emile Pouget—the overwork, unemployment, and low salaries that were, for Rabaté, intrinsic to capitalist rationalization. The CGTU leader denied that American workers received high wages and owned their own cars; he tried to refute the idea that one goal of Taylorism was to increase consumption by the working class. Yet opposing assembly-line production and new labor techniques was like "being against rain":

> We are for the principles of scientific organization of work. . . . To try to stop technical progress would not be truly revolutionary. The revolutionaries know that the working class will be the successor of capitalism and that this scientific organization will permit a much more rapid construction of socialism when the proletariat takes power.[62]

Thus the CGTU endorsed the work processes developed by capitalism, and its critique centered on the failure to distribute commodities more widely and equally. In fact, in 1927 Rabaté doubted that the French automotive industry was capable of providing cars for the masses. A decade later the Communist position had changed little: at the beginning of the great strike wave of 1936, the PCF asserted that "the masses . . . have had enough of the development of machines that benefit only the few."[63]

Like the Communists, French anarchists and anarchosyndicalists—who, as we have seen, had lost their pre-World-War-I domination of the national CGT—doubted the ability of capitalism to increase consumption. Sébastien Faure, a prominent anarchist, wanted an increase in wages to remedy the economic crisis of 1932. Faure believed that "under-consumption" was the danger to combat and that "the capacity of consumption, which constantly multiplies needs, . . . is going to progress forever."[64] The anarchist leader was quite skeptical of capitalism's ability to augment wages and decrease worktime. Other libertarians called for one month of vacation and even complained that French capitalists were rationalizing too slowly.[65]

The Socialists had been longtime advocates of increased consumption through rationalization. Prominent party members like André Philip and Jules Moch viewed rationalization favorably because it boosted workers' consumption. The Socialist solution to the economic stagnation of the depression—to boost the purchasing power of the masses—was "already contained in the comprehensive Socialist program of 1927."[66] According to Blum, the economic crisis of the 1930s was caused not by overproduction but by insufficient demand. The Socialists, Blum thought, must use the power of the state to augment the buying power of the masses. Revolution might have been the ultimate raison d'être for many in the SFIO, but increasing *pouvoir d'achat* (purchasing power) was first on the list of priorities for the majority of Socialists.

Other sectors of the Socialist movement—the "planners" and nonconformist Socialists—moved even further away from a revolutionary alternative based on the Soviet or anarchosyndicalist model. Nonconformist Socialists and neo-Socialists who had split from the SFIO in 1933 welcomed the ideas of the planners, who believed that orthodox Marxism and, of course, anarchosyndicalism were outmoded. They rejected not only revolutionary models but also Blum's distinction between the conquest and exercise of power. Instead, planners—individuals such as Henri de Man and groups like Combat marxiste and Révolution constructive—wanted to begin the construction of a socialist society with the collaboration of the middle classes. Planners distinguished between various groups within the bourgeoisie and considered certain of its elements, particularly industrial technicians, to be potential allies against the "parasitic" oligarchy of big or financial capital.[67] Many planners advocated limited nationalizations and slow evolution toward socialism. In keeping with their desire to ally with sympathetic sectors of the middle classes, they favored a mixed economy composed of public and private sectors and generally rejected the rhetoric of class war and revolution that the mainstream of the SFIO sometimes employed. Revolutionary syndicalists both inside and outside the CGT attacked the planners' repudiation of their own *ouvriériste* position, which based hopes for change on the working class alone.[68]

In 1934 the SFIO mainstream rejected planning for both political and ideological reasons. Blum believed that a commitment to planning would compromise his party's ultimate, if distant, goal of socialist revolution and lead to increased division within the SFIO. However in February the CGT began to devise its own plan; like the plan of the Belgian Workers' party, it demanded an augmentation of consumption by the masses to combat the economic crisis. As had the SFIO in 1932, the CGT favored nationalizing banks and key industries.[69] In the CGT plan issued in 1935, private management retained its control on the shop floor, and workers' control merited only passing mention. Foreshadowing post–World-War-II planning in France, the CGT plan was more concerned with rationalization and modernization than with workers' democracy or participation. The jobless were to be employed by a reduction of the workweek—the total suggested was usually forty hours—and by large public-works projects. Mass production and consumption were the goals of the CGT.

When unity between the CGT and the smaller Communist-dominated union, CGTU, was finally realized at Toulouse in March 1936, the newly unified union supported the program of the Popular Front. The Left's agreement on a platform signified that the electoral alliance might be more cohesive than the ephemeral Socialist-Radical coalition had been in 1932. It also assured voters who feared continued governmental instability that the Left's alliance might endure. Because of Communist and Radical opposition, the program of the Rassemblement populaire, as the French Popular Front was officially known, limited the scope of nationalizations more severely than the CGT plan or the Socialist program. As it was made public in January 1936, the Popular Front's platform nevertheless demanded nationalization of the defense industries and more stringent state control of the Banque de France. In addition the Popular Front proposed, as the CGT had, large public-works projects that would get the unemployed back on the job and a reduction of the working week without a decrease of pay. An augmentation of *pouvoir d'achat* remained an essential goal of the Left.

While retaining a traditional productivism, the ideologies of the French Left in the first third of the twentieth century therefore shifted toward an emphasis on consumption. They accepted, even glorified, capitalist methods of production; the Left desired a more equitable distribution of goods and services. Replacing the old anarchosyndicalist demand for workers' control of the means of production was a call for state control, since the Left believed that it could ensure more efficient production and fairer distribution through command of government. The dominant organizations of the French Left—SFIO, PCF, CGT, CGTU—sought to increase their political power and influence, not to take direct control of the productive forces or even to establish soviets. Even before the victory of the Popular Front—when the Left captured political power at the national level—the Communist and Socialist parties already dominated a number of local governments throughout France. Unlike in Spain, where many significant working-class organizations remained politically powerless and were even periodically outlawed, French society was capable of sharing political power with the Left. During the 1930s in Spain, union and party militants—including, at times, Socialists—were jailed, whereas in France their counterparts were running municipal and communal governments.

The Left's expanding domination of the Parisian suburbs between the wars revealed its integration into French society and the strength of the French social consensus. In light of leftist, particularly Communist, ideologies of class warfare or class against class and the sporadic repression of the Communist party in the 1920s, this assertion of the integrative capacities of French society may seem unfounded. However, the actual policies of the Left in the Parisian suburbs revealed a fidelity to the kind of industrial modernization that other classes in France had practiced and encouraged. Many suburban voters expressed their discontent with the lack of local infrastructure by voting Socialist or, increasingly, Communist. The Left responded by constructing sewers and installing running water, electrical facilities, and gas lines, and by paving the streets and roads that many of the new developments (*lotissements*) lacked. Although the Loi Sarraut (1928) helped encourage some building of roads and of water and sanitation facilities, this law left important gaps in the infrastructure; these local governments attempted to fill.

The Communists were quite proud of their municipal work. One Communist historian has recently declared that in the suburbs the French Communists played the same role as their Soviet comrades did in the Soviet Union.[70] According to Maurice

Thorez, the Communist municipalities were an "invaluable expression of the Party's policies": "Our municipality [Villejuif] created a city out of a swamp: Streets built, municipal services started, water, gas, and electricity."[71] At Villejuif in 1933, the PCF proudly inaugurated the Karl Marx School. Its construction had been directed by a group of progressive and revolutionary architects, including André Lurçat, whose ideology revealed certain achievements and desires of the French Left. During the school's construction, Lurçat exposed his thoughts on modern architecture: shelter was the first priority, aesthetics were secondary. In the new era, the architect should address himself not to the individual client but to "powerful organizations" that "act in the name of the masses." These organizations did not demand beauty but a sound and economic order. Like his colleague Le Corbusier, Lurçat was a follower of modern urbanism; he advocated improving automobile circulation in the "overly narrow" streets. Against the "plastic inertia of the older cities," the new city would oppose "the dynamism of its principal elements."[72] He claimed that urbanism must become a science that investigated "the ever-increasing needs." Thus, Lurçat, with Communist support, was able to realize some of the urban policies that many in the Spanish Left could only imagine.

The PCF, often with the aid of the French government, built modern housing in working-class suburbs, such as Villejuif, where most workers commuted to their jobs.[73] The Communists offered services in the new housing developments and organized renters and property owners to obtain subsidies. At Vitry—with 48,929 inhabitants, the fifteenth largest city in France—the Communist municipality provided low-cost housing (HBM, or *habitations à bon marché*) for workers. At Bagneux the PCF took control of a HBM that philanthropists had constructed for wage earners who commuted to the large firms of the region; it organized the renters over bread-and-butter issues, such as the lack of roads and public transportation. During 1935–1936 Communists campaigned for control of the municipality as the young "generation destined to manage the commune in a modern way." To the electorate, the Communist militants appeared to be "agents of modernity." In other suburban areas they established clinics, medical services, day-care centers, showers, and even a summer camp for two hundred children, which was praised by a conservative newspaper, *Le Temps.* Communist control in various suburbs allowed a stable power base that provided jobs, housing, and other advantages for militants.

Socialists, who also desired to govern working-class municipalities, could prevent Communist penetration by enacting policies similar to those of their rivals. Following World War I at Suresnes, the home of the automaker Talbot, the Socialist mayor modernized the old village, which had up to then "anachronistically conserved its rural character."[74] Henri Sellier, mayor from 1919 to 1941, helped to create the office of HBM, built clinics, day-care centers, schools, old-age homes, libraries, gymnasiums, and swimming pools. The Socialist municipality improved automobile circulation and devised plans to widen roads. At Boulogne-Billancourt and Pantin, PCF candidates were unable to defeat efficient and popular Socialist mayors.[75]

In the 1930s France was unmistakably a pluralist society where various political parties, which claimed to represent different social classes, vied for power. Underneath the conflict and the verbal animosity of the politicians, the major political forces formed a consensus, unknown in Spain. Parties claiming to represent the working class were not only legalized but also officially shared political, administrative, and, to a lesser extent, economic power with other political groupings and social classes. In the suburbs and towns Communists and Socialists helped provide the infrastructure necessary for production. Education, transportation, health, housing, and even certain leisure facilities were built or improved by local governments of the Left. While effectively contributing to the economic development and the modernization of the nation, the political parties and unions of the Left accepted both the products of capitalist industry and its methods of organizing work. The principal division between the economic policies of the Left and the Right concerned the form of ownership—nationalization versus private control of production—but not the content or the methods of production.[76] The traditional anarchosyndicalist demand for workers' or unions' control at the point of production was largely replaced by the struggles of leftist parties and unions to augment their own power and to increase consumption by their constituencies. The workers were viewed not only as producers but also, just as important, as consumers. The French working-class militants would not occupy the factories to make a revolution for the producers, as the Spanish militants did, but instead to increase their leisure and consumption.

10
FACTORY OCCUPATIONS

Although they never developed into a social revolution, the French factory occupations constituted the largest wave of sit-down strikes in the history of the Third Republic and produced its most significant series of social reforms, including the still controversial forty-hour week. After the harsh years of the depression in the early 1930s, workers' demands for shorter hours and more pay were understandable. Yet their desires would eventually help to divide the Popular Front and harm its plans for economic recovery and growth.

To comprehend the factory occupations in the spring of 1936, we must review the demographic, economic, and political situation of France in the 1930s. France was hard hit by the carnage of World War I, and its losses, combined with a low birthrate, led to a labor shortage. In addition, although the number of peasants declined by one million between 1911 and 1936, the agrarian sector—relatively backward for an advanced industrial nation—held one-third of the active male population on the land, intensifying the labor scarcity. Throughout the interwar period foreign labor from Italy, Belgium, North Africa, and Spain was recruited to reduce the shortage. On the whole, unskilled and semiskilled jobs found workers, whether French or foreign, but those positions needing skilled labor were more difficult to fill. This lack of skilled workers was to have a profound effect during the Popular Front governments.

After 1931 the economic crisis compounded slow demographic growth as France felt the consequences of the worldwide Great Depression. In industry and commerce, production fell about 20 percent during the 1930s.[1] Between 1931 and 1936 in firms with over one hundred workers, the number of salaried personnel dropped 24 percent while industrial production declined 13 percent. Although in 1936 France had an unemployment rate of only 5 percent, joblessness was significant in the Paris region, which contained about 20 percent of the active French population but had over 50 percent of the nation's unemployed. Parisian unemployment was structurally similar to that in other industrial nations, for it too was high in the more advanced industrial sectors.

French governments attempted to combat the economic crisis in various ways. In the early 1930s they increased tariff protection and generally followed policies of deflation that lowered both wages and prices but left unemployment high in French terms. Deflation protected individuals on fixed incomes by keeping the franc costly and avoiding devaluation, but the strength of the franc in relation to other national currencies made French exports comparatively more expensive and hurt industries that sold abroad. Deflationary economic policies failed to stimulate demand and get the economy moving. Governmental expenditures dropped sharply, and many industries—for example, automobiles—were hurt by reduced governmental budgets. The discontent provoked by deflation and the government's reduced spending, particularly during the government of Pierre Laval (June 1935–January 1936), contributed to the formation of the Popular Front.

Workers experienced in diverse ways the effects of the 1930s economic crisis. Unemployment rose, most notably in the construction and metalworking industries. The rise was such that the Conseil général de la Seine refused to aid the unemployed who arrived in the region after July 1934.[2] The workers' buying power did not consistently decline, however; deflation reduced not only wages but also prices. In fact, one economist estimated a 12 percent gain in workers' buying power between 1929 and 1935.[3] At Renault, for example, the workers' real monthly wages increased slightly from 1930 to 1935. In contrast, a team of contemporary investigators saw a 7 percent drop in workers' "standard of living."[4] Overall salaries of the working class declined by 15 percent from 1930 to 1935.[5] To sum up, when unemployment is taken into account, the overall or global buying power of the class decreased even though workers who were employed gained substantially during this period.

In Paris the overwhelming majority of the employed labored forty-eight hours per week. The number of foreigners who held jobs was surprisingly low. At Renault, foreigners dropped from 16 percent of the work force in February 1932 to 8 percent in May 1936. In the latter month the percentage of non-French in the entire Parisian work force rose slightly, from 4.8 to 5 percent.[6] The percentage of women in the active population declined from 37.1 in 1931 to 34.2 in 1936.[7] The privileged majority that held jobs was decidedly French and increasingly male.

Of the unemployed, eighty-one percent lost their job for economic reasons—lack of work, trimming of payrolls, and the closing of firms.[8] Nineteen percent were dismissed for personal reasons—sickness, low output, and indiscipline. A disproportionate number were foreigners, who were often the first to be dismissed, as 1932 French legislation required. At the beginning of the economic depression older workers made up a large share of the unemployed, but as the crisis persisted, an increasing number of younger workers, who were usually more productive than their older counterparts, were also fired. Before their dismissals only 25 percent of the unemployed had had a stable job (for over five years); many were single, and they remained on the dole longer than those who were married with one or two children. Jobless workers with many children also remained unemployed for long periods, since their additional family allocations nearly equaled their wages.

Working women who were touched by joblessness had particular problems. Nearly twice as many women with unemployed husbands worked as did women in general. Nineteen percent of the jobless, male or female, lived with a mate out of wedlock, compared to 11 percent of the general population. Of unmarried females dwelling with a male, 29 percent were employed, in contrast to 16.4 percent of women in general; some of these jobholders "accepted the hospitality of a boyfriend to avoid paying rent."[9] Unemployed women, though, had much greater difficulty finding work than men did; they were often older than the jobless men, and employers preferred to hire the young. In addition, some industries that employed a high percentage of women—textiles, offices, and domestic services—were particularly affected by the depression. Generally, women had considerably lower salaries than men.

The situation, though difficult, was not entirely bleak. Even the unemployed received the necessary minimum of calories, and the quality of their food was adequate.[10] From 1929 to 1935 the general population's consumption of food rose 5 percent, thereby continuing a tendency of the early twentieth century. The consumption of sugar and butter increased 50 percent between 1919 and 1939; that of fruits doubled, and that of bread declined.[11] Despite the crisis and the consequent fall of production, the general level of consumption did not decrease and even increased slightly at the expense of investment. The economic downturn did not halt the progress that had been made in public health during the Third Republic. In spite of the aging of the French population, longevity increased. Legislation such as social security helped reduce the infant mortality rate.[12]

Both the economic and political situations encouraged an alliance of the leftist political parties in the mid-1930s. As we have seen, the Communist, Socialist, and Radical parties wanted to guard against unemployment and increase consumption. In addition, the Left feared the growth of French right-wing and fascist movements. The example of Germany, where a divided Left was unable to prevent Hitler's accession to power in 1933 and subsequent destruction of leftist parties and unions, was dramatically present in many minds. After the right-wing riots against the republic in February 1934, the Socialists, Communists, and Radicals initiated long negotiations that culminated in the formation of the Popular Front during 1935. In the elections in the spring of 1936, the Popular Front coalition gained a majority of seats, and the leader of its largest party—Léon Blum of the Socialist party—was mandated to form a new government. The Popular Front's political momentum ended the decline in the observance of May Day, which had occurred from 1926 to 1934.[13] In Paris, 120,000 of the 250,000 metallurgists went on strike in 1936, including 75 to 85 percent of the Renault workers. Construction workers almost unanimously refused to labor on 1 May. Yet not all sectors participated with equal enthusiasm. A militant of the railway workers' union complained that wage earners remained indifferent to the celebration of May Day.[14]

After the Popular Front's electoral victory and before the new Blum government took office, France was confronted by the greatest wave of factory occupations or sit-down strikes that the nation had ever experienced. Aviation workers protesting dismissals of militants who had been absent on May Day initiated the occupations in Le Havre and Toulouse. Thus respect for the workers' holiday triggered the massive movement. Sit-down strikes, however, were not an invention of aviation workers, nor did workers learn of their existence only in the pages of *Humanité* or other militant publications. Such strikes "sur le tas" or "de bras croisés" had erupted in construction during the 1930s, and they were, to borrow a phrase from Charles Tilly, part of the popular repertory of the twentieth century. Workers male and female, young and old, French and foreign used tactics of occupation in the years preceding the Popular Front governments.[15]

During the Popular Front, workers continued to employ sit-downs to prevent scabs from entering the factories, occupation tactics that were particularly well chosen as the growing unemployment began to affect younger and more skilled workers. Just as important, Blum himself had assured the working class that he would not use force against it. Workers sensed correctly that Blum did not want to be the French Noske;[16] they took advantage of the hiatus in state repression to occupy factories in the suburbs of Paris and, later, throughout France. In addition, the tactics of occupation forced employers to settle more quickly than a walkout would have. They violated property rights and put the machinery and capital goods of the factory directly in the hands of the workers. Sabotage and destruction were possibilities.

The Bloch aviation plant, with seven hundred workers in the suburb of Courbevoie, was one of the first in the Paris region to be affected. Bloch produced airplanes for the state, its principal client, and its wages were relatively high, typical of those in the Parisian aviation industry.[17] On 14 May 1936 the Bloch workers occupied and spent the night inside the factory, and on the following day management conceded a slight wage hike, paid vacations, and strike pay.[18] In Paris on 22 May, the personnel of Gnôme et Rhône, which made airplane engines, protested against overtime work and demanded respect for the eight-hour day; they soon won paid vacations and an end to overtime. Several days later, wage earners at other major aviation firms in the Paris region occupied their factories and made similar demands. On 28 May the wave of occupations hit the giant Renault factories at Boulogne-Billancourt. *Humanité* asserted that "the workers were tired of the low wages, of work speed-ups, of fines, and of the military discipline that is forced upon them."

On 28 May, the same day on which laborers at Renault struck, workers at Citroën also downed their tools. The sit-downs unfolded from the aviation companies and several firms that manufactured telephone and radio equipment to the large automobile firms. At SIMCA, the French division of Fiat, twelve hundred workers staged a sit-down strike in the "enormous factories."[19] Their demands differed only slightly from those formulated at other firms: end of overtime work, eight days of paid vacation, recognition of union delegates, and an increase in wages, especially those of lower-paid workers. On 13 May the Syndicat du bâtiment decided to agitate at the 1937 exposition for a collective bargaining agreement that would establish an eight-hour day, a forty-hour week, and union delegates. Two hundred cement workers at Trocadéro—the site of the World's Fair—demanded higher pay, a longer lunch break, the end of overtime, and dressing rooms so they could change into clothes that "would command respect."[20] The last demand illustrated the narrowing distinctions in clothing between the bourgeoisie and the working class during the Popular Front: manual workers wanted to replace their blue overalls with more stylish clothes.[21]

With the exception of dressing rooms, the demands of the construction workers basically reiterated what their union leaders had wanted at the end of April.[22] Indeed, some claims, such as the abolition of the *tâcheronnat* (contracted piecework), reached back at least to the revolution of 1848. In the system of *tâcheronnat* a general contractor employed a subcontractor (*sous-traitant*) who in turn paid workers by the piece. The subcontractors usually hired the most productive laborers and were reluctant to engage the very young or the old. Workers felt that "greedy" and "immoral" *tâcherons* exploited them. During the depression years of 1932 and 1933, construction workers' refusal to work for a *tâcheron* provoked at least three strikes.[23]

On 29 May an agreement between the union and management was reached at Renault. The accord ended overtime work, increased the lowest wages, promised the completion of toilets and dressing rooms, and guaranteed strike pay for the occupation. By 8:30 P.M. the factories were evacuated.[24] On 30 May, following the Renault example, strikers at many other factories—among them Nieuport, Caudron, Farman, Brandt, and Panhard—ended their occupations with agreements similar to that reached at Renault, although workers at Bloch, Michelin, Citroën, and Lockheed also won paid vacations. In addition, workers at Citroën received permission to smoke in the factory. The Syndicat des métaux expressed "great satisfaction" with the results of the negotiations, as sixty thousand of the seventy thousand occupiers left their factories.[25] Many observers thought that the sit-down strikes had ceased.

Although automobile, aviation, and related firms had been largely evacuated by 1 June, occupations continued at several chemical firms, tire-making plants, and various electronics firms.[26] On 2 June a renewed wave of occupations affected a significant number of industries. Among them were the aviation firms, Lioré et Olivier (1,200 workers) and Breguet. Although the industries of chemicals and metalworking (300 firms were occupied) were the most affected, other industrial sectors, such as electricity, gas, and printing, also became involved by 3 June. At Renault work stoppages continued sporadically until the occupation was resumed on 4 June. On 5 June Citroën was occupied, and even the provinces began to be touched, although the Paris region remained most active. In certain occupations, workers' solidarity assumed almost mythic proportions. At Dun and Bradstreet, in a strike that lasted at least twelve days, only 14 of 127 white-collar workers (75 percent of whom were women) refused to participate in an occupation that began on 10 June.[27]

There has been considerable debate over whether the strikes were spontaneous. The Right has claimed that subversives or Communists organized the occupations. The Left, in general, has emphasized the spontaneity and joyfulness that initially characterized the movement:

> Yes, a joy. I went to see my pals in a factory where I worked a few months ago. . . . A joy to enter the factory with the smiling permission of the worker who guards the door. A joy to find so many smiles, so many friendly words. We really feel ourselves to be among comrades in these same workshops where, when I was working, everyone felt so alone with a machine. A joy to pass freely through the workshops where we had been riveted to our machine, to form groups, to gossip, to take a snack. A joy to hear, instead of the ruthless roar of machines—a striking symbol of our submission to harsh necessity—music, songs, and laughter.[28]

More recent historiography, especially from historians close to the PCF, has challenged the notion of a joyful and spontaneous strike movement and has stressed the role of Communist militants.[29] Some evidence exists to support the assertion that Communist or union militants initiated the occupations. In aviation, for example, PCF activists seem to have exercised a degree of control in the occupations. At Renault the strike erupted in workshops where PCF and former CGTU militants were influential.[30]

According to police, however, the union leadership and the Left were startled by the timing and the extent of the movement:

> The strike wave of sit-downs in metallurgical factories of the Paris region has literally surprised the militants of the CGT who were the last to be informed. . . .
>
> Neither the *unitaires* [ex-CGTU] nor the *confédérés* [ex-CGT], both of which had few members at Citroën, sparked its strike. . . .
>
> The great wave at Renault . . . began without union officials (*militants «responsables»*) being informed. . . .
>
> The major papers wanted to believe that the strike wave was Communist-inspired. Now that seems improbable. It is possible that Communist cells . . . became some of the most avid activists, but it must be acknowledged that Communist union militants were among the first to be surprised by the movement. It is possible that

> the hopes and enthusiasm that arose after the electoral victory of the Popular Front altered the minds of those who were already discontented with their material conditions.[31]

Sensing a favorable political and social climate, many workers—sometimes led by shop-floor CGT or PCF militants, sometimes on their own initiative—impulsively left their machines or laid down their tools in May and June 1936. As one historian of the Popular Front remarks, "The only satisfactory thesis is . . . that of a largely spontaneous movement: From which [came] its unprecedented importance—nearly two million strikers. From which also the prudent behavior of the employers who went with the flow without trying to stop it."[32] Workers were happy, even joyous, to stop work and took the opportunity to relax with their co-workers in the noiseless factories and occasionally to initiate love affairs (women composed over 20 percent of the work force in metallurgy).[33] Although many occupations began spontaneously, CGT militants soon began to organize the strikers and to formulate demands. Union activists organized the safety and the feeding of the workers with assistance from Socialist and Communist municipalities.[34]

When the Blum government took power on 4 June 1936, its main task was to calm the spreading movement of occupations, which worried not only governmental officials but also union leaders and, of course, the employers themselves. According to Blum, the initiative for negotiations between the employers, the union (CGT), and the government came from representatives of the major employers' organization, Confédération générale de la production française (CGPF). With one exception, the delegates who represented the CGPF in the negotiations with the CGT and the government "headed large-scale enterprises and corporations located in Paris."[35] The employers' representatives were connected with the more advanced industries, like metallurgy and chemicals. More traditional sectors, for example, commerce, textiles, and construction, were underrepresented in the CGPF delegation.

On 7 and 8 June 1936 the three groups reached an agreement. The employers' delegates recognized the workers' right to join a union without the threat of sanctions, and, in turn, non-union members were guaranteed the right to work. The CGPF representatives agreed to the election of union delegates in firms with more than ten workers, and the three groups endorsed the principle of collective bargaining between the management and the union. The accord implicitly condemned the illegal occupations. Blum personally arbitrated the question of wages, raising them between 7 and 15 percent. He also promised to introduce legislation, which was to be approved quickly, guaranteeing paid vacations and, most important, the forty-hour week.

This agreement—providing collective bargaining, union rights, the election of union delegates on the shop floor, and higher pay—was known as the *accord Matignon*. It represented the culmination of the social legislation of the Third Republic.[36] The CGT justifiably viewed it as a great victory for the Confédération; and one of its delegates reported that the employers had yielded on all points.[37] By contrast, employers in traditional sectors such as textiles and many small businessmen opposed the *accord*; their disappointment and even outrage at the agreement provoked a strong reaction against the Popular Front and a desire for unity among employers.[38] Yet management of larger enterprises generally regarded the agreement as the best settlement that could be obtained at a time when over one million workers were occupying factories and firms throughout France. The employers hoped that collective bargaining would stabilize industry.[39] According to C. J. Gignoux, who became head of the CGPF after the signing of the agreement, "the obligation of collective bargaining contracts could soften certain shocks and permit the resolution of many questions that, if regulated precipitously, would provoke serious disorder."[40] Many on the Left believed that a collective contract could limit the "abusive" and "arbitrary" authority of the employers.[41]

The demand for recognition of elected union delegates also received wide support among several ideological currents within the CGT and even backing from certain employers. Well before the Popular Front, Albert Thomas had believed that delegates could help improve production and protect workers' interests. M. Chambelland, the leader of the small group of revolutionary syndicalists grouped around the review *La Révolution prolétarienne,* called for workers' delegates to prevent management's disregard of contracts and aid workers' participation in hiring and firing.[42] Jouhaux also endorsed the institution of union delegates on the shop floor. Some of the more progressive managements believed that union representatives could prevent disorder by resolving friction between workers and employers over wages, working conditions, and the presentation of grievances; others felt that the introduction of union delegates might become the starting point for some form of productive workers' participation.[43]

Whereas some bourgeois could agree with union officials on the potential benefits of union representation, collective bargaining, pay raises for the lowest-paid personnel, and even limited paid vacations, management differed sharply from labor over the forty-hour week. Almost all employers objected that the forty-hour week would drastically raise costs and put them at a disadvantage with foreign competitors. Thus, the assertion by the economist Alfred Sauvy that the French bourgeoisie was relatively unconcerned about the effects of the forty-hour week is questionable. Well before the Popular Front, employers fervently opposed the shorter week. In January 1933, three thousand employers' organizations resolved to combat the "peril" of the forty-hour week.[44] In 1935 C. J. Gignoux protested when the International Labor Conference approved the forty-hour proposal. Numerous bosses, their representatives, and their organizations blasted the shortened workweek in the strongest possible terms; the presidents of the chambers of commerce, for example, desired to "regenerate production by faith in labor": "The French working-class as a whole must rediscover the desire to work, which previously penetrated the entire population and which permitted, after the disasters of 1870 and the trials of the Great War, admirable recoveries."[45] In June and July 1936 *Economie nouvelle,* the publication of the Fédération des industriels et commerçants français, declared that the forty-hour week would ruin small and medium-sized firms. The owners of small firms sometimes belonged to or often voted for the Radical party, which held the key to parliamentary majorities of this period. The alienation of these employers from the leftist coalition would put increasing pressure on the Radical party to abandon the Popular Front. The bourgeoisie—owners of firms small and big—resisted the forty-hour week probably more than any other demand.

French industrialists and many economists objected that the shortage of skilled workers would cause a serious bottleneck for French production if the forty-hour week were imposed too rigorously. The lack of qualified personnel, employers asserted, would block a key goal of the forty-hour week—the hiring of the unemployed. In 1937 a St.-Etienne metallurgist who supplied Renault commented that "it is out of the question for us to create additional jobs or to work during vacations since our region lacks specialists and cannot recruit enough to establish such jobs."[46] Yet the union position on the forty-hour week did reflect a deeply rooted attitude held by many workers who, as in Spain, wanted to defend their unemployed comrades by sharing the limited work available. Wage earners went on strike even during the depression in solidarity with their laid-off or dismissed colleagues.[47] Solidarity strikes would increase after the electoral victory of the Popular Front.

Even if the CGT discourse on unemployment echoed working-class sentiment, it ignored the character of the aviation industry and other sectors. These industries depended on a considerable percentage of skilled workers who, because of the French demographic situation and the insufficiency of retraining programs, were in short supply. Thus the unemployed, most of them either old or unskilled, could not easily be employed in the many skilled jobs in aviation and other industries. Industrialists also feared that competition for the limited supply of qualified workers would raise wages dramatically; in dozens of letters, management complained of the "enticing away" of skilled workers by state-run firms that would offer higher pay and better benefits.[48]

In addition to opposing strenuously the shortened week, many employers objected to the size of the wage increases that Prime Minister Blum had arbitrated. Nevertheless, the Popular Front in general and the Blum government in particular believed that the augmentations were an essential element of the theory of *pouvoir d'achat.* The Left thought that the amplified buying power of the workers, with the reemployment of the jobless, would expand consumption and stimulate the economy, as the Popular Front's program intended. Higher demand would create economies of scale that would reduce costs per unit produced; renewed activity and the prospect of increased profits would encourage investment. Thus, higher-paid workers would be able to purchase lower-priced goods, and the economy would move out of the stagnation that had characterized it since the decade's beginning. Yet there was one catch: production had to increase if the plan was to succeed. Growth of goods and services could come only from increased investment and hard work.

Investment may have decreased nationally because of investors' reluctance to keep their money in France during periods of left-wing governments, the legendary *mur d'argent.*[49] In the industries examined in detail here, however, the effects of this wall of money seem marginal. At Renault the pace of investment into modernizing machinery increased in 1936–1937 but slowed down in 1938. Massive state funds flowed into nationalized aviation firms in 1938.[50] No lack of investment seems to have marked Parisian construction; indeed, the state committed large sums for the World's Fair.[51] In these three key industries, hard work, not capital, was in particularly short supply in the Paris region during the Popular Front governments.

Officially and publicly, the Popular Front coalition assumed that workers would labor hard and even more diligently in return for higher pay and advanced social legislation. Yet after the long years of the depression of the 1930s—which often meant a quicker pace of production, a greater threat of unemployment, and decreased mobility—workers were ready to take advantage of the shifting balance of power. The forty-hour week meant a real change in everyday lives, and workers would struggle to maintain it throughout the Popular Front. Furthermore, at whatever cost to productivity, most workers wanted to divide the forty-hour week into five days of eight hours, resulting in two free days.[52] Perhaps these workers perceived more lucidly than the politicians that the Popular Front was a fleeting opportunity whose benefits must be quickly reaped. Indeed, in certain factories where increases of productivity had been matched by pay hikes, management feared that "sure enough, at the first opportunity, the workers will ask that this salary level be preserved and proclaim that the work that they perform is excessive and must be reduced without diminishing their standard of living."[53]

According to industrialists, workers thus adapted their conception of a fair or moral wage to the new political and social climate of the Popular Front. The employers' assertion meshed with the findings of the French sociologist M. Halbwachs, who concluded that workers' salaries in the early 1930s were determined not so much by basic needs but rather by habit and custom. Habit prevented workers' standard of living from descending but not from climbing.[54] Even during the deflation of the depression, when real wages generally rose for the employed, workers would strike to defend their nominal wages.[55]

There was absolutely no assurance that higher wages, shorter working week, and paid vacations would guarantee increased or even normal productivity. Indeed, given the long history of French workers' resistance to labor, the assumption of stable productivity was problematic. Studies of nineteenth- and early twentieth-century workers have shown the importance of sabotage, lateness, drunkenness, theft, slowdowns, struggles against piecework, and insubordination.[56] In addition to these, absenteeism and unauthorized absences have been documented before World War I. Of the interwar period, less is known; in the 1930s, France's political and economic stability relative to its Iberian neighbor seems to have tempered workers' resistance to work. Instances of turnover and lateness declined, and workers became *enracinés,* more reluctant to change jobs or regions. The 1930s saw the stabilization of the working class after the destabilization of the 1920s.[57]

Yet slowdowns and faked illnesses remained favored tactics. In 1932 tense relations between construction workers and their foremen sparked work slowdowns, dismissals, and a violent confrontation between the two groups.[58] Renault workers practiced the *macadam,* a tactic in which a worker would find several witnesses to testify, falsely, that he had been injured on the job and would then take off several days at the bosses' expense.[59] In the 1930s, the French automaker attempted to stymie workers' efforts to fake illnesses or to find a permissive doctor who would allow them to remain on sick leave longer than management desired: "If we take care of our own insurance, . . . it is absolutely necessary that the insured are treated, as far as possible, by our own doctors. We must flush out the shady doctors so that our workers are not cared for in clinics where they are frequently taken advantage of at our expense."[60]

On the Renault shop floor strict surveillance, including turnstiles and identity cards, was established to reduce theft and pilfering. Certain firms regularly frisked their personnel. Workers protested against this discipline and often referred to the factory as Devil's Island or the *bagne* (convict prison), as others had done in the nineteenth century. Nor was resistance to labor limited to blue-collar workers. In the spring of 1931 Renault reported that delays in accounting were partially caused by employees, of whom "the majority work irregularly and waste a good deal of time when starting a job and when leaving it. The time devoted to preparation and arranging is enormous."[61]

Refusals to labor were not unknown among the unemployed, whom the Popular Front wished to reemploy. To avoid accepting an offer from the placement bureau, the jobless would sometimes exaggerate their physical defects and health problems to convince potential employers not to hire them.[62] This tactic permitted individuals to claim that it was management who had refused their services and thus enabled them to keep their unemployment insurance. The longer they remained on the dole, the more difficult it was to accept retraining. Many would decline a position, if it meant moving to a new city. Parisian workers refused to be enticed by guarantees of housing, transportation allowances, and bonuses to "return to the farm" or even to their native province. Married couples were particularly reluctant to depart. By 1936 unemployed Parisians remained resolutely urban and rooted in what some French intellectuals considered a rootless environment.

To eliminate fraud, the placement bureau would summon the unemployed at the normal hours of their trade. For example, it convoked bakers early in the morning; this procedure "appreciably" reduced their numbers. Sudden convocation or unannounced visits also occurred. Inspectors could even interview former employers. Some *patrons* would collaborate with their personnel to swindle officials. A few managers were known to permit workers to leave the firm so they could keep appointments with the employment bureau. One building entrepreneur who had gone bankrupt encouraged his laborers to register for unemployment assistance by paying them the difference between their former salaries and the amount they received from the government. However, only a minority of the jobless attempted to deceive the authorities. In 1930, 65 percent of the unemployed were able to prove that their right to assistance was justified. By 1935, with rising unemployment touching previously unaffected sectors of the working class, the figure had climbed to 91 percent. Yet large numbers of workers were capable of violating the spirit, if not the letter, of the regulations. Parisian metalworkers, when waiting for their strikes to end, would register en masse as jobless workers so they could obtain compensation. In 1934, "given the evidence of [these] violations," the rules were changed to prevent the practice. If found guilty of fraud, the convicted could be fined or imprisoned.

In changed economic and political circumstances, resistance to labor could easily flourish, as it had before the depression when turnover and lateness were more prevalent. Given this pattern, it is not surprising that despite the signing of the Matignon Agreements on 8 June and Blum's commitment to obtain legislative approval for the forty-hour week and paid vacations, work remained halted in many factories and workshops. Although the CGT endorsed the *accord,* it was unable to end the sit-down strikes immediately in the Paris region. Again, this failure indicated that the movement was spontaneous or, at least, not entirely under the control of the CGT: "In effect, the strikes broke out in those sectors where the organizations capable of provoking them were the weakest. This is true of the CGT, which was completely outmaneuvered (*débordée*)."[63]

However unplanned and unsuspected their commencement, the occupations immediately offered important responsibilities to union militants and elected officials of the Left. Their implantation in the Parisian suburbs during the interwar period proved decisive in certain sit-down strikes. During the occupations, the Metallurgical Employers' Association (Groupement des industries métallurgiques, or GIM) complained of "interference" not only by CGT delegates but also by Communist and Socialist elected officials.[64] A Catholic academy in Vanves—whose board of directors included Cardinal Verdier, the archbishop of Paris—had eight hundred students who were largely from "modest families of the Paris region." On 26 June approximately fifty workers occupied its kitchen. The strikers received "real encouragement from the Issy municipality, which had a Communist mayor who fed them and persuaded them to hold out until victory. The older personnel would give in readily but are carried along by the young."[65] The school administration accepted the workers' demand for higher pay but refused to recognize the union. The police superintendent feared that if he used force to end the occupation, the working-class commune might react violently.

With the help of many municipalities, activists in the occupied factories organized concerts, dances, sports, games, and films. CGT militants presented workers' demands and sometimes insisted that the forty-hour week, paid vacations, and higher salaries not only be legislated at the national level but also be inscribed in collective bargaining agreements at the local level. At Renault the Communist deputy Costes reminded the management that the workers wanted the forty-hour week and paid vacations to be included in their contract: "The workers prefer, in spite of all the advantages that an eventual law might grant them, the signing of a collective bargaining agreement that has the power of a law between the two parties: Renault management and the workers."[66]

Many, if not most, historians have attributed the end of the May and June strikes to the influence of the speech that Maurice Thorez, the leader of the French PCF, gave to party militants on 11 June 1936. While praising the order and discipline of the Parisian proletariat, the Communist leader argued:

> We do not yet have behind us, with us, ready to go with us to the end, the people of the countryside. We are risking the estrange-

> ment of sections of the bourgeoisie and peasantry that are somewhat sympathetic. What then? . . . then it is necessary to know how to end a strike once satisfaction has been obtained.[67]

Yet Thorez's influence even at Renault, where the PCF claimed to have great strength, seems to have been limited. On 5 June, the day on which Thorez told the militants not to scare "the bourgeoisie and the peasants of France," damage at Renault began.[68] Although little destruction had occurred during the strike's first days, a "mean spirit" appeared among the workers on 11 June under the pretext of a delay in signing the collective bargaining agreement.[69] After 11 June there was a "new situation, characterized by the violence of the strikers." Raw materials were "voluntarily defiled and rendered unusable," from which Renault claimed 161,201 francs of damage, a considerable sum. Windows were broken "either voluntarily or involuntarily," and thousands of francs' worth of items disappeared, including clocks, tools, and equipment of all sorts. Assembly-line workers sometimes refused requests by their foremen to complete the work at hand. In one case the superintendent (*chef d'atelier*) demanded that workers grease unfinished doors that would rust if left untreated, but the workers "categorically refused" to carry out the order. Management later spent 8,379 francs to eliminate the rust. Workers used this destruction to wring concessions from the Renault management.

Most historians have stressed the workers' calm, order, and respect for both people and property during the occupations. In many firms machines and materials were protected, and management was left untouched. The workers of the Paris region did not wish to destroy the machines and factories on which they depended for their livelihood. Nonetheless, as at Renault, in several other firms during the occupations damage to property did occur. At one electronics firm (Alsthom), telephone wires were cut.[70] At the Faïencerie de Choisy-le-Roi, theft and damage were reported. The Metallurgical Employers' Association announced threats of sabotage by workers in two firms and estimated potential damage at a minimum of 200,000 francs. In two other companies, workers threatened to extinguish furnaces, which, if accomplished, would have cost the concerns hundreds of thousands of francs. Industrialists reported some damage, usually caused by workers who abruptly stopped production or who used up supplies of raw materials during the occupations.[71] In this context of petty theft, subtle sabotage, and intimidation, union representatives in fourteen factories warned that workers would run the rms themselves if their demands were not met.[72]

There was also a limited amount of violence. At a number of firms in the Paris region, managers were forcibly conned and supervisory personnel were not permitted to enter the factories. Several foremen and executives were physically searched, verbally abused, and threatened with death.[73] Foremen were particularly detested by their underlings; some were expelled from factories.[74] A CGT declaration on 2 June stating that employers "must be free to enter and leave their firms" was either ignored or disobeyed. At Renault, administrative personnel who were "guarded as hostages" became involved in fights with other workers.

However, when shop-floor delegates' demands were satisfied and collective bargaining agreements signed, the sit-downs and strikes gradually ended, often with the government's mediation. Regardless of the fears of many and the hopes of few, revolution did not occur. In many branches, wage earners made great gains. For example, on 12 June a contract in construction established an eight-hour day, restricted overtime, and abolished the *tâcheronnat.*[75] Teams with rotating assignment of workers were to perform nightwork, and the union achieved increased control of hiring.

On Bastille Day when the strike wave was nearly over, Benoît Frachon, a Communist CGT leader, told a rally of forty thousand that the workers had returned or would return to the factories with greater class consciousness.[76] The following chapter shows that this consciousness manifested itself in modes remarkably similar to those of Spanish workers during the Revolution in Barcelona.

11
REVOLTS AGAINST WORK

After the initial factory occupations in the spring of 1936 had receded, violence, destruction, and disobedience continued. Direct and indirect revolts against work—phenomena almost always present among wage earners—intensified during the French Popular Front governments. Parisian wage earners seem to have increased their resistances, particularly strikes, when the government was led by Léon Blum, prime minister from June 1936 to June 1937 and again from March 1938 to April 1938. After May 1936 many workers took advantage of a relaxation in the military-like labor discipline that had characterized factory life in the early 1930s to arrive late, leave early, miss work, slow down production, and, on occasion, to disobey their superiors in ways that hurt output. As in Barcelona in the months following the electoral victory of the Spanish Popular Front in February 1936, some workers interpreted the alliance against fascism not in terms of politics but of everyday life. For many Parisian workers, fascism became associated with iron discipline on the shop floor, an intensive productivity, and a long and tiring workweek. A foreman who demanded strict obedience, a boss who established longer working hours, or an engineer who quickened the pace of production might be labeled a fascist by some workers. Thus, the Popular Front became an opportunity to defy the work pace and to struggle against work itself.

In a letter to his deputy, one Parisian worker revealed his conception of the relation between work and fascism. The writer, who claimed to be a "convinced partisan of the Popular Front," protested the dismissal of an employee, a young woman who had refused to labor during a legal holiday, 11 November.[1] He accused the director of the company, the luxury store Fauchon, of being a "notorious fascist" (*fascite* [sic] *notoire*) and charged that the firing of the girl was illegal and intolerable "under a government of the Popular Front, elected by the workers for the defense of their interests." Although the writer was wrong concerning the illegality of the dismissal (the prohibition on work during legal holidays applied not to luxury stores but to factories and mines), the letter—whatever its misspellings and insufficient knowledge of labor law—disclosed his identification of the Popular Front with the protection of holidays. It also significantly leveled charges of fascism against an employer who wished to recover a holiday. In Paris as in Barcelona, struggles over the treatment of holidays were widespread.

At Renault after the occupations, the guerrilla against work took a variety of forms, and workers took advantage of the new atmosphere of softened discipline: "In different workshops the workers have modified, on their own initiative, their working hours, entering an hour earlier or later and leaving accordingly."[2] In the chromium and nickel plating and polishing workshops, wage earners (mostly women) stopped production with a "disconcerting ability" and formulated their demands only after the work stoppage.[3]

The newly elected union delegates often profited from the new climate in the factory. They consistently ignored a clause in the contract that instituted a ten-hour per month maximum for the exercise of union functions; many missed work whenever possible: "The delegates do not perform any real work. Some appear in their workshops only incidentally. Most of them leave their jobs at any moment without asking the permission of their foremen. The delegates meet almost constantly and, despite the numerous warnings issued, they persist in acting this way."[4] Delegates often left the factory to go to the union hall, in complete disregard of the contract; when management offered the delegates a card to permit them to circulate freely in the factory and thus to account for the time exercised in their functions, they refused.[5]

Tensions between delegates and foremen were particularly acute at Renault and a dual power existed. Foremen who attempted to enforce work discipline often ran into the opposition of both delegates and workers who disobeyed their orders.

When a delegate returned to his workshop and his foreman reproached him for his "unauthorized absence," the delegate replied that "he had had enough, that it had to blow up, and that the next time workers would not hang foremen and bosses in effigy but for real."[6] Delegates were known to enter the factory "in a state of excessive drunkenness," "engaging in clowning, preventing workers from working normally." In February 1937 a delegate ordered that machines be turned off during his mealtime, and the result was "difficulties, if not impossibilities of working during meals."[7]

Both union representatives and workers attempted to control hiring and firing at Renault. In September 1936 the personnel of *atelier* 147 demanded the dismissal of their foreman "with the plea that he made them work too much."[8] *Syndicats,* the review of the anti-Communist faction of the CGT, complained when the Renault management refused to hire an inexperienced young worker for a highly specialized job: "The industrialists want to employ only workers capable of maximum output."[9] The journal called for CGT control of hiring. Delegates asked management to fire wage earners—regardless of their work record—who refused to join the CGT.[10] Union representatives opposed the hiring of workers associated with right-wing parties and unions. Incidents of varying degrees of violence erupted:

> 10.9 [36], *atelier* 59: The workers of metal pattern-making wait at the exit for the worker K., who has received a medal for being one of the best workers in France. He was followed as far as his residence at Billancourt by three hundred agitators who covered him from head to feet with spit. At the place Sembat the police dispersed the mob.[11]

Although union power could not always prevent layoffs and dismissals, management found it difficult to fire some workers who, in its judgment, had committed "grave professional errors."[12] A company driver who had caused three separate accidents on three consecutive days could not be dismissed:

> We had to keep this worker, under the pretext that his firing was not caused by his professional errors, but because he was the chauffeur for (PCF) Deputy Costes during the strike.

> Right now concerning the working-class personnel, each job change requires several hours of discussion with the interested parties. Each dismissal, even those that are completely justified, becomes subject to negotiations that can involve the management and even the ministry. Examples are both numerous and daily.[13]

When companies in various industries laid off workers, strikes ensued.[14] Toward the end of the Popular Front, employers still inquired about the correct procedures for dismissing CGT delegates whom they charged with responsibility for defects in production.[15]

Union representatives usurped management prerogatives concerning employment: "Certain delegates take advantage of their position for personal reasons. Example: X, delegate, changed one of his cousins from an unskilled laborer to an o.s. (*ouvrier spécialisé*), ousting an o.s. and making him an unskilled worker."[16] In *atelier* 125, rationalization of a process for car interiors had reduced the need for workers, and the management wanted to dismiss female wage earners whose rate of absenteeism was high and to retain those women who were the sole breadwinners of their families. The delegate, however, opposed management's selections and argued for the retention of three married women (whom management believed to be the favorites of the delegates). The company asserted that the women whom the delegates protected did not need the jobs as much as unmarried or divorced women with an equal or larger number of dependents.[17]

Delegates used the gains of the May and June occupations in special ways. After the strikes in the spring of 1936, regular searches of the packages and suitcases of workers leaving the factories were suspended, and in *atelier* 243 a delegate threatened "incidents" if management reinstituted the checks.[18] Nevertheless, during several months the management quietly employed "a discreet surveillance." On 4 December 1937 a delegate and his partner were arrested as they entered a taxi. Both were carrying heavy bags and were taken to a police station where they declared that, every day for several months, they had stolen five kilograms of antifriction metals, which they later resold. Renault claimed 200,000 francs in damages, including the cost of the stolen goods and the estimated price of the "disorders affecting our manufactures." A conservative newspaper reported that all except one of the "twenty or so inspectors and workers from Citroën who stole numerous parts during 1936 and 1937" had been found guilty.[19]

Work slowdowns and protests against piecework were frequent during the Popular Front. In the late summer and early fall of 1936, wage earners fought hard against production incentives and a "too rapid" production pace.[20] After June 1936 in the Renault aluminum foundry, new machinery, which was supposed to reduce costs 20 percent, was installed, but the new equipment succeeded in cutting costs by only 4 percent because after a "long discussion," workers refused to "work with this new material."[21] Slowdowns continued in various workshops and assembly lines throughout 1937 and 1938. In July 1937 a director of personnel wrote that management had to confront "a great deal of both declared and underhanded ill will that paralyzes our efforts. . . . We now have serious problems maintaining piecework and production incentives. In a number of firms, in order to avoid debates, piecework has been retained only nominally, and there is really a fixed salary."[22] He believed that the only way to increase productivity was to restore incentives of piecework. Renault management charged that output in 1938 was lower than in 1936.[23] In contrast to 1936, work did not "begin normally" at starting times. Workers in the polishing workshop stopped at 1130 instead of 1200 and at 1430 instead of 1600. In the gear section work began a half-hour late and ended a half-hour early. On the assembly line, output increased only in the delegates' absence.

According to the employers, it was necessary to watch workers very closely to obtain decent productivity.[24] In August 1937 management rationalized a Renault assembly line to produce 15 to 16 chassis per hour instead of the previous 8 to 10. An executive explained the operation.

> No worker had to do more work than previously. The increase of production was made possible by the elimination of certain operations and the amelioration of machinery and method. With regard to [workers'] health, special fans and screens were installed, which meant a real advance in working conditions. From the beginning

> [of the reorganization] we ran into ill will and systematic opposition against the work pace.[25]

The delegates charged that the work rhythm was "inhuman" and that workers could not produce more than 13 chassis per hour. Despite the resistance, management claimed to have kept its "patience" and continued to pay workers as if they had reached the production goal. In November 1937, the company became frustrated by the "arrogance" of the delegates and tried to demonstrate to the workers that it was possible to attain 15.5 chassis without difficulty. The 15.5 goal was met at the end of November only when the delegates were absent, and the executive believed that workers could exceed this target if they ceased "voluntarily" limiting their output.

In other incidents, delegates frequently encouraged workers' resistance to production speed-ups. A widow who was a semiskilled lathe worker claimed that her Renault salary was her only source of income and conceded that she wanted "to make the most possible."[26] After the strikes of June 1936, (male) union delegates limited her piecework production and prohibited her from earning more than 5 francs per hour. The woman consulted with her foreman and supervisors who encouraged her to work energetically. She then went beyond the "ceiling" imposed by the delegates and earned 8.11 francs per hour. Consequently, "the delegates and the personnel of the workshop" became hostile to her. They accused her of being a member of Colonel de La Rocque's Parti social français (or PSF, the successor to his right-wing Croix de feu) and charged that she had spied for management. She denied being a spy and indicated that she was apolitical. Her colleague, Mme B., threatened her life and on 13 January 1937 successfully aroused female co-workers against her. The widow declared that her fellow workers had angrily shouted "Death!" "Down with stool pigeons," and "Up against the wall, La Rocque." Several had inscribed "Death to fascists" in the sawdust in front of her machine. To avoid the hostile demonstration against her and possible injury, the widow was forced to leave the factory by a rarely used exit. In Renault's polishing workshops a year later, union representatives continued to require that workers show them their paychecks so that the CGT activists could determine if the workers were producing beyond the de facto quota that had been established.[27]

Although Renault's difficulties are the best documented, it was not the only automaker to experience tensions between delegates and management. In September 1937 a twenty-five-day strike erupted at SIMCA, FIAT's Parisian branch. CGT representatives accused the management of the Italian firm of being "fascist" and "Mussolinian."[28] The union charged that management had refused to pay workers the minimum required by the collective bargaining agreement and treated shop stewards unfairly. Management replied that the conflict, which involved seventeen hundred workers at its Nanterre factory, was provoked by workers' slowdowns. "Production graphs clearly demonstrate this ill will. During May and June [1937] production was systematically lowered and its rhythm fell from 64 to 40 or 42 cars per day. On 7 July the management warned that it would no longer tolerate the continuation of this situation and *suddenly production returned to normal.*"[29]

Yet after July, incidents continued to plague the factory. Management dismissed a worker who had ruined a large press —valued at a half million francs. It also fired a delegate who, it claimed, had left the factory without authorization to go to the union hall. On Friday 27 August, several days after the firings, workers protested against a new system of pay distribution and stopped laboring in certain workshops at 4:00 P.M. Two hundred wage earners then demonstrated against management and, for several hours, prevented executives from leaving their offices. On the Monday following this protest, workers returned to their posts but, according to SIMCA, in an atmosphere of "underhanded agitation." When the supervisor found defects in a number of automobiles, he stopped the assembly line. The delegate and several workers then restarted the halted line, even though management had assured them that they would have an opportunity to make up the lost time and pay. The company, claiming that it could not permit workers' usurpation of its prerogatives, suspended twelve disobedient workers for forty-eight hours. When the supervisor announced the sanctions, he was booed, hit, and violently ejected from the factory. "The majority" of his fellow foremen "spontaneously" signed a letter of protest. In response to the August incidents, management fired forty-nine workers. Supported by the delegates and high union officials, the dismissed returned to the factory on 1 September. The following day, an occupation ensued and executives and foremen were again sequestered.

Fortunately for the historian, two arbitration reports evaluated management's and union's accounts. The first decided that workers must return to the factory on Monday 27 September under the same conditions that had existed before the occupation.[30] Arbitrators eliminated the dining room used for union meetings and ended the position of the union secretary who did not labor in the factory. They also reduced the workweek to not fewer than thirty-two hours to provide for the employment of all personnel.

The second arbitration ruling was issued by Guinand, the president of the nationalized railroad company (Société nationale des chemins de fer, or SNCF), appointed arbitrator by the prime minister, Camille Chautemps of the Radical party, who had succeeded Blum in June 1937 and remained in office until March 1938.[31] Guinand determined that management had been justified in dismissing the delegate who had left the factory in defiance of orders. He supported the firing of twenty-two workers and the suspensions, for one or two weeks, of twenty-two others. His panel criticized SIMCA for tolerating indiscipline and not penalizing workers immediately after they committed infractions. After listening to testimony from both labor and management, the board concluded:

> We consider that a serious state of indiscipline, which destroyed productivity, certainly prevailed in the Nanterre factory. In particular, certain delegates went way beyond their duties as established in the collective bargaining agreement, and they interfered in technical matters against the wishes of supervisory personnel. This created deplorable incidents that hindered work efficiency. Specifically, an incident of this type occurred on 30 August during a demonstration in which a supervisor was forced to leave his workshop. This was absolutely wrong.

Even after arbitration, friction persisted between unionized workers and their foremen during the fall of 1937.

The decline of production and the unsettled state of the factories should not be entirely attributed to the actions of the delegates. Management tended to blame production problems on "troublemakers" and "agitators." Yet these *meneurs,* as employers called them, found a solid base of support among fellow workers. Many SIMCA workers backed the actions of the shop stewards, and workers at Renault elected them by overwhelming majorities. At Renault in July 1936, the CGT Fédération des métaux received 86.5 percent of the votes of those registered, whereas the other unions combined polled only 7 percent, and abstentions were 6.5 percent.[32] Generally by July 1936, *cégétistes* were pleased by the overwhelming majorities their candidates had received—despite employers' resistance—in shop-steward elections throughout the Paris region.[33] In July 1938 the CGT continued to hold its majorities; it polled 20,428 out of 27,913 votes, or 73 percent. The other unions—Syndicat professionnel français, CFTC (Catholic), and independents—obtained only 11 percent in total. Abstentions more than doubled, from 6.5 percent in 1936 to 16 percent in July 1938. Although CGT militants may have employed violence to intimidate voters, as management charged during the Popular Front, the delegates of the Fédération des métaux, which won such lopsided majorities (71 delegates out of 74 in 1938), must have expressed many of their constituencies' desires.

On occasion these constituencies did limit the power of the delegates. In one case delegates required that management end a certain incentive in return for the delegates' pledge that productivity would not suffer; nevertheless, output fell.[34] As early as 30 June 1936 during negotiations between the labor minister and metallurgical employers, a CGT delegation promised to help increase output, but this commitment also remained unfulfilled. Intervention by the delegates to improve production risked arousing "the anger of the workers against the delegates." CGT metallurgical officials were concerned that either "Trotskyists" or "fascist professional unions" would gain support among workers if the Confédération did not pursue workers' demands aggressively enough.[35]

As in Barcelona, appeals by high-ranking union and Communist party officials that workers work harder often went unanswered. On 16 September 1936 the Renault management reported a work stoppage "in spite of the intervention" of the secretary of the Fédération des métaux of Billancourt and of an important CGT leader, Timbault. Even lower-ranking delegates would sometimes disobey union superiors or renege on agreements: "With the consent of the delegates, it was agreed that the painters would work two hours overtime to finish the vehicles for the automobile show. At 6:00 P.M. the delegate M, dissatisfied with his pay, gave them an order to leave in the name of the CGT."[36] The Metallurgical Employers' Association listed a number of incidents where CGT delegates hindered production by "haranguing" and exhorting their workers. Even after offending delegates were dismissed, production slowdowns sometimes continued among the rank and file. Indeed, industrialists claimed, some delegates even resigned, "exasperated by the unjustified demands of the workers."[37]

Local CGT newspapers would occasionally acknowledge that workers were late without justification. On 1 April 1937 *L'Unité* (CGT) noted lapses in discipline at the Renault ball-bearing workshop.

> We have had only too often the opportunity to record a number of uncommon absences for reasons often frivolous and sometimes nonexistent.
>
> Moreover, it is quite natural that everyone respects the work schedule, given by the management and accepted by us. We implore you to obey our union's discipline since in no way should we lay ourselves open to our enemies.

The anti-Communist Parti populaire français agreed with its adversary. The PPF's publication, *Le Défenseur,* approved the gains that the June strikes had produced at Renault: the end of turnstiles, a "little less arrogance from the wardens" (i.e., foremen), and the ability to enter the factory a bit late without losing a half day's pay. Nevertheless, "in return, the comrades exaggerate. They arrive either at 7:30 or at 8:00, thus disturbing the starting of the assembly lines. In addition, certain [workers] stop work ten minutes before the whistle."[38]

Some Communist militants were irritated by the workers' actions, and the local PCF newspaper, *La Lutte finale,* charged that "indisciplined comrades" were falling into a trap set by management by not producing well. During a cell meeting one militant "protested against the abuses perpetrated by the comrades: work stoppages before the whistle. The punching-in at noon had been ended, but the comrades were in the streets before the noon whistle had blown. . . . [He noted] work stoppages twenty or thirty minutes early."[39] The PCF disliked "personal decisions" and refused "to tolerate, under any pretext, individual action." A militant who was seen speaking to his foreman while intoxicated and who admitted having "been a little drunk" was mildly reprimanded by his cell. Communist activists were warned not to commit violent acts against non-PCF workers since "it is better . . . to keep them in view, to fence them in, and in some way to make them prisoners in case of a movement." Besides, the militant declared, out of 34,000 CGT members at Renault only 4,000 were in the PCF. Thus, 30,000 workers remained non-Communist, according to the PCF's own figures.

Occasionally, but rarely, delegates and CGT officials would respond to management's requests and ask workers to increase their output. For example, at Renault in September 1937, new and unskilled dippers (*trempeurs*) were hired and, according to management, worked poorly. In response, veteran dippers cut their production "brutally" and began to work like their newly employed colleagues. "At this moment the intervention of the delegates, who told these workers that sanctions would be taken against them if they did not resume their normal production, was very useful to support our [management's] efforts."[40] Shortly thereafter, production returned to normal. In the spring workshop, both old and new workers engaged in slowdowns. When the delegates intervened to improve output, veteran workers then produced at a normal pace. Although intervention by delegates to augment production was sometimes successful, it had definite limits since it might jeopardize their popularity and effectiveness among their constituencies. Union representatives generally hindered production, disturbed normal factory discipline, and even intimidated the minority of workers who wanted to produce at a quicker pace. Earlier hopes that union representatives in the factories would be a stabilizing force were destroyed.

The indiscipline and insubordination of many workers and delegates provoked a sharp reaction from shop foremen, engineers, technicians, and superintendents, who objected vigorously to the decline of their authority. Those who belonged to the right-wing Syndicat professionnel declared, "Mass production can exist only when a rigorous discipline reigns. Now the agitated state that exists in our industry can result only in slipshod production and uncertain delivery."[41] The Syndicat professionnel sent a letter to Prime Minister Blum in the fall of 1936, that cited the "troubles reigning in all the metallurgical factories of Paris and its suburbs." It blamed the decline of the management's authority on "irresponsible agitators who are not qualified to substitute for the management." Foremen and superintendents claimed that they had approved the new social legislation "from its inception," but they demanded that the government end agitation in the factories.[42] The *agents de maîtrise* (supervisory personnel) contrasted the poor discipline at Renault with the "countries of order," Great Britain, the United States, and Germany.[43] In March 1937 certain disgruntled members of the *maîtrise* went on strike in four factories of the Société industrielle des téléphones to demand "absolute guarantees of safety and discipline."[44]

In January 1939, after the collapse of the general strike of 30 November 1938, the Syndicat professionnel reminded a senior Renault administrator that "since June 1936" workers had defied the authority of foremen and supervisors and that the cadres had now restored the "output and productivity of numerous workshops."[45] A letter of 1 December 1938, probably by Louis Renault, stated: "Our *maîtrise* has suffered for two years the repercussions of politics. It has frequently been forced to accept a lack of respect for discipline and systematically restrained output."[46]

Generally in automotive and metallurgical production, it was this climate of indiscipline that most disturbed industrialists and their immediate subordinates:

> Since the month of June, there are complaints of a lowering of workers' output. Most often, this reduction is not the result of the

> ill will of the workers but rather of a slackening of discipline. The intervention by the state, the unions, the delegates, and the cells provokes disorder in the workplace and also uncertainty in the minds of the workers about who is in charge.[47]
>
> Strikes of several hours' duration sabotage production less than the state of indiscipline that is being fostered in the factory and now infects the workers. Consequently, our first duty is to struggle against the institutionalization of indiscipline.[48]

Reacting to the lax discipline, many foremen and superintendents, and perhaps engineers and technicians was well, inclined toward extreme right-wing parties or fascist movements that clamored for the restoration of order and discipline in the workplace. These movements attracted those cadres who, for personal or patriotic reasons, insisted on hard work and heightened discipline: "When there is no discipline, output must be faulty. The necessity of discipline is so evident that engineers and foremen, who want the factories to operate well and who are in daily contact with the work force, are the first to demand the preservation of management's authority."[49] In response, workers who opposed a quickened production pace would sometimes charge—justly or not—that foremen who exacted increased productivity and workers who refused to participate in production slowdowns were fascists or members of right-wing organizations.[50] Those workers who continued to labor during a strike were also labeled fascists by their striking colleagues.

Despite its nationalization, the aviation industry experienced somewhat less intensively the problems that characterized automobile production during the Popular Front governments. Nationalization of the war industries and elimination of privately owned defense firms had been a goal of the Popular Front, and at the beginning of 1937 the French state assumed control of most large aviation companies. CGT representation on the administrative councils of the nationalized enterprises was quickly instituted; although in a minority position, the union did participate effectively in the management of the nationalized aviation companies during 1937 and 1938. These enterprises retained their former owners and managers, men like M. Bloch and H. Potez, to direct the day-to-day operations of the firms.

Nationalization brought workers significant changes, raising salaries and guaranteeing better benefits and more job security. Increasingly in 1938, the government also set out to rationalize production in an industry that often conserved its artisanal character. Its goals were to specialize production, eliminate craftsman-like methods, and promote assembly-line organization. The state encouraged the formation of specialized factories that mass-produced aircraft parts; this "rational organization of work" produced excellent results that in 1938 cut the time necessary for certain operations.[51] Engineers were employed to determine the ideal duration of specific tasks; one process, for instance, was reduced from twenty-five thousand hours of labor to four thousand.[52]

Nationalization also led to a further standardization of manufacturing processes. New machines were purchased in France or abroad to offset shortages of qualified personnel. Buildings were constructed and more workers—many of them attracted by the offer of higher salaries—were hired. The state promoted the concentration of previously dispersed branches while encouraging the establishment of new factories outside the Paris region, which in 1936 contained 65 to 90 percent of French aviation plants and featured relatively generous wages and frequent agitation.

In nationalized aviation, workers received good wages for several reasons. Despite expanding rationalization, many operations in the industry required highly skilled workers, in contrast to the automobile sector where work was generally less precise and less complicated. Because the French demographic situation kept skilled laborers in short supply, to attract and keep them industrialists paid qualified workers well. Aviation managers were forced to hire many new workers who, according to a supporter of the Popular Front and its nationalizations, were often poorly qualified.[53]

In addition to the industry's need for qualified labor, CGT representation on its administrative councils and the industry's vulnerability to strikes that could paralyze national defense all gave the union considerable influence on contract negotiations. Many workers in nationalized aviation were therefore relatively privileged, and private employers complained that they could not match the elevated wages and improved benefits that were attracting their best workers into this sector.[54] Qualified workers increased not only their wages but also their mobility during the Popular Front; knowing that their skills were in demand, workers could easily move from one firm to another. High rates of turnover were hardly conducive to rigorous discipline or heightened productivity.[55] Indeed, one prudent manager recommended that time-measurement controllers be more lenient with skilled workers, thereby encouraging them to stay. Employers were obliged to tolerate acts of indiscipline as well as disputes between qualified workers and experienced time-measurement controllers who refused to "bend . . . to the demands of the skilled." In possession of greater bargaining leverage, skilled workers were sometimes (as in the spring of 1938) more willing to strike than their less skilled companions.

Perhaps because of employees' greater pride in workmanship and improved working conditions, nationalized aviation firms experienced less agitation and social tension than either aviation firms that remained in private hands or the automobile industry. Although the tensions were somewhat mitigated, the nationalized sector still confronted labor difficulties. CGT delegates, who were supposed to facilitate labor-management relations, took advantage of their position to escape from the factory.[56] An anonymous whistle-blower, whose charges were generally confirmed by state inspectors, wrote that the authority of union delegates at SNCASO at Suresnes (Société nationale de constructions aéronautiques du sud-ouest, formerly Blériot) often surpassed that of the foremen.[57] Union representatives and even other union members had stopped working; according to this informant, forty to fifty workers out of fourteen hundred no longer produced. "Contrary to the orders of management," the delegates slowed work rhythms and left the factory whenever they wished without receiving permission.

A military technician, who inspected a number of nationalized aviation companies in the Paris suburbs, assessed the situation at SNCASO in Courbevoie.

> The authority of the *maîtrise* is now nearly nonexistent. The major part of the supervisory personnel and technicians, seeing that they

were not supported by management, joined the CGT and cooperated (*faire corps*) with the workers to maintain the slowdown of production. However, some would like to demonstrate their authority.[58]

At the Courbevoie plant, delegates had four rooms, desks, and a telephone at their disposal. On the walls, a list of all personnel was posted, and union representatives could summon a worker during working hours. Delegates left the factory when they desired and were able to paralyze production very quickly, as the 30 November 1938 strike would show. They had also organized a cooperative that could provision workers during factory occupations. At Sautter-Harlé—an armaments maker with approximately a thousand workers—the management agreed to permit six union delegates to use a room but soon concluded "that what the delegates wanted was a room at their disposal the entire day and beyond the control of management."[59]

Even when aviation delegates attempted to aid production, their advice often went unheeded. For instance, in September 1938, despite delegates' promises that workers would labor Saturday and Sunday, many failed to appear for weekend duty.[60] Discipline in the plants became lax and authority was frequently defied. At Gnôme et Rhône, an aviation firm in which the government had partial control (*participation minoritaire*), a worker complained of the reinforced work discipline that followed the Jacomet arbitration agreement of the spring of 1938.[61] Before the arbitration over worktime and wages, workers could move freely in the factory and go to the toilet when they desired. After the Jacomet decision, however, thirty guards were posted, toilets and dressing rooms were closely watched, and the authority of the foremen was strengthened. The atmosphere had changed considerably since June 1936, according to Trotskyists; management became bold enough to fire workers, hire informers, and employ guards who were former boxers and street fighters. It increased the number of time clocks and imposed "insolent and definitive workshop rules" against "entering the dressing rooms before the whistle." Workers could be dismissed for eating on the job or making unauthorized trips to the toilets. The foremen were returned to their previous role as "prison guards," and, of course, the power of the delegates was restricted. The CGT protested in June that it had lost control over hiring, which was now in the hands of the company union, Association des ouvriers Gnôme et Rhône.[62] CGT membership dropped 25 percent as workers abandoned the Confédération for the company union, which the Left linked to the right-wing Syndicat professionnel.[63] Prior to the Jacomet arbitration, all ten men in one shift had been in the CGT, but in July only five remained and seven had joined the company union (two wage earners apparently belonged to both unions); a revolutionary syndicalist estimated that at least 10 percent of the union members at the factory belonged to both organizations. Thus, as in Barcelona, a worker's membership in a union did not mean a commitment to its ideology. In addition, after the Jacomet decision the forty-five-hour week was established and divided into five weeks of six days' labor followed by three weeks of five working days. Recovery, or the making up, of holidays was facilitated, and workers were assured of only one full weekend every eight weeks.

Indiscipline was not limited to blue-collar workers. Early in the Popular Front, R. Caudron, an aviation industrialist, criticized the "poor output" of white-collar workers in his research department and emphasized the need for reinforced discipline and order:

> We must have a responsible person who can watch output, who forces [the personnel] to be on time, who restrains their overly indulgent exits and absences, who controls visits . . . in a word, who puts our house in order.
>
> Our 170 employees have missed a total of 1,239 hours of work in November [1936], of which 458 hours were attributed to sickness.[64]

Unproductive aviation workers, like lax autoworkers, could not easily be dismissed.

In aviation firms under greater governmental control, senior administrators condemned "la vague générale de paresse" and planned to use overtime and "especially to strengthen the authority of the factories' management."[65] In the Paris region, it should be noted, the tension between workers and their immediate superiors was intensified by the narrowing of pay differentials between the two categories. Workers sometimes earned more money than the foreman who directed them. An engineering professor, who advocated "scientific" organization of work, inveighed against the "tendency to level wages, which therefore discouraged the best [workers]."[66]

Aviation workers resisted piecework and incentives for production. At the beginning of 1938 the Minister of Aviation declared that aircraft production had been hindered, not primarily because of the forty-hour week, but rather because of the "insufficiency of hourly production in the nationalized factories."[67] Aviation industrialists, like state engineers, demanded that output be augmented. At Gnôme et Rhône, workers agreed among themselves to limit production: when management wanted to quicken output, "unforeseeable incidents and machine stoppages showed the impossibility of increasing the pace."[68] Gnôme et Rhône workers knew how many pieces per hour their neighbors had completed, and pro-Communist *La Vie ouvrière* declared that these workers refused "to accept an incentive to overproduce."[69] After the Jacomet decision of April 1938, Gnôme et Rhône personnel were no longer able to learn the amount that their colleagues earned from piecework, and pay was distributed in secret.[70] By September, Gnôme et Rhône's production rhythm was much greater but used fewer personnel than that of the Société nationale de constructions de moteurs (SNCM), whose nationalization in May 1937 was responsible for increased union power on the shop floor. At Salmson, a privately owned aviation firm employing twelve hundred workers, the CGT claimed that its secretary had been unjustly dismissed and that its delegates were prevented from exercising their functions.[71] These actions by the management did not "encourage the workers to augment the pace of production," and the CGT asserted that "to obtain a normal output, one must have a normal attitude toward the workers." Even the president of the SNCM at Argenteuil, who was a strong advocate of nationalization, alerted his personnel that "in the factory, one works."[72] Although René Belin, the CGT leader who represented the union on the administrative council of the

SNCM, denied that he had "imposed" a resolution concerning the length of the workday and output on workers, he nonetheless stated that "a satisfactory output" should be maintained "in the aviation factories and especially at the Lorraine [SNCM]."[73]

While managers of the nationalized aviation firms granted workers increased wages, high overtime pay, August vacations, improved health and safety conditions, professional reeducation, special transportation to work, and even CGT participation in hiring, they nevertheless insisted on tying pay levels to production through a system of piecework or incentives. Officials in both public and private enterprises were convinced that incentives were necessary in a situation where, despite the purchase of new machinery and the addition of new personnel, productivity frequently declined. A detailed investigation of one factory in 1937 placed the decline at 5 percent, which appears to be slight.[74] However, given that aviation was attracting some of the highest paid workers in a period of growing international tension, even a 5 percent drop was significant. Furthermore, the 5 percent figure did not take into account social conflicts or strikes. Although other reports claimed that individual output had not decreased, more detailed and voluminous documentation indicates that extremely serious problems of output and productivity existed in Parisian aviation plants during the Popular Front. Officials determined that productivity had dropped sharply between June and October 1936 and then stabilized at relatively low levels in 1937.[75] At the still private Breguet plant at Vélizy "the work teams usually labored lethargically . . . slowdowns, negligence, and pilfering (*freinage et coulage*) became widespread."[76] At the Riom trial, Stéphane Thouvenot—a young engineer who obtained high positions in the nationalized sector both during the Popular Front and the liberation—stated that "nationalization took place in a troubled political and social atmosphere and failed industrially. The main cause of the failure was the relations between workers and bosses." A recent study of the industry concurs.

> On the whole, the nationalized enterprises produced 395 airplanes in 1937 in contrast to 483 in 1936 in the workshops that they inherited. During this period, their average yearly personnel rose from

> 14,220 to 14,894 workers and foremen, or 37.7 employees per plane as opposed to 29.44 in the preceding year, which meant a 28 percent reduction of output. Certainly, this was offset by retooling and reorganization. . . . Certainly, the planes were more complicated: For all that, the net reduction of output was 11 percent. More than their private competitors because of their role as "social showcases," the nationalized firms experienced problems resulting from the balance of forces established after the strikes of 1936. According to a confidential report of February 1938, the production of Morane-Saulnier fighters at the Bourges plant was thus delayed because of the reluctance of the work teams to change from traditional Hanriot manufactures to the Morane-Saulnier, which had been subcontracted fifteen months earlier.[77]

In 1938 the employers' organization, Constructeurs de cellules, appealed to the Minister of Aviation for "the development of piecework."[78] The president of the Chambre syndicale de moteurs also recommended piecework. In November 1938 a handwritten memo on the departure of skilled workers from Renault established that one major reason for the skilled workers' mobility was that work was less strenuous in airplane production and "in aviation, piecework is only a disguised hourly wage. Since competition is minimal, the taxpayer pays the bill."[79] Renault listed twenty-three skilled drillers (*fraiseurs*) whose piecework earnings were substantially less than management desired. Metallurgical employers charged that "piecework [in aviation] is practically abandoned. The Fédération des métaux (CGT) constrains workers not to go beyond a 'ceiling' of fixed salaries."[80]

An unnamed informant denounced piecework in aviation as "a mockery." He cited the example of a task performed by several workers in four minutes. When one worker completed the same job in sixteen minutes, the others consequently reduced their pace.[81] A report written by an engineering professor complained that "deplorable habits" had become rooted in aviation; workers were appealing over the heads of their own management directly to the Minister of Aviation.

> Thanks to the atmosphere in the aviation ministry and thanks also to the demagogy of certain directors, consulting committees [composed of an equal number of labor and management representatives], which could have promoted collaboration in another era,

> helped to disorganize the firms. Certain workers went so far as to call for complete control of the administration [of the factory].[82]

In a personal letter to the minister, B. Rouzé (the production manager of the SNCAN [Société nationale de constructions aéronautiques du nord] and a member of the Radical party) criticized union delegates who interfered when foremen disciplined workers.[83]

A military technician, visiting nationalized factories in the Paris suburbs, reported deliberate slowdowns by workers. The SNCASO plant at Courbevoie was "a model of passive resistance to production."[84] One worker who was expected to produce one piece every hour made only six pieces in seven hours. When challenged, he demanded that the production manager finish the part in the allotted time. The manager then produced the piece in front of the worker in "21 minutes without hurrying." The military technician concluded that the worker's slowness more than tripled costs and that sanctions should be applied if he did not increase his output.

A young engineer made even graver charges concerning the Courbevoie plant, which was headed by Marcel Bloch. The engineer's letter was forwarded to the Minister of Aviation by Lucien Lamoureux, a Radical party deputy, who had supported the Popular Front at its inception. Lamoureux became increasingly hostile to the coalition of the Left and was eventually one of its most resolute opponents in the Radical party. An investigation undertaken by an important official of the ministry, Thouvenot, verified the engineer's charges.[85] A prototype of the fighter plane M.B. 150, which had taken 18,000 hours to build at the beginning of 1936, required 40,000 hours in 1938. The unnamed technician believed that productivity had declined for several reasons. First, since May 1936 salaries were no longer linked to output. Thus, "the good and the bad worker had equal pay." Second, "the unions became strong" and effectively threatened strikes if dissatisfied; the disciplinary authority of the supervisory personnel had therefore been decisively weakened. Other reports concerning nationalized aviation reiterated that "ill will" reigned in certain plants and recommended increasing the weight of piecework in the workers' total salary.[86] They remarked that the work rules of the collective bargaining agreement assigned workers to a specific *atelier,* thereby obstructing management's flexibility.[87] An admiral criticized a nationalized company for high costs, which were caused partially by a lack of planning and by what he termed "ouvriers peu travailleurs."[88]

Aviation workers vigorously defended the weekend and the forty-hour week. As a result, French aviation production was slowed and weakened in comparison with the German industry, where workers labored between fifty and sixty hours per week.[89] In some German metallurgical factories, wage earners worked ten hours per day, and several mechanical construction firms were permitted to operate sixty to seventy-two hours per week. The point here is not to echo simplistic Vichyite accusations that the Popular Front was responsible for the French defeat in 1940 but rather to show the tenacity of resistance to work in a period of heightened international tension. The persistence of refusals suggests that in 1938 the nationalization of the masses was still incomplete in France. Given the history of the Second World War, it is regrettable that German workers did not imitate their French comrades.

In 1938 the French government and employers pressured the workers to work overtime to close the gap. However workers resisted these demands for several reasons of varying importance. The ideology of both the Communist and anti-Communist factions of the CGT clearly asserted that overtime was unnecessary and exploitative when unemployment existed. This discourse on unemployment regarded overtime as an attack on unemployed workers' right to and need for a job. Nevertheless the CGT position, shared of course by the rest of the Popular Front, did not take into account the conditions in an advanced economy, where the lack of skilled workers and technicians created bottlenecks in production. The short supply of skilled workers was aggravated by the participation of the CGT in hiring: "In the nationalized aviation factories, delegates controlled employment. From a professional point of view this recruitment left something to be desired, and a CGT or PCF card was often required."[90] At a SNCASO factory in the Parisian suburbs, CGT delegates hired only union members who (it was charged) were often Communists. Although the regional hiring office (Office départemental de placement) protested CGT hiring practices, it proved incapable of reducing CGT control.[91] Employers feared even lower productivity if the unions took complete control of hiring and firing.

Workers in aviation and other industries not only resisted overtime and attempts to lengthen the workweek through solidarity with the unemployed but, more important, because they wanted to protect their weekend and the forty-hour week. Despite claims by many in the Popular Front that workers would be willing to sacrifice for national defense, the authorities found it difficult to extend the workweek beyond forty hours. A governmental report affirmed that one reason planes were not being completed on schedule was that legislation had restricted overtime.[92] It attributed insufficient exports, in part, to inflexibility concerning extra hours. In February 1938 high government officials claimed that only several thousand aviation workers were performing overtime, and more effort was needed if delays were to be reduced.[93] On 2 March 1938 *Syndicats* reported that the "metallurgical workers are too attached to the forty-hour week to let it be violated." Pressure grew in March as Henry Potez, other aviation industrialists, and military officers demanded more hours of labor without compensatory time off: in a schedule of five days of eight hours, they requested that a worker who worked nine hours one day would no longer be able to labor only seven hours the next.[94] Again in June 1938, top aviation officials stressed "the extreme difficulty that they confronted in making overtime acceptable in private industry."

An investigation claimed that workers' refusal of overtime had "nearly paralyzed overall production."[95] The inquiry calculated that on average aviation workers performed only three hours of overtime per year and had the right to recover these hours. Wage earners' insistence on this right made overtime "nothing more than a costly shift of the schedule."[96] In public, Popular Front organizations continued to insist that the union was willing to make the workers labor overtime for national defense. The workers, it stated, were willing to contribute to the antifascist cause, giving to the Spanish republic an extra hour without pay. In private, though, the CGT leader, Ambroise Croizat, admitted that the forty-hour week hindered aircraft production and that overtime was necessary, but he considered that "the working masses" were "insufficiently informed of industrial necessities."[97] Looking back during the Second World War, a clandestine issue of the Socialist newspaper, *Le Populaire,* reproached workers for failing to work overtime during the Popular Front.[98]

In March 1937 and again in the spring of 1938, strikes erupted in various Parisian metallurgical firms, including aviation plants, over wage issues and the extension of the forty-hour week. During these strikes and others, aviation workers sometimes demonstrated an indifference to quality and even a hostility toward the means of production. In many workshops, work was halted without concern for the consequences that the stoppage would have on production rhythms.[99] After the March–April 1938 strikes, the privately owned Société des avions Caudron reported 6,379 francs of damages. At the Société industrielle des téléphones, an electrical installation damaged during the occupation accidentally electrocuted one worker.[100] Renault also claimed extensive "violence," "damages," and "thefts" during these occupations: windows were broken; raw materials wasted; and spark plugs, lamps, scissors, clothes, thermometers, and batteries were either missing or stolen.[101]

Historians of various political persuasions have stated that during the strikes of the spring of 1938 the managements of both public and private aviation companies rejected the union's offer to work forty-five hours per week.[102] The aviation employers' rejection of the forty-five-hour week was altogether exceptional, however, and stemmed from the high costs of the CGT demands. The Jacomet arbitration later reduced the costs of overtime pay, and the forty-five-hour week was accepted, though only in aviation.[103] Thus, aviation directors—both public and private—supported changes in the forty-five-hour week. Their attitude was similar to that of the vast majority of the French bourgeoisie, who felt that the forty-hour week was legislated laziness that put France at a disadvantage in international competition or that the forty-hour week should at the very least be modified to suit the needs of each specific industry in order not to hinder production. Throughout the spring and summer of 1938 aviation managements pushed for longer working hours. In March 1938 the administrator of a nationalized enterprise, the SNCASE (Société nationale de constructions aéronautiques du sud-est), insisted on "the necessity, in order to accelerate production, to work forty-five hours . . . in the planning department and in tool fabrication."[104] Other aviation industrialists asserted that, to be effective, the forty-five-hour week had to be extended to suppliers of raw materials, semifinished products, and accessories.[105] In July 1938 the Chambre syndicale des constructeurs de moteurs d'avions debated whether to accept only one hundred hours of overtime per year or to strive for "a permanent end" to the restrictions on the workweek:

> Mr. X thinks that it is not more overtime but a permanent repeal that must be obtained.
>
> I would share his opinion if this permanent repeal had some possibility of being enacted, which it does not. Therefore if we insist on it, which we will certainly not get, we risk losing the advantages of the extra credit of one hundred hours of overtime. Sometimes when you want to do something better, it turns out worse.[106]

Again in the summer and fall of 1938, aviation workers fought against overtime and battled to save the weekend or at least two consecutive days without work. The forty-five-hour week in aviation was generally divided into five days of nine hours each, despite the desires of many employers—and Léon Blum—who would have preferred to divide the forty-five- and even the forty-hour week into six days.[107] They argued that productivity and the likelihood of overtime were often greater in a six-day week. Important industrialists claimed that work during Saturday was preferable to working at night for several reasons. Productivity was lower at night, and it was harder to watch the shop floor since fewer supervisory personnel were available. In addition, public transportation was infrequent, and female workers were prohibited by law from work at night. Union activists nevertheless asserted that workers would "until the bitter end . . . resolutely defend" the workweek arranged in five days of eight hours each against that in six days of six hours and forty minutes each.[108] In June 1938 the anti-Communist CGT members of the firm La Précision moderne were determined to defend "the 5 × 8, threatened by decrees."[109] The Fédération des métaux also opposed the extension of the workday. In October 1938 workers at both public and private aviation firms left their jobs at 5:00 P.M. instead of 6:00 P.M. to protest overtime: "The workers of a number of aviation companies—Farman, Caudron, Potez, Breguet—refused to do more than 8 hours of work. Completely disregarding ministerial decisions and in violation of the law, they left their workshops when their 8 hours were finished."[110]

Sanctions were taken against aviation workers at Hispano-Suiza and Caudron who had "as early as 15 October refused to do overtime allowed by the Jacomet [arbitration] decision." Lasting less than a week, these sanctions were effective; 93 percent of the personnel was soon working forty-five hours per week. At Caudron the government authorized the dismissal of six hundred fifty workers who refused to do the legally authorized overtime. Shortly thereafter, most workers accepted the forty-five-hour week, significantly divided into five days of nine hours. Thus the weekend was conserved.

It should be mentioned that this agitation against extra work came after the Munich agreements of 30 September 1938, which the PCF actively opposed; the walk-outs and work stoppages in October may indicate some PCF influence among aviation workers. Employers asserted that the unions, in a large number of cases, prevented workers from performing overtime. Before the agreements were signed, union opposition had softened somewhat, but after Munich, the *syndicats* became intransigent. "We can cite examples of factories where workers now refuse to do the hours of overtime that they had accepted before 1 October. In aviation, this change of attitude is public."[111] The unions had agreed to work on 1 October, a Saturday, but then reneged and refused.

In light of the attempts by workers in aviation and other industries to defend the forty-hour week and the weekend—both before and after the Munich agreements—the Communist influence had only marginal importance. Workers, most of whom were not party-affiliated, fought to defend the gains of June 1936 regardless of party positions. Employers listed thirteen firms where workers refused, well before the Munich agreements, to perform overtime that had been approved by the Inspecteur du travail.[112] Even when legally required to do so, aviation workers sometimes refused to work Saturdays and Sundays to recover holidays that had occurred during the working week. In May 1937, Gnôme et Rhône personnel nearly unanimously opposed work on Saturday and the recovery of holidays: in a referendum, 95 percent refused to work on Saturday and desired a normal weekend.[113] In the week that followed Easter vacation, "certain workers refused Saturday labor, which was intended to recover the loss of worktime caused by the Monday closing."[114] The Gnôme et Rhône management dismissed twenty-four workers who allegedly did not work on Saturday.[115] In May 1938 and again in August 1938, *La Vie ouvrière* reported workers' resistance to the end of the forty-hour week.

On 1 September 1938, when international tensions were rising, the Société d'optique et de mécanique de haute précision—which made instruments used in national defense—received an authorization from the government permitting five hours of overtime and a workweek of forty-five hours.[116] The management established that the workday would begin at 0730 instead of 0800 and finish at 1800 instead of 1730. On Monday 5 September, at the workshops on the boulevard Davout, 59 percent of the workers disobeyed the new work schedule by arriving late and 58 percent departed early. On Tuesday, 57 percent of the workers arrived late. At the Croix Nivert shops, 36 percent arrived late on Monday, and 59 percent on Tuesday. On Wednesday, 59 to 72 percent of the work force were absent for part of the day.[117] Significantly, management noted that "the great majority" of skilled workers disregarded the new schedule and lacked discipline. Thus as in Barcelona, revolts against work were not limited to the lower strata of the working class during the Popular Front. Skilled workers' disobedience "made it impossible to work normally during the overtime ordered by the prime minister." Other companies reported numerous refusals by workers to obey the legal extension of the work week. Throughout 1938 a poor "social climate" prevented intensive aircraft production, and the inferior quality and quantity of labor caused a "bottleneck" in the aviation industry.[118]

The threat of retaliatory strikes often prevented aviation management from firing disobedient or unnecessary laborers. CGT participation in hiring new personnel in the aviation industry made the problem of featherbedding nearly insoluble. By the beginning of 1938 many aviation firms had "a personnel larger than their needs, whereas for social reasons they were not able to lay off any worker. Output has been affected and production has fallen to half of what it could be considering the true capacity of the factories."[119] In February 1938 the chief administrator (*administrateur-délégué*) of Gnôme et Rhône stated that the aviation industry could double production without hiring additional workers. *Usine,* the employers' periodical, remarked that aviation workers "produce much less than previously but earn twice as much."[120] The readiness of wage earners in aviation and other industries to defend their jobs and sources of income should not, of course, be confused with their eagerness to work in factories, as the continuing problems of output and discipline have demonstrated.

The Parisian construction industry, especially the large projects like the extension of the métro, the building of a stadium, and the erection of the exposition for the 1937 World's Fair, exhibited problems similar to those of the aviation and automotive industries. Yet the construction firms' smaller size may have made their struggles over the length of the working day, overtime, output, CGT control of hiring, and discipline even more violent than in other industries. As has been seen, the May and June strike movements, which began in metallurgy, quickly affected construction workers who demanded an ambitious program of public works, the forty-hour week, improved working conditions, an end to overtime, the limitation of piecework, and the abolition of the *tâcheronnat.* Workers and their unions were particularly concerned with job security in a sector where structural and seasonal unemployment affected 23 percent of the work force in February 1936. Yet even after many demands were granted, agitation persisted. The May and June movements created a new social situation in which productivity and output dropped significantly on construction sites. At the beginning of October 1936 in a conversation with Joseph Caillaux, the president of the control commission of the World's Fair (*exposition*) of 1937, M. Labbé, who was the commissioner for the exposition, noted that since the "events" of the spring, workers had lost their eagerness (*ardeur*) to work and had engaged in slowdown strikes (*grèves perlées*).[121] Labbé doubted that the exposition could open on the scheduled date of 1 May 1937, and he appointed two CGT representatives to boost the work effort. In the second half of 1936 and in 1937, almost all firms still complained of "the insufficiency of workers' output."[122] Laborers took twice as long to complete certain jobs in 1937 as they had early in 1936.[123] A letter from the Minister of Commerce and Industry declared that if output between February and May 1936 had been maintained, a job that actually required 264,700 hours to complete could have been finished in only 78,710 hours.[124] Piecework was effectively ended on many construction sites, and employers lamented that their personnel had lost "le goût du travail."[125] The *Rapport général,* presented by Commissioner Labbé in 1938, declared that the exposition's most serious difficulty was "the slowing down of output," which resulted from "an impairment of the willingness, of the conscientiousness of the labor" of the building workers.[126] Before May 1936 many projects were one month ahead of schedule, whereas by December 1936 delays of five months were reported.

Companies that were extending the métro and building a stadium in the suburbs experienced similar declines in output and productivity. In October 1937 the management of the métro extension to the Gare d'Austerlitz contrasted "the frame of mind of 1934, when the tendency was to increase output, with the frame of mind of 1936."[127] In the fall of 1936, the masons quit work early and engaged in slowdown strikes that reduced output 90 to 95 percent. Many workers increased their snack time from ten to thirty minutes.[128] Output dropped approximately 37 percent and even further as "our workers began to foresee the completion of certain jobs and, consequently, layoffs." The enterprises charged with the construction of the stadium at St.-Cloud finished in March 1938 instead of July 1937, as originally planned.[129] Bricklayers needed 256 hours to complete a chimney that should have taken only 123 hours.[130] Employers complained that workers took longer to dress, undress, eat, go to the toilet, and take a break.

The rapid fall of productivity can be partially attributed to the climate of disobedience that reigned at the construction sites. Workers were able to defy the normal industrial chain of command without fear of reprisals. According to *Usine,* at the World's Fair, "no one" was "able to command, not the bosses, not the government, not the unions."[131] On many construction sites at the exposition the employers' authority had disappeared, but the question of the union's authority was more complex. Although workers often disobeyed or ignored high-ranking CGT leaders, lower-ranking union delegates did exercise considerable power at the fair and at other large construction projects where they controlled both hiring and speed of production. An exposition administrator testified that "during the entire project, a day did not pass without the site being disturbed by the arrival (during working hours) of CGT officials and delegates who set up meetings, gave orders, and organized production."[132] Other unions charged that the CGT monopolized the exposition and constantly violated their right to organize on other construction sites in the Paris region. In July 1936 the secretary of the Masons' Union asked his delegates to check the union cards of workers who had been in arrears for a significant time ("depuis trois assemblées générales"), implying that construction workers were reluctant to pay dues. If behind in payments, members were to be sent to the union hall before they started their jobs.[133]

In August, Albert Bedouce, the Socialist Minister of Public Works, wrote a warning to Blum.

> On a certain number of sites the contractors cannot complete their projects because of a significant decrease in workers' output. I have been informed that in some trades the decline of output stems from methodical acts by delegates. I cannot believe that they are legitimate representatives of working-class organizations. I think that under these circumstances it is indispensable to ask the CGT to intervene immediately through the representatives of the Fédération du bâtiment so that the decline of output—which nothing can justify—does not prevent the execution of the government's plan [of public works for the unemployed]. Action is even more urgent since I have been told that employers' organizations, in order to finish work in progress, would be willing to accept contracts that limit output. This output, even if higher than presently, would be much lower than before the recent [social] legislation.[134]

Early in 1937, Prime Minister Blum sent his right-hand man, Jules Moch, to deal with the chaotic situation at the World's Fair, which was becoming an acute embarrassment to the CGT-supported government. In March 1937 Moch endorsed the de facto control of the CGT over many sites and "counseled hiring by the unions in order to avoid incidents."[135] The Socialist government evidently believed that it would be more fruitful to work with the CGT, not against it, in the battle to finish the exposition on schedule. The PCF and the CGT were also anxious to have the fair open on its 1 May scheduled date in order not to embarrass the Popular Front. *La Vie ouvrière* asserted that all comrades wished for the success of the fair, and R. Arrachard, the secretary general of the Fédération du bâtiment, declared that the exposition "*must be . . . and will be ready on the first of May.*"[136] *Syndicats,* the anti-Communist rival of *La Vie ouvrière,* wanted the World's Fair to be renamed the *exposition de travail* instead of the *exposition des arts et techniques* and stated that it would open on 1 May. The Communists also asserted that the construction must be accelerated and that the project must be inaugurated on its planned date.[137] Writing in *Humanité,* H. Raynaud, secretary of the Union des syndicats ouvriers de la région parisienne, was certain that "*the Parisian workers*" were "*capable of finishing the fair on the determined date*" (italics in original). On 12 February the Communist journalist Paul Vaillant-Couturier assured his readers that "the exposition will open 1 May. It will be a holiday of work." In March the CGT leader, Toudic, formulated the slogan, The World's Fair is a battle of the workers and of the Popular Front against fascism and the bosses.

Yet, as in Barcelona, despite published appeals production lagged, and on 1 February 1937 the major leaders of the Popular Front gathered to address the assembled workers of the World's Fair. Blum declared, "The exposition will be the triumph of the working class, the Popular Front, and liberty. It will show that a democratic regime is superior to dictatorship. . . . The reputation of the Popular Front is at stake, and I tell you frankly that work on Saturday and Sunday is necessary."[138] Léon Jouhaux, the head of the CGT, told the crowd that "sacrifices must be made." Marcel Gitton, one of the PCF's top officials, addressed the audience: "The exposition will open 1 May, the day of the *fête du travail.* Its success will be a factor in the strengthening of the Popular Front. The fair will be a victory of thousands of workers and all the laboring masses. The enemies of the Popular Front yearn for the failure of the exposition. The workers want it to be an unprecedented success."

Regardless of the pleas and exhortations of the leaders, the exposition opened far behind schedule. The CGT refused to lengthen the forty-hour week. Thus, two or three shifts per day had to be organized, and the output of these additional shifts declined significantly for several reasons. First, the shortage of skilled laborers led to the hiring of inexperienced workers for the second and third shifts. The CGT wholeheartedly endorsed this practice and even forbade employers to utilize some of their most qualified personnel who did not belong to the union. Of the four cement workers one firm was forced to hire, only one had real experience.[139] Much of the work completed by the second and third shifts was poorly executed and often had to be redone. Second, the night shift had inherent difficulties with lighting, and its abnormal schedule was typically much less productive than the day shifts. Third, the unions opposed the use of technical advances and preferred manual techniques in order to create jobs; they refused, for instance, to operate spray-painting machines.[140]

Although high-ranking CGT officials promised that work on Saturday and Sunday would be permitted within the framework of the forty-hour week, in practice CGT delegates at the exposition largely banned weekend work. Delegates and workers ignored pleas from both the CGT and *Humanité* that weekend work was necessary to open the fair on time. Several weeks after Blum's speech, a carpenters' delegate insisted that no work be done on Saturday and Sunday.[141] The painters of the American pavilion were denied permission to work Saturday and Sunday; shortly afterward, an electric transformer was damaged, presumably to protect the right to a work-free weekend.[142] According to the official report of the exposition, the union leaders were unable to "deliver" on their promises of weekend labor: "Even when an understanding [on weekend work] was reached . . . the following Saturday a counterorder, frequently inexplicable, prohibited the shifts from entering the sites."[143] In addition, workers refused to recover days lost to inclement weather or holidays that occurred during the working week.[144]

CGT delegates often set production quotas and limited

piecework. Many of the workers, hired through the CGT's *bourse du travail,* had little interest in improving their output. It was quite difficult to fire these wage earners because of the power of the union and the administration's fear of incidents, which sometimes did occur. When the management of the Algerian exhibit dismissed nine roofers, workers retaliated by occupying the site, despite the presence of police.[145] Officials then decided to keep the dismissed laborers on the job. Although Arrachard, secretary general of the Fédération du bâtiment, claimed that he intervened frequently so that workers would produce normally, his interventions seem to have been ineffective.[146] On 13 May 1937, almost two weeks after the scheduled opening date had passed, Jules Moch told Arrachard that the "comedy had gone on long enough," and that order must be restored.[147] In June 1937 Moch threatened to "go public" and tell the press that the union was responsible for the delays if work on the museums were not quickly completed. Some foreign nations attempted to employ non-French workers to finish their pavilions, but the CGT effectively opposed not only this practice but even the hiring of provincial French workers.[148] The Americans wanted to finish their pavilion by 4 July, their Independence Day, and they concluded a contract with a Belgian firm to finish a metal roof because of the "impossibility of obtaining a sufficient output from French workers."[149] With the agreement of the exposition's labor inspector, however, the CGT demanded the hiring of a certain number of its workers. These newly employed French laborers "have only disorganized the [construction] site and discouraged the Belgian workers by their absolute inactivity, resembling a slowdown strike." The erection of the roof took twice as much time as planned. When provincial workers were employed, Parisian unions insisted that they return to the provinces immediately after the building was finished.[150]

Struggles over the control of hiring, production rhythms, and weekend work produced a climate of violence at the exposition and other construction sites. The tense atmosphere is easy to understand since workers and union delegates consistently undermined the authority of employers and their foremen; moreover, many employers at the exposition headed small firms and could not afford the cost overruns that higher salaries, low productivity, and CGT control of hiring entailed. One particularly combative employer, Jules Verger, had dismissed a shop steward and had apparently ignored the collective bargaining agreement. When his firm was hit by a strike, he asserted that the fair had become a "revolutionary experiment." "Since last October [1936], I have been fighting against the revolutionary unions. These last ten months have been marred by a thousand incidents of various kinds. The majority of my [construction] sites have been attacked and sometimes sabotaged."[151] Arbitrators condemned these violations of the right to work and agreed that the *chantiers* of Verger and Delporte must be protected by the authorities.[152] Verger, later to become a militant *pétainiste,* reported that nearly finished work was sabotaged at the Pavillon des vins.

On construction sites other than Verger's, CGT members physically prevented non-union personnel from working and obstructed their legal right to work. Sometimes police were called to protect non-union personnel; certain workers even carried arms on the job.[153] At a stadium construction site in St.-Cloud, a worker knifed his foreman.[154] The World's Fair of 1937 opened on 24 May with much work incomplete, two and one-half months behind schedule; the CGT finally inaugurated its own pavilion, the Maison du travail, on 1 July 1937, two months late.[155]

Publicly, the Popular Front coalition attempted to ignore the workers' reduced productivity, violence, and struggles against work. According to the Left, the bosses were to blame for delays and production problems in the industries examined. The Communists, the CGT, and even the Socialists charged innumerable times in their publications that fascist bosses were sabotaging production to damage the Popular Front and deliver the nation to Hitler and Mussolini. *Syndicats* accused employers of staging work slow-downs in a "deceitful struggle" against the Popular Front.[156] *Humanité* declared that Renault workers only wanted to work, and *Le Populaire* charged that the goal of the bosses was to slow down and sabotage production. These charges were largely polemical; the bosses and the "two hundred families"—the Radical slogan for the wealthiest families in supposed control of the French economy—were a convenient symbol. Undoubtedly some businessmen and cautious savers did export their capital, but as yet little evidence exists to sustain accusations that the French bourgeoisie, perhaps the founder of modern nationalism, willingly sabotaged its own industries for the benefit of foreign powers.

The Left's charges and its ideology of sabotage and conspiracy by the bosses or the 200 families hid the structural problems of boring, repetitive, and sometimes dangerous wage labor in a modern industrial society. Even with regard to the World's Fair, the Left continued its triumphant discourse. Significantly, the CGT's pavilion was named la maison du travail.

> [It is] eminently representative of the entire conception of the French union movement. [The working class] will continue to be at home in the maison du travail. Workers from all over the world will be coming to Paris, and all the visitors will discover there a specifically working-class environment. . . . They will not be able to avoid the conclusion that a new world is being built and that a new civilization, based on work, is being created under our eyes.[157]

With few exceptions, the Left refused to admit that work discipline sometimes collapsed amid the new social situation created by the May and June strikes and the inauguration of the more lenient Popular Front governments. This new social environment encouraged workers' defiance of management and sometimes even of the union. It was usually not bosses but workers who refused weekend work, who were inexperienced in their jobs, who defied authority, and who often slowed production. After the war, Léon Blum criticized workers at the exposition and in armaments for refusing overtime and decreasing productivity. He asserted that workers should have risen above a backward and egoistic *patronat* and, by laboring hard, set an example for the entire nation.[158]

Like their Barcelonan counterparts, Parisian wage earners continued to avoid workspace and struggled to lessen worktime during their Popular Front. Direct and indirect resistance persisted under the governments of the Left. Perhaps the most fundamental and difficult problems for the Popular Fronts came not from their declared enemies but from those they purportedly represented. An analysis of the Left's encounter with popular and more specifically working-class culture continues in the next chapter.

12
THE PROBLEMS OF UNEMPLOYMENT AND LEISURE

Publicly and officially, both Popular Fronts fought not only against workers' resistances but against licentious popular culture as well. Both leftist coalitions used their own resources and those of the state to solve what they considered the problems of unemployment and leisure. Unlike its Spanish counterpart, which was engaged in a civil war, the French Left was joined by some of its right-wing opponents who also wished to civilize, domesticate, and curb the idleness, drinking, gaming, and smoking of the workers. To replace these practices, both the French Left and Right attempted to promote new desires and new consumerist needs, while struggling against workers' indifference to production.

In the industries examined, the French Left did put one important part of its productivist ideology into practice: employment of the jobless. As in Barcelona, the desire to share worktime was deeply rooted among many Parisian workers, who continued to initiate strikes to defend the jobs of colleagues who had been dismissed. Because of the genuinely popular effort to share employment, the payrolls of the exposition increased from 5,000 workers in December 1936 to 24,800 at the end of April 1937. Renault and the aviation firms in the Paris area added literally thousands of new workers. Despite these additions, the World's Fair opened considerably behind schedule, productivity at Renault did not improve, and airplane production was sluggish. The Left nevertheless continued to assert that the unemployed wanted only to work. More accurately, the unemployed had less desire to labor in factories than need of jobs, or more precisely, steady incomes. Some industrialists asserted that hiring the jobless did more economic harm than good: in May 1936 the Third Employers' Conference on Apprenticeship declared that in 1933 sugar producers had hired 4,100 unemployed workers and that their labor was characterized by low productivity, "inaptitude" for work, and high turnover.[1] In addition, certain of the newly engaged demonstrated little "ardor for their work" and became "elements of discord and agitation in the factories." At construction sites throughout the Paris region, workers deliberately slowed their pace as the projects approached completion in order to receive an income for a longer period. At one project, CGT delegates opposed the hiring of qualified workers from other construction sites so that their own workers could take turns sharing unemployment benefits.[2] As in Spain, the Left's discourse on unemployment masked the reality of a situation in which many workers, both employed and unemployed, often wanted a source of income more than they desired to produce in jobs from which they derived little satisfaction or social prestige.

Throughout the Popular Front, officials in the Ministry of Labor lamented the lack of discipline among the jobless. A naval engineer working in this ministry concluded that employed, skilled workers had a "physical endurance" and an "eagerness to work" that were "generally much greater" than those of the unemployed.[3] On 1 July 1936 sanctions were established to encourage the unemployed to complete their reeducation.[4] The authorities wanted to reduce the propensity of the jobless to abandon training centers in spring and summer, a phenomenon that paralleled the increase in strikes by the employed during the same seasons. The labor committee believed that "it seems absolutely necessary to have a wide range of punishments at our disposal" to reduce "indiscipline."

Even when the unemployed completed their training, they were too few in number and the quality of their work was often deficient. According to the Comité de décentralisation industrielle, the forty-hour week had created the need for fifteen thousand additional mechanics, in part because the skilled were leaving the shop floor for desk jobs or promotions to supervisory positions.[5] The newly trained lacked dexterity and quickness and were, of course, less familiar with machinery.[6] Some managers claimed that the unemployed who had been retrained worked not like skilled workers but rather like the unskilled.[7] The labor ministry admitted that even after three months of instruction, an unemployed worker was unable "to produce the same number of pieces as a skilled worker" and could continue to receive unemployment insurance.[8] Employers and government officials alike generally considered retraining programs to be failures.

To further complicate matters, a serious struggle between employers and the CGT arose over the reeducation of the unemployed. Industrialists charged that the jobless who were being trained in the centers of the Syndicat des métaux (a CGT union) were unconcerned with productivity. Even though these workers sincerely believed that they were professionals, "they were absolutely incapable of completing their work in a normal length of time."[9] Therefore, they could be hired only as semiskilled personnel (*ouvriers spécialisés*). According to employers, the CGT school was producing fitters (*ajusteurs*) for aviation plants, "who are only, in truth, semiskilled (*manœuvres spécialisés*) whose training is relatively limited." Industrialists criticized the government for promoting the CGT center and charged that the administration "facilitates the infiltration (*noyautage*) of firms by the Communist Syndicat des métaux." Also, industrialists feared even lower productivity if the union took complete control of hiring and firing. To combat the union's influence, employers wanted to promote their own reeducation centers and to expand them beyond the size of the CGT's program. Employers thought that companies "should become aware of the need to favor workers" who had been retrained in their own centers.

Throughout the Popular Front the Left continued to demand the employment of the jobless not only to increase consumption but also to modernize and rationalize the infrastructure of work and leisure in Paris and its suburbs. The unions and the leftist parties lobbied for a vast campaign of public works and urbanization. The PCF called for the construction of day-care centers, stadiums, and bathing and showering facilities.[10] It argued that projects must be built rapidly to give work to the jobless. *Humanité* praised the accomplishments of PCF municipalities that provided health facilities and social assistance, and it stressed Communists' role as "doers" (*réalisateurs*). *Syndicats,* the CGT review, demanded similar types of projects, and it lauded the work of the Socialist mayor of Suresnes, Henri Sellier, who organized his municipality "rationally," improved health and safety conditions, and built schools.[11] In addition, *Syndicats* esteemed the work of Tony Garnier, the modern architect who built the city hall or, as it was called, *usine municipale* for the Socialist government of Boulogne-Billancourt, where Renault and other major metallurgical firms were located. Thus, unlike its Spanish counterpart, the French Left was able to realize certain reforms within the framework of capitalism and without revolution.

Leftist organizations lauded the modern and progressive urbanism that would replace old residential areas where inadequate housing and unhealthy sanitary conditions promoted high rates of tuberculosis. *Humanité* complained that the destruction of the traditional *quartiers* came "belatedly," and the PCF newspaper desired to improve traffic circulation at the expense of the picturesque.[12] It did not "lose hope that one day skyscrapers which could compete in height with those of New York, would be erected" in Paris. The anti-Communist *Syndicats* joined a dissident Communist, Boris Souvarine, who wholeheartedly endorsed Le Corbusier's *ville radieuse* and wanted to update Parisian roads for automobiles.[13] The Fédération du bâtiment (CGT) also approved Le Corbusier's Pavilion of New Times at the World's Fair of 1937, where the renowned Swiss architect offered "modern civilization the housing that it merits."[14] The progressive architect designed a *ville radieuse* from which workers could "joyously" commute to their factories, a neo-Saint-Simonian city of high rises that was to be inhabited by producers and was characterized by a "stark division between work and play."[15] Toudic, secretary of the regional committee of the Syndicat du bâtiment, admired Le Corbusier's film, *Les bâtisseurs,* praised concrete structures, and believed that the buildings erected by Communist and Socialist municipalities combined both beauty and utility.[16]

Members of the Popular Front frequently appealed for the construction of HBM, which often took the form of high-rise apartments for workers in the suburbs. From 1928 to 1933 France built more low-cost housing than ever before, and by 1936 eighteen thousand HBM housed approximately one hundred thousand people in Paris.[17] Because of the economic crisis and consequent joblessness, the PCF demanded a continued effort to build HBM, which, it claimed, had been particularly beneficial for workers by providing them employment and shelter.[18] Anti-Communist CGT militants praised Baron Haussmann's fight against slums during the Second Empire and demanded the building of HBM to provide work for the unemployed.

The modern urbanism advocated and adopted by the Left emphasized increased mobility and expanded circulation. In this sense, the Left's policies followed the tradition of Haussmann, who had also improved mobility and traffic circulation. Communists, Socialists, and *cégétistes* campaigned for large public works projects to transport people more rapidly around the Paris region. Planners such as Le Corbusier and Lurçat, who were employed by the Left, stressed the advantages of a highly developed system of roads for automobiles. In 1925 Le Corbusier had identified the health of the city with its capacity for movement: "The city that achieves speed achieves success."[19] The architect saw himself bringing order and mobility to the city, as Haussmann had. To fight against unemployment, *Syndicats* advocated "a plan of roads to facilitate the circulation of Parisians in and around their city."[20] Union activists criticized the government for building only one highway when five were needed, and they asserted that great expressways with their own police were necessary to solve "the problem of circulation." *La Vie ouvrière* believed that improved circulation saved lives and that "the builder of roads" was "the bringer of health."[21] According to the militants, the urbanist should illuminate the slums and move traffic through the city. The vision of the pro-Communist activists resembled in some ways that of Louis Renault and other capitalists who also urged "beautiful roads" for automobiles and better circulation in the Paris region.[22]

In addition to highway construction, the partners of the Popular Front recommended improvements in public transportation. The Communists, in particular, advised that the costs of traveling to and from work be substantially reduced; *Humanité* attacked the anarchy of suburban transportation.[23] The PCF insisted on the extension of the métro into the outskirts of Paris and on 22 January 1937 celebrated the inauguration of the métro station of Plaisance. It argued that buses must replace tramways since the latter did not always get workers to their jobs on time.

The Left's vision of the city contained four distinct, but interconnected, urban spaces: work, housing, transportation, and leisure. Work was, of course, the most important space, by which the others were defined. Housing was to be clean, healthy, and inexpensive. According to Le Corbusier, it should be mass-produced, like any other machine-made object. Housing and work were to be linked by transportation, preferably that of the automobile, supplemented by the métro and buses. Circulation had to be improved so that workers could efficiently commute from housing to work, from apartment to factory. The final space was devoted to leisure. Parks, recreation areas, tourist facilities, swimming pools, sporting fields, and stadiums were all clearly separated from work. Leisure was defined in opposition to work. The urbanism of the Left reproduced spatially the separation between work and play that is characteristic of industrial civilization.

Play meant leisure, the principal growth industry of the Popular Front and one of the fastest growing sectors of the twentieth century. The mass leisure pioneered by the French Popular Front was a clear indication of an economy that was capable of generating and partially satisfying new needs. The terms, leisure (*loisir*) and spare-time activities (*loisirs*), are themselves significant because they reflected fundamental changes in social attitudes. In the nineteenth century Paul Lafargue, the French socialist leader and son-in-law of Karl Marx, spoke and wrote of *le droit à la paresse*; however, in the twentieth century leaders of working-class organizations never mentioned *paresse,* idleness, or laziness. Blum argued that "leisure is not laziness, it is rest after work."[24] The Left urged a shorter working week both to provide more jobs for the unemployed and to promote new spare-time activities that it made an intense effort to organize.

Before and especially during the Popular Front, the Left attempted to dominate *loisirs* and to reduce management's role in the organization of spare-time activities. In the nineteenth century, French employers had often provided libraries, leisure facilities, and even theater space for their personnel; stadiums were frequently named after wealthy entrepreneurs. Before World War I, Catholics had sponsored sporting and gymnastic associations.[25] After the Great War Catholics' and employers' control of leisure activity was increasingly challenged by the organized Left. Both sides realized that sports were a relatively easy way to mobilize and influence adolescents. Political parties, unions, and *patrons* fought to dominate sporting activities to demonstrate their symbolic and real control of youth. The intense battles between the employers and the CGT during the interwar period indicated the development of a growing social need.

With regard to leisure activities, a number of Parisian metallurgical industrialists followed an antirevolutionary strategy, not based on the clergy as was often the case in Barcelona, but on secular social works. By 1936, five thousand French summer camps—many of which were supported by industrialists—received one hundred thousand urban youth from humble backgrounds.[26] During the Popular Front, Benoît Frachon, a leader of the pro-Communist tendency in the CGT, acknowledged that "there is not one aspect of the everyday life of the workers that has escaped the care of the management."[27] In this case, Frachon's assertion seems plausible, since a study undertaken in 1935 demonstrated that of eighty-five factories surveyed, eighty had sporting facilities.[28] Nonetheless, according to Frachon, workers often distrusted employers' initiatives, and he advocated that the union capture control over the organization of leisure activities from industrialists.

Following their electoral victory, the elements of the Popular Front increased their efforts for workers' sporting and leisure activities. Blum established a new chair on the history of work and leisure at the Paris law school; he founded a subministry of "sports et loisirs," despite the incomprehension and opposition of many bourgeois who persisted in calling the new post "le ministère de la *paresse*" and who had not yet realized the industrial or commercial potential of this growing new sector.[29] The extreme Right declared that the worker did not possess the "inalienable right to dress badly, to shout the *Internationale* when a Rolls passed, and to litter everywhere."[30] Disregarding the scorn, Blum appointed Léo Lagrange as "undersecretary of state for the organization of spare-time activities and sports," and the thirty-six-year-old Socialist deputy began to democratize sports by instituting "islands of leisure" throughout the nation.[31] His new position was under the authority of the Ministry of Public Health, an indication that the Popular Front designed leisure to improve the workers' health or, in the terminology of the time, "the race." Paid vacations were also to ameliorate the "physical condition of workers."[32]

In fact the Left, like the Right, was determined to civilize the workers and to wage war on licentious popular culture. Lagrange argued that the working class had known how to win more leisure but now must learn how to use it.[33] *Humanité* too opposed *paresse* and insisted upon *loisirs intelligents.*[34] As part of this intelligent leisure, union activists wanted workers to reduce their intake of alcoholic beverages. *La Vie ouvrière* declared that "we are capable of organizing our days of rest," and it warned workers against "frequenting bars and losing the inclination to work." The CGT's newly established Tourist Bureau urged "healthy utilization" of leisure to permit workers to achieve "well-being and culture."[35] The head of the CGT's educational program, which collaborated with the Tourist Bureau, advocated "universities of work"—supported by the government—to train workers how to control the productive forces.[36] According to *Syndicats,* the fears of those who had predicted "the perils of idleness" had been alleviated by the "organization of spare-time activities" (*organisation des loisirs*) that the CGT had undertaken. Non-Communist union militants asserted that a shorter working week would permit male workers to spend more time with their families.

The unions nourished the growth of tourist traffic. Emilie and Georges Lefranc, a married team of trade-union intellectuals and educators, recommended that all workers "try *to go away*" during their annual paid vacations, and they saw the same need to escape after a normal workday: "Workers who have finished their working day . . . want a change of place, to forget their job, and to flee from everything that reminds them of it."[37] Sunday should become the "day of departure." The Lefrancs advocated leisure as relief from boring work and an ugly urban environment, which lacked air and light: "*Leisure must permit* [workers] *to regain the balance broken by our civilization.*" Leftist theoreticians of leisure attempted to solve the problem of *loisirs* by defining leisure activities as compensation for the alienating conditions at work and in the city.

The Lefrancs also encouraged sporting activities, physical sports that must eliminate the "cult of the star" and supplement intellectual activity. Socialists believed sports to be the key element of leisure activities: "Physical exercise—controlled and channeled naturally—compensates wonderfully for a sedentary life and overspecialization at the workplace."[38] During the Popular Front the tremendous growth of the Fédération sportive et gymnique du travail, a new organization of Socialist and Communist sports enthusiasts, mirrored the expansion of the unions.[39] In 1935 it had 732 clubs and 42,706 members; by 1938 it possessed 1,687 clubs and 102,694 members. Football was undoubtedly a major activity in many workers' clubs. Originally used to train a nineteenth-century elite, the sport became increasingly popular among workers in the Paris region between the wars.

As early as the 1920s the Communists were keenly interested in organizing the sporting activities of wage earners; during the Popular Front they demanded a billion francs to promote this form of leisure activity.[40] The PCF urged the construction of gymnasiums, stadiums, swimming pools, and athletic fields. Sports were a means of rational development, and many Communists argued—as did certain syndicalists and industrialists—that an expansion of sporting activities could produce a physical well-being that would increase workers' productivity. Communists gave considerable attention to their party's sporting events, which sometimes received more coverage in their press than did major strikes.

Anti-Communist CGT militants feared that the PCF and employers would monopolize workers' leisure. They believed that the "application of the forty-hour week and paid vacations compels us to organize spare-time activities" and advised their fellow activists to anticipate the actions of employers by creating libraries, theaters, outings, and sporting games. Leisure activities that the bosses organized had only one goal—to prevent workers from thinking, a charge that Communists had voiced in the 1920s and 1930s. When the forty-hour week was granted to clerks, *Syndicats* noted, "Today, joy fills their hearts. . . . Tomorrow, the problem of the organization of spare-time activities will be posed."[41]

Working-class organizations and the Popular Front governments endorsed and planned the flight of workers from their workplaces and urban homes into specialized leisure spaces. In 1936 Lagrange approved 253 projects for the construction of stadiums, in addition to plans for numerous athletic fields.[42] By the end of 1937, 400 projects were in progress. It must be recalled that many traditional places where workers spent their free time had already been destroyed by 1936. Before the Popular Front and the organization of mass tourism, many Paris workers had spent their days off in the nearby countryside where they fished in the Seine or the Marne or passed their time in rural bistros. By 1936 the waters of the Seine and the Marne were polluted, and many of the suburbs had lost their rustic flavor. At Boulogne-Billancourt, home of Renault, "there are now gray, thick walls where before, during holidays, working-class families frolicked on the grass under the poplars."[43] The Socialist government, the CGT, and the PCF began to organize excursions from urban to increasingly distant vacation sites. The government introduced special price reductions for transportation—called popular or Lagrange tickets—to move workers from their homes to leisure areas such as the French Riviera. In 1936, 600,000 used Lagrange tickets, 1,200,000 in 1937, and nearly as many in 1938.[44] Over 100,000 traveled to the Riviera in the winter, but even more took advantage of the reduced fares to visit their relatives in the countryside.[45]

Lagrange's office also planned special trains: Paris–Nice, Paris–Toulouse and cruises to Corsica, Algeria, and even Barcelona.[46] Likewise, the union initiated tourisme CGT, its official tourist agency, coordinating activities from ski trips to North African cruises. The CGT established a Vacations for All organization, which merged with the Tourist Bureau in December 1937. The agency booked trips at reduced prices, reserved rooms at modest hotels, and established campgrounds. It also created a Vacations-Savings plan, which encouraged workers to put aside a small sum every week and accumulate enough for holidays. According to the union, its savings plan would alter the habits of certain workers: "They will drink perhaps fewer *apéritifs* and smoke fewer cigarettes, but, anyway, that will not be so bad."[47] The CGT's bureau offered package deals on credit ("buy now, pay later").[48] Transforming the mythological conspirators of anti-Communist literature, the Left developed a new identity—that of travel agents. The Communists frequently propagated the slogan, The Riviera for all, and urged the expansion of mass tourism into all provinces. The PCF deputy from Nice instituted a bus service from Paris to the Côte d'Azur.[49] Other more politically neutral organizations also participated in the leisure boom. Catholic groups set up their own youth hostels to compete with the lay hostels, which, Catholics objected, mixed the sexes and encouraged dangerous opinions. In 1938 new travel agencies—forerunners of today's low-budget charter companies—began to cater to a more popular clientele to whom it offered moderately priced package deals. Still, only a minority of workers were able to take advantage of the discounts and special opportunities. In 1936 employed Parisian workers spent three times more on laundry than on vacations and trips.[50]

During the 1930s and especially during the Popular Front, certain leisure activities encouraged the mixing of young people from various backgrounds.[51] Lagrange actively promoted the youth hostel movement, but it attracted many more teachers than workers. In 1935, 90 youth hostels provided 10,000 overnight stays. In 1936, the numbers rose to 229 hostels and 26,800 nights. Participation in scouting among the more modest sections of the population also grew significantly during the Popular Front. Donning uniforms, waving banners, and marching in processions tended to level social differences—at least momentarily—among scouts. In 1935, 80,000 were involved, by 1939, 108,000. Of the three major scouting groups, Catholic, Protestant, and secular, the last experienced by far the most rapid growth. Perhaps many parents with few means encouraged their children to join so the adults could spend their vacations by themselves. Lagrange and Jean Zay, the education minister in the Blum government, collaborated in bringing sports into public schools and universities.[52] By the fall of 1937, over 100,000 popular-sporting diplomas, which tested competence in various activities, had been issued.

The Popular Front offered young people the chance to learn to fly a plane. The Minister of Aviation, Pierre Cot, who had the cooperation of Lagrange, promoted Popular Aviation and air clubs that aimed to teach flying to youngsters from various social backgrounds. In September 1937 four thousand young delegates representing ten thousand club members attended the first fête of popular aviation at Vincennes. The clubs trained four thousand new pilots from all over the nation.[53] The PCF took a prominent role in publicizing and recruiting for Popular Aviation and enthusiastically declared that "a healthy and strong youth" was being created. Yet important government officials had a different idea. They complained of the low intellectual level and poor physical condition of the new recruits, boys and, after 1936, girls between the ages of fourteen and twenty-one. According to their report, many of these youngsters naively assumed that their training in Aviation populaire would enable them to pursue careers as military pilots. But only 50 percent passed a simple written examination, and their responses shocked the examiners: the *Marseillaise* was the wife of the president of the republic, the Baltic a river, the Versailles treaty an eighteenth-century document, and Lyon north of Paris. Physical tests were no more positive.

Furthermore, aviation clubs were rife with generational and class conflicts. The new sections of Popular Aviation merged with the established Aéro-clubs, which had an older and wealthier membership. The elite in the Aéro-clubs had invested considerable resources in the organizations and did not welcome the poorer, less educated newcomers.[54] Every section experienced tensions; when peace reigned it was usually because the new members followed the "better trained" leaders of the old Aéro-clubs. In 1938 government officials concluded that Aviation populaire had not been worth the financial effort—each pilot produced had cost 750,000 francs. Growing international tension increased the need for trained aircraft personnel and led to the replacement of Popular Aviation by Premilitary Aviation. The Popular Front's desire to strengthen French youth and democratize flight quickly turned in a more militaristic direction, but it nevertheless prefigured the rise of a mass airline industry in the 1960s.

In addition to flying, other new rights appeared during the Popular Front as the CGT claimed "le droit à la neige" or the right to bring the city to the mountains: "Winter sports have become a necessity. . . . After vacations at the ocean, why not ski vacations?"[55] During the Christmas season of 1936, fifty thousand persons (approximately one-fourth of all French skiers) left Paris for the snow; Lagrange himself, equipped with skis, inaugurated a youth hostel in the mountains. Special weekend tickets gave workers a chance to ski in Auvergne. The government attempted to lower the prices for ski rentals and hotels, to open the sport to less privileged individuals. Rumors concerning these new rights spread among some metallurgical workers who believed (it appears wrongly) that they could take an extra day of paid vacation for every month they worked.[56] According to a union leader, SIMCA workers sincerely thought that they were allowed to extend their vacations from 23 to 30 August. When they took the extra week, management fired them.

The mass tourism and leisure generalized by the Popular Front inaugurated the era of the weekend and the vacation. On 17 August 1936 *Humanité* presented both a photograph of Paris deserted, showing the place de la Concorde with neither automobiles nor pedestrians, and an article entitled, "Murderous Day," which confirmed that on the highways six people had been killed and thirty injured in traffic accidents.[57] Overcrowding became an issue during the summer months as urban dwellers rushed to escape from their homes and workplaces. Workers' publications demanded that new roads be constructed to ease the difficulties of tourist travel and complained that traffic jams had discouraged many from traveling on Sunday, the chosen day of departure; union militants complained that the "rush of bathers," which "jammed the majority of beaches," created an "intolerable crush." Overcrowding and inflated prices discouraged workers from visiting cities such as Nice in August. Employers too desired paid vacations without traffic jams.[58] A law passed in November 1938 attempted to correct the "disorder" of vacation scheduling that risked harming national production. The legislation stipulated, apparently without much success, that firms in the same industry stagger paid vacations.

In factories the more or less traditional struggle—both official and unofficial—over working on Monday was supplemented by new conflicts over work on Saturday. As has been seen, many workers refused to accept work on weekends, preventing employers from organizing shifts and thereby, according to one prominent Socialist, diminishing weekly production.[59] The automobile workers of SIMCA at Nanterre "considered that their two days of rest were an invaluable gain" and did not wish to work four days one week and six days another.[60] Employers at Saint-Denis complained about the difficulties of unloading trains on Saturdays and refused to pay for storage.[61] In 1937 strikes, demonstrating that Holy Saturday was becoming as revered as Holy Monday, erupted in six metallurgical firms over working Saturday to recover Easter Monday. Employers reported that the Compagnie électro-mécanique at Bourget—which fulfilled contracts for the Navy—decided to recover Easter Monday on Saturday 3 April with the approval of the Inspection du travail; however 437 of its 472 workers did not appear.[62] Vouret et fils in Le Bourget claimed that a "cell of agitators" reneged on a previous agreement to recover Easter Monday on Saturday 3 April, with the result that 105 of its 136 workers refused to compensate for lost worktime. The firm insisted that its supervisory personnel, "tired of seeing its authority flouted, shares our point of view."[63] Workers' propensity to fight for a free weekend was encouraged by very popular weekend tickets, issued to such places as the seashore and picturesque villages as well as ski resorts.

The scheduling of paid vacations became another arena of struggle. As has been mentioned, union activists advised the staggering of vacations, which the Minister of Labor also advocated, so that the tourist industry could expand and workers could enjoy their holidays as comfortably as the bourgeois did. The president of the Metallurgical Employers' Association (GIM) noted "the difficulties that have arisen inside the firms especially because of workers' demands about scheduling their vacations."[64] Conflicts over vacation dates arose because of the different motivations of the workers, management, and the unions. Individually, the workers wanted to choose their dates. Summer was particularly desirable not only for its sun and warmth but also because children were out of school. Single workers might favor summer for various reasons, including acquiring a good tan, an increasingly popular symbol of health and leisure. The unions often supported the workers' preference, though at times the CGT opposed the complete shutting down of factories during one or two weeks in the summer; the union objected to the forced unemployment of workers who did not possess the minimum six-months' seniority to be eligible for vacation. On the other side, managers' main priority was to coordinate vacations with market conditions and their suppliers. Employers also wanted to avoid the complications of organizing shifts and subsequent fights over vacation dates.

Middle-class skeptics remained unpersuaded by the Left's discourse on leisure, believing that the workers had become idle and were wasting time.[65] The employers feared that increased spare time would lead only to more drinking in cabarets. It should be noted that in France in the 1930s alcoholism was a serious problem, particularly among males. In 1933 the French consumed 2.61 liters of hard liquor per person compared to .56 liters for the English and .77 for Germans. The French also drank twice as much wine per person as the Spanish and three times more than the Italians.[66] France possessed one establishment licensed to serve alcoholic beverages for each 80 inhabitants compared to one for 430 in Great Britain. In 1936 the unemployed spent a larger percentage of their income on wine and coffee (6.1 and 2.1 percent, respectively) than on rent (7.2) or on clothing (5.5).[67] The jobless considered these drinks to be inelastic expenses; their percentage of the budget increased only marginally as workers' income rose.

Logré, the chief physician at the police infirmary in Paris, noted an increase in alcoholism since the new social legislation had been enacted "because potential alcoholics have experienced, at least temporarily, a rise in their purchasing power, and they have more time to drink."[68] According to another source, the social reforms of the Popular Front did not diminish alcoholism, at least not in Paris. Despite a national decline in consumption of alcohol, the number of alcoholics treated by the psychiatric clinic of the Paris police increased steadily from 1935 (421 cases), to 1936 (494), 1937 (517), and 1938 (535).[69] A delegate of the Ligue anti-alcoolique complained that, in the absence of repressive measures, increased leisure and higher pay had encouraged insobriety during the Popular Front.[70] He cited as evidence the increasing number of establishments serving alcoholic drinks and the growing profits of large distillers, such as Pernod and Cinzano. Other backers of temperance advocated women's suffrage as a way of diluting the political influence of drinking males.

An investigation conducted from 1934 through 1937 in one large Parisian power plant found that at least 16 percent of the work force were alcoholics.[71] According to the physician, the personnel of the enterprise had good working conditions—a collective bargaining agreement, employment security, paid vacations, generous sick leave, and a retirement plan. Their housing too was considered more than adequate. The 173 cases of alcoholism out of a total work force of 1,092 (that contained only 15 women) were therefore not caused by "the habitual excuses of slums, unemployment, and insecurity." Forty-seven of the alcoholics were from Brittany, which meant that 32 percent of the Bretons working at the plant were dipsomaniacs. The alcoholic 16 percent of the personnel were responsible for approximately 25 percent of the sicknesses and accidents both on and off the job. These workers missed 31 days of work per year compared to 17 for nonalcoholics.[72]

Another physician characterized French workers as "the most alcoholic in the world."[73] Admissions of alcoholics and others with alcohol-related illnesses to mental institutions rose almost 16 percent from 1936 through 1938. In the interwar period in many homes, the apéritif, especially anise-based beverages, began to complement the traditional popularity of wine and beer.[74] Some families believed that the two liters of wine per day, apéritifs excluded, were the necessary minimum for working adults.

Activists complained that "the same workers who do not feel rich enough to buy a union educational brochure, which could lead them from moral misery, do not hesitate paying in a bar for expensive alcoholic poisons that destroy their health and stupefy them."[75] Militants criticized "unaware comrades, who before joining the CGT passed their time playing cards and betting on the horses."[76] A CGT official lamented that all too often only students visited the youth hostels, whereas workers spent "their Sundays in a smoke-filled café." The bars, music halls, and dances of Montmartre seemed to be more attractive to wage earners than the universities of work or other improving occupations.[77] In terms of monies spent, horse racing was by far the most popular sport.

The tourist industry's conception of leisure was often little different from the CGT's. The industry criticized the lack of "social tourism" in France and urged that all classes participate in leisure activities.[78] These activities should compensate for the unnatural labor of modern times through a "momentary return to nature," which would eventually improve the workers' capacity to work. A new company, Union française des loisirs, offered its services to employers who wanted to respond to a new need, the organization of leisure in aid of "social pacification." Thus, both the dynamic sector of the tourist industry and the Left agreed that organized leisure was a necessary alternative both to the harshness of the workers' laboring life and to the licentiousness of traditional popular culture.

So did the employers. Following the precedent of management-sponsored summer camps, the bourgeois elite desired to remake workers' leisure in ways similar to those suggested by working-class organizations. For them, workers' free time had to be organized and channeled to produce a cleaner, healthier, and happier working class. Louis Renault advocated "public works necessary for the organization of leisure."[79] The tough-minded employers did not object to the sporting and leisure activities sponsored by the CGT and the PCF but rather to their alleged attempts to indoctrinate youth with "Marxism."[80] The review, *L'Europe nouvelle,* which vigorously fought the forty-hour week, nevertheless asserted that workers' rest (*repos*) must be converted into spare-time activities, and it hoped that in the future the dream of a Paris surrounded by stadiums might be realized. One authority called for "scientific organization of leisure" so that workers might return to their post with more energy. Sports, in particular, would improve body and mind and therefore output.[81] Municipalities were urged to continue their construction of bathhouses and day-care centers. In the tradition of nineteenth-century philanthropy, it was asserted that new and clean housing would encourage workers to spend more time with their families. Workers wanted not socialism but property, specifically homes with gardens.

During the 1930s the more traditional activities, such as gardening, began to be replaced or complemented by the car. On the Left and Right many argued that the future of transportation for both leisure and work should be the private automobile. Pervasive propaganda glorified the machine and its drivers. For example, in the summer of 1938, various newsreels featured "the Grand Automobile Rally at Trocadéro," where "the most recent and most elegant cars" were presented by their owners, "whose dress," it was announced, "matched the colors and lines of the autos."[82] For its part, *Humanité* criticized French automobile builders for failing to "democratize" the automobile.[83] The PCF daily complained that "the car, this marvelous newborn that provides so much work for laborers," was too expensive for the proletariat. Communist and union militants agreed that the automobile was beautiful and that the prosperity of the nation depended on the motor-vehicle industry. The Fédération des métaux urged nationalization of the industry if capitalist automobile manufacturers proved incapable of providing a "democratic car."[84] *Syndicats* asked, "What good does it do to build more automobiles, if most people cannot buy them?"[85] Both literally and figuratively, working-class organizations helped to pave the way to a future in which the private car would become the centerpiece of work, leisure, and transportation. Louis Renault concurred with his class enemies that the price of automobiles must be lowered so that "one day every family in France can have its own little car."[86] *Usine,* published by the metallurgical industrialists, wanted to popularize cars as Kodak had cameras.

Workers were encouraged to consume commodities more accessible than automobiles. Advertising in both leftist and rightist publications propagated the virtues of consumption and awakened desires that many were able to satisfy only after World War II. Nevertheless, in the 1930s a whole range of goods—cameras, radios, bicycles, watches, sewing machines, vacuum cleaners, hunting rifles, bedroom sets, gourmet foods, cosmetics, and still other articles—were temptingly offered to French workers. Bargain stores in Paris—Prisunic, Monoprix, and Multiprix—encouraged mass consumption of many of these items. If cars remained merely a wish for most French workers, the purchase of a motorcycle, almost nonexistent in Spain, was easier. The most obtainable means of transportation remained the bicycle; its numbers doubled from four million in 1920 to eight million in 1939. Many wage earners commuted to work—and to strikes—on their bikes.

Radios became more available to those with modest incomes, and their sales rose from 1.3 million in 1933 to 5 million in 1939.[87] Over 65 percent of working Parisians and 28.2 percent of those unemployed possessed a radio in 1936. Twice as many Parisian working-class households owned radios than books.[88] Employed workers spent over 50 percent more on tobacco than on books and newspapers, thus demonstrating the continuing vitality of the oral component of French working-class culture. The CGT believed—not entirely without reason, it seems—that the "average working-class family" could purchase household items such as "costly" vacuum cleaners if it reduced spending on wines and apéritifs.[89] The union could have added cigarettes.

Yet some workers saved and labored to acquire healthier commodities and services. After the First World War, many men who had become familiar with arms in the trenches took up hunting as a sport, and the number of permits issued between the war and the early 1930s tripled.[90] Advertisements for rifles in the working-class press showed that many Parisian workers were interested in shooting. As in the Aéro-clubs, sportsmen from the upper classes, however, disdained the new hunters and refused them admittance into exclusive associations. To prevent the democratization of the sport, these wealthy enthusiasts desired to raise the price of a hunting license.

Women of all classes participated in a new world of consumption, continuing to frequent beauty salons and using more cosmetics than earlier generations had. Over one-third of working-class households in Paris contained a sewing machine;[91] with the spread of electricity into urban homes, many consumers acquired an electric iron. Many young families bought furniture on credit. Even when workers earned relatively high wages, they spent less of their income on housing than lower middle-class employees did. The result was substandard housing, and the size of apartments and the number of rooms were insufficient. The possibilities of spending both time and money on lodgings were limitless.

Given the need and appetite to consume, wage hikes were workers' key demand during almost all strikes. Metallurgical employers charged that the Communist leaders of the Syndicat des métaux hid the "political" nature of their strikes by emphasizing economic and professional grievances.[92] On occasion, workers refused a workweek that fell below forty hours. In 1937 one delegation of workers protested against a thirty-five-hour week that management attributed to a lack of orders.[93] It is significant that the delegation's protest came less than two weeks before Christmas, a period of heightened consumption. In contrast to celebrations of *noël* before the Great War, festivities during the Popular Front included expanded gift giving and more widespread use of Christmas trees.

In order to meet new and old needs, some workers demanded overtime; others approved piecework. When at the end of 1936 upholsterers went on strike to eliminate piecework, a minority of workers in certain firms favored pay incentives but "lacked the courage to speak up."[94] As in Barcelona, an undetermined number of wage earners engaged in moonlighting (*travail noir*) despite the unions' hostility. The CGT would sometimes accuse workers in company unions like the Association des ouvriers Gnôme et Rhône of moonlighting and thereby stealing work from the unemployed.[95] Penalties were established not only for workers who labored during their paid vacations but also for those who hired them.[96] Yet the extent of working off the books remains unknown.[97]

An expanding range of leisure possibilities induced others to work hard for future vacations and weekend outings. In most working-class families, both parents had to be wage earners in order to afford a vacation.[98] At SIMCA—where work slowdowns were common even among those paid by the piece—workers increased production to earn higher piecework wages as summer vacations neared.[99] Wage earners' roles as producers and consumers sometimes conflicted. In July 1936 women who shopped in Parisian working-class neighborhoods "were delighted that the forty-hour week allowed them to finish their housekeeping chores during the week and to keep the weekend intact."[100] However the application of the forty-hour week also resulted in the closing of food shops from Sunday noon until Tuesday morning. The Monday closings severely limited the possibilities of a weekend outing since perishables bought on Saturday would not last until Tuesday in the summer heat. Without refrigerators, discontented workers were forced to shop on Sunday morning. Shop clerks, though, insisted on dividing the forty-hour week into five days of eight hours with Sunday and Monday free, against their employers' desire for six working days. The clerks' representative justified their decision by asserting, "Sales no longer depend on the opening of stores but on the purchasing power of the masses."[101]

The discourses on the problems of unemployment and leisure revealed that many on the Right and on the Left shared the values of the "civilizing offensive." Unemployment they solved by putting the jobless to work building roads to improve traffic circulation, apartment houses to lodge workers, and automobiles to move the masses. The unions and parties of the Popular Front found the answer to the issue of leisure in organizing healthy and wholesome activities. The Left defined unemployment and leisure as problems whose solutions would be found in the development and construction of a city of *habita-*

tions à bon marché and of productive factories from which workers could commute to specialized leisure areas. In this sense, the Left's views on leisure meshed with its vision of the working class as devoted producers and potentially salubrious consumers. It reduced the working week so that the unemployed, who were supposedly eager to work, could obtain jobs and increase their buying power. Leisure for the workers had value not just for its own sake but also to make the class better producers in the workplace. Like some sectors of the *patronat,* the CGT, SFIO, and PCF argued for the restorative powers of *loisirs.*

At the same time, the leaders of the Left were genuinely moved by labor's new right to leisure. In a well-known speech at the Vichy regime's show trial at Riom in 1942, Léon Blum described what he perceived as one of his major accomplishments:

> I did not leave my office very much . . . but when I did and crossed the Parisian suburbs, I saw the roads lined with old jalopies, motorbikes, and tandems with working-class couples wearing matching sweaters. It all showed that the idea of leisure awakened in them a natural and simple style, and I had the sense, in spite of everything, of having brought sun and light into dark and difficult lives. We not only took workers away from the bars and provided them with more opportunity for family life but gave them hope for the future.[102]

Discounting Blum's repetition of leftist rhetoric on alcoholism and the family, we can nonetheless agree that workers did become very attached to the Popular Front's reforms granting a shorter working week and paid vacations. This desire to reduce worktime produced difficulties for the coalition. The Popular Front was trapped between its productivist promises to the nation and its consumerist constituents. Parisian workers did not show their gratitude to the Left for its advanced social legislation by working harder and producing more efficiently. Although at Renault resistance to work decreased before August vacations, it increased in the fall, after the first summer vacations had ended. Despite the restorative discourse of the Left, alcoholism did not decline in Paris and may have become more pervasive. Paralleling their lack of subordination in the workplace, many Parisian workers, like their Barcelonan counterparts, continued to use their free moments in ways that both union officials and employers condemned.

Ironically, it was the workers' attachment to the reduced working week, perhaps the major reform of the Popular Front, that helped disrupt the unity of the leftist coalition and greatly contributed to its downfall. The Popular Front was popular because of its expansion of leisure, and it was hardly surprising that its end was provoked by the workers' actions to resist more worktime.

13
THE END OF THE POPULAR FRONT

The shifting attitude of the Radical party, which was often the key to parliamentary majorities in the latter years of the Third Republic, caused the rupture of the Popular Front. Although Radical deputies depended on the votes of Socialists and Communists to win elections, many Radical constituents remained skeptical of the leftist coalition's economic policies.[1] Peasants, owners of small firms, and members of the middle classes who accepted the Radicals' defense of anticlericalism and republican liberties had never fully consented to the Popular Front's economic program, particularly the forty-hour week. Employers resented being forced to close two days per week or being unable to adapt the shorter workweek to their seasonal needs. In the spring of 1937, Radicals complained of union power and violations of the right to work. In June 1937 immediately before the fall of the first Blum government, Edouard Daladier, the Radical leader who had promoted the formation of the leftist coalition, reflected increasing anti–Popular Front sentiment in his own party by calling for the reestablishment of "order"—which was, significantly enough, an anti–Popular Front code word. Although Camille Chautemps, a veteran Radical politician who succeeded Blum in June 1937, was committed to maintaining the Popular Front, he nevertheless established an investigatory commission on production with the goal of modifying the forty-hour week. At the party congress in October 1937, Chautemps, Daladier, and other Radical party officials agreed to remain in the leftist coalition only if it maintained "order" and defended the middle classes.

After the fall of the second Blum government in April 1938, Daladier became prime minister. His government gradually shifted further to the Right as it faced accelerating internal and international pressures on production to overcome the stagnation of the French economy and prepare for the coming war. Domestically, this shift reflected the estrangement of the middle classes whose anger over the forty-hour week intensified as inflation did. Rising prices resulted from the constant wage increases, the slowdown of production in many industrial branches, and the successive devaluations of the franc, which had lost almost 60 percent of its value in less than two years. If unionized workers were largely able to keep up with the 75 percent rise in wholesale prices and a 47 percent increase in retail prices, retired persons on fixed incomes, *rentiers,* and even many *fonctionnaires* were economically injured by inflation they blamed on the Popular Front.[2] In addition, many owners of small businesses became increasingly receptive to the anti–Popular Front positions of large employers' organizations and moved toward "republican authoritarianism."[3]

Supplementing the economic grievances of important Radical constituents, the French and their allies who wanted a strong defense were concerned with the sluggishness of military production. In April 1938 General Armengaud complained of the low rate of aircraft production and cited as one of its causes "the quantity—relatively inadequate—of the weekly labor of each worker."[4] The general lamented that the productivity of French aviation workers was considerably below that of German workers, and he called upon his fellow citizens to sacrifice for the *patrie.*

The general's fears were shared by many bourgeois and industrialists. Low aircraft production compelled the government to purchase American planes, despite objections from organizations of employers and workers alike. At the end of September 1938, the newly elected president of the SNCASO declared that the closing of the factories on Saturdays and Sundays was "unacceptable" during a period of international tension.[5] He cited the "very serious" problem of output and urged more incentives for production. The employers' periodical, *La Journée industrielle,* blamed the lack of qualified personnel, the disappearance of incentives, and the erosion of the authority of the *maîtrise* for what it claimed was a 30 percent decrease in aviation productivity.[6]

Toward the end of the Popular Front, the Inspecteur général du travail alluded to the hostile social climate in a speech to representatives of management and labor. This high government official was certain that no employer wanted the return of a *patronat du droit divin* (divine-right bossism) but that on their side the union militants should "strive to make their comrades understand" the obligations and advantages of a collective bargaining agreement. Yet the militants "were not always understood as they should have been. Their directives were sometimes not respected because those to whom they spoke were not conscious of collective responsibility."[7] The Inspecteur général argued that working-class organizations must make workers comprehend that the collective bargaining agreement was a "pact of non-aggression"; once it was signed, they should labor as hard as possible for their employers:

> The unions must use every opportunity to demand that the collective bargaining agreement be obeyed [by their members]. No work is possible without discipline, and there is no discipline without authority. Now after the bargaining agreement has defined this authority, which must rule in the workplace, the workers must submit to it.

In November 1938 Daladier appointed a conservative, Paul Reynaud, to the Ministry of Finance. Throughout the Popular Front, Reynaud had opposed the forty-hour week and had fought to increase French production. He had continually warned that the constraints imposed on the French economy would lead to stagnation and weak defense. In June 1937 Reynaud declared, "We have progressively tried to diminish labor, but we have forgotten output, and we have raised simultaneously the cost of living and the costs of production."[8] As minister, Reynaud quickly attacked the application of the forty-hour week and destroyed the weekend. He established a six-day working week, authorized overtime up to nine hours per day within the limits of a forty-eight-hour week, and reduced overtime pay by 10 to 25 percent.[9] To encourage a longer workweek, Reynaud's decrees forbade the five-day week of eight hours per day without the authorization of the Ministry of Labor. He also declared null and void collective bargaining agreements that banned piecework, and he envisaged sanctions for workers who refused to work overtime in defense industries. In a radio address, Reynaud, who had opposed the Munich agreements and argued for a tough stance against Germany, told his countrymen:

> In 1933 France produced more cast iron than Germany. Today it produces four times less [than Germany]. . . . Our production must increase 30 to 40 percent. Now, all the unemployed together, even if they could be hired tomorrow, could only increase our production 7 to 8 percent. Therefore the workweek must be lengthened. Do you believe that in Europe today France can simultaneously maintain its standard of living, spend 25 billion on arms, and rest two days per week? No. You want action. I tell you that the week of two Sundays has ceased to exist.[10]

Reynaud's attack on the weekend along with other aspects of his program aroused great opposition among workers. The Socialist Jules Moch remarked that the minister's address provoked "amazement and fury in the working class."[11] The industrialists noted "strike threats" in factories that planned to work on Saturday 26 November; nevertheless, many entrepreneurs were grateful for Reynaud's assault on a labor-free Saturday, which had quickly become a cherished tradition in the Parisian working class.[12]

On the other side, René Belin, the leader of the anti-Communist group within the CGT, had wondered in August 1938 if Daladier would cross the Rubicon by terminating the forty-hour week.[13] The PCF which, it was claimed, was initially hesitant to defend the forty-hour week became more determined "when it realized that the masses were resolutely hostile to [Reynaud's] project of mutilation"; some unions even charged that Daladier's program was fascist.[14] As early as September 1938, the National Federation of Paper Workers equated Daladier's radio speeches, which called for more work, with those of Hitler and Mussolini. CGT militants in the paper industry insisted that Daladier's program was a replica of that of the right-wing PSF of Colonel de La Rocque. According to *La Vie ouvrière,* Daladier was a representative of "big capital," which was in turn connected to fascism. One CGT leader, H. Raynaud, charged that Daladier had "yielded to the wishes of internal [French] fascism."[15] The same issue of the CGT publication displayed a cartoon in which Hitler and Mussolini advised the French prime minister to use "our methods with the workers." In the pages of *Syndicats,* R. Froideval, secretary of the CGT Construction Union of Paris, accused Paul Reynaud of plagarizing Hitler.[16]

At the CGT's congress of Nantes the Confédération's three principal factions—Communist, anti-Communist, and the small number of revolutionary syndicalists—unanimously agreed on the need for union actions to prevent enactment of Reynaud's decrees. They planned a general strike on 30 November that "expresses the protest of the working class against the decrees that especially hurt it both by terminating the day off on Saturday without any reason and without any benefit for the national economy and by establishing a reorganization of overtime that is totally unjustified."[17] E. Jacoud, the secretary of the Federation of Transportation (CGT), noted "the general indignation that the decrees aroused shortly after they appeared" and asked, "What federation could have resisted such a justifiable response?"[18] Anti-Communist militants asserted that "sportsmen" also would "defend the week of two Sundays," which was "the most satisfactory reform of all."[19]

Even before the planned date of 30 November wildcat strikes erupted against the six-day week. New schedules that obliged personnel to work Saturday or Monday generated intense opposition among a multitude of workers, many of whom, including Catholics, were not known for their militancy.[20] At the Hutchinson tire factory in Puteaux, at the chemical firm of Kuhlmann in Aubervilliers, and at Matières colorantes of St.-Denis, workers engaged in *grèves sauvages* protesting the new work schedules.[21] Other major chemical, aviation, and metalworking firms in the suburbs were hit by wildcats, and the CGT was forced to appeal to its militants to restrain the strikers. On 24 November at aviation plants in the Paris region, wildcat strikes occurred before Reynaud's decrees were applied.[22] The president of the nationalized aviation sector declared that "after the establishment of the contract and the social laws, recourse to a strike is a revolutionary measure that risks arousing the majority of the nation against the workers."

He announced, "According to the statistics, fifty-five hours per week of work are necessary to ensure the existence of the country."

On 24 November the largest and most violent wildcat strike erupted in Renault. Although the PCF and its followers claimed that Renault workers were not responsible for the violence or attributed it to Trotskyists, the automobile workers did engage in sabotage and physical aggression. Some foremen and superintendents were beaten, and forty-two bludgeons or blackjacks and one dagger (which had been made in the factories) were found in the workshops occupied by the strikers.[23] Workers used new cars and trucks to construct barricades, broke windows, and destroyed a clock. Strikers left the basement of the infirmary full of gasoline. Police had to evacuate the factories by force and were greeted by a barrage of various automobile parts ranging from carburetors to pistons. Forty-six policemen and at least twenty-two strikers were injured in the confrontations. Many works in progress were ruined, and management claimed almost 200,000 francs in damages.[24]

Approximately two hundred eighty workers were arrested, mainly for failure to respect the right to work (*entraves à la liberté du travail*).[25] From the available police reports on thirty-one workers, only five were described as "political" and members of the PCF. Twenty-one were judged "nonpolitical" (*pas s'occuper de politique*) by police inspectors, and reports on five others contained no mention of political activity.[26] Only two out of the thirty-one workers had a criminal record. Three of the thirty-three persons whom the Renault management accused of violating the "right to work" and engaging in violence and sabotage were women.[27] The female suspects sometimes equaled their male counterparts in violence. One threw a pot of benzine at a widow who continued to work during the strike; the two others threatened to "smash in the face" of their female colleagues who failed to stop work.

The Renault statistics are extremely significant because they contradict the claims by the management and the Daladier government that the 24 November strike was "political," that is, a protest by PCF militants against the government that had signed the Munich accords. These statistics roughly mirrored the percentage of PCF members in the Renault factories; according to the militants' unofficial numbers, the PCF had four thousand adherents out of thirty-four thousand workers.[28] The figures thus reflect an unexpectedly low rate of PCF membership among some of the presumably most militant workers and tend to refute assertions by historians that the PCF controlled Renault during the Popular Front.[29] The police reports indicate that nonpolitical workers were the essential force behind the 24 November strike to defend the weekend against Reynaud's decrees. The lack of criminal records among the workers who committed violent acts against both people and property implied that violence in a huge, rationalized plant like Renault was caused not by criminals, or even PCF militants, but by a disgruntled minority that was outraged by the longer workweek.

Indeed, throughout the Popular Front, the PCF and the CGT—like their counterparts in Barcelona—were well aware of the generally low degree of political militancy among the majority of French workers. The PCF had difficulty finding devoted militants to lead its cells and lamented the passivity of its Renault adherents who usually neglected to purchase party publications.[30] Generally, the bulk of PCF members were less interested in the party's politics or projects for the future than in its defense of their bread-and-butter demands. The CGT itself was careful to give priority to specific economic grievances rather than political demands during the most important strikes. The Syndicat des métaux even denied that the one-hour strike of Monday, 7 September 1936, in solidarity with Spain was exclusively "political." Of course, the union did not dispute that a major purpose of the work stoppage was to elicit support for the Spanish Republicans, but it also demanded wage hikes and protested the "violations of the collective bargaining agreements," "firings of personnel," and "nonpayment of vacations."

After 1936, workers generally responded without great enthusiasm to other political movements. Despite the strong support of the Syndicat des métaux, the demonstration of 24 June 1937 against the Senate—which had blocked Blum's financial initiatives and contributed to the fall of his first government—generated a relatively low turnout.[31] Yet at certain moments many workers mobilized for political causes. After all, the Popular Front coalition had been propelled in 1934 by the mass political strikes and demonstrations of 12 February that protested against the right-wing riots of 6 February. A Bastille Day unity demonstration in 1935, May Day marches in 1936 and 1937, and the commemoration in 1936 of the 1871 Paris Commune drew several hundred thousand on each occasion. Tens of thousands of Parisian workers also participated in a demonstration against the fascist attack on Léon Blum in February 1936. In November 1936 hundreds of thousands took to the streets to protest against the right-wing press whose slanders had caused the suicide of Roger Salengro, the Socialist Minister of the Interior.

The strike following the Clichy massacre was one of the rare occasions during the period of Popular Front governments when impressive numbers of workers participated in an essentially political work stoppage. In the evening of 16 March 1937, six thousand to ten thousand left-wing demonstrators met to protest a gathering of La Rocque's Parti social français (PSF), which was the largest and most rapidly growing formation of the extreme Right. The crowd clashed with police who had been sent to separate the two hostile groups. The confrontations caused the deaths of five or six antifascists and injuries to approximately two hundred persons. The deaths and injuries aroused "a profound emotion in working-class circles."[32] On the morning of Thursday 18 March, large numbers of Parisian workers responded to a CGT strike call. The protest against the fascist movement of La Rocque and against the police shootings became the most important political strike of the Popular Front.[33]

The political character of the 30 November 1938 general strike was less important than its defense of the forty-hour week, but it, nevertheless, failed decisively. Employers were well prepared, and they warned their personnel that strikers would lose seniority and paid vacations.[34] Some industrialists declared that striking would constitute a clear violation of the contract and that those who did not come to work would be fired or rehired on an individual basis after an examination of their records. The government also acted with force and shrewdness to end the strikes in the most vital public services. In Parisian public transportation, the walkout was a failure.[35] The strike was supported by only a few railroad and postal workers.

Troops were stationed in the métro, train, and bus stations to ensure traffic circulation, and employers asserted that where a *service d'ordre* (police force) protected the right to work, participation in the general strike was minimal.[36] René Belin reported that Daladier had effectively prevented a walkout in public services by threatening potential strikers with military tribunals.[37] *Humanité* asserted that the state had created "an atmosphere of terror" by placing soldiers in the centers of public transportation. The revolutionary syndicalists charged that "the fascistization of the French state continues rapidly."[38] Even the relatively moderate Léon Jouhaux concluded that "Daladier . . . wanted to demonstrate that he could take the same attitude toward the working class as Hitler."[39]

Whether fascist or not, the Daladier government foreshadowed contemporary practices by an astute manipulation of the state-controlled radio that intimidated strikers and potential strikers. As were other government workers, radio employees were requisitioned. News broadcasts, which the radio monopolized since newspapers failed to appear during the strike, openly encouraged strikebreaking.[40] One railroad union official admitted that the "bombardment of the airwaves was unquestionably effective." Other union leaders concluded that the government's use of the radio had aided the bosses and confused the workers.[41] Coercion by military and police supplemented a clever employment of the means of communication to break the 30 November general strike. During the Popular Front, the radio became an outlet for the propaganda not only of consumption but also of production.

The advanced industries examined actively participated in the movement in defense of the forty-hour week and against the Reynaud plan. In the suburbs, where the most important aviation and automobile firms were located, the percentage of strikers was relatively high. Figures varied widely according to sources: the Fédération des métaux declared that 80 percent of workers participated in the strike, whereas the government and employers estimated 25 percent.[42] A document in the Renault archives reported that 30 to 40 percent of the workers and 2 to 3 percent of the office workers of the Paris region participated; it stated that at Citroën 35 percent of the workers were absent and at SIMCA 70 percent.[43] In private aviation companies at Issy-les-Moulineaux, more than 33 percent of the workers participated in the general strike.[44] In nationalized aviation the strike was nearly total in the SNCASO factories at Villacoublay, Suresnes, and Courbevoie, and the walkout continued in these plants until 9 December when management reported that only 20 to 50 percent of the personnel were working.[45] The president of the firm was especially disappointed by the workers of the CGT-dominated Courbevoie factory who, he said, had broken their promises. Aviation strikers threatened nonstriking personnel and refused to respect their right to work (*liberté du travail*). Buses that carried laborers to the Villacoublay plant were sabotaged, and over 50 percent of the aviation personnel reportedly participated in the strikes.

An effective, if controversial, repression followed the failure of the general strike. Workers who had caused production problems during the Popular Front were dismissed. Leftist historiography largely regards this post-November repression as an almost irrational act of vengeance by employers.[46] It presents the dismissed workers as innocent passive victims who wanted only to exercise their legal union rights. Yet considering the workers' fight against work and factory discipline, the employers' repression seems exceedingly rational. An estimated eight hundred thousand workers were either locked out or laid off immediately after the failed strike of 30 November. According to management, "only" thirty-four out of one hundred forty Citroën delegates were fired.[47] At Renault, management dismissed those "troublemakers" (*meneurs*) who had limited production in the workshops; after these workers were fired, productivity jumped 10 to 25 percent in many workshops.[48] Despite a general reduction of personnel from thirty-four thousand to thirty-two thousand, production did not decline.[49] On 1 December 1938 Louis Renault noted that during the Popular Front the power of the working class had prevented layoffs of several thousand workers, many of whom had been hired in the autumn and winter of 1936. Frequently, these newly employed laborers were poorly qualified, inadequate producers who were "insufficiently adapted" to the factory. Yet Renault had been unable to dismiss them because he feared retaliatory strikes and other actions. The failed strikes of November provided him with the opportunity to trim his payrolls, reinforce discipline, and increase productivity. In the body assembly workshops, fifty-four out of approximately seven hundred workers were dismissed, but production remained stable.[50] In the woodworking *atelier,* the work force was reduced from seventy-one to fifty-eight, yet production did not fall. In these and other Renault workshops, wages actually increased since workers were no longer able or forced to limit their piecework production.[51] During the Popular Front, Renault workers had often sacrificed higher pay for a less intensive work pace. At the end of 1938, factory discipline was reinforced by the reestablishment of turnstiles and inspections to prevent thefts, which had increased since the spring of 1936. In addition, workers were no longer able to exercise their "right" to leave the factory for a snack.[52]

Yet the employers' response was not totally unrestrained. When M. G. Claude of Action française advocated a return to a forty-eight-hour week with wages based on forty hours, *Usine* objected that, given the workers' struggle for the forty-hour week, Claude's proposal was unrealistic.[53] The management of Caudron calculated that 65 percent of its workers had participated in the 24 November wildcat but stated that many would be rehired, and on 12 December 1938, "work began again normally."[54] According to one report, the Ministry of War "definitively" fired only 209 workers out of 100,000, and those dismissed—many of whom had worked in aviation—were soon reemployed by private industry.[55] At the beginning of January 1939, 10,000 workers remained without jobs, but many of them were rehired in the following weeks as renewed economic expansion increased industrial production, which climbed 15 percent from November 1938 to June 1939 as unemployment fell from 416,000 in January 1939 to 343,000 in June 1939.[56]

In nationalized aviation, selective dismissals eliminated those workers who had hindered production. On 9 December 1938 the president of the SNCASO noted that all would be rehired "except for those persons having committed violations of the right to work, or serious errors, or those not having a normal output before the strike." According to the chief administrator of the same enterprise, fewer than 10 percent of the personnel would be suspended but even some of them would be reemployed in the following weeks. A high executive of the SNCAN declared that wage earners who had not violated the right to work would be recalled as quickly as possible.[57] The president of the SNCAN fully approved the executive's position, which he explained:

> An examination of all the important cases must be undertaken in an extremely serious manner, with the goal to avoid the slightest injustice. For the personnel who can be reproached with serious errors, their individual records will be constituted and submitted to a commission composed of persons who are independent of the nationalized company and who will make the final decision.

By January 25 1939 the SNCAN executive desired "to make humanitarian gestures as quickly as possible," and he told the administrative council that he had, "studied for certain cases, the possibility of reemployment in a different factory than the one where the concerned person was working before 30 November. Already several positions have been offered and accepted under these conditions."[58]

In addition to selective dismissals, management now tied wages more closely to production by increasing the weight of monetary incentives. On 9 December 1938 the president of SNCASO stated that "the reduction of the base salary must be compensated by bonuses or production incentives."[59] In addition, employers probably reduced the CGT's control over the hiring of new personnel. The poststrike policies of aviation management were at least partially effective, since the monthly delivery of airplanes doubled within several months after the disturbances of November 1938: "From the end of 1938 . . . production increased considerably. . . . The effort to equip the industry, the augmentation of the number of suppliers, the lengthening of the working week . . . were fruitful."[60]

Thus the rapid increase in production did not derive entirely from the end of the forty-hour week since aircraft production depended on long-term planning and large-scale capital investment. Paradoxically, as the Popular Front governments rearmed and rationalized the defense industries, pressures increased to end the forty-hour workweek, which was, of course, one of the workers' major gains in the Blum period. During

1938, as the machinery of mass production was put into place, industrialists lobbied intensely to lengthen the workweek.[61] Reynaud and Daladier responded positively, and a month after the failed strike of November, the official week of motor manufacturers was six days of eight hours. At the end of 1938 productivity increased 6.4 percent. In February 1939, workers in all nationalized firms were laboring at least forty-four hours, and Gnôme et Rhône employed three shifts, each working forty-eight hours. If the end of the forty-hour week was not solely responsible for the gains in production and productivity, the post-November climate of longer hours, tightened discipline, and union busting undoubtedly contributed to the increases in output.

Once a climate of work discipline had been reestablished, the great majority of dismissed workers, whose skills were frequently needed, was reintegrated into the labor force. Private firms seem to have been more punitive than the nationalized sector or the arbitration courts, however. Capitalists saluted the "return of good sense, of calm, and of the only doctrine that is healthy—work." It should be noted that striking foremen and *agents de maîtrise,* who were a small minority of this stratum, were, exceptionally, not rapidly rehired.[62] In nationalized aviation, of the approximately 835 dismissed workers who remained jobless in the spring of 1939, only 7 were foremen (*contremaîtres*) and 25 were technicians or engineers. Aviation management believed that it was not possible to reopen the factories without a sufficiently powerful police force. In December 1938 the foremen and supervisors of Renault wrote to the Socialist daily, *Le Populaire,* protesting its article of 23 December, which claimed that the demand for dismissals of the *meneurs* was the work of a "minority of malcontents." The foremen asserted that the firings were supported by almost all their colleagues; their petition against the *meneurs* had collected 2,500 signatures of supervisory personnel. The foremen claimed to be satisfied by the "restoration of order" that followed the November strikes.[63]

As for the fascist political tendencies of employers and their immediate subordinates, these ideological impulses grew during the Popular Front at least partially in response to the workers' challenge of authority, their refusal to work diligently, and the government's inability to reestablish order in the factories or on the construction sites. The extreme right-wing Parti social français made CGT control of hiring one of its major issues during the electoral campaign of early 1937.[64] At Renault, large numbers of foremen and *agents de maîtrise* gravitated toward right-wing unions. Among *collaborateurs,* a category that included not only foremen but also white-collar sales and administrative personnel, the CGT lost support. In December 1936 in elections for delegates, the Confédération had obtained 64.2 percent (3,248 votes) while other unions had received 35.8 percent (1,812 votes).[65] Two years later in November 1938, CGT votes fell to 45 percent of the total, whereas that of the other unions rose to 55 percent. Support for right-wing professional unions was greater among foremen and supervisory personnel than other *collaborateurs.* In November 1938 all the sections of the *agents de maîtrise* elected non-CGT representatives. Supervisors and foremen chose ten delegates of the SACIAT, an authoritarian and anti-Communist organization that had complained about the loss of authority of the cadres throughout the Popular Front. While heatedly denying it was in the bosses' camp, the SACIAT claimed that it defended "the only means by which we can assure our future: our work."

Calls for the restoration of order and discipline in the workplace were the common denominator among the numerous factions of the Right.[66] The PSF pledged to safeguard "the right to work." The electricity magnate Ernest Mercier, a promoter of Redressement français, condemned "disorder"; the Ligue des patriotes demanded discipline; the Bonapartists desired "a very firm central authority"; and Francisme wanted a leader who led and followers who did what they were told. Bertrand de Jouvenal, an intellectual in Jacques Doriot's Parti populaire français, which some historians have called fascist, admired the Third Reich for undertaking "the gigantic task of reconciliating man and his work." Yet the extreme Right had by no means a monopoly on appeals for order and discipline. Some initial supporters of the Popular Front, such as the neo-Socialists and Frontistes, also complained about the lack of government authority. As has been seen, in November 1938 republicans in the *clemenciste* tradition, led by Paul Reynaud, reestablished an atmosphere of order that led to disciplined production in certain sectors of the economy.

Yet it should not be inferred that all industries experienced a rise in productivity only after the failure of the general strike and the ensuing repression. As in Barcelona, industrial and political periodizations cannot be completely identified; greater output in a number of firms did not always depend solely on the results of the national confrontation between the CGT and the government on 30 November 1938. For example, productivity increased dramatically in private Parisian bus and transportation companies after the forty-four-day drivers' strike and occupation at the end of 1937 and beginning of 1938.[67] Furthermore, the Jacomet arbitration of the spring of 1938 had the effect of tightening discipline in certain aviation firms.

Considerably before November 1938, Jules Verger, a *patron de combat,* adopted what he claimed was an effective strategy against CGT militants. Verger was the president of the employers' organization, Chambre syndicale de l'entreprise électrique de Paris; of its 700 members only a handful employed more than 100 workers.[68] He replaced about 130 workers who had struck in October 1936 with new personnel who were "very happy to work after a hard period of unemployment." His loyal workers were heads of households, determined "not to let their jobs be stolen from them because, above everything, they had to provide for their families." The entrepreneur desired to create a family atmosphere in his firm.

In the electricians' strike, verbal and physical violence was a near constant. In early November, approximately 2,200 workers out of 3,500 in the Syndicat des monteurs-électriciens struck in solidarity with the 130 whom Verger had fired in October.[69] Verger's own personnel, who now numbered 166, continued laboring and, along with other *jaunes* (scabs) became targets for the strikers. Verger "asked his staff to respond to violence with violence." The police correctly surmised that confrontations would multiply. The strikers were determined to prevent the *jaunes* and members of the professional union from working, and they made a special effort to halt Verger's own enterprise.[70] On 13 November police arrested 4 strikers for obstructing the right to work. The following day police intervened when 15 strikers attempted to stop the work of 20 nonstrikers. At a meeting, a certain Thomas, presumably a member of the CGT Electricians' Union, stated that force was the only way to make the *jaunes* understand. The union complained that the police were present whenever the strikers were, and it accused the government of being as reactionary and as repressive as the German Social Democrats had been.

The strikers used old and new tactics to achieve their goals. Their intelligence network seems to have functioned well, and they employed rapid modern transportation—cars, trucks, and bicycles—to appear at sites where nonstrikers were active. In one incident, 100 or so *grévistes* arrived by automobiles, surprised 30 of Verger's men, injured 3, and disappeared before police arrived. Strikers usually attacked only when they considerably outnumbered their adversaries, as at the Jardin des Plantes where 100 strikers forced 12 electricians to abandon their jobs. At Malakoff 12 strikers, who had arrived on bicycles, fought with 4 workers. Furthermore, as in the nineteenth century, scabs' tools might be mislaid, materials confiscated, and work sabotaged.

On several occasions, strikers abducted one or two strikebreakers and interrogated them at a union hall for several hours. When militants questioned why he broke the strike, one worker replied that he was the father of five children and had to labor to feed them. The average age of the strikers who were arrested by police was 22.9, whereas the average age of the nonstrikers was 29.3; the latter likely had more dependents than the former. However exaggerated, Verger's rhetoric about the family did reflect one reality of the conflict. During other strikes industrialists claimed that a parent was less likely to stop work than a single or younger worker.[71]

By the second week of December, familial constraints may have contributed to slowing the strike's momentum. In addition, the Minister of the Interior, the Socialist Marx Dormoy, was apparently determined to protect the right to work, even at the risk of alienating the CGT:

> Regarding the incidents caused by striking electricians who prevent nonstrikers from working and who abduct them: The minister asks

them to stop and wishes us to station officers around each site so that the right to work is protected.

The director of the municipal police has been informed.[72]

As in Spain, in France during the first half of the twentieth century a powerful state, ready to employ its forces to guarantee social order, may have been a prerequisite for labor discipline in certain industries.

Unlike its Spanish counterpart, the French Popular Front became the birthplace of the weekend and mass tourism, not of revolution. The Soviet or anarchosyndicalist alternative of workers' control and development of the means of production had declining appeal for French working-class activists. The core of union and left-wing militants, who were the central force behind the collectivizations in Barcelona, played an entirely different role in Paris. Communists and Socialists in France no longer called for soviets or revolutionary workers' control, and the remaining anarchosyndicalist and Trotskyist militants were largely ignored. In France, the demand for revolution was superseded by guerrilla warfare against work.

The divergent paths of France and Spain influenced the actions and the desires of militants in working-class organizations in Paris and Barcelona. More than its Spanish counterpart, the French bourgeoisie developed the means of production, created a solid agricultural base, and achieved national unity and independence. In addition, by the twentieth century the state had separated itself from the Church and had replaced the values of tradition and religion with those of science and technology. In short, unlike its Iberian peers, the French bourgeoisie had achieved many of the prerequisites of a modern economic order.

French trade unions and left-wing parties were directly affected by the dynamism of their bourgeoisie. Since the issues of separation of Church and state, jurisdiction of military and civilian power, and regionalism had been largely resolved in the France of the 1930s, conflicts over these matters were less significant for French working-class organizations than for their Spanish counterparts. The understandable resentment and violence that Spanish workers and militants manifested toward a largely Catholic bourgeoisie—which had literally and figuratively abandoned its factories—was less evident in Paris. Parisian employers and industrialists were not forced to flee for their lives. The French political consensus was wide and even permitted a sharing of power with major left-wing and working-class organizations, in the legislature and also in many local governments in the interwar years. Thus, instead of outlawing and repressing the major working-class groups, French society was strong enough to integrate labor organizations to the extent that revolution became more a rhetorical artifice than a real possibility. Communist and Socialist municipalities helped build and modernize the infrastructures necessary for production. French syndicalists slowly dropped their insistence on workers' control of the productive forces and pushed for greater consumption. Therefore, by 1936, France no longer contained that nucleus of revolutionary syndicalists who in Spain took control and developed the means of production. On the contrary, in Paris union militants would often encourage or acquiesce in the desires of the rank and file who wanted to avoid constraints of workspace and worktime. If the more developed French political and social system limited the revolutionary option, it likewise reduced the chances for a reactionary or fascist coup d'état.[73] Despite all the problems of production and social unrest, extreme right-wing plots failed miserably during the French Popular Front, in direct contrast to the Spanish situation.[74] The French officer class maintained its grudging loyalty to the republic, and sincere republicans proved capable of breaking major strikes and reducing refusals to labor.

Although resistance to work has accompanied all stages of industrialization, the character of the advanced productive forces, which the French bourgeoisie has continually developed from the second half of the nineteenth century, aggravated struggles against industrial labor. Workers wanted to escape from environments pictured in *A nous la liberté* and *Modern Times.* Their revolts took forms of indifference, slow-downs, indiscipline, lateness, absenteeism, theft, and even sabotage and outright violence. After the electoral victory of the Popular Front, Parisian wage earners took advantage of the easing of repression by state and police to occupy factories and, later, to greatly intensify their struggles against work. At the end of 1938 a strong government, willing to use the forces at its disposal, was needed to restore labor discipline and to increase production. Thus political changes profoundly influenced both economic performance and social relations.

The examination of the Paris workers' struggles during the Popular Front questions assertions by some historians that the twentieth-century French working class had "accepted the industrial system" and that it had adapted to the factory.[75] The process of adaptation to the industrial system is, of course, extremely complex. The French working class had adapted to the industrial system to the extent that it did not destroy the factories during its occupations and that it labored to acquire many of the goods and services produced by industrial society. Sabotage and destruction of property did however exist during and after the occupations. Violence was not infrequent at the end of 1936 and throughout 1937 and 1938. Although CGT membership jumped from around 800,000 in 1935 to nearly 4,000,000 in 1937—one sign of adaptation to the factory system—the union was often ignored or disobeyed by its rank and file. As we have seen, apathy toward union leaders and directives was not unknown during the Popular Front. As in Spain, union membership seldom meant ideological commitment but was rather "an expression of a new conformism."[76] For many French workers, joining the union was a way to realize their hopes to work less and to consume more.

In short, coercion had to supplement adaptation in order to make workers work. At moments during the Popular Front and particularly at the end of 1938, the employers and the state realized that adaptation was insufficient, and they employed force—police, military, dismissals, legal proceedings, and court trials—to make workers labor harder and produce more. The weekend vanished, but only temporarily. Although it has now become a fixture of contemporary Western civilization and appears in the cinema of Jean-Luc Godard as the factory did in the 1930s films of René Clair and Chaplin, the weekend's painful birth and violent infancy were consequences of the workers' lack of adaptation to the factory system.

The Communists, the Socialists, and the CGT attempted to control the struggles against work by organizing the weekend and paid vacations and also by fighting for the forty-hour week. These parties and unions argued that the shorter workweek would help solve the problem of unemployment by putting the jobless to work. Nationally, the forty-hour week was only marginally successful in eliminating joblessness. In fact, unemployment began to decline dramatically after the failed general strike of 30 November 1938 when the forty-hour week was eradicated, arms spending increased, and private investment encouraged. It is difficult to determine which factor most stimulated the economy, although it is clear that the forty-hour week disregarded the specific French demographic situation in which the lack of skilled workers impeded production.

If only marginally successful in increasing employment nationally, the forty-hour workweek did force employers in the Paris region in many industries to hire more workers. But this larger work force did not lead to the increased production that the Popular Front assumed would raise the purchasing power of the workers. Indeed, employment of the jobless and corresponding measures limiting worktime led to higher costs that passed to consumers through inflation and heavier taxes. The wage increases won by the workers of the Paris region, which were also partly responsible for rising costs, were largely wiped out by this inflation. Higher prices resulted in strikes for increased pay and ultimately in greater social tensions.

The Left tried to mask the problems of the forty-hour week with productivist ideology. It claimed that the unemployed wanted only to work and that the bosses were sabotaging production. It refused to admit that many unemployed and employed workers too, for that matter, were more interested in securing a steady income than in improving output. Even when, on rare occasions, union and leftist political leaders concurred with the opposition's charges that the lack of skilled labor was harming output or that production had declined, the leaders' calls for more work and improved production went unheard.

The Left refused to acknowledge the workers' active resistance to factory discipline and wage labor. Its press ignored the workers' violence toward their foremen and those colleagues who refused to join the union. The Left attempted to portray the workers as sober, hardworking, disciplined, and willing to sacrifice for the good of the *patrie* and, of course, production. Many historians of varying political beliefs and scholarly orientations have often continued this tradition and have therefore ignored social realities and essential aspects of working-class life.

Conclusion

An examination of what I have called workplace utopianism will clarify workers' resistance to work during the Popular Fronts. The productivist utopian tradition grew during the eighteenth and nineteenth centuries and, although it retains a certain vigor, has gradually been breaking down in the twentieth. Given the differences between France and Spain, it is easy to understand why this tradition was born in France, the home of the Enlightenment and its carrier throughout Europe during the revolutionary and Napoleonic periods. In Spain, the influences of the Enlightenment and the revolutionary era were much weaker. In the nineteenth century Marx, Proudhon, and Bakunin built on the Enlightenment legacy and elaborated their own productivist utopias, which became the basis for the ideologies of organized working-class movements in both France and, somewhat later, Spain. Productivist utopianism has undergone questioning in developed European nations during this century, especially in France in 1968. The tradition's persistence in Spain beyond the 1930s indicated the country's distinct development.

The roots of workplace utopianism are in the Enlightenment's insufficiently critical conception of work. The *philosophes* linked labor to progress; civilization meant effort, not idleness. The illustrations of the *Encyclopédie,* like Spanish socialist realist art, idealized the productive forces and those who made them function. The shop-floor reality, of course, was more complex than either the images or ideology suggested. Historians have discovered that the eighteenth-century workshop held no golden age of labor. Class conflict, absenteeism, turnover, and drunkenness were common. Coercion by guilds and state power proved necessary to keep workers working.

Abbé Sieyès's *What Is the Third Estate?* continued the glorification of labor and the producers. Idleness characterized the nobles, who were of no use to the nation. The nation meant, in fact, the useful classes, a concept that included everyone who worked, even intermediaries and ecclesiastics. In attacking the idleness of the nobility, Sieyès's pamphlet served immediate political and polemical purposes but, just as important, reflected French bourgeois dynamism and desires to create a new, more kinetic, nation that would include industrious foreigners. His vision outlined the revolutionary and Napoleonic project that would appeal to Europe of the middle classes. In Spain, however, sectors of the population, often led by clerics, fought a guerrilla against the French model. As has been seen, the bourgeois or liberal revolution remained stymied in the Iberian Peninsula. Instead, in the nineteenth and the first half of the twentieth century, Spain provided the model of the pronunciamiento to its former colonies and other areas of the Third World.

The anarchosyndicalists and Marxists built on the French revolutionary and Enlightenment inheritance. This is no place to examine in detail their attitudes to labor. It is enough to say that both groups tended to take Enlightenment and revolutionary positions on work to an extreme, more narrowly defining producers as wage laborers and eliminating bourgeois and clerics from the useful classes. Instead of merely identifying work with progress, civilization, and the nation, Marxists and anarchosyndicalists wished to construct their utopias in the workplace with the enthusiastic cooperation of the workers. The preceding pages have shown the difficulties, if not the impossibilities, of such a project. Nevertheless, varieties of Marxist and anarchosyndicalist thinking became the basis for the ideologies of working-class organizations in France and Spain. Concerned with the differences between these ideological rivals, historians have often ignored their shared workplace utopianism.

It is important to point out that these ideologies were frequently elaborated in France or with reference to French conditions. The more advanced French social, economic, and political development in the nineteenth century stimulated reflection on the place of the proletariat in industrializing society. Paralleling their trading patterns, Spain often imported modern working-class ideologies from France. The workplace utopianism of Proudhon had an important impact on both Spanish anarchists and republicans; through the agency of the French socialists Paul Lafargue and Jules Guesde, Marxism was transported over the Pyrenees. The revolutionary movements persisted in Spain during the first third of the twentieth century as they were losing their impact in their countries of origin.

Although workplace utopians in France and Spain called on workers to take over the productive forces and construct a socialist or libertarian society, everyday contact with wage earners mitigated the Left's theoretical commitment to productivism. During the nineteenth century and when out of power in the twentieth, working-class organizations usually supported their own constituents' demands for less worktime. In fact, the organizations would probably have had fewer members if they had ignored workers' demands to avoid work. But the advocacy of idleness per se never became a publicly proclaimed platform of the Left. In the 1930s leisure was frequently defended in productivist terms as restoration after work or as effective employment of the jobless. The more subversive forms of resistance—absenteeism, malingering, and sabotage—were officially ignored, except in situations like the Spanish Revolution and, to a much lesser extent, the French Popular Front, when the parties and the unions of the Left assumed some responsibility for the smooth functioning of the productive forces and were thus forced to combat resistance. Even in this period, complaints by union and party leaders concerning the quantity and quality of work carried out by the rank and file were never sufficient to challenge the ultimate goal of taking over and developing the productive forces.

For social historians, this lack of a public political articulation of resistance to work by working-class organizations does not lessen its significance. Rather than dismiss the hidden or write it off as secondary, historians must analyze the reasons for the absence of a clear statement on sabotage, absenteeism, lateness, and malingering. Like theft or alcohol and drug consumption, resistance to work arouses fears and possesses a subversive side that invites repression. In societies—such as those of Barcelona and Paris during the Popular Fronts—officially devoted to the development of the productive forces, refusal to work borders on the criminal. Historians cannot assume that the discourse of the parties and unions of the Left truly reflected the actions and beliefs of the workers; organizations had their own reasons for ignoring and concealing the struggles against labor. After all, the unions depended on the workplace for their organizational existence, and Socialist and Communist parties advocated the control of the productive forces, not their destruction. Their rhetoric about the potentialities of labor was not wholly disinterested. Thus, perhaps inevitably, workplace utopianism dominated the Left.

Yet even in the nineteenth century, dissident voices were heard. The most famous was Paul Lafargue's *Droit à la paresse* (1880), which, it has been said, has been translated into more languages than any other socialist work except for the *Communist Manifesto.* The pamphlet remains a vigorous and humorous defense of idleness, but it reveals a partial, perhaps distorted, view of the nineteenth-century French working class. Its often forgotten original subtitle was "A Refutation of the 'Right to Work' of 1848." Lafargue believed that the demand for employment articulated during the revolution of 1848 represented the wishes of an implicitly unitary working class. Like other Marxists, he did not see that the demands of working-class parties and unions often disguised more than they revealed. Lafargue interpreted the demand for work literally and therefore presented a questionable portrait of wage earners. According to the French socialist leader, the workers, possessed by a "strange madness," loved labor. A "resigned" and "guileless working class" permitted itself to be indoctrinated by the bourgeois dogmas of effort and abstinence. Lafargue and many others who followed him ignored the nineteenth-century workers' struggles against labor, which could be seen even in the famous national workshops of 1848. He misjudged the workers, most of whom would not have objected to his vision of a society where the machines did the hard labor once performed by human beings. His cybernetic utopia, in which wage labor would be abolished, suggests a way beyond workshop utopianism.

In the twentieth century, the questioning of work continued. During the Popular Fronts, leisure (not idleness or laziness) acquired a certain legitimacy, especially in France, where a de facto Ministry of Leisure (with no Spanish equivalent) was established. However other forms of resistance to work remained hidden until after 1968. Particularly in France, that year symbolized a young generation's desire to change everyday life and its confrontation with accepted Western values. Given this context, one of the slogans of the French May—Never work—may not be less shocking but is more clear. One should note that the questioning of productivist utopianism (which has survived 1968 in its councilist or democratic forms) occurred first in a nation that had developed into a consumer society. The critique of labor was slower to arrive in Spain, preoccupied in 1968 with political protest against an authoritarian system and only beginning to explore consumerism. Only after 1975—in Spain's model of a transition to consumerism and democracy that replaced the old model of pronunciamiento—would criticism of workplace utopianism emerge.

Although signs of its breakdown have multiplied after 1968, the productivist utopian tradition has continued to influence Western conceptions of work. Not all labor historians want to build the utopia in the workplace, but most share a positive or insufficiently critical conception of work. Marxists view the working class as desiring to take over the productive forces and make itself by overcoming its undisciplined, backward, or immature behavior. Modernization theorists argue that workers' resistance will inevitably disappear during the adaptation to a modern workplace. Culturalists deemphasize resistance by claiming that workers find meaning in wage labor. They argue that the inculcation of the values of consumption, of responsibility, of patriotic and political conviction motivate wage earners. Yet these seductive forces proved inadequate in the 1930s and had to be complemented by forms of coercion. In the workplace, managers formulated strict rules and controls to improve output. On a larger scale the repressive powers of states and governments countered struggles against work.

Thus, an analysis of resistance contributes to an understanding of a key function of the state in industrial societies and to the conclusion that one of the most vital functions of the state is to make workers work. During the 1930s, a weakened or permissive state encouraged resistance, whereas a repressive state —bourgeois or proletarian—reduced refusals to work. The growth and use of state power in Barcelona and Paris during the Popular Fronts cast doubt on the argument of the workplace utopians that in socialism or libertarian communism the state will wither away. Accepting labor uncritically and believing that it provided meaning for workers, the productivist utopians logically concluded that the state would be superfluous once workers had taken control of the productive forces. Yet the actual historical experience of the Left in power in Paris and Barcelona questions such a vision. Despite the presence of working-class parties and unions in government, workers continued to resist constraints of workspace and worktime, thereby provoking state intervention to increase production. Historians may conclude that the state can be abolished only when Lafargue's cybernetic utopia has been realized.

Notes

ABBREVIATIONS USED IN NOTES

AD	Ministère des affaires étrangères
AGA	Archivo general de administración
AHN	Archivo histórico nacional
AN	Archives nationales
APP	Archives de la préfecture de police
AR	Archives des usines Renault
AS	Archivo histórico nacional, sección guerra civil
BN	Bibliothèque nationale
CE	Archives du commissariat de l'exposition
GIM	Archives du groupement des industries métallurgiques
IISH	Internationaal Instituut voor Sociale Geschiedenis
PC	Pujol Collection
SHAA	Service historique de l'armée de l'air
SNA	Société nationale aérospatiale
SNCA	Société nationale de constructions aéronautiques

INTRODUCTION

1. For Marxist historiography see Georg Lukács, *History and Class Consciousness* (Cambridge, Mass., 1971), pp. 46–82; George Rudé, *Ideology and Popular Protest* (New York, 1980), pp. 7–26; see also the recent restatement of Lukács's position in Eric Hobsbawm, *Workers: Worlds of Labor* (New York, 1984), pp. 15–32. The views of modernization theorists can be found in Peter N. Stearns, *Revolutionary Syndicalism and French Labor: A Cause without Rebels* (New Brunswick, N.J., 1971), and Stearns, *Lives of Labor: Work in a Maturing Industrial Society* (New York, 1975). For a critique of Lukács's approach, see Richard J. Evans, ed., *The German Working Class* (London, 1982), pp. 26–27. For

another interesting critique of Lukács, see John Clarke, Chas Critcher, and Richard Johnson, eds., *Working-Class Culture: Studies in History and Theory* (London, 1979), pp. 209–11.

2. The term is from Annie Kriegel, "Le parti communiste français sous la Troisième République (1920–1939): Evolution de ses effectifs," *Revue française de science politique* 21, no. 1 (February 1966): 10.

3. Stearns, *Revolutionary Syndicalism.*

4. Evans, *German Working Class;* John Bodnar, *Workers' World: Kinship, Community, and Protest in an Industrial Society, 1900–1940* (Baltimore, 1982).

5. Clarke et al., eds., *Working-Class Culture;* Gareth Stedman Jones, *Languages of Class: Studies in English Working-Class History, 1832–1982* (New York and London, 1983); Patrick Joyce, ed., *The Historical Meanings of Work* (Cambridge, 1987), pp. 1–31.

CHAPTER ONE

1. B. R. Mitchell, *European Historical Statistics, 1750–1970* (New York, 1975). It should be noted that French statistics were taken in the summer and Spanish statistics in the winter, perhaps exaggerating the differences between the two agricultures.

2. Le tourisme, Conseil national économique, AN, F^{12}8800.

3. Jordi Nadal, *El fracaso de la revolución industrial en España, 1814–1913* (Barcelona, 1975), p. 210; Carles Sudrià, "La exportación en el desarrollo de la industria algodonera española, 1875–1920," *Revista de historia económica,* no. 2 (1983): 371–76; cf. Jordi Nadal, "La industria fabril española en 1900: una aproximación," in *La economía española en el siglo XX: Una perspectiva histórica,* ed. Jordi Nadal, Albert Carreras, and Carles Sudrià (Barcelona, 1987), p. 38.

4. Joseph Harrison, *An Economic History of Modern Spain* (Manchester, 1978), p. 70.

5. N. Sánchez Albornoz, "La integración del mercado nacional," in *Agricultura, comercio colonial y crecimiento económico en la España contemporánea,* ed. Jordi Nadal and Gabriel Tortella (Barcelona, 1974), p. 187.

6. Nadal, *El fracaso,* pp. 30–39; see also Gabriel Tortella Casares, *Los orígenes de capitalismo en España* (Madrid, 1975).

7. Harrison, *Modern Spain,* p. 72.

8. Jaime Vicens Vives, *An Economic History of Spain,* with Jorge Nadal Oller, trans. Frances M. López Morillas (Princeton, 1969), p. 658.

9. Jaime Vicens Vives, *Cataluña en el siglo XIX,* trans. E. Borras Cubells (Madrid, 1961), p. 65.

10. P. Romeva Ferrer, *Història de la indústria catalana,* 2 vols. (Barcelona, 1952), 2:378; Julian Amich, *Historia del puerto de Barcelona* (Barcelona, 1956), pp. 215–17; Nadal, *El fracaso,* p. 158; Ivan T. Berend and Gyorgy Ranki, *The European Periphery and Industrialization, 1780–1914,* trans. Eva Palmai (Cambridge, 1982), p. 94.

11. Berend and Ranki, *European Periphery,* p. 154.

12. A. Broder, G. Chastagnaret, and E. Temime, "Capital et croissance dans l'Espagne du XIXème siècle," in *Aux origines du retard économique de l'Espagne, XVIe–XIXe siècles* (Paris, 1983), p. 78.

13. Nadal, *El fracaso,* p. 158.

14. Guillermo Graell, *Programa económico, social y político para después de la guerra* (Barcelona, 1917), pp. 175–77; Fomento de trabajo nacional, *Memoria* (Barcelona, 1932).

15. Santiago Roldán and José Luís García Delgado, *La formación de la sociedad capitalista en España,* with Juan Muñoz (Madrid, 1973), 1:23–38.

16. Juan Antonio Lacomba, *Introducción a la historia económica de la España contemporánea* (Madrid, 1972), p. 424. Gaston Leval, a French anarchist who worked in both countries, observed that the division of labor in Spain remained primitive in comparison to French industry. See his work, *El Prófugo* (Valencia, 1935).

17. Jordi Maluquer de Motes, "De la crisis colonial a la guerra europea: Veinte años de economía española," in *La economía española en el siglo XX,* ed. Jordi Nadal et al. (Barcelona, 1987), p. 88; see Pedro Gual Villabí, *Memorias de un industrial de nuestro tiempo* (Barcelona, 1922), for valuable insights into the Barcelonan bourgeoisie during World War I; see also Pau Vila Dinarés and Lluis Casassas Simó, *Barcelona i la seva rodalia al llarg del temps* (Barcelona, 1974), p. 394; Guillermo Graell, *Ensayo sobre la necesidad de la vuelta a las prácticas religiosas* (Barcelona, 1921), p. 309; Pedro Gual Villabí, *La economía en la industria textil* (Barcelona, 1950), p. 18; Joan Sardà and Lluc Beltran, *Els problemes de la banca catalana* (Barcelona, 1933), p. 22; Jordi Nadal and Carles Sudrià, *Història de la caixa de pensions* (Barcelona, 1981), p. 172.

18. Francisco Comín, "La economía española en el período de entreguerras (1919–35)," in *La economía española en el siglo XX,* ed. Jordi Nadal et al. (Barcelona, 1987), p. 107; Cristina Borderías Mondéjar, "La evolución de la división sexual del trabajo en Barcelona, 1924–1980: Aproximación desde una empresa del sector servicios—La Compañía Telefónica Nacional de España" (Ph.D. diss., University of Barcelona, 1984).

19. Fomento, *Memoria,* 1919–1920. These annual reports and minutes of employers' organizations are indispensable for the history of the Catalan entrepreneurs after World War I. In 1919 there were ap-

proximately two hundred thousand employers in Catalonia, of whom eighty thousand were "producers." According to its figures, in 1925 the Fomento had more than twenty thousand members who were in almost every branch of Catalan industry. Many declarations concerning important issues were signed jointly by the dozens of employers' organizations in Catalonia, which generally agreed on questions of order and discipline.

20. Actas de la junta directiva de la asociación Fomento de trabajo nacional, 24 November 1922 (hereafter cited as Fomento, Actas).

21. *El Trabajo nacional,* August 1923.

22. *Homenaje tributado por las fuerzas vivas y autoridades de Barcelona al General de Brigada Excmo. Señor Don Miguel Arleguí y Bayonés* (Barcelona, 1922); on Martínez Anido, see Gerald Meaker, *The Revolutionary Left in Spain, 1924–1923* (Stanford, 1974), pp. 328–34, 456–58. Colin M. Winston (*Workers and the Right in Spain, 1900–1936* [Princeton, 1985], p. 139) has called Arleguí "an authentically cruel individual."

23. *El Trabajo nacional,* August 1923.

24. Fomento, *Memoria,* 1934. For general remarks on the Catholicism of Spanish elites, see Stanley Payne, *Spanish Catholicism* (Madison, 1984), p. 110. On religiosity in the early twentieth century, see Joaquín Romero Maura, *La rosa de fuego: Republicanos y anarquistas: La política de los obreros barceloneses entre el desastre colonial y la semana trágica, 1899–1909* (Barcelona, 1975), p. 37.

25. Graell, *Ensayo,* p. 250; Guillermo Graell, *La cuestión religiosa* (Barcelona, 1911), pp. 16, 36; ibid., *Ensayo,* p. 383.

26. Víctor González de Echávarri y Casteñeda, *Objeto del catecismo: Su interés para todas las clases sociales* (Barcelona, 1934), p. 48.

27. Graell, *Ensayo,* pp. 76–77; *Cuestión,* p. 32; the following paragraphs are based on *Ensayo.*

28. Sholomo Ben-Ami, *Fascism from Above: The Dictatorship of Primo de Rivera in Spain, 1923–1930* (Oxford, 1983), p. 332.

29. Ibid., p. 262.

30. Josep Fontana and Jordi Nadal, "Spain 1914–1970," in *Fontana Economic History of Europe: Contemporary Economies,* ed. Carlo Cipolla (Glasgow, 1976), 2:472.

31. *El Trabajo nacional,* September 1924. See also the discussions in Fomento, Actas, 24 November 1922; Federación de fabricantes de hilados y tejidos de Cataluña, *Memoria,* (Barcelona, 1931); Federación de industrias nacionales, *Memoria* (Madrid, 1935).

32. C. Montoliu, *El sistema de Taylor y su crítica* (Barcelona, 1916), p. 63.

33. Josep M. Tallada, *L'organització científica de la industria* (Barcelona, 1922), p. 9.

34. Antido Layret Foix, *Organización de una oficina para el cálculo de los tiempos de fabricación* (Barcelona, 1931), p. 85.

35. *El Trabajo nacional,* October 1927.

36. *Exito,* January 1931.

37. Ibid.; cf. F. W. Taylor, *The Principles of Scientific Management* (New York, 1967), p. 85, who demands "the elimination of all men who refuse to or are unable to adopt the best methods."

38. Pedro Gual Villabí, *Principios y aplicaciones de la organización científica del trabajo: Obra de vulgarización* (Barcelona, 1929), p. 11.

39. Telegram, 6 July 1931, Leg. 7A, no. 1, AHN.

40. Telegram, Gobernador civil a ministro, 13 November 1931, Leg. 7A, no. 1, AHN.

41. Comín, "Entreguerras," p. 136; Maluquer de Motes, "De la crisis," p. 70.

42. Fomento, *Memoria,* 1930; see also Mercedes Cabrera, *La patronal ante la II República: Organizaciones y estrategia, 1931–1936* (Madrid, 1983), p. 206.

43. Francisco Madrid, *Ocho meses y un día en el gobierno civil de Barcelona: Confesiones y testimonios* (Barcelona, 1932), pp. 242–43.

44. Telegram from Bosch Labrus, president of Fomento, 22 July 1931, Leg. 7A, no. 1, AHN.

45. Federación de fabricantes, *Memoria,* 1932.

46. Telegrams, July–October 1931, Leg. 7A, no. 1, AHN.

47. Fomento, *Memoria,* 1931.

48. Ibid.

49. Comín, "Entreguerras," p. 112.

50. *Annuaire statistique de la France,* 1934, p. 477; Nadal and Sudrià, *Caixa,* pp. 131, 138, 249.

51. Fomento, *Memoria,* 1932.

52. Ibid., 1934; 1935.

53. Fomento, Actas, 21 September 1931; Fomento, *Memoria,* 1931.

54. Fomento, Actas, 27 May 1932.

55. On religious education of the elite, see Gary Wray McDonogh, *Good Families: A Social History of Power in Industrial Barcelona* (Ann Arbor, 1982), pp. 376–77.

56. Ignasi Terrada Saborit, *Les colònies industrials: Un estudi entorn del cas de l'Ametlla de Merola* (Barcelona, 1979), p. 168. The author calls the colony "paternalistic-religious." Historians of Spanish Catholicism have underlined this alliance between the Spanish capitalist elite and

the Church. See Joan Connelly Ullman, *The Tragic Week: A Study of Anticlericalism in Spain (1875–1912)* (Cambridge, Mass., 1968); José M. Sánchez, *Reform and Reaction* (Chapel Hill, 1964), p. 44; Payne, *Spanish Catholicism,* pp. 110–12.

57. Bernat Muniesa, *La burguesía catalana ante la Segunda República española (1931–1936)* (Barcelona, 1986), 2:46–47.

58. Elena Posa, "Cada dona un vot," *L'Avenç,* no. 4 (July–August 1977): 45.

59. See Alberto Balcells, *Crisis económica y agitación social en Cataluña de 1930 a 1936* (Barcelona, 1971); John Brademas, *Anarcosindicalismo y revolución en España (1930–1937),* trans. Joaquín Romero Maura (Barcelona, 1974); G. Blanco Santamaría and E. Ciordia Pérez, *La industria textil catalana* (Madrid, 1933), for statistics on workers in various industries in Barcelona and Catalonia.

60. See Pere Gabriel, "La població obrera catalana, una població industrial?," *Estudios de historia social* 32–33 (January–June 1985): 191, 204.

61. Enrique Diumaró y Mimó, *El problema industrial textil: El maquinismo y la cuestión social* (Barcelona, 1939), p. 68.

62. Josep Maria Bricall, *Política econòmica de la Generalitat (1936–1939)* (Barcelona, 1978–1979), 1:31–32.

63. See Alberto del Castillo, *La Maquinista Terrestre y Marítima: Personaje histórico (1855–1955)* (Barcelona, 1955), pp. 418, 461; see also Pedro Fraile, "Crecimiento económico y demanda de acero: España, 1900–1950," in *La nueva historia económica en España,* ed. Pablo Martín Aceña y Leandro Prados de la Escosura (Madrid, 1985), p. 71.

64. Joaquín Ciuró, *Historia del automovil en España* (Barcelona, 1970), pp. 94–95.

65. *Cuadernos de historia económica de Cataluña* (1969–1970): 130; *El Trabajo nacional,* September 1924, listed eight companies that failed.

66. M. Schwartz, "L'industrie automobile," Conseil national économique, AN, F^{12}8797.

67. *Metalurgia y construcción mecánica* (January 1936).

68. *Conselleria d'economia* (October 1936); F. F. Sintes Olives and F. Vidal Burdils, *La industria eléctrica en España* (Barcelona, 1933), pp. 48, 128–51.

69. Comín, "Entreguerras," p. 136; Carles Sudrià, "Un factor determinante: La energía" in *La economía española en el siglo XX,* ed. Jordi Nadal et al. (Barcelona, 1987), p. 322.

70. *Electricidad* (January 1936).

71. UGT statistics are in 1426, AS.

72. Comín, "Entreguerras," p. 116; Jesús Sanz, "La agricultura es-

pañola durante el primer tercio del siglo XX: Un sector en transformación," in *La economía española en el siglo XX,* ed. Jordi Nadal et al. (Barcelona, 1987), pp. 248–50; cf. Proyecto de ley de protección a la industria nacional de productos nitrogenados sintéticos, 320, AS.

73. Francesc Roca, "La 'gross Barcelona': Dues introduccions," *Recerques: Ideologia i creixement industrial,* no. 6 (1976): 123.

74. *Estadísticas básicas de España, 1900–1970* (Madrid, 1975); *Annuaire,* 1934, pp. 425–26.

75. *Industria catalana* (March 1933).

76. Pierre Vilar, *Historia de España,* trans. Manuel Tuñón de Lara and Jesús Suso Sola (Barcelona, 1978), p. 121.

CHAPTER TWO

1. For fine distinctions among these categories, see Gaston Leval, *Precisiones sobre el anarquismo* (Barcelona, 1937).

2. See Gerald Brenan, *The Spanish Labyrinth* (Cambridge, 1964). See also Gerald Meaker, *The Revolutionary Left in Spain, 1914–1923* (Stanford, 1974).

3. Peter N. Stearns, *Revolutionary Syndicalism and French Labor: A Cause without Rebels* (New Brunswick, N.J., 1971), pp. 10, 105.

4. Joaquín Maurín, *La revolución española* (Barcelona, 1977), p. 154.

5. Alberto Balcells, *Crisis económica y agitación social en Cataluña de 1930 a 1936* (Barcelona, 1971), p. 18, would put the figure at 37 percent. My own random sample from AS indicates that less than one-third of Barcelonan workers were non-Catalans. In 1930, 37.14 percent of the Barcelonan population was born outside of Catalonia. See A. Cabre and I. Pujades, "La població de Barcelona i del seu entorn al segle XX," *L'Avenç,* no. 88 (December 1985), p. 35.

6. Stanley Payne, *Falange* (Stanford, 1967), p. 2; "Direction des affaires politiques et commerciales," 3 January 1934, AD.

7. Henri Paechter, *Espagne, 1936–1937* (Paris, 1986), p. 85; Pierre Conard and Albert Lovett, "Problèmes de l'évaluation du coût de vie en Espagne: Le prix du pain depuis le milieu du XIX siècle, une source nouvelle," *Mélanges de la casa de Velásquez* 5 (1969): 419; Gabrielle Letellier, Jean Perret, H. E. Zuber, and A. Dauphin-Meunier, *Enquête sur le chômage* (Paris, 1938–1949), 3:35.

8. Joaquín Arango, "La modernización demográfica de la sociedad española," in *La economía española en el siglo XX,* ed. Jordi Nadal et al. (Barcelona, 1987), p. 209.

9. Figures from B. R. Mitchell, *European Historical Statistics, 1750–1970* (New York, 1975), p. 20; Paris and Barcelona comparisons are

based on the *Gaseta municipal de Barcelona, 1935* and *Annuaire statistique de la ville de Paris, 1935–1937.*

10. Cécile Tardieu-Gotchac, "Les fléaux sociaux," in *Histoire économique de la France entre les deux guerres,* ed. Alfred Sauvy (Paris, 1972), 3:290.

11. Balcells, *Crisis económica y agitación social,* p. 70.

12. *Anuario estadístico de España,* 1934, pp. 782, 982.

13. Ibid., pp. 802–6; *Annuaire de Paris,* 1934, p. 62. These figures are approximations and exclude first-aid stations.

14. Julio Ruiz Berrio and Angeles Galino, "L'éducation en Espagne," in *Histoire mondiale de l'éducation,* ed. Gaston Mialaret and Jean Vial (Paris, 1981), 3:205.

15. Ramón Tamames, *La república, la era de Franco* (Madrid, 1980), p. 132; R. Aubert, M. D. Knowles, and L. J. Rogier, eds., *L'Eglise dans le monde moderne* (Paris, 1975), 5:110.

16. Ruiz Berrio and Galino, "L'éducation," p. 202.

17. John M. McNair, *Education for a Changing Spain* (Manchester, 1984), p. 26; Tamames, *La república,* p. 66; Harry Gannes and Theodore Repard, *Spain in Revolt* (London, 1936), p. 228.

18. Ramón Safón, *La educación en la España revolucionaria (1936–1939),* trans. María Luisa Delgado and Félix Ortega (Madrid, 1978), p. 30.

19. Guillermo Graell, *Programa económico, social y político para después de la guerra* (Barcelona, 1917), p. 227.

20. Fomento de trabajo nacional, Actas de la junta directiva, 24 November 1922.

21. Javier Tusell Gómez, *Las elecciones del frente popular en España* (Madrid, 1971), 2:210.

22. Figures from Safón, *Educación,* pp. 82–84.

23. Juan Peiró, *Trayectoria de la CNT* (Madrid, 1979), p. 11; see León Ignacio, "El Pistolerisme dels anys vint," *L'Avenç,* no. 52 (September 1982), which claims that the CNT leader learned to read at age sixteen.

24. McNair, *Education,* p. 25; *Estadísticas básicas,* pp. 430–31; Joseph N. Moody, *French Education since Napoleon* (Syracuse, N.Y., 1978), p. 142. See also *La industria eléctrica* (March 1936).

25. Angel Marvaud, *La question sociale en Espagne* (Paris, 1910), p. 413.

26. Xavier Cuadrat, *Socialismo y anarquismo en Cataluña (1899–1911: los orígenes de la CNT)* (Madrid, 1976), p. 56.

27. For anarchist faith in progress, see José Alvarez Junco, *La ideología política del anarquismo español, 1868–1919* (Madrid, 1976), p. 75.

28. Cited in Mary Nash, *Mujer, familia y trabajo en España, 1875–1936* (Barcelona, 1983), p. 300.

29. Cited in Alberto Balcells, *Trabajo industrial y organización obrera en la Cataluña contemporánea (1900–1936)* (Barcelona, 1974), p. 14.

30. Georges Lefranc, *Le mouvement syndical sous la Troisième République* (Paris, 1967), p. 163.

31. Georges Sorel, *Réflexions sur la violence* (Paris, 1972), p. 320; on Sorel's influence in Spain, see E. Giralt i Raventos, ed., *Bibliografia dels moviments socials a Catalunya, país Valencià i les illes* (Barcelona, 1972).

32. Léon Jamin, *La lutte pour les 8 heures* (Paris, 1906), pp. 28–41.

33. E. Pouget, *L'organisation du surmenage: Le système Taylor* (Paris, 1914), p. 55.

34. Ibid., pp. 20–21, 45.

35. David F. Noble, *America by Design* (New York, 1977), p. 275.

36. Angel Pestaña, *Terrorismo en Barcelona,* ed. Xavier Tusell and Genoveva García Queipo de Llana (Barcelona, 1979), p. 67.

37. Antonio Elorza, *La utopía anarquista bajo la Segunda República española* (Madrid, 1973), pp. 391–468.

38. Diego Abad de Santillán, *El anarquismo y la revolución en España: escritos 1930–1938,* ed. Antonio Elorza (Madrid, 1976), pp. 280–96. The following paragraphs are based on this text.

39. Xavier Paniagua, *La sociedad libertaria: Agrarismo e industrialización en el anarquismo español, 1930–1939* (Barcelona, 1982), p. 254; Issac Puente, *La finalidad de la CNT: El comunismo libertario* (Barcelona, 1936); Walther L. Bernecker, *Colectividades y revolución social: El anarquismo en la guerra civil española, 1936–1939,* trans. Gustau Muñoz (Barcelona, 1982), p. 83.

40. Angel Pestaña, *Normas orgánicas* (Barcelona, 1930), p. 18.

41. Civera quoted in Paniagua, *Sociedad,* p. 187.

42. Juan López, *Cómo organizará el sindicato a la sociedad* (Barcelona, n.d.), p. 5.

43. Puente, *Finalidad,* p. 15.

44. Ramón Segarra Vaqué, *Qué es el comunismo libertario* (Madrid, n.d.), p. 10.

45. CNT, *El congreso confederal de Zaragoza, 1936* (Madrid, 1978), pp. 231–33. The congress guaranteed limited autonomy for communes that rejected industrialization or adopted nudism.

46. Christian Cornelissen, *El comunismo libertario y el régimen de transición,* trans. Eloy Muñiz (Valencia, 1936).

47. Cornelissen cited in Paniagua, *Sociedad,* p. 143.

48. Bernecker, *Colectividades,* p. 86.

49. The following is derived from Pierre Besnard, *Le monde nouveau: Organisation d'une société anarchiste* (Paris [reprint, 1934]), p. 10.

50. Guillaume quoted in Besnard, *Monde*, p. 70.

51. Gaston Leval [Pedro R. Piller, pseud.], *Problemas económicos de la revolución social española* (Rosario de Santa Fe, 1932), p. 28.

52. Gaston Leval, *Nuestro programa de reconstrucción* (Barcelona [1937?]), p. 12.

53. Leval, *Problemas económicos*, p. 16.

54. Leval quoted in Paniagua, *Sociedad*, p. 206. See also Leval's discussion in *Precisiones*, p. 221.

55. *Solidaridad Obrera*, 8 January 1937. On workers' resentment of priests who were exempted from military service, see Jacques Valdour, *L'ouvrier espagnol: Observations vécues* (Paris, 1919), 1:284.

56. Juan Peiró, *Problemas y cintarazos* (Rennes, 1946), p. 143; Gonzalo de Reparaz, *La tragedia ibérica* (Barcelona, n.d.), p. 113; See also José Alvarez Junco, "El anticlericalismo en el movimiento obrero," in *Octubre 1934* (Madrid, 1985), pp. 283–300.

57. Valdour, *L'ouvrier espagnol*, 1:208, 328–31.

58. Anselmo Lorenzo, *Contra la ignorancia* (Barcelona, 1913), p. 13.

59. Pere Solà Gusiñer, "La escuela y la educación en los medios anarquistas de Cataluña, 1909–1939," *Convivium* 44–45 (1975): 52.

60. Diego Abad de Santillán, *El organismo económico de la revolución: Cómo vivimos y cómo podríamos vivir en España* (Barcelona, 1938). For similar critiques by libertarian militants, Gonzalo de Reparaz, [hijo], *Pobreza y atraso de España* (Valencia, 1932) and Ricardo Sanz, *El sindicalismo y la política: Los solidarios y nosostros* (Toulouse, 1966), p. 38.

61. Sindicato de la industria siderometalúrgica de Barcelona, *¿Colectivización? ¿Nacionalización? No socialización* (Barcelona, 1937), p. 13.

62. This quotation and the following come from *Sidero-Metalurgia*, July and August 1937.

63. *CNT Marítima*, 13 May 1937.

64. Ibid., 23 October 1937.

65. *Hoy*, December 1937 and January 1938 (*Hoy* was a CNT building workers' review).

66. See Alfonso Martínez Rizo, *La urbanística del porvenir* (Valencia, 1932), which would reduce the congestion of overly large cities and avoid skyscrapers; in practice the CNT rejected this libertarian militant's different "rational urbanism," as it did decentralization.

67. *Boletín del Sindicato de la industria fabril y textil de Badalona y su radio*, February 1937 (Badalona was an industrial suburb of Barcelona).

68. *Conferència de la indústria tèxtil del POUM* (Barcelona, 1937), pp. 11–13.
69. Federico Melchor, *El frente de la producción: Una industria grande y fuerte para ganar la guerra* (Valencia? 1937?), pp. 6, 12.
70. *CNT Marítima,* 11 September 1937; 18 December 1937.
71. *Horizontes,* 1 February 1937.
72. *Aeronáutica,* May–June 1938.
73. *Solidaridad Obrera,* 3 March 1938; *Butlletí de la Federació catalana d'indústries químiques–UGT,* November 1937, p. 22.
74. *Síntesis,* October 1938.
75. Telegrams, 9 and 13 July 1931, Leg. 7A, no. 1, AHN.
76. *CNT Marítima,* 16 January 1938.
77. *Luz y fuerza,* April 1937.
78. Ibid., February 1937.
79. See also Francisco Madrid, *Ocho meses y un día en el gobierno civil de Barcelona: Confesiones y testimonios* (Barcelona, 1932), p. 14; Murray Bookchin, *The Spanish Anarchists: The Heroic Years, 1868–1936* (New York, 1978), pp. 177–78; Juan Gómez Casas, *Historia del anarcosindicalismo español* (Madrid, 1973), p. 115; César M. Lorenzo, *Los anarquistas españoles y el poder, 1868–1969* (Paris, 1972), p. 34; Sanz, *Sindicalismo,* pp. 34–35.
80. Abad de Santillán, *El organismo económico,* p. 180; Elorza, *La utopía anarquista,* p. 430.
81. Puente, *Finalidad de la CNT,* p. 14.
82. Gaston Leval, *Conceptos económicos en el socialismo libertario* (Buenos Aires, 1935), p. 100.
83. Besnard quoted in Paniagua, *Sociedad,* p. 137.
84. Abad de Santillán, *El organismo económico,* p. 58; Leval, *Precisiones,* p. 222.
85. Paniagua, *Sociedad,* pp. 171, 172–77.
86. CNT, *El congreso de Zaragoza,* p. 236; italics added.
87. *Solidaridad Obrera,* 12 May 1936.

CHAPTER THREE

1. Murray Bookchin, *The Spanish Anarchists: The Heroic Years, 1868–1936* (New York, 1978), p. 160; see also César M. Lorenzo, *Los anarquistas españoles y el poder 1868–1969* (Paris, 1972), p. 37 and Juan Gómez Casas, *Historia del anarcosindicalismo español* (Madrid, 1973), p. 94; Antonio Bar Cendón, "La confederación nacional del trabajo frente a la II República," in *Estudios sobre la II República española,* ed. Manuel Ramírez (Madrid, 1975), p. 222.

2. Lorenzo, *Los anarquistas españoles,* p. 33. On the definition of direct action, see Ricardo Sanz, *El sindicalismo y la política: Los solidarios y nosotros* (Toulouse, 1966), p. 43, who argues that many workers misinterpreted direct action to mean a systematic use of force to solve labor disputes; Sanz defines direct action as face-to-face bargaining between labor and capital.

3. Bookchin, *The Spanish Anarchists,* p. 168; see also Lorenzo, *Los anarquistas españoles,* p. 43; Gerald Meaker, *The Revolutionary Left in Spain, 1914–1923* (Stanford, 1974), p. 63.

4. José Peirats, *La CNT en la revolución española* (Paris, 1971), 1:26. On the weakness and compromises of Spanish anticlericals, see Raymond Carr, *Spain 1808–1975* (Oxford, 1982), pp. 490–94.

5. Paul Preston, "The Origins of the Socialist Schism in Spain, 1917–1931," *Journal of Contemporary History* 12, no. 1 (January 1977): 125.

6. Lorenzo, *Los anarquistas españoles,* pp. 35–36.

7. Fomento de trabajo nacional, *Memoria,* 1921–1922.

8. Lorenzo, *Los anarquistas españoles,* p. 50.

9. John Brademas, *Anarcosindicalismo y revolución en España (1930–1937),* trans. Joaquín Romero Maura (Barcelona, 1974), p. 31.

10. Enric Ucelay Da Cal, "Estat català: Strategies of Separation and Revolution of Catalan Radical Nationalism (1919–1933)" (Ph.D. diss., Columbia University, 1979), pp. 266–68. On cooperation between the Confederación and Catalan nationalists, see also Sanz, *Sindicalismo,* pp. 129, 184.

11. Bookchin, *The Spanish Anarchists,* pp. 217–18; see also Brademas, *Anarcosindicalismo y revolución,* p. 31; Susanna Tavera, "La CNT i la 'República catalana,' " *L'Avenç,* no. 13 (February 1979): 46.

12. Brademas, *Anarcosindicalismo y revolución,* p. 50.

13. The remainder of this paragraph is based on Telegrama oficial, 21 January 1932, gobernador a ministro, caja 2412, AGA.

14. Lorenzo, *Los anarquistas españoles,* p. 57.

15. G. Munis, *Jalones de derrota: Promesa de victoria, España 1930–1939* (Mexico City, 1948), p. 92.

16. Brademas, *Anarcosindicalismo y revolución,* pp. 98–103; Bookchin, *The Spanish Anarchists,* p. 245; Lorenzo, *Los anarquistas españoles,* p. 58; Gómez, *Historia del anarcosindicalismo,* p. 169.

17. Durruti, quoted in Bookchin, *The Spanish Anarchists,* p. 250; see also Brademas, *Anarcosindicalismo y revolución,* p. 108.

18. Lorenzo, *Los anarquistas españoles,* p. 61; José A. González Casanova, *Elecciones en Barcelona (1931–1936)* (Madrid, 1969), p. 26.

19. CNT, 9 December 1933, quoted in Brademas, *Anarcosindicalismo y revolución*, pp. 114–15.

20. Susanna Tavera, "Els anarcosindicalistes catalans i la dictadura," *L'Avenç*, no. 72 (July 1984): 65; Sanz, *Sindicalismo*, p. 123; for the growth of the CNT in Asturias at the end of Primo's dictatorship and the beginning of the Second Republic, see Adrian Shubert, *Hacia la revolución: Orígenes sociales del movimiento obrero en Asturias, 1860–1934*, trans. Agueda Palacios Honorato (Barcelona, 1984), pp. 178–79.

21. Cited in Peirats, *La CNT*, 1:83–87; italics added.

22. Ibid., p. 88.

23. Edward E. Malefakis, *Agrarian Reform and Peasant Revolution in Spain* (New Haven, 1970), pp. 301–2.

24. Francisco Madrid, *Ocho meses y un día en el gobierno civil de Barcelona: Confesiones y testimonios* (Barcelona, 1932), p. 198.

25. Ibid., p. 238; Jordi Sabater, *Anarquisme i catalanisme: La CNT i el fet nacional català durant la guerra civil* (Barcelona, 1986), pp. 31–37.

26. Brademas, *Anarcosindicalismo y revolución*, p. 133. The CNT's daily newspaper, *Solidaridad Obrera*, was banned. See Peirats, *La CNT*, 1:101; see also Alberto Balcells, *Crisis económica y agitación social en Cataluña de 1930 a 1936* (Barcelona, 1971), p. 179.

27. Shubert, *Hacia*, p. 202.

28. Ricard Vinyes, "Sis octubre: Repressió i represaliats," *L'Avenç*, no. 30 (September 1980); Sanz, *Sindicalismo*, p. 260.

29. Circular 17, 14 April 1935, 2416, AGA.

30. For the manifesto, Javier Tusell Gómez, *Las elecciones del frente popular en España* (Madrid, 1971), 2:352–58. It is also reproduced in Santos Juliá, *Orígenes del frente popular en España, 1934–1936* (Madrid, 1979), pp. 216–23.

31. Tusell, *Las elecciones*, 1:222; Santos Juliá, *Orígenes*, p. 131.

32. Brademas, *Anarcosindicalismo y revolución*, p. 163.

33. Lorenzo, *Los anarquistas españoles*, p. 72.

34. Acció catòlica quoted in Tusell, *Las elecciones*, 1:114–15.

35. Elena Posa, "El front d'esquerres de Catalunya," *L'Avenç*, no. 1 (April 1977): 52.

36. Bar Cendón, "La confederación," p. 247, attributes the victory of the Popular Front to the CNT.

37. González Casanova, *Elecciones*, pp. 26, 67. The effect of the CNT's abstentionist campaign is still a subject of dispute; see Mercedes Vilanova, "El abstencionismo electoral y su relación con las fuerzas políticas en la provincia de Gerona durante la Segunda República:

Un ejemplo, La Escala," in *Homenaje a Dr. D. Juan Reglà Campistol* (Valencia, 1975), 2:500–503; Vilanova concludes that the CNT's antipolitical position had little influence on its sympathizers.

38. Bar Cendón, "La confederación," p. 232; see also A. Cucó Giner, "Contribución a un estudio cuantitativo de la CNT," *Saitabi* 20 (1970).

39. Balcells, *Crisis económica y agitación social,* p. 12.

40. Fomento de trabajo nacional, Actas de la junta directiva, 24 November 1922.

41. Sindicato único de la metalurgia, *Informe sobre su reorganización y desenvolvimiento* (Barcelona, 1931), p. 19; Sanz, *Sindicalismo,* p. 194.

42. Actas, pleno de juntas, federación local de sindicatos únicos de Barcelona, 31 December 1931, 501, AS.

43. Quoted in Balcells, *Crisis económica y agitación social,* pp. 201–2.

44. Madrid, *Ocho meses,* p. 154.

45. Balcells, *Crisis económica y agitación social,* p. 203; Anna Monjo and Carme Vega, *Els treballadors i la guerra civil* (Barcelona, 1986), p. 14.

46. Valdour, *L'ouvrier espagnol,* 1:45, 329.

47. Gaston Leval, *El prófugo* (Valencia, 1935), p. 142.

48. Antido Layret Foix, *Organización de una oficina para el cálculo de los tiempos de fabricación* (Barcelona, 1931), pp. 16, 42.

49. Fomento, *Memoria,* 1934. In France the issue was a workweek of forty hours, not of forty-four hours.

50. Balcells, *Crisis económica y agitación social,* pp. 220–24; Alberto del Castillo, *La Maquinista Terrestre y Marítima: Personaje histórico (1855–1955)* (Barcelona, 1955), pp. 460–61.

51. Castillo, *La Maquinista Terrestre y Marítima,* pp. 464–65.

52. Fomento, *Memoria,* 1932.

53. Valdour, *L'ouvrier espagnol,* 1:52. On dechristianization, see the brief remarks in Josep Massot i Muntaner, *Aproximació a la història religiosa de la Catalunya contemporània* (Barcelona, 1973), pp. 119–24.

54. G. Blanco Santamaría and E. Ciordia Pérez, *La industria textil catalana* (Madrid, 1933), p. 36.

55. Fomento, Actas, 14 February 1927.

56. Federación de fabricantes de hilados y tejidos de Cataluña, *Memoria* (Barcelona, 1930); Fomento, *Memoria,* 1932.

57. Figures in Rosa María Capel Muñoz, *La mujer española en el mundo del trabajo, 1900–1930* (Madrid, 1980), p. 32.

58. Fomento, *Memoria,* 1928.

59. Gobernador a ministro, 10 August 1931, Leg. 7A, no. 1, AHN.

60. Madrid, *Ocho meses,* p. 194.

61. Rosa María Capel Martínez, ed., *Mujer y sociedad en España, 1700–1975* (Madrid, 1982), p. 213.

62. Fomento, Actas, 2 June 1922.

63. Capel, *Mujer y sociedad,* p. 214. There is also evidence that married women continued as wage earners (Cristina Borderías Mondéjar, "La evolución de la división sexual del trabajo en Barcelona, 1924–1980: Aproximación desde una empresa del sector servicios—La Compañía Telefónica Nacional de España" [Ph.D. diss., University of Barcelona, 1984], pp. 379–80). The figures for men were 39.13 percent single, 52.65 married, and 4.86 percent widowed.

64. 6, 9, and 15 July 1931, Leg. 7A, no. 1, AHN; 4,300 female workers were employed in the communications sectors—telephone, telegram, and post office—in 1930. In 1933 almost 40 percent of telephone workers were women.

65. Capel, *Mujer y sociedad,* p. 236; Mary Nash, *Mujer, familia y trabajo en España, 1875–1936* (Barcelona, 1983), p. 53.

66. The following paragraph is based on Federación de fabricantes, *Memoria* (Barcelona, 1933).

67. Fomento, Actas, 16 July 1934; Fomento, *Memoria,* 1934; Balcells, *Crisis económica y agitación social,* pp. 223–24.

68. Fomento, *Memoria,* 1934.

69. Gobernador civil a ministro, Leg. 40A, no. 2, AHN.

70. The following paragraphs are based on telegrams, October 1930, Leg. 40A, no. 2, AHN.

71. Telegram, 20 April 1931 and Gobierno civil de Barcelona, Leg. 7A, no. 1, AHN.

72. Gobernador civil a ministro, 19 November 1931, Leg. 7A, no. 1, AHN; 23 August 1932, Leg. 6A, no. 35, AHN. See also Manuel Ramírez Jiménez, "Las huelgas durante la Segunda República," *Anales de sociología* (1966): 81.

73. Balcells, *Crisis económica y agitación social,* p. 227.

74. See series of telegrams in Leg. 7A, no. 1 and Leg. 40A, no. 2, AHN.

75. Balcells, *Crisis económica y agitación social,* p. 207.

76. Adolfo Bueso, *Recuerdos de un cenetista* (Barcelona, 1978), 2:93.

77. Ibid., p. 135; Fomento, *Memoria,* 1934; Mercedes Cabrera, *La patronal ante la II República: Organizaciones y estrategia, 1931–1936* (Madrid, 1983), p. 101.

78. Balcells, *Crisis económica y agitación social,* p. 230.

79. 20 March 1936, 147, AS.

80. The following is derived from Balcells, *Crisis económica y agitación social,* pp. 231–88.

81. Acta de la reunión, CNT caldereros, 12 May 1936, 1428, AS; Asamblea, CNT cargadores, 29 May 1936, 1404, AS; 14 January 1937, 182, AS.

82. Fomento, *Memoria,* 1934.

CHAPTER FOUR

1. José Peirats, *La CNT en la revolución española* (Paris, 1971), 1:160. Felix Morrow (*Revolution and Counterrevolution in Spain* [New York, 1974]) has remarked on the similarity between the Bolshevik program of 1917 and that of the Central Committee of Antifascist Militias. Unlike the Bolsheviks, however, the CNT and the FAI ended up sharing power with other political parties and unions.

2. *Tierra y Libertad,* 10 September 1936. On the Church, see Frances Lannon, "The Church's Crusade against the Republic," in *Revolution and War in Spain, 1931–1939,* ed. Paul Preston (London, 1984); Enric Ucelay Da Cal, *La Catalunya populista: Imatge, cultura i política en l'etapa republicana, 1931–1939* (Barcelona, 1982), p. 140; Mary Vincent, "The Spanish Church and the *Frente Popular*" (Paper presented at Popular Fronts Conference, University of Southampton, April 1986); Hilari Raguer i Suñer, *La unió democràtica de Catalunya i el seu temps (1931–1939)* (Montserrat, 1976).

3. Pierre Vilar, *La guerre d'Espagne, 1936–1939* (Paris, 1986), p. 24.

4. *Solidaridad Obrera,* 23 July 1936; Gabriel Jackson, *The Spanish Republic and the Civil War* (Princeton, 1967), p. 289.

5. Josep Massot i Muntaner, *Aproximació a la història religiosa de la Catalunya contemporània* (Barcelona, 1973), p. 128. See also Vilar, *La guerre,* p. 108; the author adds, "Il faut remonter à la révolution française pour trouver l'équivalent." For a recent study, José M. Sánchez, *The Spanish Civil War as a Religious Tragedy* (Notre Dame, 1987), p. 8.

6. Agustin Souchy and Paul Folgare, *Colectivizaciones: La obra constructiva de la revolución española* (Barcelona, 1977), p. 75; Direction des affaires politiques et commerciales, 3 November 1936, 244, AD.

7. Junta, 16 January 1937, 1204, AS; Caldereros en cobre, 9 September 1936, 1428, AS; Junta de secciones, 24 September 1936, 1446, AS.

8. Antoni Castells i Durán, "La colectivización-socialización de la industria y los servicios en Barcelona ciudad y provincia" (Manuscript, Barcelona, Centre d'estudis històrics internacionals, 1986), p. 131.

9. See files in Generalitat 240, AS.

10. Comité, 26 November 1936, 182, AS.

11. Although this firm depended on the contracts awarded by the CNT, the personnel opposed collectivization (Informe, contables UGT-CNT, 5 March 1938, 1219, AS).

12. For the text in Catalan, see Albert Pérez Baró, *30 meses de colectivismo en Cataluña (1936–1939)* (Barcelona, 1974), pp. 193–200; for a contested Spanish version, Souchy and Folgare, *Colectivizaciones,* pp. 36–38.

13. César M. Lorenzo, *Los anarquistas españoles y el poder, 1869–1969* (Paris, 1972), p. 103.

14. Juan P. Fábregas, *Les finances de la revolució* (Barcelona, 1937), p. 87.

15. Juan P. Fábregas, *Los factores económicos de la revolución española* (Barcelona, 1937).

16. See Noam Chomsky, *American Power and the New Mandarins* (New York, 1969), pp. 72–158; Burnett Bolloten, *The Spanish Revolution, the Left, and the Struggle for Power during the Civil War* (Chapel Hill, 1979); John Brademas, *Anarcosindicalismo y revolución en España (1930–1937),* trans. Joaquín Romero Maura (Barcelona, 1974); Carlos Semprún-Maura, *Revolución y contrarrevolución en Cataluña, 1936–1937,* trans. Julia Escobar (Barcelona, 1974); James W. Cortada, ed., *A City in War: American Views on Barcelona and the Spanish Civil War, 1936–1939* (Wilmington, Del., 1985).

17. Lorenzo, *Los anarquistas españoles,* p. 223; *Butlletí interior de la Unió general de treballadors,* January 1937. These figures, especially those of the UGT, must be used with caution.

18. *Boletín del Comité nacional de la CNT para exclusivo uso de los sindicatos,* 1 November 1937; Lorenzo, *Los anarquistas españoles,* p. 225. On the Generalitat's formal control, see José Arias Velasco, *La hacienda de la Generalidad, 1931–1938* (Barcelona, 1977), p. 211.

19. *De Companys a Indalecio Prieto: Documentación sobre las industrias de guerra en Cataluña* (Buenos Aires, 1939), pp. 77–91. The defense sector was obviously a bastion of power for whichever organization controlled it, and its workers had privileged access to food supplies.

20. L'industrie de guerre de la république espagnole, box 54, Burnett Bolloten Collection, Hoover Institution; UGT sindicato de madera, 6 May 1938, 1411, AS.

21. Informe al comité ejecutivo, 23 April 1938, 1084, AS.

22. *Solidaridad Obrera,* 10 May 1938.

23. Ramón Tamames, *La república, la era de Franco* (Madrid, 1980), p. 310.

24. *Solidaridad Obrera,* 11 November 1938.

25. Peirats, *La CNT,* 2:173.

26. Joan Fronjosà, *La missió dels treballadors i la dels sindicats en la nova organització industrial* (Barcelona, 1937), p. 5.

27. Actes de reunió del consell general de la indústria química, Generalitat 252, AS.

28. The Generalitat had decreed a 50 percent reduction in rents and wanted to restrict union control of urban property (Josep Tarradellas, *L'obra financera de la Generalitat de Catalunya* [Barcelona, 1938], pp. 42–44).

29. Walter Tauber, "Les tramways de Barcelone collectivisés pendant la révolution espagnole, 1936–1939," *Bulletin d'information, Fondation internationale d'études historiques et sociales* (March, 1977): 14.

30. Castells, "Colectivización," p. 74.

31. Walther L. Bernecker, *Anarchismus und Bürgerkrieg: Zur Geschichte der Soziale Revolution im Spanien, 1936–1939* (Hamburg, 1978), pp. 234, 245, 254; Walther L. Bernecker, *Colectividades y revolución social: El anarquismo en la guerra española, 1936–1939,* trans. Gustau Muñoz (Barcelona, 1982), p. 76.

32. *Solidaridad Obrera,* 26, 27, 28 July 1936; Tauber, "Tramways," p. 25.

33. Anna Monjo and Carme Vega, *Els treballadors i la guerra civil* (Barcelona, 1986), p. 44.

34. Tauber, "Tramways," p. 39.

35. Comité central de gas i electricitat, 19 August 1936, 182, AS.

36. Tauber, "Tramways," p. 38.

37. Adolfo Bueso, *Recuerdos de un cenetista* (Barcelona, 1978), 2:162.

38. Pérez Baró, *30 meses,* p. 46.

39. Quoted in Bernecker, *Colectividades,* p. 315; *Solidaridad Obrera,* 2 June 1937.

40. Comité, 12 November 1936, 182, AS.

41. Al Sindicato, 18 February 1937, 1446, AS; Comité, 4 January 1937, 182, AS; *Solidaridad Obrera,* 15 May 1937.

42. Comité, 2 and 16 March 1937, 181, AS.

43. Reunión de junta, 23 February 1204, AS; Acta de asamblea, 21 February 1937, 469, AS; Reunión, organización telefónica, 1170, AS.

44. Comité, 16 March 1937, 181, AS.

45. Manuel Azaña, *Obras completas* (Mexico City, 1967), 3:488.

46. United Shoe, Generalitat 252, AS.

47. Informe, 22 June 1938, 9, Leg. 18, AS.

48. Monjo and Vega, *Els treballadors,* p. 156; Al Sindicato, 29 January 1938, 9, Leg. 18, AS. See also the concluding remarks of Michael

Alpert, *El ejército republicano en la guerra civil* (Paris, 1977), pp. 299–335.

49. Letters from militants in 933 and other *carpetas,* AS; on the legitimacy of "indispensable" status in a metallurgical factory, see Trefilerías (n.d.), 887, AS.

50. Alberto Balcells, *Crisis económica y agitación social en Cataluña de 1930 a 1936* (Barcelona, 1971), p. 198.

51. Pérez Baró, *30 meses,* p. 47.

52. The following information is from Actas de sindicato de trabajadores de canódromos, 861, AS.

53. 18 October 1936, 1322, AS.

54. Societat de moços, 20 September 1936, 1170, AS.

55. Comité, 17 October 1938, 182, AS.

56. H. Rüdiger, "Materiales para la discusión sobre la situación española en el pleno de la AIT," 8 May 1937, Rudolf Rocker Archives, 527–30, IISH.

57. Acta de asamblea (n.d.), 469, AS.

58. *CNT Marítima,* 7 August 1937; *Boletín del Sindicato de la industria de la edificación, madera y decoración,* 10 October 1937; *Sidero-Metalurgia,* September 1937.

59. Acta de asamblea ordinaria, 4 December 1936, PC.

60. See report, 1219, AS.

61. Monjo and Vega, *Els treballadors,* pp. 91–92; Anna Monjo and Carme Vega, "Les col.lectivitzacions industrials a Barcelona durant la guerra civil," *L'Avenç,* no. 70 (April 1984): 37.

62. Asamblea general extraordinaria, sindicato de artes gráficas CNT, 18 October 1936, 1204, AS. At the same meeting a motion was presented to require members to purchase the union's journal so it "would be successful"; the motion failed, perhaps because the union press lacked support among the rank and file.

63. Acta, 21 February 1937, 469, AS; Acta, 22 August 1937, 1404, AS.

64. Reunión de junta, 2 October 1936, 1204, AS; Comité ejecutivo, 10 December 1937, 501, AS.

65. See J. García Pradas, *Antifascismo proletario: Tesis, ambiente, táctica* (Madrid, 1938?), 1:24.

66. Juan López, *Seis meses en el ministerio de comercio: Conferencia pronunciada el 27 mayo 1937* (Valencia, 1937), p. 14; Jordi Sabater, *Anarquisme i catalanisme: La CNT i el fet nacional català durant la guerra civil* (Barcelona, 1986), p. 55.

67. M. Cardona Rossell, *Aspectos económicos de nuestra revolución* (Barcelona, 1937), p. 13.

68. Juan Peiró, *Problemas y cintarazos* (Rennes, 1946), pp. 124–25, 53; Sabater, *Anarquisme,* pp. 55, 63.

69. A. Schapiro, "National-Anarchisme," *Le Combat syndicaliste,* 11 June 1937, Rudolf Rocker Archives, 566, IISH.

70. See CNT/AIT circulars, "Nacional-Anarquismo," in ibid. The CNT was not exempt from a xenophobia that occasionally degenerated into a rather familiar antisemitism. *Solidaridad Obrera,* 31 January 1937, accused Franco of looking like a Jew and criticized "Jewish plutocrats" and financiers of working with Hitler. In May 1938 when Ben-Krimo, a Sephardic Jew, asked the CNT to aid persecuted Jews, he received a very cold response from Mariano Vázquez, the secretary of the national committee. Vázquez refused to open Spain's doors "to all the Jews who wish to come here. It is impossible because it would undoubtedly be one of the most counterrevolutionary decisions that we could take. We are sure that [admission of the Jews] would mean the immediate revival and strengthening of capitalism and the old exploitation" (See the exchange of letters in 811, AS).

71. Helmut Rüdiger, *El anarcosindicalismo en la revolución española* (Barcelona, 1938), p. 7.

72. *CNT Marítima,* 11 September 1937.

73. *Solidaridad Obrera,* 15 September 1937.

74. Ibid., 14 September 1937.

75. Comité de serveis correccionals, 14 January 1937, Generalitat, leg. 25, AS.

76. *Solidaridad Obrera,* 31 December 1936.

77. Lorenzo, *Los anarquistas españoles,* p. 124.

78. Luis López de Medrano, *986 días en el infierno* (Madrid, 1939), pp. 178–84. This author's opinion cannot always be taken at face value; at one point in his tirade against the Popular Front, he claims that Guernica was destroyed by "Red Basque separatists allied with criminals of the CNT."

79. *Motiu,* 24–30 July 1937, Generalitat 69, AS.

80. Files in 352, AS; the following statistics are from Estances dels reclosos, Generalitat 88, AS. See also A los compañeros, 26 January 1938, 1446, AS.

81. See files in 615, AS.

82. Eric Hobsbawm, *Workers: Worlds of Labor* (New York, 1984), p. 87. See also Carmen Grimau, *El cartel republicano en la guerra civil* (Madrid, 1979), p. 208, for images of women.

83. *Tierra y Libertad,* 20 November 1937; Henri Paechter, *Espagne, 1936–1937* (Paris, 1986), p. 110.

CHAPTER FIVE

1. Report of the textile unions, 17 May 1937, 1352, AS; *Boletín del Sindicato de la industria fabril y textil de Badalona y su radio,* February, 1937; Acta de la tercera sesión del pleno nacional de regionales de la industria fabril, textil, vestir, 626, AS; A. Pérez, "La concentración industrial," *CNT Marítima,* 15 September 1938; sastrería, 7 October 1937, 1219, AS.

2. Antoni Castells i Durán, "La colectivización-socialización de la industria y los servicios en Barcelona ciudad y provincia" (Manuscript, Barcelona, Centre d'Estudis històrics internacionals, 1986), pp. 319–36. See figures in Josep Maria Bricall, *Política econòmica de la Generalitat (1936–1939)* (Barcelona, 1978–1979), 1:224; Francesc Roca, "El decret de municipalització de la propietat urbana de l'2 de juny del 1937 i la nova economia urbana," *Recerques: Política i economia a la Catalunya del segle XX,* no. 2 (1972): 225.

3. *Solidaridad Obrera,* 4 and 5 September 1937; Burnett Bolloten, *The Spanish Revolution, the Left, and the Struggle for Power during the Civil War* (Chapel Hill, 1979), p. 63.

4. UGT-CNT comisión organizadora de la conferencia nacional de la industria de piel y de calzado, 163, AS.

5. *Boletín de información,* 10 April 1937; cf. Bolloten, *Revolution,* pp. 63–64, which claims that seventy-one factories were reduced to twenty.

6. Acta, 6 July 1937, Generalitat 252, AS. Yet the Chemical Council ignored the French consul's objection to establishing industrial federations; see Acta, 31 December 1937, Generalitat 252, AS.

7. Acta, 24 August 1937, Generalitat 252, AS.

8. Actas, 4 June and 5 October 1937, Generalitat 252, AS; on Pirelli, see Jordi Maluquer de Motes, "De la crisis colonial a la guerra europea: Veinte años de economía española," in *La economía española en el siglo XX,* ed. Jordi Nadal et al. (Barcelona, 1987), p. 89.

9. Acta, 2 June 1938, Generalitat 252, AS.

10. Junta, 15 and 23 February 1937, 1204; Actas, 27 August and 15 October 1937, Generalitat 252, AS. On the "blind egoism" of firms that refused to aid less successful enterprises, see Walther L. Bernecker, *Colectividades y revolución social: El anarquismo en la guerra española, 1936–1939,* trans. Gustau Muñoz (Barcelona, 1982), pp. 378, 439.

11. Federació local de Barcelona, comité, 9 and 12 January 1937, 1311, AS.

12. 12 November 1936, 182, AS.

13. Actas, 24 August and 31 December 1937, Generalitat 252, AS.

14. Acta, MZA, 8 April 1937, 531, AS.

15. Reunión, 17 April 1938, 1049, AS.

16. Minutes of the CNT sección metales no-ferrosos, 1 September 1937, 847, AS; minutes of the CNT sección caldereros en hierro y sopletistas, 6 December 1936, 1385, AS. See also Comité, 9 April 1937, 181, AS; Reunión, 5 November 1936, 1122, AS; PSUC, radio 8, 12 December 1936, 1122, AS.

17. Acta de reunión del pleno del comité central de control obrero del ramo gas y electricidad, 27 November 1936, 182, AS.

18. 14 and 26 April 1937, 181, AS.

19. 1, 2, 12 September and 5 December 1936, 182, AS; Castells ("Colectivización," pp. 575–76) claims that the multinational SOFINA coerced technicians into leaving by threatening to blacklist them.

20. 5 and 9 October 1936, 182, AS.

21. 12 October 1936, 182, AS.

22. 15 December 1936, 182, AS; January 1937, 181, AS.

23. 30 October 1936, 182, AS.

24. 9 January 1937, 182, AS.

25. 5 December 1936, 182, AS; 29 September 1936, 182, AS.

26. 12 November and 1 December 1936, 182, AS.

27. 29 September and 29 December 1936, 182, AS.

28. *Luz y fuerza,* October 1937.

29. 14 April, 1 and 29 June 1937, 181, AS.

30. 27 September 1937, 181, AS; Federación catalana de gas y electricidad, UGT, July–September 1937, 482, AS.

31. Consell general, 31 March 1938, Generalitat 252, AS.

32. Acta, 5 April 1937, 531, AS; Hispano-Radio (n.d.), 1175, AS.

33. CNT questionnaires, 387, AS; see also Pere Gabriel, "¿La població obrera catalana, una població industrial?" *Estudios de historia social* 32–33 (January–June 1985): 206.

34. Proyecto de socialización de la industria siderometalúrgica CNT-UGT, June 1937, 505, AS; Sindicato de la industria siderometalúrgica de Barcelona, *¿Colectivización? ¿Nacionalización? No socialización* (Barcelona, 1937), p. 11.

35. *Horizontes,* June–July 1937.

36. *Sidero-Metalurgia,* November 1937.

37. Ibid., September 1937.

38. This paragraph is based on Hoja de control y estadística, CNT sindicato único de la metalurgia de Barcel[illegible] 871, AS; Al Consejo local técnico administrativo de la industria siderometalúrgica (*carpeta*

unknown), AS. See also *Les collectivitzacions a Catalunya,* Secció d'estudis econòmics, polítics i socials, Institucions Francesc Layret (Barcelona, 1938).

39. *Las Noticias,* 3 September 1938.

40. *Hoy,* January 1938.

41. *Boletín del Sindicato de la industria de la edificación, madera y decoración,* 10 October 1937 and 15 August 1938.

42. *Hoy,* December 1937.

43. The following paragraph adheres to the minutes of the meeting of the Pleno del comité central de control obrero, 181, AS.

44. 4 January, 11 March, and 19 April 1937, 181, AS.

45. 20 November 1936, 182, AS.

46. 19 September 1936, 182, AS. Early in the Revolution, peasants invaded not only property of large landowners but also that of worker-controlled enterprises; when peasants presented the Central Committee with a bill for "cultivation," it refused to pay (31 August 1936, 182, AS).

47. The following information comes from 26 November 1936, 182, AS.

48. 25 December 1936, 182, AS.

49. 20 March and 28 May 1937, 181, AS.

50. 9 April 1937, 182, AS.

51. 12 May 1937, 181, AS.

52. 26 April 1937, 182, AS.

53. Acta, 18 March 1937, 531, AS.

54. Acta, 14 September 1937, Generalitat 252, AS.

55. Junta, 5 February 1937, 1204, AS.

56. Acta de reunión, comité central, 12 March 1937, 531, AS.

57. Agustin Souchy and Paul Folgare, *Colectivizaciones: La obra constructiva de la revolución española* (Barcelona, 1977), p. 102.

58. Castells, "Colectivización," p. 467; Libro de actas de comité UGT, sociedad de albañiles, acta de reunión de la junta, 2 January 1937, 1051, AS.

59. Acta de asamblea, cargadores, 31 January 1937, 1404, AS.

60. 19 April 1937, 181, AS; Acta, MZA, 9 April 1937, 531, AS; Acta, comité central, 26 March 1937, 531, AS; 26 January 1937, 181, AS.

61. Vicente Guarner, *Cataluña en la guerra de España, 1936–1939* (Madrid, 1975), pp. 219–28. The following information is from Sugerencias, Fábrica LL, 1446, AS, and circular no. 53, 1084, AS.

62. En Badalona el sindicat metal.lurgic UGT, 1453, AS.

63. *Sidero-Metalurgia,* November 1937; *Horizontes,* May 1937.

64. *CNT Marítima,* 7 August, 11 and 25 September 1937; Alberto

Baró, *30 meses de colectivismo en Cataluña (1936–1939)* (Barcelona, 1974), p. 85.

65. Martha A. Ackelsberg, "Separate and Equal? Mujeres Libres and Anarchist Strategy for Women's Emancipation," *Feminist Studies* 11, no. 1 (Spring 1985).

66. See Murray Bookchin, *The Spanish Anarchists: The Heroic Years, 1868–1936* (New York, 1978), pp. 4–5, 56–57; Frank Mintz, *La autogestión en la España revolucionaria* (Madrid, 1977), p. 69. Ricardo Sanz (*El sindicalismo y la política: Los solidarios y nosotros* [Toulouse, 1966], p. 83) notes that some militants abstained from smoking and drinking while others did not. On CENU, see Ramón Safón, *La educación en la España revolucionara (1936–1939),* trans. María Luisa Delgado and Félix Ortega (Madrid, 1978), pp. 91–95; Discurso of Juan Puig Elias (n.d.), Generalitat 266, AS.

67. Floreal Ocaña quoted in Safón, *Educación,* p. 150.

68. Floreal Ocaña, "La escuela moderna: Conferencia pronunciada el 30 de julio 1937," *Tiempos nuevos* (Oct.–Nov. 1938).

69. *Economia: Butlletí mensual del departament d'economia de la Generalitat de Catalunya,* September 1937.

70. See files in 798, AS.

71. *Luz y fuerza,* October 1937.

72. *CNT Marítima,* 26 February, 23 April, 25 June 1937, 15 August and 20 November 1938.

73. *Solidaridad Obrera,* 19 January 1938.

74. 12 January 1937, 182, AS.

75. Joint CNT-UGT declaration in *UGT Edificación,* 15 August 1937; italics added.

76. Acta, 28 September and 5 October 1937, Generalitat 252, AS.

77. *De Companys a Indalecio Prieto: Documentación sobre las industrias de guerra en Cataluña* (Buenos Aires, 1939), pp. 21–31.

78. 26 and 29 September 1936, 182, AS.

79. Reunión del pleno, 5 October 1936 (tarde), 181, AS.

80. *CNT Marítima,* 26 February, 8 and 23 April 1937 and 11 September 1938.

81. *Boletín del Comité nacional de la CNT para exclusivo uso de los sindicatos,* 1 November 1937.

82. *CNT Marítima,* 2 April 1938.

83. Ibid., 19 February 1938. The UGT did not have enough dependable militants to fill positions of responsibility in the power industry (14 December 1936, 182, AS).

84. Comité nacional de relaciones de la industria fabril y textil CNT-AIT, Valencia, 626, AS.

85. Comité central de España industrial, 10 December 1936, 626, AS; see H. E. Kaminski (*Los de Barcelona,* trans. Carmen Sanz Barberá [Barcelona, 1976], p. 181), who reports that directors who remained as technicians received 1,000 pesetas per month.

86. Industria Olesana, S.A., companys de la ponencia del sindicato único del arte fabril i textil, 626, AS.

87. Cf. Ramón Tamames, *La república, la era de Franco* (Madrid, 1980), p. 307, for a Euro-Communist analysis. The payment of salaries often depended on a firm's economic situation; an engineer in a firm without resources might earn less than an unskilled laborer in an enterprise with contracts or influence (Consell de la federació local, 25 June 1937, 501, AS; Actas del pleno regional de industrias químicas, July 1937, 531, AS).

88. Comité, 22 May and 1 September 1937, 501, AS.

89. March 1937, Generalitat 282, AS.

90. Kaminski, *Barcelona,* p. 181.

91. Anna Monjo and Carme Vega, *Els treballadors i la guerra civil* (Barcelona, 1986), p. 87.

92. Acta de asamblea (n.d.), 469, AS.

93. Acta de asamblea, 21 February 1937, 469, AS.

94. Reunión, 22 December 1936, 1204, AS.

95. Mujeres libres, 17 February 1938, 529, AS; A todos los sindicatos, 25 April 1938, 1084, AS.

96. Dr. Félix Martí Ibáñez, *Obra: Diez meses de labor en sanidad y asistencia social* (Barcelona, 1937), p. 77; *Ruta,* 1 January 1937.

97. Quoted in Kaminski, *Barcelona,* p. 67; Dorsey Boatwright and Enric Ucelay Da Cal, "La dona del barrio chino," *L'Avenç,* no. 76 (November 1984): 29. On legalization of abortion, see Mary Nash, "L'avortament legal a Catalunya," *L'Avenç,* no. 58 (March 1983): 188–94.

98. Consejo de la federación local UGT, 2 and 5 October 1937, 501, AS; Informe al ple, 7 August 1937, 1322, AS.

99. Asamblea, R. Pujol Guell, 11 November 1937, 1085, AS.

100. Reglamento interior, Eudaldo Perramon, 1 September 1938, 1219; Secciones modistas UGT-CNT, 2 July 1937, 1336, AS.

101. UGT, letter from Elissa Uris and militants' replies, August–September, 1049, AS.

102. These citations are from F. W. Taylor, *The Principles of Scientific Management* (New York, 1967); original italics.

103. *CNT Marítima,* 15 September 1938.

104. Letter from Francisco Cuinovart, 887, AS.

105. Letter (signature unclear) to Junta administrativa del sindicato de la industria siderometalúrgica, 887, AS.

106. *Sidero-Metalurgia,* September 1937.
107. *Horizontes,* May 1937.
108. *Institut de ciències econòmiques de Catalunya,* October 1937.
109. *Horizontes,* February 1937.

CHAPTER SIX

1. A tots els sindicats obrers de la indústria tèxtil de Catalunya, 163, AS.
2. *Boletín de información,* 9 April 1937.
3. Informe que presenta el consejo económico de la industria siderometalúrgica; Informe que presenta el consejo de empresa de la material para ferrocarriles, 1186, AS.
4. The following paragraph adheres to the minutes of the CNT metallurgists, 1179, AS.
5. Sección de estaciones colectivizadas, 29 November 1936 and 13 January 1937, 1404, AS.
6. Sindicato nacional ferroviario, 23 January 1937, 1482, AS.
7. PSUC, radi 8, 22 July 1937, 1122, AS.
8. F. Vehils Vidal, 23 February 1937, 1099, AS.
9. 26 October 1937, 1219, AS.
10. Red nacional de ferrocarriles, servicio de material y tracción, sector este, May 1938, 1043, AS (original emphasis).
11. *Boletín del Sindicato de la industria de la edificación, madera y decoración,* 10 August 1937.
12. Joint CNT-UGT declaration in *UGT Edificación,* 15 August 1937.
13. Libro de actas de comité UGT, sociedad de albañiles, 20 November 1937, 1051, AS.
14. *UGT Edificación,* 1 February 1938.
15. Josep Maria Bricall, *Política econòmica de la Generalitat (1936–1939),* (Barcelona, 1978–1979), 1:101–18.
16. *Hoy,* January 1938.
17. *Solidaridad Obrera,* 7 May 1937; Juzgado general de contrabando, 1336, AS. On women's demonstrations, see Enric Ucelay Da Cal, *La Catalunya populista: Imatge, cultura i política en l'etapa republicana, 1936–1939* (Barcelona, 1982), 309–23; Temma Kaplan, "Female Consciousness and Collective Action: The Case of Barcelona, 1910–1918," *Signs* 7, no. 3 (Spring 1982): 548–65.
18. *Estadística: Resúmenes demográficos de la ciudad de Barcelona, 1936–1939,* p. 22.
19. This paragraph follows the minutes of the Comité central de control obrero, 181–82, AS; see Walther L. Bernecker, *Colectividades y*

revolución social: El anarquismo en la guerra civil española, 1936–1939, trans. Gustau Muñoz (Barcelona, 1982), p. 363.

20. The next two paragraphs are based on the minutes of the Cros assembly, 1421, AS.

21. Consejo obrero de coches camas, 10 November 1936 and 13 March 1937, 467, AS.

22. 29 September 1936, 182, AS.

23. 25 August 1937, 181, AS.

24. Actas de metalúrgicos, 3 July and 9 April 1937, 1179, AS.

25. Comité ejecutivo de la federación local UGT, 27 November 1937, 501, AS; the federation agreed to pay half the salaries.

26. Acta, 18 March 1937, 531, AS.

27. Reunión de junta, 13 November and 8 December, 1936, 1204, AS.

28. Actas del sindicato único de la metalurgia, sección joyería, platería, relojería, 16 January 1937, 1352, AS.

29. 12 December 1936, 182, AS.

30. Acta, 29 November 1936, 1404, AS.

31. Anna Monjo and Carme Vega, *Els treballadors i la guerra civil* (Barcelona, 1986), pp. 64, 170.

32. Informe, 14 August 1936, 182, AS; Junta de distribución, CNT, 15 June 1937, 1446, AS.

33. Letter from the Consejo obrero de MZA, sindicato nacional ferroviario UGT, 24 November 1937, 467, AS.

34. Asamblea, 13 January 1937 and Acta, 24 July 1937, 1404, AS. The assembly agreed that if the three paid the fine, they could keep their vacations.

35. Comité regional, sección defensa, 17 July 1938, 1049, AS.

36. The following information is from *Boletín del Sindicato de la industria de la edificación, madera y decoración,* 10 November 1937.

37. Sanitaria, 12 February 1938, 1203, AS; Libro de actas de comité UGT, sociedad de albañiles, reunión de junta, 7 November 1937, 1051, AS.

38. Comité ejecutivo de la federación local UGT, 29 September 1937, 501. In November 1936 the prosecuting attorney of the Tribunal popular, Adolfo Bueso, labeled "as fascist the majority of the members of the Insurance Union" (Federació local UGT, 27 November 1936, 1311, AS).

39. Actas, 13 June, 6 June, and 22 August 1937, 1404, AS. Sick pay varied according to collective and union.

40. Sindicato de la industria siderometalúrgica, sección lampistas, asamblea general, 25 December 1936 and 15 January 1937, 1453, AS.

41. Actas de metalúrgicos, 15 February 1937, 1179, AS.

42. Comité central, 22 August 1936, 182, AS; see also Acta de reunión del comité de control, 19 March 1937, 467, AS.

43. Reglamento interior, Eudaldo Perramon, 1 September 1938, 1219, AS.

44. Consejo de la federación local, 4 November 1937, 501, AS.

45. The following information is derived from PSUC, radi 8, (July?) 1937, 1122, AS.

46. Reunión de junta, 2 October 1936, 1204, AS; Actas de junta y los militantes de las industrias construcciones metálicas CNT, 7 December 1937, 921, AS; Acta, MZA, 9 April 1937, 531, AS.

47. Reunión de junta, 23 October 1936, 1204, AS; 9 October, 12 November, and 12 December 1936, 182, AS.

48. Acta de reunión, 19 March 1937, 467, AS; Acta de reunión, 16 March 1937, 531, AS.

49. Proyecto de estatuto interior, sastrería Casarromona (n.d.), 1219, AS.

50. J. García Pradas, *Antifascismo proletario: Tesis, ambiente, táctica* (Madrid, 1938?), pp. 129–30.

51. 14 January 1937, 181, AS.

52. A la junta, 25 June 1938, 1084, AS; see also two letters, 20 January 1938, 1084, AS.

53. This paragraph follows the letter from the Collective M.E.Y.D.O., 854, AS.

54. The following information is from Acta de asamblea, 24 July 1937, 1404, AS.

55. Societat de moços, 20 September 1936, 1170, AS.

56. Actas de construcciones metálicas CNT, 7 December 1937, 921; Junta de teléfonos UGT, 9 January 1937, 1170, AS; *Solidaridad Obrera*, 30 December 1937.

57. Federación local, 4 April 1938, 1084, AS.

58. Compañeros, 11 February 1938, 1084, AS; militants rejected a proposal to expel the accused but refused to allow him to hold union office.

59. *Solidaridad Obrera*, 3 February 1937.

60. The following information is based on a series of documents in 181, AS.

61. A todos, 30 September 1938, 1084, AS.

62. Sección de coordinación, informe de la Barriada Prat Vermel, CNT, 11 July 1938, 830, AS.

63. *Solidaridad Obrera*, 24 June 1938.

64. Comissió consultiva, 13 July 1938, Generalitat 277, AS.

65. PSUC, célula 9a, 7 January 1938, 1122, AS.

66. Comissariat d'assistència als refugiats, informe, Reus, 30 October 1938, Generalitat 277, AS.
67. Comissió, 27 July 1938, Generalitat 277, AS.
68. *Estadística,* 1936–1939.
69. Joan Fronjosà, *La missió dels treballadors i la dels sindicats en la nova organització industrial* (Barcelona, 1937), p. 15; see also Asamblea, 29 October 1937, 1219, AS.
70. Sindicato nacional ferroviario, acta, 23 January 1937, 1432, AS.
71. Consejo de la federación local, 4 November 1937, 501, AS; Comité ejecutivo de la federación local UGT, 26 July 1937, 501, AS.
72. 5 October 1936, 182, AS.
73. The following information is found in minutes of 16 July and 27 September 1937, 181, AS.
74. *Solidaridad Obrera,* 24 July 1937.
75. Consell general, reunió extraordinària, 181, AS.
76. Reunió extraordinària del consell, 4 October 1937, 181, AS.
77. Actas de metalúrgicos CNT, 27 May and 14 July 1937, 1179, AS.
78. Sindicato de la industria siderometalúrgica, sección lampistas, 2 July 1937, 1453, AS.
79. Reunión de junta, 29 December 1936, 1204, AS; Industria del automóvil, 14 October 1936, 1049, AS.
80. Minutes of the Secció de paletes i manobres del sindicat de l'edificació, 1052, AS.
81. Letter from UGT militants to UGT secretary general, 24 September 1937, PC.
82. Consejo de la federación local, 2 October 1937, 501, AS.
83. Actas, cuarta sesión del pleno regional de las industrias químicas de Cataluña, July 1937, 531, AS.
84. Acta de reunión de militantes, 3 June 1938, 531, AS.
85. Sindicat d'obrers metal.lúrgics UGT, secció de joieria, argenteria i anexes, assamblea, 3 July 1937, 505, AS.
86. Federació local UGT, 9 January 1937, 1311, AS.
87. Comité ejecutivo, 21 December 1937, 501, AS.
88. Federació catalana, 1 September 1938, 1049; Comité d'enllaç, secció sastreria, 25 June 1937, 1219, AS.
89. Fronjosà, La missió, p. 28.
90. *III Congrés de la UGT a Catalunya, informe de Josep del Barrio* (Barcelona, 1937), p. 26.
91. Consejo de la federación local, 16 December 1937, 501, AS; Informe, 7 August 1938, 1322, AS.

92. José Peirats, *La CNT en la revolución española* (Paris, 1971), 3:37–39.

93. Quoted in Bernecker, *Colectividades*, p. 136.

94. Gonzalo Coprons y Prat, empresa colectivizada, vestuarios militares, 1099, AS.

95. The following information is based on Projecte de reglamentació interior de l'empresa, 1099, AS.

96. Projecte d'estatut interior per el qual hauran de regir-se els treballadors, 1099, AS.

97. Assamblea ordinaria dels obrers de la casa Artgust, 6 September 1938, 1099, AS.

98. Acta aprobada por el personel de la casa Antonio Lanau, 15 August 1938, 1099, AS; for an analogous prohibition on singing, Reglamento, Costa colectivizada, 22 September 1938, 1219, AS.

99. *Boletín del Sindicato de la industria fabril y textil de Badalona y su radio*, February 1937; Reglamento interior, confecciones casa Parareda, empresa colectivizada, 1219, AS; Reglamento interior, Eudaldo Perramon, 1 September 1938, 1219, AS.

100. See Reglamentos, 1219, AS; Circular no. 37, 19 March 1938, 1084, AS.

101. Informe de la casa Mallafré hecho por el contable del CADCI, 15 June 1937, 1099, AS.

102. Letter from Artgust to Sección sastrería CNT, 9 February 1938, 1099, AS.

103. Informe revisión J. Lanau (signed by accountant), 15 November 1937, 1099, AS.

104. Informe, August 1938, 1219, AS.

105. Acta, 12 July 1938, 1219, AS.

106. Casa Alemany, 23 June 1937, 1219, AS; Rabasso Palau, 25 October 1938, 1219, AS; 8 July 1938, 1219, AS; letter from Comité de la fábrica no. 7 (n.d.), 1085, AS.

107. Consejo nacional de ferrocarriles, circular no. 3, primas de regularidad, 26 February 1938, 1043, AS.

108. Acta, MZA, 8 April 1937, 531, AS.

109. Acta de la reunión, comité central, 16 and 18 March 1937, 531, AS.

110. Peirats, *La CNT*, 3:21.

111. Décret instituant un "certificat du travail," 4 March 1937, 259, AD. For the certificates themselves, Generalitat 252, no. 13, AS.

112. Luis López de Medrano, *986 días en el infierno* (Madrid, 1939), pp. 192–93.

113. PSUC, radi 8, 26 July 1937, 1122, AS.

114. CNT junta de distribución, 8 June 1937, 1446, AS; Sindicato nacional ferroviario, 23 January 1937, 1482, AS.

115. Reunión de junta, 29 December 1936, 1204, AS.

116. Actas del sindicato único de la metalurgia, sección joyería, platería, relojería, 8 December 1936, 1352, AS.

CHAPTER SEVEN

1. *La España industrial: Libro del centenario* (Barcelona, 1947).
2. Alberto del Castillo, *La Maquinista Terrestre y Marítima: Personaje histórico (1855–1955)* (Barcelona, 1955), p. 508.
3. Josep Maria Bricall, *Política econòmica de la Generalitat (1936–1939)* (Barcelona, 1978–1979), 1:61.
4. [Author unknown] *Franco in Barcelona* (London, 1939).
5. Anna Monjo and Carme Vega, *Els treballadors i la guerra civil* (Barcelona, 1986), p. 189.
6. Bricall, *Política econòmica de la Generalitat,* 1:47–56.
7. *Solidaridad Obrera,* 26 December 1937.
8. Sindicato de la industria siderometalúrgica de Barcelona, *¿Colectivización? ¿Nacionalización? No socialización* (Barcelona, 1937), p. 6.
9. The following is derived from Felipe Alaiz, "Hacia el estajanovismo," *Tiempos nuevos* (Oct.–Nov. 1938).
10. Informe confidencial, 1 January 1938, 855, AS.
11. *Solidaridad Obrera,* 28 and 29 August 1937.
12. *Boletín del Sindicato de la industria fabril y textil de Badalona y su radio,* June 1937.
13. *Hoy,* January 1938.
14. *Síntesis,* December 1937; *Petróleo,* January 1938.
15. *CNT Marítima,* 29 March, 3 July, and 13 November 1937; Libro de actas de gerencia de la flota mercante española, 30 July 1938, 183, AS.
16. *CNT Marítima,* 11 June and 15 August 1938.
17. Ricardo Sanz, *El sindicalismo y la política: Los solidarios y nosotros* (Toulouse, 1966), pp. 98–99.
18. *Hoy,* January 1938.
19. *Boletín del Sindicato de la industria fabril y textil de Badalona y su radio,* February 1937. As mentioned earlier, some members of the CNT opposed Stakhanovism, but they, like their colleagues who favored decentralization, were frequently ignored during the Revolution (J. García Pradas, *Antifascismo proletario: Tesis, ambiente, táctica*

[Madrid, 1938?], p. 120, which argued against Communists' proposals for incentives and Stakhanovism).

20. *Síntesis,* January and December 1937. In the workplace the emphasis on medals and distinctions roughly corresponded with that in the Republican army (Ramón Salas Larrazábal, *Los datos exactos de la guerra civil* [Madrid, 1980], p. 151).

21. *Horizontes,* June–July 1937.

22. UGT Metallurgical Congress, September 1938, 901, AS; *Hoy,* January 1938.

23. Federico Melchor, *El frente de la producción: Una industria grande y fuerte para ganar la guerra* (Valencia? 1937?), p. 21.

24. Informe al ple, 7 August 1938, 1322, AS.

25. PSUC, radi 8, 22 July 1937, 1122, AS.

26. *Sidero-Metalurgia,* September 1937.

27. *Hoy,* December 1937.

28. *Boletín del Sindicato de la industria de la edificación, madera y decoración,* 10 September 1937; *Sidero-Metalurgia,* July 1937.

29. *Petróleo,* January 1938.

30. *Boletín de información,* 5 May 1937; *Amanecer: Organo de la escuela de militantes de Cataluña, CNT-FAI,* October 1937.

31. Gobernación A, caja 2412, AGA; see also *El mundo deportivo* (1936–1938).

32. Lliga amateur de futbol, 13 November 1936, Generalitat 89, AS.

33. José A. González Casanova, *Elecciones en Barcelona (1931–1936)* (Madrid, 1969), p. 73.

34. Sindicato único de espectáculos públicos, December 1936, Generalitat 89, AS.

35. Reunión de junta, 23 October 1936, 1204, AS; *Solidaridad Obrera,* 1 June 1937.

36. 12 February 1937; PSUC, célula 9a, 7 January 1938, 1122, AS; minutes of CNT metallurgists, 11 March 1937, 1179, AS.

37. F. Montseny quoted in H. E. Kaminski, *Los de Barcelona,* trans. Carmen Sanz Barberá (Barcelona, 1976), p. 66.

38. Floreal Ocaña, "La escuela moderna: Conferencia pronunciada el 30 de julio 1937," *Tiempos nuevos* (Oct.–Nov. 1938).

39. Michael Alpert, *El ejército republicano en la guerra civil* (Paris, 1977), p. 211; Junta, 23 February 1937, 1204, AS.

40. Alpert, *El ejército,* p. 210.

41. 11 December 1936, 182; 3 February 1937, 181, AS.

42. *Los amigos de Durruti,* 22 June 1937.

43. Alaiz, "Hacia el estajanovismo."

CHAPTER EIGHT

1. René Rémond, *Histoire de l'anticléricalisme en France de 1815 à nos jours* (Paris, 1976), pp. 225–30; Michel Winock, *Histoire politique de la revue «Esprit», 1930–1950* (Paris, 1975), p. 37.
2. Adéline Daumard, "Caractères de la société bourgeoise," in *Histoire économique et sociale de la France,* ed. Fernand Braudel and Ernest Labrousse (Paris, 1976), 3:839.
3. Maurice Lévy-Leboyer, "Le Patronat français a-t-il été malthusien?" *Le Mouvement social,* no. 88 (July–September 1974): 28; Ingo Kolboom, "Patron et patronat: Histoire sociale du concept de patronat en France au 19e et 20e siècles," *Mots,* no. 9 (October 1984): 98.
4. J.-J. Carré, P. Dubois, and E. Malinvaud, *French Economic Growth,* trans. John P. Hatfield (Stanford, 1976), p. 150.
5. Tom Kemp, *Economic Forces in French History* (London, 1971), p. 223. See Patrick O'Brien and Caglar Keyder, *Economic Growth in Britain and France, 1780–1914: Two Paths to the Twentieth Century* (London, 1978), p. 21: "Our central point is that something called relative backwardness cannot be inferred from characteristic features of French industrialization."
6. Rondo Cameron, "L'économie française: Passé, présent, avenir," *Annales Economies, Sociétés, Civilisations,* no. 5 (Sept.–Oct. 1970): 1418–33.
7. Alfred Sauvy, ed., *Histoire économique de la France entre les deux guerres* (Paris, 1972), 1:304.
8. Jacques Néré, *La Troisième République, 1914–1940* (Paris, 1967), p. 84; André Armengaud, "La population," in *Histoire économique de la France entre les deux guerres*, ed. Alfred Sauvy (Paris, 1972), 3:31.
9. Sauvy, ed., *Histoire économique*, 1:265.
10. Richard F. Kuisel, *Capitalism and the State in Modern France* (New York, 1981), pp. 31–51; Gerd Hardach, "La mobilisation industrielle en 1914–1918: Production, planification et idéologie," in *1914–1918: L'autre front*, ed. P. Fridenson (Paris, 1977), p. 88.
11. François Caron and Jean Bouvier, "Guerre, crise, guerre," in *Histoire économique et sociale de la France*, ed. Fernand Braudel and Ernest Labrousse (Paris, 1976), 4:648.
12. François Caron, *Histoire économique de la France, XIXe–XXe siècles* (Paris, 1981), p. 158.
13. Albert Carreras, "La industria: Atraso y modernización," in *La economía española en el siglo XX,* ed. Jordi Nadal, Albert Carreras, and Carles Sudrià (Barcelona, 1987), p. 293.

14. Jean-Charles Asselain, *Histoire économique de la France* (Paris, 1984), 2:78.

15. C. J. Gignoux, *L'économie française entre les deux guerres, 1919–1939* (Paris, 1942), p. 104.

16. Charles P. Kindleberger, *Economic Growth in France and Britain, 1851–1950* (Cambridge, Mass., 1964), p. 122; Sauvy, ed., *Histoire économique,* 1:232; François Caron and Jean Bouvier, "Structure des firmes—emprise de l'état," in *Histoire économique et sociale de la France,* ed. Fernand Braudel and Ernest Labrousse (Paris, 1976), 4:771; Gérard Noiriel, *Les ouvriers dans la société française* (Paris, 1986), p. 123; Pierre, George, "Etude statistique des dimensions des établissements industrielles," in *Matériaux pour une géographie volontaire de l'industrie française,* Gabriel Dessus, Pierre George, and Jacques Weulersse (Paris, 1949), p. 123; Kemp, *Economic Forces,* p. 54; Lévy-Leboyer, "Le patronat," pp. 46–48; Asselain, *Histoire économique,* 2:73; Ingo Kolboom, *Frankreichs Unternehmer in der Periode der Volksfront, 1936–1938* (Rheinfelden, 1983).

17. M. Schwartz, "L'industrie automobile," Conseil national économique, AN, F^{12}8798; Patrick Fridenson, *Histoire des usines Renault* (Paris, 1972), pp. 10–11; Noiriel, *Ouvriers,* p. 123.

18. M. R. Musnier, "Le problème des transports," Conseil national économique, AN, F^{12}8798.

19. Edmond Petit, *La vie quotidienne dans l'aviation en France au début du XXe siècle (1900–1935)* (Paris, 1977), p. 58.

20. M. Dautry, "Rapport sur l'aéronautique marchande française," Conseil national économique, AN, F^{12}8798.

21. A. Matagrin, *L'industrie des produits chimiques et ses travailleurs* (Paris, 1925), p. 67.

22. M. Fleurent, "Les industries chimiques," Conseil national économique, AN, F^{12}8796.

23. Claude Fohlen, "France 1920–1970," in *Fontana Economic History of Europe,* ed. Carlo Cipolla (Glasgow, 1976), 1:85.

24. Ernest Mercier Collection, Hoover Archives; Charles Malégarie, *L'électricité à Paris* (Paris, 1947), p. 67; Noiriel, *Ouvriers,* p. 123.

25. Caron and Bouvier, "Guerre, crise, guerre," 4:650.

26. "La question des industries," Conseil supérieur de défense nationale, 19 September 1925, AN, F^{22}316; Marcel Ulrich, rapport, Conseil national économique, AN, F^{12}8796; *L'Europe nouvelle,* 15 February 1936.

27. Judith A. Merkle, *Management and Ideology: The Legacy of the International Scientific Management Movement* (Berkeley, 1980), chap. 5.

28. Henry Le Chatelier, preface to F. W. Taylor, *La direction des ateliers* (Paris, 1913); F. W. Taylor, *Etudes sur l'organisation du travail dans les usines* (Angers, 1907); F. W. Taylor, *Principes d'organisation scientifique des usines* (Paris, 1912).

29. [Commander] Hourst, *Le problème de la main d'œuvre: La taylorisation et son application aux conditions industrielles de l'après-guerre* (Paris, 1916), pp. 46–47.

30. Maurice Daumas, "Les techniques industrielles," in *Histoire économique de la France entre les deux guerres,* ed. Alfred Sauvy (Paris, 1972), 3:158–59.

31. Michel Collinet, *L'ouvrier français: Essai sur la condition ouvrière (1900–1950)* (Paris, 1951), p. 69.

32. Alain Touraine, *L'évolution du travail ouvrier aux usines Renault* (Paris, 1955), pp. 28, 84.

33. Georges Lefranc, *Histoire du travail et des travailleurs* (Paris, 1975), p. 335.

34. Touraine, *Evolution du travail,* p. 42.

35. Simone Weil, *La condition ouvrière* (Paris, 1951), pp. 20, 28.

36. Annie Fourcaut, *Femmes à l'usine en France dans l'entre-deux-guerres* (Paris, 1982), p. 99.

37. Campagne contre le gaspillage, March 1932, AN, 91AQ3; Jules Moch, *Socialisme et rationalisation* (Brussels, 1927), pp. 38–49.

38. Du chapitre des économies, AN, 91AQ3.

39. Note de service no. 816, 22 October 1931, AN, 91AQ22.

40. Résumé de notes de M. Renault, Jan.–Feb. 1931, AN, 91AQ22.

41. Note 391, 14 April 1931, AN, 91AQ22.

42. Note de service, no. 2093, 29 April 1932, AN, 91AQ22.

43. Note concernant le service d'économies, 1937–1938, AN, 91AQ3; Conférence de M. Renault du 10 novembre 1937, AN, 91AQ3.

44. Note 975, 1 July 1931, AN, 91AQ22.

45. Rapport général du voyage de M. Reynaud en Amérique, 11 November–16 December 1936, AN, 91AQ69.

46. L'apprentissage aux usines Renault, 2 March 1937, AN, 91AQ3.

47. Recherche des moyens propres à améliorer les prix de revient, 10 May 1937, AN, 91AQ3.

48. Résumé d'un entretien avec un agent de service des économies de l'usine Citroën, AN, 91AQ3.

49. Visite à la maison Ford (1929), AN, 91AQ67.

50. La fabrication automobile en Amérique (n.d.), AN, 91AQ77; Résumé—voyage aux Etats-Unis de M. Guillemon (1929), AN, 91AQ67.

51. Visite de la G.M., AN, 91AQ24.

52. Rapport sur la mécanisation comptable dans les départements, 8 July 1938, AN, 91AQ3.

53. The following paragraph is derived from Petit, *La vie quotidienne dans l'aviation.*

54. Arnold Brémond, *Une explication du monde ouvrier: Enquête d'un étudiant-ouvrier dans la banlieue parisienne* (Saint-Etienne [Loire], 1927), p. 47; Sauvy, ed., *Histoire économique,* 1:232; Félix Battestini, L'industrie française du gros matériel mécanique et électrique (Paris, 1937); M. Hervé Detton, "Les industries des matériaux de construction, du bâtiment et des travaux publics," 1 May 1931, Conseil national économique, AN, F^{12}8797.

55. Sauvy, ed., *Histoire économique,* 1:268; Adolphe Hodée, *Les travailleurs devant la rationalisation* (Paris, 1934), p. 17.

56. Jean Bastié, *La croissance de la banlieue parisienne* (Paris, 1964), p. 141; Schwartz, "L'industrie automobile,"AN, F^{12}8798.

57. Pierre Cot, *Triumph of Treason* (Chicago, 1944), p. 322.

58. Philippe Ariès, *Histoire des populations françaises* (Paris, 1971), p. 130.

59. Ibid., p. 145.

CHAPTER NINE

1. See Eugen Weber, "Un demi-siècle de glissement à droite," *International Review of Social History* 5, no. 2 (1960): 165–201.

2. Michel Winock, *Histoire politique de la revue «Esprit», 1930–1950* (Paris, 1975), pp. 121, 159; Réunion organisée par le club de faubourg, 14 May 1936, AN, F^{7}13983; Les milieux catholiques, 22 May 1936, AN F^{7}13983; Paul Christophe, *1936: Les catholiques et le front populaire* (Paris, 1986), pp. 25–32.

3. Georges Dupeux, *Le front populaire et les élections de 1936* (Paris, 1959), p. 113.

4. Joseph N. Moody, *French Education since Napoleon* (Syracuse, N.Y., 1978), pp. 99, 146; Rondo Cameron, "Por qué fue tan desigual la industrialización europea," in *La industrialización europea: Estadios y tipos,* Pierre Vilar, Jordi Nadal, Rondo Cameron, and Peter Mathias (Barcelona, 1981), pp. 312–17, Ivan T. Berend and Gyorgy Ranki, *The European Periphery and Industrialization, 1780–1914,* trans. Eva Palmai (Cambridge, 1982), p. 58.

5. B. R. Mitchell, *European Historical Statistics, 1750–1970* (New York, 1975).

6. Formation des illetrés, AN, 39AS387.

7. Madeleine Rebérioux, *La république radicale, 1898–1914* (Paris, 1975), p. 76.

8. Madeleine Rebérioux and Patrick Fridenson, "Albert Thomas, pivot du réformisme français," *Le Mouvement social,* no. 87 (April–June 1974); Alain Hennebicque, "Albert Thomas et le régime des usines de guerre, 1915–1917," in *1914–1918: L'autre front,* ed. P. Fridenson (Paris, 1977), pp. 122–44; Gerd Hardach, "La mobilisation industrielle en 1914–1918: Production, planification et idéologie," in *1914–1918: L'autre front,* ed. P. Fridenson, p. 108.

9. See documents in AN, 91AQ57.

10. M. Fleurent, "Les industries chimiques," Conseil national économique, AN, F^{12}8796.

11. Medical results reported in *La Vie ouvrière,* 24 November 1938; *Syndicats,* 16 October 1936.

12. Jacques Juillard, "Diversité des réformismes," *Le Mouvement social,* no. 87 (April–June 1974): 4; Martin Fine, "Toward Corporatism: The Movement for Capital-Labor Collaboration in France, 1914–1936" (Ph.D. diss., University of Wisconsin, 1971).

13. Peter M. Arum, "Du syndicalisme révolutionnaire au réformisme: Georges Dumoulin (1903–1923)," *Le Mouvement social,* no. 87 (April–June 1974): 39.

14. Bernard Georges and Denise Tintant, *Léon Jouhaux: Cinquante ans de syndicalisme* (Paris, 1962–1979), 1:1.

15. Georges Lefranc, *Le mouvement syndical sous la Troisième République* (Paris, 1967), p. 198; Georges Lefranc, *Le mouvement socialiste sous la Troisième République (1875–1940)* (Paris, 1963), 2:227. On Spanish libertarian reaction to World War I, see Gerald Meaker, *The Revolutionary Left in Spain, 1914–1923* (Stanford, 1974), pp. 28–29, and Gaston Leval, *El prófugo* (Valencia, 1935).

16. Hardach, "Mobilisation," p. 235; Fine, "Corporatism," p. 42.

17. See Annie Kriegel (*Aux origines du communisme français: Contribution à l'histoire du mouvement ouvrier français* [Paris, 1969]), who concludes that the organized working-class movement (a minority of the class) had revolutionary aspirations in 1919–1920 but that the situation in France was not revolutionary because of the strength of the French bourgeoisie and the victory of the nation. For an emphasis on workers' revolutionary activity, see N. Papayanis, "Masses révolutionnaires et directions réformistes: Les tensions au cours des grèves des métallurgistes français en 1919," *Le Mouvement social,* no. 93 (Oct.–Dec. 1975): 51–73; B. Abherve, "Les origines de la grève des métallurgistes parisiens, juin 1919," *Le Mouvement social,* no. 93 (Oct.–Dec. 1975): 77–85. For views stressing the limits of revolutionary activity,

see Jean-Paul Brunet, *Saint-Denis: La ville rouge, 1890–1939* (Paris, 1980), pp. 210–32; Robert Wohl, *French Communism in the Making, 1914–1924* (Stanford, 1966), p. 167.

18. Lefranc, *Mouvement syndical,* p. 216.

19. Michel Collinet, *L'ouvrier français, esprit du syndicalisme* (Paris, 1951), p. 157.

20. Charles Maier, *Recasting Bourgeois Europe* (Princeton, 1975), pp. 148–49.

21. Lefranc, *Mouvement syndical,* p. 230.

22. Jacques Amoyal, "Les origines socialistes et syndicalistes de la planification en France," *Le Mouvement social,* no. 87 (April–June 1974): 158; see also Richard F. Kuisel, *Capitalism and the State in Modern France* (New York, 1981), p. 79.

23. Lefranc, *Mouvement syndical,* p. 249.

24. Georges and Tintant, *Jouhaux,* 1:326.

25. Quoted in Lefranc, *Mouvement syndical,* p. 224.

26. René Mouriaux, *La CGT* (Paris, 1982), p. 63.

27. Georges and Tintant, *Jouhaux,* 2:43.

28. Antoine Prost, *La CGT à l'époque du front populaire, 1934–1939* (Paris, 1964), p. 34.

29. Jean-Paul Depretto and Sylvie V. Schweitzer, *Le communisme à l'usine: Vie ouvrière et mouvement ouvrier chez Renault, 1920–1939* (Paris, 1984), p. 107.

30. Herrick Eaton Chapman, "Reshaping French Industrial Politics: Workers, Employers, State Officials, and the Struggle for Control in the Aircraft Industry, 1938–1950" (Ph.D. diss., University of California, Berkeley, 1983), p. 81.

31. Jean Rabaut, *Tout est possible: Les «gauchistes» français, 1929–1944* (Paris, 1974), p. 224, which concludes that the CGTSR never initiated an important strike; see Kathryn E. Amdur, "La tradition révolutionnaire entre syndicalisme et communisme dans la France de l'entre-deux-guerres," *Le Mouvement social,* no. 139 (April–June 1987): 48, which emphasizes the persistence of revolutionary syndicalism in this period.

32. Raymond Carr, *The Spanish Tragedy: The Civil War in Perspective* (London, 1977), pp. 52–53.

33. Lefranc, *Mouvement socialiste,* 2:267; Tony Judt, *La reconstruction du parti socialiste* (Paris, 1976), p. 81; Gilbert Ziebura, *Léon Blum et le parti socialiste, 1872–1934,* trans. Jean Duplex (Paris, 1967), p. 286.

34. Léon Blum, *L'œuvre* (Paris, 1972), pp. 451–60.

35. Donald N. Baker, "The Politics of Socialist Protest in France: The Left Wing of the Socialist Party, 1921–1939," *Journal of Modern*

History 43, no. 1 (March 1971): 24, 36–41, which views the *pivertistes* more as protesters than revolutionaries. For a recent interpretation of the SFIO's reformism, see Jacques Kergoat, *Le parti socialiste* (Paris, 1983); see also Tony Judt, *Marxism and the French Left: Studies on Labour and Politics in France, 1930–1981* (New York, 1986), p. 158, which contrasts the "doctrinal intransigence" of the SFIO with its political compromises.

36. Donald N. Baker, "The Socialists and the Workers of Paris: The Amicales Socialistes, 1936–1940," *International Review of Social History* 24 (1979): 8; Nathanael Greene, *Crisis and Decline: The French Socialist Party in the Popular Front* (Ithaca, 1969), p. 141; Helmut Gruber, *Léon Blum, French Socialism, and the Popular Front: A Case of Internal Contradictions* (Ithaca, 1986), p. 40, emphasizes the moderation of Pivert.

37. Pivert quoted in Jean-Paul Joubert, *Révolutionnaires de la SFIO: Marceau Pivert et le pivertisme* (Paris, 1977), p. 141.

38. Pivert quoted in ibid.; Rabaut, *Tout,* pp. 242–43.

39. Résultat des élections législatives, 29 April 1936, AN, $F^7$13983.

40. Pivert, 13 March 1937, quoted in Greene, *Crisis,* p. 136.

41. Greene, *Crisis,* p. 194.

42. Baker, "Amicales," pp. 20, 29; Jean-Pierre Rioux, "Les socialistes dans l'entreprise au temps du front populaire: Quelques remarques sur les amicales socialistes (1936–1939)," *Le Mouvement social,* no. 106 (January–March 1976): 3–24; see also Joubert, *Révolutionnaires,* pp. 102–3, 145.

43. Rabaut, *Tout,* p. 273.

44. Joubert, *Révolutionnaires,* p. 155. It is interesting to note that the social composition of the POUM, unlike that of the Gauche révolutionnaire, was working-class (Victor Alba, *Histoire du POUM,* trans. Noémie Pagés [Paris, 1975]).

45. Kriegel, *Origines,* p. 61.

46. Griffuelhes quoted in Lefranc, *Mouvement syndical,* p. 248.

47. Jean Touchard, *La gauche en France depuis 1900* (Paris, 1977), chap. 2; Nicole Racine and Louis Bodin, *Le parti communiste français pendant l'entre-deux-guerres* (Paris, 1972), p. 209, give figures of 180,000 PCF members at Tours and 30,000 in 1933.

48. Tom Kemp, *Stalinism in France: The First Twenty Years of the French Communist Party* (London, 1984), 1:88–89; Jacques Fauvet, *Histoire du parti communiste français, 1920–1976* (Paris, 1977), p. 77.

49. P. Semard quoted in Racine and Bodin, *Parti,* p. 171.

50. Fauvet, *Parti,* p. 81; Jean-Paul Brunet, *Histoire du parti communiste français (1920–1982)* (Paris, 1982), p. 41.

51. Thorez quoted in Dupeux, *Elections,* p. 70.

52. Fauvet, *Parti,* p. 97; Brunet (*PCF,* p. 44) states that the PCF had 6.7 percent of registered voters and 6.3 percent of votes cast.

53. Fauvet, *Parti,* p. 146; Brunet, *PCF;* figures vary slightly.

54. Instructions données par la direction du parti communiste à ses organismes de base pour le 2e tour de scrutin, 30 April 1936, AN, $F^7$13983.

55. Irwin M. Wall, *French Communism in the Era of Stalin* (Westport, Conn., 1983), p. 16; see also Jacques Kergoat, *La France du front populaire* (Paris, 1986); Henri Heldman, "Le parti communiste français à la conquête de la classe ouvrière: Les cellules d'entreprise, 1924–1938" (Thèse, 3e cycle, University of Nanterre, 1979), p. 187.

56. Résultat des élections législatives, 29 April 1936, AN, $F^7$13983.

57. Annie Kriegel, "Le parti communiste français sous la Troisième République (1920–1939): Evolution de ses effectifs," *Revue française de science politique* 21, no. 1 (February 1966): 33; Brunet, *PCF,* p. 52.

58. For the PCF, see Louis Bodin, "De Tours à Villeurbanne: Pour une lecture renouvelée de l'histoire du parti communiste français," *Annales Economies, Sociétés, Civilisations,* nos. 2–3 (March–June 1975).

59. Pierre Saint-Germaine, "La chaîne et la parapluie: Face à la rationalisation (1919–1935)," *Les Révoltes logiques,* no. 2 (1976): 98.

60. *Humanité,* 26 April and 17 May 1936; italics added. One can only agree with this particular evaluation by *Humanité.*

61. Ibid., 24 May 1936.

62. O. Rabaté, *Rationalisation et action syndicale: Discours prononcé au congrès fédéral des métaux (CGTU)* (Paris, 1927), pp. 66–67.

63. *Humanité,* 22 May 1936. On miners, see Aimée Moutet, "La rationalisation dans les mines du nord à l'épreuve du front populaire," *Le Mouvement social,* no. 135 (April–June 1986): 79.

64. Sébastien Faure, *La crise économique: Le chômage, origines—conséquences—remèdes* (Paris, 1932), p. 12.

65. Madeleine Pelletier, *Le travail: Ce qu'il est, ce qu'il doit être* (?, 1930), pp. 20–21.

66. Julian Jackson, *The Politics of the Depression in France, 1932–1936* (Cambridge, 1983), p. 39; see also Jules Moch, *Socialisme et rationalisation* (Brussels, 1927).

67. Amoyal, "Origines," p. 150; see also Jean-François Biard, *Le socialisme devant ses choix: La naissance de l'idée de plan* (Paris, 1985).

68. Georges Lefranc, "Le courant planiste dans le mouvement ouvrier français de 1933 à 1936," *Le Mouvement social,* no. 54 (January–March 1966): 85.

69. For the program of the CGT see Georges Lefranc, *Histoire du*

front populaire (Paris, 1974), pp. 465–66; Henri Noyelle, "Plans d'économie dirigée: Les plans de reconstruction économique et sociale à l'étranger et en France," *Revue d'économie politique,* no. 5 (September–October 1934): 1602; Georges Lefranc, "Histoire d'un groupe du parti socialiste S.F.I.O.: révolution constructive (1930–1938)," in *Mélanges d'histoire économique et sociale en hommage au professeur Antony Babel* (Geneva, 1963), pp. 401–25.

70. Jacques Girault, *Sur l'implantation du parti communiste français dans l'entre-deux-guerres* (Paris, 1977), p. 114.

71. *Humanité,* 30 April 1929, cited in ibid., p. 114.

72. André Lurçat, *Projets et réalisations* (Paris, 1931), p. 5; André Lurçat, "Urbanisme et architecture," *Cahiers de l'école de Rochefort, collection Comprendre la ville* (Paris, 1942) p. 12. See also Jean-Louis Cohen ("Lurçat au pays de soviets," *Architecture, mouvement, continuité,* no. 40 [September 1976]: 10), who emphasizes Lurçat's commitment to increased urban circulation. Lurçat admired the Soviet Union of the 1930s because "there work becomes easy."

73. This paragraph is based on Girault, *Sur l'implantation,* 17–129.

74. René Sordes, *Histoire de Suresnes* (Suresnes, 1965), p. 530.

75. Depretto and Schweitzer, *Communisme,* p. 53.

76. In theory, the Left did oppose defense production and argued for increased social expenditures.

CHAPTER TEN

1. Alfred Sauvy, ed., *Histoire économique de la France entre les deux guerres* (Paris, 1972), 2:121.

2. Gabrielle Letellier, Jean Perret, H. E. Zuber, and A. Dauphin-Meunier, *Enquête sur le chômage* (Paris, 1938–1949), 1:250.

3. Sauvy, ed., *Histoire économique,* 2:133; cf. Georges Lefranc, *Histoire du front populaire* (Paris, 1974), p. 50, who has concluded that workers' buying power declined; see also Julian Jackson, *The Politics of the Depression in France, 1932–1936* (Cambridge, 1983), p. 58.

4. Jean-Paul Depretto and Sylvie V. Schweitzer, *Le communisme à l'usine: Vie ouvrière et mouvement ouvrier chez Renault, 1920–1939* (Paris, 1984), p. 16; Letellier et al., *Enquête,* 1:60.

5. Jean Lhomme, "Le pouvoir d'achat de l'ouvrier français au cours d'un siècle: 1840–1940," *Le Mouvement social,* no. 63 (April–June 1968): 41–69.

6. Au sujet du chômage dans la région parisienne, 3 May 1936, AN, $F^7$13983.

7. Annie Fourcaut, *Femmes à l'usine en France dans l'entre-deux-guerres* (Paris, 1982), pp. 46–47.

8. The following is based on Letellier et al., *Enquête,* 2:86.

9. Quoted in Fourcaut, *Femmes,* p. 131.

10. Sauvy, ed., *Histoire économique,* 2:122.

11. Jean and Françoise Fourastié, "Le genre de vie," in *Histoire économique de la France entre les deux guerres,* ed. Alfred Sauvy (Paris, 1972), 3:215.

12. André Armengaud, "La démographie française du XXe siècle," in *Histoire économique et sociale de la France,* ed. Fernand Braudel and Ernest Labrousse (Paris, 1976), 4:619; Jacques Godard, "A propos de la mortalité infantile," Georges Lefranc Collection, Hoover Institution.

13. Graphique du nombre des grévistes du 1er mai, AN, 39AS864–870; Jacques Kergoat, *La France du front populaire* (Paris, 1986), p. 98; Depretto and Schweitzer, *Communisme,* p. 182.

14. Meeting organisé par le syndicat unifié des cheminots à Vitry-sur-Seine, 2 May 1936, AN, F^7 13983.

15. Grève d'ouvriers peintres, 17 May 1930, APP 1870; Grève d'ouvriers outilleurs, 13 September 1933, APP 1870; Grèves d'ouvriers cimentiers, 28 March 1934 and 17 March 1936, APP 1873; Grève d'ouvriers et ouvrières toliers et ferblantiers, 30 March 1934, APP 1870; Grève d'ouvriers manœuvres, 27 July 1934, APP 1873; Charles Tilly, *The Contentious French* (Cambridge, Mass., 1986); Depretto and Schweitzer, *Communisme,* pp. 131–49; Sylvie V. Schweitzer, *Des engrenages à la chaîne* (Lyon, 1982), p. 164; *Humanité,* 30 and 31 March, 4 April 1934.

16. Gustav Noske (1868–1946) was the German Social Democratic leader who reestablished order in Germany by suppressing the insurrection of early 1919 that attempted to extend the German revolution. Blum made it clear that he would not follow Noske's precedent.

17. Henri Prouteau, *Les occupations d'usines en Italie et en France* (Paris, 1938), p. 103.

18. *Humanité,* 17–29 May 1936; Jacques Danos and Marcel Gibelin, *Juin 36* (Paris, 1972), 1:41–44; *Usine,* supplements of 23 May and 4 June 1936; *Le Petit Parisien,* 27–28 May 1936.

19. *Le Petit Parisien,* 29 May 1936.

20. *Humanité,* 17 and 27 May 1936.

21. Barcelonan workers also were ambivalent toward their work clothes. Employees of the power industry—meter readers and collectors—demanded a removable insignia on their company-supplied uniforms so that they could wear them both on and off the job.

22. Activité de l'union des syndicats de la région parisienne, 29 April 1936, AN, F^7 13652.

23. Louis Danty-Lafrance and René Villmer, *La rémunération de la main d'œuvre dans l'organisation du travail* (Paris, 1937), p. 35; see also Bernard Mottez, *Systèmes de salaires et politiques patronales: Essai sur l'évolution des pratiques et des idéologies patronales* (Paris, 1966); Grève d'ouvriers cimentiers, 13 March 1933; Conflit dans une entreprise de travaux publics, 20 January 1932; Incidents sur un chantier de construction à Malakoff, 8 January 1932, all in APP 1873; Grèves de manœuvres, 7 May 1936, AN, $F^7$13983.

24. Danos and Gibelin, *Juin 36,* 2:50; Bertrand Badie, "Les grèves du front populaire aux usines Renault," *Le Mouvement social,* no. 81 (October–December 1972): 98; *Usine,* 4 June 1936; *Humanité,* 30 May 1936.

25. *Le Petit Parisien,* 31 May 1936.

26. Ibid., 1–4 June 1936; *Humanité,* 5 June 1936; Danos and Gibelin, *Juin 36,* 1:62–66.

27. Trois tentatives, (n.d.), AN, F^{60}996.

28. Simone Weil, *La condition ouvrière* (Paris, 1951) p. 231.

29. Badie, "Les grèves," pp. 83–84.

30. Herrick Eaton Chapman, "Reshaping French Industrial Politics: Workers, Employers, State Officials, and the Struggle for Control in the Aircraft Industry, 1938–1950" (Ph.D. diss., University of California, Berkeley, 1983), p. 135; Depretto and Schweitzer, *Communisme,* pp. 181–84.

31. Occupation des usines, 30 May 1936, AN, $F^7$13983.

32. Antoine Prost, "Les grèves de juin 1936," in *Léon Blum, chef du gouvernement,* ed. Pierre Renouvin and René Rémond (Paris, 1981), p. 74.

33. Sian Reynolds, "Women and Men: Different Experiences of the Popular Front in France" (Paper presented at Popular Fronts Conference, University of Southampton, April 1986); Renseignements: Répartition du personnel entre les diverses fabrications, 8 July 1936, AN, 39AS830/831.

34. Compte-rendu de la délégation, 6 June 1936, AN, 91AQ16.

35. Henry W. Ehrmann, *Organized Business in France* (Princeton, 1957), p. 7; Georges Lefranc, *Juin 36* (Paris, 1966), pp. 143–58.

36. Edouard Dolléans and Gérard Dehove, *Histoire du travail en France: Mouvement ouvrier et législation sociale de 1919 à nos jours* (Paris, 1955), 2:13; Miniconi, *Ce qu'il faut savoir sur les assurances sociales* (Paris, 1937); Joel Colton, *Compulsory Labor Arbitration in France* (New York, 1951), p. 17.

37. André Delmas, *A gauche de la barricade* (Paris, 1950), p. 101; see Ingo Kolboom, *La revanche des patrons: Le patronat face au front populaire,* trans. Jeanne Etoré (Paris, 1986), for small employers' opposition

to the agreement; also Serge Berstein, *Histoire du parti radical* (Paris, 1980–1982), 2:449–50.

38. Activité des groupements patronaux, 29 July 1936, AN, $F^7$12961.

39. Charles Jeanselme, *Le nouveau régime des conventions collectives en France* (Paris, 1938), p. 25.

40. C. J. Gignoux, *L'économie française entre les deux guerres, 1919–1939* (Paris, 1942), p. 304.

41. Léon Jouhaux quoted in Danos and Gibelin, *Juin 36,* 2:87.

42. Lefranc, *Juin 36,* p. 67.

43. Jean Coutrot, *L'humanisme économique* (Paris, 1936), p. 20; Pierre André, *Les délégués ouvriers* (Paris, 1937), p. 3.

44. *La Journée industrielle* quoted in Martin Fine, "Toward Corporatism: The Movement for Capital-Labor Collaboration in France, 1914–1936" (Ph.D. diss., University of Wisconsin, 1971), p. 226.

45. *L'Economie nouvelle,* June–July 1936 and in 1938. On the opposition of the *patronat* throughout the Popular Front see letters AN, 39AS977 and AN, 91AQ15; C. J. Gignoux, *Patrons, soyez des patrons!* (Paris, 1937), p. 7; Activité des groupements patronaux, 29 July 1936, AN, $F^7$12961; Adrian Rossiter, "Popular Front Economic Policy and the Matignon Negotiations" (Paper presented at Popular Fronts Conference, University of Southampton, April 1986); Joel Colton, *Léon Blum: Humanist in Politics* (Cambridge, 1966), pp. 167–70.

46. Letter from Aciéries et forges de Firminy to L. Renault, 22 July 1937, AN, 91AQ83.

47. Grève d'ouvriers cimentiers et ferrailleurs, 7 June 1932, APP 1873; Grève d'ouvriers cimentiers, 22 November 1934, APP 1873; Fin de grève d'ouvriers en articles de voyage, 3 September 1935, APP 1870.

48. Letters collected in AN, 39AS948/949.

49. Jean-Noël Jeanneney, *François de Wendel en république: L'argent et le pouvoir, 1914–1940* (Paris, 1976), 2:815; François Bloch-Lainé, *Profession fonctionnaire* (Paris, 1976), pp. 122–23; see also the discussion in Irwin M. Wall, "Teaching the French Popular Front," *The History Teacher* (May 1987): 366–69.

50. Patrick Fridenson, *Histoire des usines Renault* (Paris, 1972), pp. 278–80; Emmanuel Chadeau, *L'industrie aéronautique en France, 1900–1950* (Paris, 1987), pp. 252–333; Robert Frankenstein, *Le prix du réarmement français, 1935–1939* (Paris, 1982), pp. 81–86, 160–69, 257.

51. Jean-François Pinchon, "La conception et l'organisation de l'exposition," in *Cinquantenaire de l'exposition internationale des arts et des techniques dans la vie moderne* (Paris, 1987), pp. 41–43.

52. La commission administrative de la CGT, 18 July 1936, AN, $F^7$12961.

53. Note sur les salaires à la S.A.F.E., 16 January 1937, AN, 91AQ37.

54. Conversely, workers' refusals to work a thirty-hour week during the Popular Front may be attributed to their reluctance to see their buying power decline precipitously (M. Halbwachs, *L'évolution des besoins dans les classes ouvrières* [Paris, 1933], p. 137).

55. Compagnie du ciment Verre, 13 December 1934, APP 1873; Grève d'ouvriers cauoutchoutiers, 18 May 1934, APP 1870.

56. See Michelle Perrot, *Les ouvriers en grève: France 1871–1890* (Paris, 1974); Roland Trempé, *Les mineurs de Carmaux, 1848–1914* (Paris, 1971), 1:229; Yves Lequin, *Les ouvriers de la région lyonnaise* (Lyon, 1977); Jacques Valdour, *Ouvriers parisiens* (Paris, 1921), pp. 24–31, which concludes that workers would not work unless forced.

57. Noiriel, *Ouvriers,* pp. 174–75.

58. Grève d'ouvriers cimentiers, 5 July 1936, APP 1873.

59. Depretto and Schweitzer, *Communisme,* p. 98; "Les lendemains d'octobre: La jeunesse ouvrière française entre le bolchévisme et la marginalité," *Les Révoltes logiques,* no. 1 (1975): 74.

60. Etude sur l'assurance 'Accidents du travail,' 24 September 1931, AN, 91AQ57.

61. Cause de ce retard, AN, 91AQ3.

62. The following is derived from Letellier et al., *Enquête,* 1:255, 310–17.

63. Prost, "Les grèves," p. 73.

64. Grèves de juin 1936, GIM.

65. Letter from Commissaire de police de Vanves, 27 June 1936, APP 1873.

66. Costes cited in Compte-rendu de la délégation, 6 June 1936, AN, 91AQ16.

67. Thorez quoted in Lefranc, *Juin 36,* p. 172.

68. See numerous documents and letters from Renault management, its insurance company, and the arbitrator in AN, 91AQ115.

69. See three signed statements and Affaire: usines Renault grève du 5 au 14 juin 1936, in AN, 91AQ115; Arbitrage, état des dommages, détériorations, et soustractions constatés, AN, 91AQ115; Letter to X. 3 November 1936, AN, 91AQ115. Cf. Badie, "Les grèves," p. 92, which calls the Renault occupation "a model of a self-managed society."

70. Grèves de juin 1936, GIM; Occupation des usines, GIM.

71. AN, $F^2$2760, $F^2$2761; Occupation des usines, GIM.

72. Etablissements où il existe une menace de mise en marche par les ouvriers, (n.d.), GIM.

73. Extraits de correspondances, (n.d.), Incidents—Bennes Pillot, Als-Thom, La Flamme bleue, Dunlop, Bretin, Edoux Samain, S.E.V., Montupet, D.A.V.U.M., Bronzavia, SOUMA, GIM; Faits signalés, (n.d.), GIM.

74. Renvoi d'ouvriers terrassiers et mineurs, 28 May 1936, AN, $F^7$13983; for the CGT statement, see Kergoat, *France*, p. 115; Extraits de correspondances, Bretin, lettre du 10 juin 1936, GIM; Grèves de juin 1936, GIM; Faits signalés, Als-Thom, GIM; A la maison de couture Chanel, 24 June 1936, APP 1872; *Le Petit Parisien*, 29 May 1936.

75. Convention collective, 12 June 1936, AN, F^{60}996.

76. Manifestation populaire organisée par le parti communiste au vélodrome Buffalo, APP 1862.

CHAPTER ELEVEN

1. Letter to J. Garchery, 9 December 1936, AN, F^{22}396.

2. Autres manquements, 4 September 1936, AR.

3. Incidents, AR. Simone Weil (*La condition ouvrière* [Paris, 1951], p. 152) noted between 1934 and 1936 that supervisors complained of "momentarily unoccupied" female workers who met "in large numbers to gossip"; foremen feared the talk would create "indiscipline" and wanted to fine the "gossipers."

4. Note, 11 September 1936, AR.

5. Rôle et compétence des délégués, 21 October 1936, AR; Incidents, AR.

6. Les violations, 21 October 1936, AR.

7. Incident de . . . 12 janvier 1937, AN, 91AQ16; 5 février 1937, AN, 91AQ16.

8. Les violations, AR.

9. *Syndicats*, 18 November 1937.

10. Autres manquements, 4 September 1936, AR.

11. Les violations, 23 September 1936, AR.

12. 9 September 1936, AR.

13. Autres manquements, 4 September 1936, AR; Note 1, Comment se pose le problème, (Spring 1937?), AN, 91AQ3.

14. Grève d'ouvriers d'une fabrique de chaudières, 20 August 1936, APP 1873; Etablissements Vitrix. Sentence de M. Pontremoli, 17 April 1937, AN, 39AS1012.

15. Letter from Groupement des industriels de Poissy, 18 May 1938, AN, 39AS802.

16. Autres manquements, 4 September 1936, AR.

17. Rapport concernant le licenciement du personnel de l'atelier 125, (n.d.), AN, 91AQ15.

18. Note de service no. 21.344, 6 December 1937, AN, 91AQ16.

19. *L'Intransigeant,* 5 November 1938.

20. Quelques manquements, 9 September 1936, AR; Incidents, AR.

21. Note from M. Penard, 22 April 1938, AN, 91AQ65.

22. Letter to M. Thiebaud from H. Duvernoy, directeur de personnel des usines Renault, 16 July 1937, AN, 39AS836.

23. The following information is taken from Séries de diagrammes de puissance absorbée par les ateliers, 22 April 1938, AN, 91AQ65.

24. Freinage . . . des cadres camionettes, Freinage . . . des cadres Celta et Prima, AN, 91AQ116.

25. Chronométrage, 9 November 1937, AN, 91AQ65; this citation and comments are based on Difficultés rencontrées, 22 April 1938, AN, 91AQ65.

26. Déclaration de Madame X, 14 January 1937, AN, 91AQ65.

27. Note by L., "Limitation de la production," 21 April 1938, AN, 91AQ65.

28. CGT fédération des techniciens, 27 September 1937, GIM; *La Vie ouvrière,* 27 May 1937, and letter to GIM, 21 October 1937.

29. Notes sur les incidents survenus, 8 September 1937, GIM; italics in original. The following is based on this document and Conflit SIMCA, (n.d.), GIM.

30. Compromis d'arbitrage, 23 September 1937, GIM.

31. Décision arbitrale, 1 October 1937, GIM. For tensions in October, see *Syndicats,* 14 October 1937; on the selection of arbitrators, see Joel Colton, *Compulsory Labor Arbitration in France* (New York, 1951), pp. 33–50.

32. Résultat des élections des délégués ouvriers, AN, 91AQ116; see Projet de lettre à M. Ramadier, 9 March 1938, AN, 39AS830/831, which blames trouble on a "handful of agitators."

33. Correspondance, 17 July 1936, APP 1862.

34. Atelier: Evacuation des copeaux, 30 September 1936, AN, 91AQ16. For a similar problem in the mines, see Aimée Moutet, "La rationalisation dans les mines du nord à l'épreuve du front populaire," *Le Mouvement social,* no. 135 (April–June 1986): 90–93.

35. 30 June 1936, AR; AN, 91AQ116; La situation dans la métallurgie, 12 February 1937, AN, $F^7$12966.

36. Les violations, 21 October 1936, AR.

37. Grèves de juin 1936, GIM; Note from Rosenblatt, 22 April

1938, AN, 91AQ65; Syndicat des industries mécaniques de France, 6 October 1936, AN, 39AS848.

38. *Le Défenseur,* December 1936.

39. Assemblée générale des sections et cellules d'ateliers, (n.d.), AN, 91AQ16. The following is based on this document (probably the report of a management informer) and Réunion de 28/9/36, sousrayon communiste Renault, AN, 91AQ16.

40. Note from Penard, 22 April 1938, AN, 91AQ65.

41. Syndicat professionnel quoted in Jacques Delperrié de Bayac, *Histoire du front populaire* (Paris, 1972), p. 315.

42. Les techniciens, ingénieurs, (n.d.), AR.

43. Letter from Syndicat professionnel des agents de maîtrise, AR.

44. *Usine,* 18 March 1937.

45. Letter to chief administrator from Syndicat professionnel des agents de maîtrise, techniciens, et employés, AN, 91AQ15.

46. Note au sujet des effectifs, AN, 91AQ15.

47. L'arbitrage obligatoire et le problème de l'autorité, 22 December 1936, AN, 39AS1012.

48. Notes pour la préparation de l'assemblée générale du 5 novembre 1937, AN, 39AS857.

49. Bulletin quotidien, L'arbitrage obligatoire, 22 December 1936, AN, 39AS1012.

50. Déclaration de Madame X, 14 January 1937, P., 1 February 1937, AN, 91AQ65; Incidents, AN, 91AQ16; see also documents on various incidents in AN, 91AQ116.

51. SNCAN, 25 January 1939. SNA (from minutes of the *comité de direction*).

52. SNCASO, 26 April 1938, SNA (from minutes of the *conseil d'administration*).

53. Robert Jacomet, *L'armement de la France (1936–1939)* (Paris, 1945), p. 55, 251; cf. Robert Frankenstein, *Le prix du réarmement français, 1935–1939* (Paris, 1982), p. 242.

54. Letter from Aciéries et forges de Firminy, AN, 91AQ83; letter from Etablissements L. Douzille, 21 January 1939, SNA.

55. Départ des ouvriers professionnels, 23 November 1938, AN, 91AQ31; for an earlier period see S.A.F.E., 27 December 1934, AN, 91AQ37.

56. SNCAN, "Objet: Déplacements," 4 March 1937, SNA.

57. La situation des établissements, (n.a., n.d.), and Eléments de réponse, 31 December 1938, SHAA, Z11607, which agreed with the unknown author.

58. These assertions concerning the Courbevoie plant were sec-

onded by an engineer and confirmed by Air Ministry investigators (Rapport du capitaine Testas, SHAA, Z12935).

59. Letter to Inspecteur général du travail, 13 September 1938, AN, 39AS830/831.

60. SNCASO, 9 December 1938, SNA.

61. Pierre Couturet, "Un exemple bien typique: Gnôme et Rhône," *La Révolution prolétarienne,* 25 July 1938; *Le bolchevik de chez Gnôme-Rhône,* June 1938, AN, $F^7$12966. A (CGT?) document complained that thirty policemen were "paid to do nothing" at Gnôme et Rhône (Arrêté, SHAA, Z12939).

62. On demande des nationaux, June 1938, AN, $F^7$12966.

63. Couturet, "Un exemple."

64. Note 18 dec. 1936, AN, 91AQ31; Comment se pose le problème, (Spring 1937?), AN, 91AQ3.

65. SNCAN, 19 October 1938, SNA.

66. M. Métral, "L'industrie aéronautique française," (March?) 1938, SHAA, Z12935; letter from Jean Coutrot, 3 March 1938, SHAA Z12935. See also Comité de production, 4 February 1938, SHAA, Z12946.

67. *Usine,* 19 February 1938; letter from Chambre syndicale, 4 April 1938, AN, 91AQ80.

68. Couturet, "Un exemple typique."

69. *La Vie ouvrière,* 3 March 1938.

70. Couturet, "Un exemple typique"; Emmanuel Chadeau, *L'industrie aéronautique en France, 1900–1950* (Paris, 1987), p. 320.

71. *La Vie ouvrière,* 21 July 1938.

72. C. Bonnier, "Huit mois de nationalisation," AN, 91AQ80.

73. *Syndicats,* 22 June 1938.

74. M. Roos, "Situation de l'industrie aéronautique," 1937, SHAA, Z11606.

75. See Rendement, (n.a., n.d.), SHAA, Z11507; Réponse au questionnaire du comité de contrôle financier, 16 December 1937, SHAA Z12936. Note pour M. le ministre de l'air, 26 November 1937, SHAA Z12936 claimed that nationalization had not adversely affected output; an unnamed and undated document (Arrêté d'extension de la convention nationale de l'aviation, SHAA, Z12939) asserted the workers and delegates produced normally.

76. Chadeau, *L'industrie aéronautique,* p. 320.

77. Ibid., pp. 242–44.

78. Conseil d'administration, chambre syndicale de constructeurs, 17 March 1938, AN, 91AQ80; Frankenstein, Réarmement, p. 278.

79. Départ and Paye aux pièces, 23 November 1938, AN, 91AQ31.

80. *Usine,* 9 June 1938.

81. La situation des établissements, SHAA, Z11607.

82. M. Métral, "L'industrie aéronautique," (March?) 1938, SHAA, Z12935.

83. B. Rouzé, letter to Guy La Chambre, 7 March 1938, SHAA, Z12936.

84. Rapport du capitaine Testas, (January?) 1939, SHAA, Z12935.

85. The following information is derived from the Lamoureux file, SHAA, Z12935.

86. L'industrie des cellules, (n.d.), SHAA, Z12937.

87. Chadeau, *L'industrie aéronautique,* p. 321.

88. Comité du matériel, 20 May 1938, SHAA, Z12946.

89. Métral, "L'industrie aéronautique," March 1938, SHAA, Z12935. For specific information on worktime in Germany, see "La durée effective du travail en Allemagne," *Revue internationale du travail,* no. 3 (March 1939): 393–406.

90. Pomaret (ministre du travail) quoted by Elisabeth du Reau, "L'aménagement de la loi instituant la semaine de quarante heures," in *Edouard Daladier: Chef du gouvernement,* ed. René Rémond and Janine Bourdin (Paris, 1977), p. 145.

91. La situation des établissements, SHAA Z11607; Bulletin quotidien, l'arbitrage obligatoire, 22 December 1936, AN, 39AS1012.

92. Roos, "La situation," 1937, SHAA, Z11606.

93. Comité de production, 4 February 1938, SHAA, Z12946.

94. Comité du matériel, 15 March 1938, SHAA, Z12946; Comité de production, 22 June 1938, SHAA, Z12946.

95. Les causes, 13 September 1938, in Les insuffisances actuelles de la production aéronautique, SHAA, Z11606.

96. Roos, "La situation," 1937, SHAA, Z11606.

97. Croizat quoted by Reau, "L'aménagement," p. 136.

98. Jacomet, *L'armement,* p. 260.

99. Constat, 10 March 1937 (signed by *hussier*), and Dégâts commis et liste du matériel, outillage et matières volés ou détériorés, 22 April 1938, AN, 91AQ115.

100. Letter from Syndicat général de la construction électrique, 13 April 1938, GIM.

101. Etat des déprédations, disparitions, 24 April 1938, AN, 91AQ16; letter to Doyen des juges d'instruction, AN, 91AQ16.

102. Georges Lefranc, *Histoire du front populaire* (Paris, 1974), p. 274; Delperrié de Bayac, *Histoire du front populaire,* p. 449; Alfred Sauvy, ed., *Histoire économique de la France entre les deux guerres* (Paris, 1972), 2:276.

103. Reau, "L'aménagement," p. 133; see also Frankenstein, *Réarmement,* p. 277.

104. SNCASE, 29 March 1938, SNA. See Chadeau (*L'industrie aéronautique,* p. 321), which makes a distinction between *motoristes,* who made airplane engines and wanted more worktime, and *avionneurs,* who made plane bodies and became dissatisfied with the shortened workweek only later in the year; see also Frankenstein, *Réarmement,* pp. 277–78.

105. Note de la chambre syndicale des industries aéronautiques remise à M. le ministre du travail, 31 March 1938, AN, 91AQ80; see also Chadeau, *L'industrie aéronautique,* pp. 339–40.

106. Note, 8 July 1938, AN, 91AQ80.

107. Rapport et annexes sur la production aéronautique, SHAA, Z11606; Comité du matériel, 15 March 1938, SHAA Z12946; Jean-Charles Asselain, "Une erreur de politique économique: la loi de quarante heures de 1936," *Revue économique,* no. 4 (July 1974): 688–90. See also *Usine,* 24 November 1938; letter from Louis Masson, 10 May 1937, AN, 39AS802. On Blum, see Lefranc, *Histoire du front populaire,* pp. 211–12.

108. *Syndicats,* 25 February 1937; *La Vie ouvrière,* 6 May 1937, on railroad workers who demanded the 5 × 8 and opposed the 6 × 6 : 40; on department-store employees' preference for the 5 × 8 over 6 × 6 : 40, see Annie Fourcaut, *Femmes à l'usine en France dans l'entre-deux-guerres* (Paris, 1982) p. 220.

109. Préparation du congrès de la fédération des métaux, AN, $F^7$12966.

110. The following is taken from *Usine,* 10 October 1938; *La Journée industrielle,* 19–26 October 1938.

111. Les heures supplémentaires pour la défense nationale, 17 October 1938, AN, 39AS974–975.

112. Refus d'effectuer les heures autorisées, 19 March 1938, GIM. Interestingly enough, eight of thirteen incidents occurred during *la belle saison*—May, June, and July. On recovery, SNCAN, procès-verbal, Conseil d'administration, 24 December 1936, SNA.

113. *Syndicats,* 13 May 1937.

114. Circulaire aux inspecteurs du travail, (n.d.), AN, 91AQ64.

115. *La Vie ouvrière,* 23 June 1938.

116. The following information is from a letter to the ministre du travail, 6 September 1938 and Note de service no. 210, 2 September 1938, AN, 39AS830/831. This firm's history of labor conflict included strikes in June 1926, January 1930, and April 1938. On 25 March 1937 *La Vie ouvrière* charged that the "fascist" executives of Optique et

précision at Levallois believed themselves "authorized to watch workers day and night."

117. Letter from Société des magnétos R. B. au ministre du travail, 7 September 1938, AN, 39AS830/831.

118. J. Truelle, "La production aéronautique militaire française jusqu'en juin 1940," *Revue d'histoire de la deuxième guerre mondiale,* no. 73 (January 1969): 90.

119. Note sur la crise de l'aéronautique française, AN, 91AQ80.

120. *Usine,* 17 February and 13 January 1938.

121. Commission permanente, 2 October 1936, AN, CE.

122. Ibid., 11 June 1937.

123. Comité de contentieux, 19 June 1939, Contentieux, 35, AN, CE.

124. Letter from ministère du commerce et de l'industrie, 6 February 1941, Contentieux, 34, AN, CE.

125. Rapport by B., (n.d.), Contentieux, 34, AN, CE.

126. Edmond Labbé, *Rapport général* (Paris, 1938), 2:68. Labbé, frustrated by workers' strikes and "strolls into the city," had threatened to resign but was dissuaded by President Lebrun (Lefranc, *Histoire du front populaire,* p. 240).

127. Comité de direction, AN, 89AQ2025.

128. Entreprises de grands travaux, May 1938, AN, 89AQ2026.

129. Conseil d'état: section du contentieux, letter of 1946, Contentieux, 35, AN, CE.

130. Comité de contentieux, 19 June 1939, Contentieux, 35, AN, CE.

131. *Usine,* 6 May 1937.

132. Letter from administrator, 21 April 1939, Contentieux, 40, AN, CE.

133. Réunion organisée par le syndicat des maçons et cimentiers d'art, 19 July 1936, AN, F^{7}13652.

134. Ministre des travaux publics à M. le président du conseil, 21 August 1936, AN, F^{60}639.

135. Commission tripartite, 11 March 1937, AN, CE. On the relations between the Blum government and the CGT, see Bernard Georges, "La CGT et le gouvernement Blum," *Le Mouvement social,* no. 54 (January–March 1966): 67.

136. *La Vie ouvrière,* 18 February 1937; original italics.

137. *Syndicats,* 18 January 1937; *Humanité,* 12 August 1936.

138. Blum quoted in Delperrié de Bayac, *Histoire du front populaire,* p. 368.

139. Rapport des établissements Cabirol, 19 April 1939, Contentieux, 40, AN, CE.

140. Labbé, *Rapport,* 1:80.

141. Réunion organisée par les ouvriers du bâtiment à Clichy, 23 February 1937, AN, F[7] 12966.

142. Letter to Labbé, 3 July 1937, Contentieux, 38, AN, CE.

143. Labbé, *Rapport,* 2:67. The workers of the métro extension project also refused weekend work (AN, 89AQ2025).

144. Letter from Société de Canal et Schuhl, 6 July 1942, Contentieux, 35, AN, CE; *Usine,* 22 April 1937.

145. Rapport by B., (n.d.), Contentieux, 34, AN, CE; Comité de contentieux, 20 July 1939, Contentieux, 41, AN, CE.

146. *La Vie ouvrière,* 30 March 1939.

147. Commission tripartite, 13 May 1937, AN, CE.

148. Note des ingénieurs-constructeurs, (n.d.), Contentieux, 37; letter from administrator, 21 April 1939, Contentieux, 40, AN, CE.

149. The following is from note, (n.d.), Contentieux, 37, AN, CE.

150. Assemblée générale des charpentiers en bois, 25 February 1937, AN, F[7] 12966.

151. Discours prononcé par M. Jules Verger, 11 August 1937, AN, 39AS843.

152. Compte-rendu et décisions d'arbitrage, 6 August 1937, in Communication des établissements Verger et Delaporte, BN.

153. Commission tripartite, 29 April 1937; letter to Labbé, 3 July 1937, Contentieux, 38, AN, CE.

154. Letter from Société de Canal et Schuhl, 6 July 1942, Contentieux, 35, AN, CE.

155. *Syndicats,* 1 July 1937, celebrated the occasion: "A l'exposition 1937 l'édifice grandiose élevé par la CGT à la gloire du travail a été inauguré."

156. *Syndicats,* 27 November 1936, 24 June 1937; *Humanité,* 14 April 1938; *Le Populaire,* 3 April 1937. For a recent repetition of these accusations, see Benoît Frachon, *Pour la CGT: Mémoires de lutte, 1902–1939* (Paris 1981), p. 198.

157. *Le Peuple,* 5 July 1937.

158. Léon Blum, *A l'échelle humaine* (Paris, 1945), pp. 117–19; see also Joel Colton, *Léon Blum: Humanist in Politics* (Cambridge, 1966), p. 171.

CHAPTER TWELVE

1. Maurice Joly, *Productivité et discipline dans la profession* (Paris, 1939), pp. 57–58.

2. Comité de contentieux, 19 June 1939, Contentieux, 35, AN, CE.

3. Ministère du travail, 10 January 1938, AN, 39AS991.

4. Comité de décentralisation industrielle pour la main d'œuvre, 26 September 1936, AN, 39AS991; Comité de reclassement professionnel, 16 July 1937, AN, 39AS991.

5. Comité de décentralisation, (n.d.), AN, 39AS991.

6. Ministre du travail, 10 January 1938, AN, 39AS991.

7. Note pour M. Pluyette, 2 May 1938, AN, 39AS839.

8. Letter from Ministre du travail, 4 January 1937, AN, 39AS830/831.

9. Note—comité de reclassement professionnel, 30 September 1937, AN, 39AS990; Le vendredi 5 novembre, AN, 39AS991.

10. *Humanité,* 17–24 May 1936.

11. *Syndicats,* 23 December 1937, 28 December 1938, and 10 June 1937.

12. *Humanité,* 13 August 1936, 5 April and 5 May 1938.

13. *Syndicats,* 16 March 1938; *Nouveaux Cahiers,* 15 June 1937.

14. *La Vie ouvrière,* 14 October 1937; Le Corbusier, *Des canons, des munitions . . . merci! Des logis, s.v.p.* (Paris, 1938), pp. 7–9.

15. Robert Fishman, *Urban Utopias in the Twentieth Century* (New York, 1977), p. 233.

16. *La Vie ouvrière,* 12 May 1938.

17. Roger-Henri Guerrand, *Le logement populaire en France: Sources documentaires et bibliographie (1800–1960)* (Paris, 1979), p. 128.

18. *Humanité,* 22 August 1936 and 3 March 1938; *Syndicats,* 23 December 1937.

19. Le Corbusier quoted in Fishman, *Utopias,* p. 191.

20. *Syndicats,* 15 and 23 December 1937.

21. *La Vie ouvrière,* 21 January 1937.

22. For Renault's attitude, see Patrick Fridenson, *Histoire des usines Renault* (Paris, 1972), pp. 318–19, and AN, 91AQ16.

23. *Humanité,* 29 October 1936, 18 June 1937, and 9 March 1938.

24. Léon Blum, *A l'échelle humaine* (Paris, 1945), p. 112.

25. Richard Holt, *Sport and Society in Modern France* (London, 1981), pp. 70–78.

26. Françoise Cribier, *La grande migration d'été des citadins en France* (Paris, 1969), p. 41. P. A. Rey-Herme (*Les colonies de vacances en France, 1906–1935* [Paris, 1961], 1:294) offers figures of one hundred fifty thousand children who left Paris for vacation camps in 1936.

27. Benoît Frachon, *Le rôle social des syndicats* (Paris, 1937), pp. 7–8.

28. Holt, *Sport,* p. 204.

29. Henri Noguères, *La vie quotidienne en France au temps du front populaire (1935–1938)* (Paris, 1977), p. 150.

30. *Je suis partout* quoted in Paul Christophe, *1936: Les catholiques et le front populaire* (Paris, 1986), p. 10.
31. *La Flèche de Paris,* 6 February 1937.
32. Jean-Victor Parant, *Le problème du tourisme populaire* (Paris, 1939), p. 217.
33. Lagrange quoted in Noguères, *Vie quotidienne,* p. 188.
34. *Humanité,* 5 September 1937; *La Vie ouvrière,* 18 March 1937.
35. Parant, *Problème,* p. 86.
36. Emilie Lefranc and Georges Lefranc, *Le syndicalisme devant le problème des loisirs* (Paris, 1937), pp. 36–37; *Syndicats,* 8 April 1937 and 15 June 1938.
37. The following is derived from E. and G. Lefranc, *Syndicalisme,* pp. 14–43; italics in original.
38. *Le Populaire,* 12 January 1937.
39. Holt, *Sports,* pp. 205–6.
40. *Humanité,* 25 and 28 May 1936.
41. *Syndicats,* 11 December 1936 and 8 April 1937.
42. Benigno Cácères, *Loisirs et travail: Du moyen âge à nos jours* (Paris, 1973), pp. 192–93; Holt, *Sport,* p. 207; Jacques Kergoat, *La France du front populaire* (Paris, 1986), p. 362.
43. *Humanité,* 20 July and 29 November 1936.
44. Cácères, *Loisirs et travail,* p. 189; Jules Moch, *Le front populaire: Grande espérance* (Paris, 1971), p. 160. Parant, *Problème,* pp. 83–84, gives figures of 550,000 in 1936 and 900,000 in 1937.
45. *La Vie ouvrière,* 13 May 1937.
46. Noguères, *Vie quotidienne,* p. 154; Parant, *Problème,* p. 92.
47. *Le Peuple,* 3 December 1937.
48. *Syndicats,* 25 March 1937.
49. *Humanité,* 21 June and 6 December 1936, 29 January 1937.
50. Gabrielle Letellier, Jean Perret, H. E. Zuber, and A. Dauphin-Meunier, *Enquête sur le chômage* (Paris, 1938–1949), 3:69.
51. Aline Coutrot, "Youth Movements in France in the 1930s," *Journal of Contemporary History* 5, no. 1 (1970): 23–35; Kergoat, *France,* p. 314; Eugène Raude and Gilbert Prouteau, *Le message de Léo Lagrange* (Paris, 1950), p. 105.
52. Jean-Louis Chappat, *Les chemins de l'espoir, ou combats de Léo Lagrange* (Liévin, 1983), pp. 184–256.
53. Noguères, *Vie quotidienne,* pp. 168–69; Aviation populaire, 17 February 1937, AN, F^7 12966; *Humanité,* 1 June 1936; Exposé, SHAA, Z12944; Comité du matériel, 10 June 1938, SHAA, Z12946; see Roger Bordier (*36 la fête* [Paris, 1985], p. 98) on PCF reaction to fears that a proletarian wave would engulf aviation.

54. See Holt, *Sport,* pp. 175, 186.

55. *Syndicats,* 18 March 1937; Noguères, *Vie quotidienne,* p. 159; Kergoat, *France,* p. 337.

56. Letter from Etablissements Reinhard et Chapuiset, 9 June 1938, AN, 39AS836; M. Doury, SIMCA-FIAT à Nanterre, violations de la convention collective, 3 September 1937, GIM.

57. *Humanité,* 17 August 1936 and 15 December 1937; *Syndicats,* 9 September 1937.

58. *Usine,* 10 September 1936; Parant, *Problème,* p. 217.

59. Moch, *Espérance,* p. 298.

60. *Syndicats,* 20 May 1937.

61. Letter from the Groupement des industriels de la région de Saint-Denis, 8 July 1937, AN, 39AS803; Réunion du comité du 14 avril 1937, AN, 39AS852.

62. *Usine,* 8 April and 6 May 1937; Refus de récupérer en violation de la loi de 40 heures, 19 March 1938, GIM.

63. Vouret, 12 May 1937, GIM.

64. Procès-verbal, GIM, 14 April 1937, AN, 39AS852.

65. Parant, *Problème,* p. 10; Yvonne Becquet, *L'organisation des loisirs des travailleurs* (Paris, 1939), p. 20.

66. *Annuaire statistique de la France,* 1934; Cécile Tardieu-Gotchac, "Les fléaux sociaux," in *Histoire économique de la France entre les deux guerres,* ed. Alfred Sauvy (Paris, 1972), 3:232.

67. Letellier et al., *Enquête,* 3:51–75.

68. *Usine,* 27 January 1938.

69. Sully Ledermann, *Alcool, alcoolisme, alcoolisation* (Paris, 1956–1964), 2:306.

70. "Cahiers de la santé publique," *L'Hygiène sociale,* 12 March 1938. For women's suffrage and alcoholism, "Rapport sur le concours militaire antialcoolique," *L'Etoile bleue* (March 1939).

71. The following information is derived from René Barthe, "Alcoolisme et personnel d'une entreprise: Bilan médico-social," *Annales d'hygiène publique, industrielle et sociale* 16 (December 1938): 525–33.

72. Ledermann, *Alcoolisme,* 2:379. These figures on absenteeism do not include work accidents. In this enterprise, absenteeism did not increase during the Popular Front perhaps because the flu epidemic of the winter of 1935 was particularly severe.

73. Patricia E. Prestwich, "Antialcoholism in France since 1870" (manuscript), p. 59; Tardieu-Gotchac, "Les fléaux sociaux," p. 235.

74. Jean and Françoise Fourastié, "Le genre de vie," in *Histoire économique de la France entre les deux guerres,* ed. Alfred Sauvy (Paris, 1972), p. 215; Barthe, "Alcoolisme," p. 538.

75. *L'Unité,* September 1936, quoted in Jean-Paul Depretto and Sylvie V. Schweitzer, *Le communisme à l'usine: Vie ouvrière et mouvement ouvrier chez Renault, 1920–1939* (Paris, 1984), p. 221.

76. *La Vie ouvrière,* 29 October 1936; E. and G. Lefranc, *Syndicalisme,* p. 33.

77. Louis Chevalier, *Montmartre du plaisir et du crime* (Paris, 1980), p. 445; *Annuaire statistique de la ville de Paris,* 1935–1937, pp. 613–15.

78. E. Milhaud, "Intervention," 12 April 1935, AN, F^{12}8800; Union française des loisirs, AN, 39AS399.

79. 28 May 1936, AN, 91AQ16.

80. *L'Elan social,* 21 and 28 October 1937; *L'Europe nouvelle,* 22 May 1937.

81. Becquet, *L'organisation des loisirs,* pp. 21–23, 64.

82. Actualités cinématographiques de la semaine, 29 June 1938, AN, $F^7$13019.

83. *Humanité,* 8 and 13 October 1937.

84. *Le Guide du métallurgiste,* July 1938.

85. *Syndicats,* 23 September 1937.

86. 22 June 1936, AN, 91AQ16; *Usine,* 3 March 1938.

87. Fourastié, "Le genre," p. 223.

88. Letellier et al., *Enquête,* 3:134.

89. Centre confédéral d'éducation ouvrière, cycle de conférences sur la condition et le rôle de la femme: Hygiène et logement, (n.d., 1937?), Georges Lefranc Collection, Hoover Institution.

90. Holt, *Sport,* pp. 174–75.

91. Letellier et al., *Enquête,* 3:133–218; Fourastié, "Le genre," p. 217.

92. Résumé, p. iv, April 1938 (?), GIM.

93. Note de service, no. 13.091, 13 December 1937, AN, 91AQ83.

94. 22 December 1936, APP 1871. The worker who defended piecework also denounced "the intrusion of women into the profession."

95. Ce que les décolleteurs doivent savoir, June 1938, $F^7$12966.

96. See A. Lorch, *Les congés payés en France* (Paris, 1938), p. 61. Fines were turned over to the unemployment fund.

97. It seems that, for example, only 2 percent of the budget of the unemployed came from odd jobs (Letellier et al., *Enquête,* 3:11).

98. Parant, *Problème,* p. 198.

99. Réponse de la direction SIMCA à la note remise au groupe par M. Doury, 3 September 1937, GIM.

100. Fermeture des magasins d'alimentation, Paris, 25 July 1936, AN, $F^7$12961.

101. Assemblée générale organisée par la chambre syndicale des employés, section du Bon Marché, 13 February 1937, AN, $F^7$12968.

102. Blum quoted in Georges Lefranc, *Histoire du front populaire* (Paris, 1974), p. 339.

CHAPTER THIRTEEN

1. The following is based on Serge Berstein, *Histoire du parti radical* (Paris, 1980–1982), 2:455–518.
2. See Alfred Sauvy, ed., *Histoire économique de la France entre les deux guerres* (Paris, 1972), 2:286, for figures. See also Jean-Charles Asselain, *Histoire économique de la France* (Paris, 1984), 2:66; Joel Colton, *Compulsory Labor Arbitration in France* (New York, 1951), pp. 82–86.
3. Ingo Kolboom, *La revanche des patrons: Le patronat face au front populaire,* trans. Jeanne Etoré (Paris, 1986), p. 291.
4. *L'Europe nouvelle,* 9 April and 21 May 1938.
5. SNCASO, 27 September 1938, SNA.
6. *La Journée industrielle,* 20 November 1938.
7. Speech to Congrès national des commissions paritaires d'offices publics de placement, 8 September 1938, AN, 39AS830/831.
8. Reynaud quoted in Jacques Delperrié de Bayac, *Histoire du front populaire* (Paris, 1972), p. 396.
9. *L'Europe nouvelle,* 19 November 1938; *Usine,* 17 November 1938; Asselain, *Histoire économique,* 2:68.
10. Reynaud quoted in Delperrié de Bayac, *Histoire du front populaire,* p. 462. See also Paul Reynaud, *Pourquoi ferait-on la grève? Discours radiodiffusé, prononcé le 26 novembre 1938* (Paris, 1938).
11. Jules Moch, *Le front populaire: grande espérance* (Paris, 1971), p. 310.
12. Procès-verbal, 22 November 1938, AN, 39AS852; on Saturday closing, see letter from Groupement des industriels de la région de Saint-Denis, 8 July 1937, AN, 39AS803.
13. *Syndicats,* 31 August 1938.
14. Ibid., 14 September 1938; *Le Travailleur du papier-carton,* September 1938.
15. *La Vie ouvrière,* 17 November and 3 November 1938.
16. *Syndicats,* 29 November 1938.
17. Ibid., 19 November 1938.
18. *Le Travailleur des transports,* December 1938.
19. *Syndicats,* 29 November 1938.
20. *L'Echo des syndicats,* (CFTC) December 1938. During the Popu-

lar Front, even working-class organizations had problems making workers appear on Monday. For example, to protest lay-offs from Chausson at Gennevilliers, on 21 August (1937?) *Humanité* called on all the workers of this firm—including those dismissed—to demonstrate at the company on Monday, 23 August. Only seven arrived (Note concernant l'incident Chausson, AN, 39AS836).

21. *Usine,* 24 November 1938; *Humanité,* 22 November 1938. Workers considered the new work schedule at Hutchinson—seven hours Monday through Friday and nine hours on Saturday—an insult.

22. *Humanité,* 25 November 1938; *La Vie ouvrière,* 24 November 1938; SNCASO, 25 November 1938, SNA.

23. Report from M. B., 6 December 1938, AN, 91AQ116. Also see the photographs of weapons in this file; report of Préfecture de police, January 1939, AN, $F^2$2760 and documents in AN, 91AQ117.

24. Guy Bourdé, *La défaite du front populaire* (Paris, 1977), p. 148.

25. Liste des individus arrêtés à l'usine Renault, AN, 91AQ116. Of those arrested, 194 were sentenced to prison terms—in some cases, of two months (Jacques Kergoat, *La France du front populaire* [Paris, 1986], p. 292).

26. Reports by police inspectors, December 1938, AN, 91AQ117.

27. Exposé, AN, 91AQ117.

28. See the report by a management informer in AN, 91AQ16. Of the five CGT delegates listed in police reports in AN, 91AQ117, only one was a Communist militant and another was known as sympathetic to the PCF; the other three delegates were described as "nonpolitical." Estimates of PCF membership vary; Jean-Paul Depretto and Sylvie V. Schweitzer (*Le communisme à l'usine: Vie ouvrière et mouvement ouvrier chez Renault, 1920–1939* [Paris, 1984], pp. 186, 230) offer figures of 120 members in May 1936, 1,300 in June 1936, 4,200 in September, 5,500 in December, and 7,675 in March 1937. The PCF's own numbers in *Tout faire pour servir le peuple de France,* 5e conférence de la région Paris-ouest du PCF à Gennevilliers (16–17 January 1937) and 6e conférence régionale à Argenteuil (4–5 December 1937) put the membership at over 7,650 during 1937 and 6,000 in December 1936. Another firm, the Bouguenais aviation plant, had lower than expected PCF membership: of 700 workers, 60 were members of the PCF, according to Résumé des rapports, (n.d.), SHAA, Z11607.

29. See Bertrand Badie, "Les grèves du front populaire aux usines Renault," *Le Mouvement social,* no. 81 (October–December 1972); Robert Durand, *La lutte des travailleurs de chez Renault* (Paris, 1971).

30. Henri Heldman, "Le parti communiste français à la conquête de la classe ouvrière: Les cellules d'entreprise, 1924–1938" (Thèse, 3e cycle, University of Nanterre, 1979), pp. 194–213; Sections syndicales Hotchkiss, GIM.

31. See file on this *manifestation* in APP 1867. For an overview, see Julian Jackson, *The Popular Front in France: Defending Democracy, 1934–1938* (Cambridge, 1988), p. 115.

32. Incidents de Clichy et de leurs conséquences, 19 March 1937, APP 1865.

33. Telegrams in APP 1866, dossier, Grève générale du 18–3–37; Historique de l'affaire Clarisse, AN, 91AQ16; Rapport des sections syndicales, AN, 91AQ16 (?); *Le Jour, Le Journal,* and *Action française,* 19 March 1937; letter to *Le Populaire,* 26 December 1938, AN, 91AQ16; Contre-manifestation, 15 March 1937, APP 1865.

34. *Usine,* 8 December 1938; SNCASO, 25 November 1938, SNA.

35. Grève générale 30–11–38, 3 December 1938, AN, F^{60}640. This document asserts that only 191 in a work force of 10,842 in Parisian public transport obeyed the strike order; the figure seems too low.

36. Grève du 30 novembre 1938, AN, 39AS804.

37. *Le Travailleur des transports,* December 1938; *Syndicats,* 7 December 1938.

38. *Humanité,* 1 December 1938; R. Louzon, "De l'état démocratique à l'état autoritaire," *La Révolution prolétarienne,* 10 December 1938.

39. Jouhaux quoted in Bourdé, *La défaite,* p. 161.

40. André-Jean Tudesq, "L'utilisation gouvernementale de la radio," in *Edouard Daladier: chef du gouvernement,* ed. René Rémond and Janine Bourdin (Paris, 1977), pp. 256–63.

41. *Syndicats,* 21 December 1938; *La Vie ouvrière,* 8 December 1938; *Le Travailleur du papier-carton,* December 1938.

42. See Bourdé, *La défaite,* pp. 204–5. Nationally, participation was 72.48 percent in metallurgy and 80 percent in construction (Kergoat, *France,* p. 286).

43. Renseignements obtenus, 30 November 1938, AN, 91AQ16.

44. Note sur la grève partielle, 7 December 1938, AN, 91AQ115. Another report claimed that at Renault-Aviation and at Salmson, work continued normally on 30 November (Note, 23 January 1939, SHAA Z12947).

45. The following is based on SNCASO, 9 December 1938, SNA.

46. Cf. Bourdé, *La défaite,* pp. 223–28; cf. also Richard F. Kuisel, *Capitalism and the State in Modern France* (New York, 1981), p. 125.

47. *Usine,* 8 December 1938.

48. Exemples d'augmentation du rendement, AN, 91AQ116. Depretto and Schweitzer (*Communisme*, p. 268) assert that 843 union officials were dismissed at Renault.

49. Patrick Fridenson, *Histoire des usines Renault* (Paris, 1972), pp. 270–72.

50. Exemples d'augmentation du rendement, AN, 91AQ116.

51. Ibid.; Un horaire provisoire, AN, 91AQ15: "The Renault factories were practically shut down from noon on 24 November to 16 December 1938. During this period, backed-up orders could not be filled, and workers lost a considerable portion of their wages that they really needed, especially during this time of year. . . . A large number of our workers have signed a petition asking for overtime."

52. Réponse au rapport fourni à tous les groupements du front populaire, 20 December 1938, AN, 91AQ116; *La Vie ouvrière*, 22 December 1938 and 9 February 1939.

53. *Usine*, 16 December 1938.

54. Note sur le débrayage du 24 novembre 1938, AN, 91AQ115.

55. Robert Jacomet, *L'armement de la France (1936–1939)* (Paris, 1982), p. 271.

56. Bourdé, *La défaite*, p. 230; Antoine Prost, "Le climat social," in *Edouard Daladier: Chef du gouvernement*, ed. René Rémond and Janine Bourdin (Paris, 1977), p. 109; Sauvy, ed., *Histoire économique*, 2:338; Delperrié de Bayac, *Histoire du front populaire*, pp. 513–15.

57. SNCASO, 9 December 1938, SNA.

58. SNCAN, 25 January 1939, SNA.

59. SNCASO, 9 December 1938, SNA.

60. Jacomet, *L'armement*, p. 287.

61. Emmanuel Chadeau, *L'industrie aéronautique en France, 1900–1950* (Paris, 1987), p. 313–22; Robert Frankenstein *Le prix du réarmement français, 1935–1939* (Paris, 1982), pp. 237–38.

62. SNCASO, 25 January 1939, SNA. For nationalized aviation, see Liste nominative du personnel des établissements de l'armée de l'air exclu définitivement à la suite de la grève du 30 novembre 1938, AN, F^{60}640.

63. Letter, 26 December 1938, AN, 91AQ16.

64. See various reports of February 1937 in AN, F^{7}12966.

65. *Bulletin du Syndicat professionnel et amicale des agents de maîtrise, techniciens, et employés des usines Renault*, February 1937; *SACIAT* (Syndicat et amicale des chefs de service, ingénieurs, agents de maîtrise et techniciens des industries métallurgiques, mécaniques et connexes), November–December 1938. On SACIAT see *L'Indépendance syndicale*, August–September 1937.

66. Philippe Machefer, *Ligues et fascismes en France, 1919–1939* (Paris, 1974), pp. 91–104; Philippe Burrin, *La dérive fasciste: Doriot, Déat, Bergery, 1933–1945* (Paris, 1986), pp. 219–93.

67. Société anonyme des transports, assemblée générale du 12 juin 1939, AN, 91AQ52.

68. Agitation, 4 November 1936, APP 1870; Discours prononcé par M. Jules Verger, 11 August 1937, AN, 39AS843; letter from Verger, président de la chambre syndicale de l'entreprise électrique de Paris, 12 August 1937, AN, 39AS843.

69. Grève générale possible des monteurs-électriciens, 10 November 1936, APP 1870; 12 November 1936, APP 1870; Grève de monteurs-électriciens, 19 November 1936, APP 1870.

70. The following is based on telegrams of November 1936 in APP 1870.

71. Suggestions des adhérents, 14 April 1938, GIM.

72. Préfecture de police, cabinet du préfet, 3 December 1936, APP 1870. On this handwritten note the date is partially illegible.

73. Cf. Robert Paxton, *Vichy France* (New York, 1982), which refers to "the incipient civil war" (p. 49), "the virtual French civil war" (p. 245), and "climate of civil war" (p. 246) that supposedly existed during the Popular Front.

74. See Delperrié de Bayac, *Histoire du front populaire,* pp. 407–9, for a description of the failure of the plots of the Cagoule; Martin S. Alexander, "Hommes prêts à tout accepter: The French Officer Corps and the Acceptance of Leftist Government, 1935–1937" (Paper presented at Popular Fronts Conference, University of Southampton, April 1986).

75. See Peter N. Stearns, *Revolutionary Syndicalism and French Labor: A Cause without Rebels* (New Brunswick, N.J., 1971) p. 106; Stearns, *Lives of Labor: Work in a Maturing Industrial Society* (New York, 1925); see also Edward Shorter and Charles Tilly, *Strikes in France, 1830–1968* (London, 1974), pp. 67–75. Many other authors—such as Claude Fohlen (*La France de l'entre-deux-guerres [1917–1939],* [Tournai, 1972], p. 157)—have written that the forty-hour week was a symbol to workers.

76. Michel Collinet, *L'ouvrier français, esprit du syndicalisme* (Paris, 1951), p. 118.

Primary Sources

OFFICIAL ARCHIVES

Spain

Archivo histórico nacional—sección guerra civil, Salamanca (Barcelona and Generalitat)
Archivo histórico nacional, Madrid (Gobernación)
Archivo general de administración, Madrid (Gobernación)

France

Ministère des affaires étrangères, Paris (Spain, 1930–1940)
Ministère du commerce, Archives nationales, Paris (F^{12})
Ministère de l'intérieur, Archives nationales, Paris (F^{2}, F^{7})
Travail et sécurité sociale, Archives nationales, Paris (F^{22})
Secrétariat général du gouvernement, Archives nationales, Paris (F^{60})
Archives d'entreprise, Archives nationales, Paris (AQ)
Archives d'associations, Archives nationales, Paris
Archives du commissariat de l'exposition, Archives nationales, Paris
Service historique de l'armée de l'air, Vincennes
Archives de la préfecture de police, Paris

BUSINESS AND LABOR ARCHIVES

Spain

Archivos de Fomento de trabajo nacional, Barcelona (Actas de la junta directiva)

France

Collection Jules Verger, Bibliothèque nationale, Paris
Archives du groupement des industries métallurgiques et mécaniques de la région de Paris, Neuilly
Société nationale aérospatiale, Paris (SNCAN, SNCASO, SNCASE)
Archives des usines Renault, Billancourt

OTHER DEPOSITORIES

Colección Pujol, Barcelona
Internationaal Instituut voor Sociale Geschiedenis, Amsterdam (Rudolf Rocker Collection)
Hoover Institution, Stanford, California (Burnett Bolloten, Ernest Mercier, and Georges Lefranc Collections)

GOVERNMENT PUBLICATIONS

Spain

Anuario estadístico de España, 1934 (Madrid, 1935)
Estadística: resúmenes demográficos de la ciudad de Barcelona (Barcelona, 1935–1939)
Estadísticas básicas de España, 1900–1970 (Madrid, 1975)
Gaseta municipal de Barcelona (Barcelona, 1934–1939)

France

Annuaire statistique de la France, 1934 (Paris, 1935)
Annuaire statistique de la ville de Paris, 1932–1937 (Paris, 1937–1942)

PERIODICAL LITERATURE

Spain

Aeronáutica
Amanecer
Los amigos de Durruti
Boletín del Comité nacional de la CNT para exclusivo uso de los sindicatos
Boletín de información
Boletín del Sindicato de la industria de la edificación, madera y decoración
Boletín del Sindicato de la industria fabril y textil de Badalona y su radio
Butlletí de la Federació catalana d'indústries químiques-UGT
Butlletí interior de la unió general de treballadors
CNT Marítima
Conselleria d'economia
Electricidad
Exito
La Hispano-Suiza
Horizontes
Hoy
Industria catalana

La Industria eléctrica
Institut de Ciències econòmiques de Catalunya
Luz y fuerza
Metalurgia y construcción mecánica
El Mundo deportivo
Las Noticias
Petróleo
Ruta
Sidero-Metalurgia
Síntesis
Solidaridad Obrera
Tierra y Libertad
El Trabajo nacional
UGT Edificación

France

Annales d'hygiène publique, industrielle et sociale
Le bolchevik de chez Gnôme-Rhône
Le Bulletin du Syndicat professionnel et amicale des agents de maîtrise, techniciens, et employés des usines Renault
Le Défenseur
L'Echo des syndicats
L'Economie nouvelle
L'Etincelle
L'Etoile bleue
L'Europe nouvelle
La Flèche de Paris
Le Guide du métallurgiste
L'Humanité
L'Hygiène sociale
L'Indépendance syndicale
La Lutte finale
Nouveaux Cahiers
Le Petit Parisien
Le Peuple
Le Populaire
La Révolution prolétarienne
Revue internationale du travail
SACIAT
Syndicats
Le Travailleur du papier-carton

Le Travailleur des transports
La Vie ouvrière

SELECTED BUSINESS PUBLICATIONS

Spain

Federación de fabricantes de hilados y tejidos de Cataluña, *Memoria* (Barcelona, 1930–1933)
Federación de industrias nacionales, *Memoria* (Madrid, 1931–1936)
Fomento de trabajo nacional, *Memoria* (Barcelona, 1919–1936)

France

Les Ailes
L'Elan social
La Journée industrielle
L'Usine

Index

Compositor: BookMasters, Inc.
Text: 11/13 Baskerville
Display: Baskerville
Printer: Braun-Brumfield, Inc.
Binder: Braun-Brumfield, Inc.